INSURABILITY OF EMERGING RISKS

This book brings together leading experts in the fields of insurance and the law of obligations to consider how insurance law is attempting to deal with emerging risks.

Emerging risks pose significant challenges for the insurance industry. Apart from difficulties in quantifying such risks, the availability of insurance capacity is often a concern. The book looks at these issues from philosophical, economic, and actuarial perspectives. It asks how far existing private law rules can cope with emerging risks, and in so far as they cannot, how the law should be developed by courts and lawmakers to deal with the emerging legal issues.

The book questions the suitability of the current insurance business models in insuring climate-related risks, autonomous systems, insurance of fines and penalties; and how mass or systemic risks (eg pandemics or cyber risks) can be made insurable through 'add on' coverages to the conventional insurance policies. It also evaluates governments' roles to encourage insurers to provide cover for such risks and discusses how a balance can be struck between the need to regulate and the insurance markets' dynamics.

The book will be of academic interest to anyone working in the field of insurance and also relevant for market participants, policy-makers and regulators.

Insurability of Emerging Risks

Law, Theory and Practice

Edited by
Barış Soyer
and
Özlem Gürses

•HART•
OXFORD • LONDON • NEW YORK • NEW DELHI • SYDNEY

HART PUBLISHING

Bloomsbury Publishing Plc

Kemp House, Chawley Park, Cumnor Hill, Oxford, OX2 9PH, UK

1385 Broadway, New York, NY 10018, USA

29 Earlsfort Terrace, Dublin 2, Ireland

First published in Great Britain 2025

A catalogue record for this book is available from the British Library.

A catalogue record for this book is available from the Library of Congress.

Library of Congress Control Number: 2024946797

ISBN: HB: 978-1-50997-871-7
ePDF: 978-1-50997-873-1
ePub: 978-1-50997-872-4

Typeset by Compuscript Ltd, Shannon

ACKNOWLEDGEMENTS

The editors wish to express their gratitude to all participants in the workshops held at King's College London in November 2022 and Freie Universität Berlin in June 2023, especially to **Professors Armbrüster, Hunter and Brownsword**, who provided inspiration and invaluable guidance for this collection.

We are grateful to **Xinge Li** (Research Assistant at the Institute of International Shipping and Trade Law at Swansea) for her assistance in putting this volume together, especially dealing with the daunting task of putting tables together in a professional manner.

We also would like to thank **Dr Roberta Bassi** (Publisher, Hart Publishing) and **Verity Stuart** (Assistant Editor, Hart Publishing) for their assistance and practical suggestions that helped us immensely during the publication process of this collection.

CONTENTS

ABOUT THE CONTRIBUTORS

Editors

Barış Soyer

Professor of Commercial and Maritime Law, Director of the Institute of International Shipping and Trade Law, Swansea University

Professor Soyer directs the Institute of International Shipping and Trade Law at Swansea University and is a member of the British Maritime Law Association and British Insurance Law Association. He is the author of *Warranties in Marine Insurance* (2001), *Marine Insurance Fraud* (2014), and many articles published in journals such as *Cambridge Law Journal*, *Law Quarterly Review*, *Edinburg Law Review*, *Lloyd's Maritime & Commercial Law Quarterly*, the *Journal of Business Law*, the *Torts Law Journal* and the *Journal of Contract Law*. *Warranties in Marine Insurance* won the Cavendish Book Prize 2001 and was awarded the British Insurance Law Association Charitable Trust Book Prize in 2002 for its contribution to insurance literature. *Marine Insurance Fraud* also won the latter prize in 2015.

He has also edited large numbers of collections of essays on commercial, maritime and insurance law. In addition, he sits on the editorial boards of the Journal of International Maritime Law, Shipping and Trade Law and editorial committee of the Lloyd's Maritime and Commercial Law Quarterly (International Maritime and Commercial Law Yearbook). Professor Soyer currently teaches Charterparties: Law and Practice and Marine Insurance on the LLM Programme at Swansea.

Özlem Gürses

Professor of Law, King's College London

Professor Gürses is the author of *Marine Insurance Law* (3rd ed 2023), *The Law of Compulsory Motor Vehicle Insurance* (2019) and *Reinsuring Clauses* (2010), as well as several articles on insurance and reinsurance law. She recently edited a *Research Handbook on Marine Insurance Law* (Edward Elgar, 2024). Professor Gürses sits in the Presidential Council of International Association of Insurance Law (AIDA), and the British Insurance Law Association Committee, and chairs the Reinsurance Working Party of AIDA. Özlem frequently presents her research at international and national conferences, and she teaches insurance, marine insurance, and reinsurance law at higher education institutions at home and abroad, including Australia, Singapore, Germany and China.

Contributors

Christian Armbrüster

Professor of Law, Freie Universität Berlin

Christian Armbrüster is a tenured Professor of Private Law at Freie Universität Berlin, a leading University in Germany where he previously held the Dean and Vice Dean positions at the Law Faculty. Prior to taking up his role in Berlin Christian held the Chair of private law at Bucerius Law School in Hamburg. Christian studied law in Germany and Switzerland and conducted his PhD in liability and property insurance. He then completed his habilitation in corporate law. Alongside his academic career, Christian sat as a Court of Appeal judge at the Kammergericht (Court of Appeal) in Berlin from 2007 until 2013, with a specialisation in Company and Commercial Law. He acts as an arbitrator, and he undertook expert witness duties in several disputes in Germany, UK, USA and France. Christian was also involved in various German legislative processes in contract, tort and insurance law.

Roger Brownsword

Professor of Law, King's College London and Bournemouth University

Roger Brownsword has professorial positions in Law at King's College London (where he was the founding Director of TELOS) and at Bournemouth University. His many books and articles are known throughout the English-speaking world; and, he also has publications in Chinese, French, German, Italian, and Portuguese. His most recent books are: *Law, Technology and Society: Reimagining the Regulatory Environment* (2019), *Law 3.0: Rules, Regulation and Technology* (2020), *Rethinking Law, Regulation and Technology* (2022), *Technology, Governance and Respect for Law: Pictures at an Exhibition* (2022), *Law, Regulation and Governance in the Information Society* (co-edited with Maurizio Borghi) (2023), *Technology, Humans, and Discontent with the Law: the Quest for Better Governance* (2024) and *The Future of Governance: A Radical Introduction to Law* (2025).

Fred Hawke

Consultant, Clayton Utz

Fred has amassed a wealth of experience and a career spanning more than 40 years in insurance law. He has conducted comprehensive policy reviews and counselled insurance disputes across all major general and life insurance classes. He served as an insurance company Claims Manager and General Counsel, negotiating and settling insurance and reinsurance disputes involving some of Australia's most significant liability losses for the first half of his career. Since joining Clayton Utz 25 years ago, Fred has practised extensively in insurance and reinsurance law with focus on regulatory and compliance issues, captive insurer arrangements, Bankers Bonds, crime and financial liability insurances, facultative and treaty reinsurance, and retrocession arrangements. He has extensive experience in trade credit insolvency and political risk insurance, both in the insurance industry and legal practice. He also advises government clients on the insurance provisions and procurement of major infrastructure and development projects.

Fred is a well-recognised and prolific writer and presenter on insurance law and insurance industry related legal matters and occasional lecturer in the Graduate Studies Program at several Australian universities. He is a member of the Editorial Board, a former General Editor of the Insurance Law Journal published by Lexis Nexis, and the former Chair of the Journal Advisory Council of the Australian Insurance Institute. He is also the Australian Reporter for the Center for International Legal Studies and the author of the Chapter on Australia in Oceana Publications Inc's loose-leaf publication International Insurance Law and Regulation, as well as a number of other papers and articles on insurance law and claims management.

Erik S Knutsen

Professor of Law, Queen's University Kingston

Erik S. Knutsen (LLM, Harvard Law School; JD, Osgoode Hall Law School; BA (Hons), Lakehead University) is a Professor at the Queen's University Faculty of Law in Kingston, Ontario, Canada. He served as Associate Dean (Academic) for the Queen's Faculty of Law from 2018–2020. His areas of academic interest include tort, insurance law, health law, medical liability, civil procedure and the civil litigation system.

He is the author of *Halsburys Laws of Canada – Insurance*, a co-author of the treatises *Canadian Tort Law* (with Linden, Feldthusen, Hall and Young) and *Stempel and Knutsen on Insurance Coverage*, as well as the casebooks *The Civil Litigation Process* and *Principles of Insurance Law*. He is also the author or co-author of more than 70 scholarly articles, papers and other publications on the topics of tort, insurance, and civil litigation. He has presented his work at venues in Canada, the United States, Europe, the United Kingdom, and China. He is frequently involved with professional and judicial education initiatives. His work has been cited by Canadian, American, and European appellate and trial courts.

Professor Knutsen is an elected member of the American Law Institute (the leading American law reform organization), the European Law Institute (the leading European law reform organization), and an Honorary Fellow of the American College of Coverage Counsel (the leading American insurance coverage litigation organization). He is appointed to Ontario's Civil Rules Committee, the group that oversees reform to the rules of civil procedure for the province.

Professor Knutsen was awarded the university-wide Queen's University Baillie teaching award in 2018. He has also three times earned the law faculty's teaching award. He was previously a Visiting Assistant Professor at Florida State University College of Law, where he also earned a teaching award.

He has practised tort and insurance litigation in New York at Paul, Weiss LLP where he assisted with 9/11 World Trade Center cases, in Toronto at Fasken Martineau LLP, and in Thunder Bay at Carrel + Partners LLP. He is a member of the bar of Ontario, Canada. Professor Knutsen regularly consults with lawyers on cases heading to trial or appeal, including cases at the Supreme Court of Canada, American courts, and other courts and tribunals around the world.

George Leloudas

Professor of Law, Member of the Institute of International Shipping and Trade Law, Swansea University

Professor Leloudas is a graduate of the National and Kapodistrian University of Athens and holds LLM degrees in Commercial Law from the University of Bristol, and in Air and Space Law from the McGill Institute of Air and Space Law. He also completed his PhD in air law with emphasis on liability and insurance at Cambridge University.

His principal teaching and research interest is the carriage of passengers and goods by air, road and sea, but his interests extend to multimodal transport, insurance law, the regulation of autonomous transport systems, including cyber risks and artificial intelligence, and arbitration law. He has published two monographs, the first one on *Risk and Liability in Air Law* and the second one on *Air Cargo Insurance* with Professor Malcolm Clarke of Cambridge University. He is also the General Editor of the preeminent air law publication, *Shawcross and Beaumont on Air Law* and has numerous peer-reviewed publications and grants in the areas of private (international) law and regulation.

Before joining the Institute, George worked as a Solicitor at Gates and Partners in London for several years where he advised airlines and their insurers on liability and regulatory matters. He was also an assistant to the legal counsel of the International Union of Aviation Insurers (IUAI) providing support in relation to the replacement of the Rome Convention on Surface Damage with the 2009 Montreal Conventions. George is an instructor at the Training and Development Institute of the International Air Transport Association (IATA) where he teaches international air law for lawyers and legal professionals, law of aviation insurance and air cargo liability law.

Peter MacDonald Eggers KC

Barrister

Peter is a barrister practising at 7 King's Bench Walk, specialising in all aspects of commercial law, with a particular emphasis on insurance and reinsurance. Previously a solicitor, he took silk in 2011. He is co-author of *Good Faith and Insurance Contracts* and editor of *Carver on Charterparties*, the author of *Deceit: The Lie of the Law* and *The Vitiation of Contractual Consent*, and a contributing editor of *Chitty on Contracts*. A previous chair of BILA, Peter teaches part time at UCL and Queen Mary. He is in addition the immediate past Chair of BILA.

Gary Meggitt

Associate Professor of Law, The University of Hong Kong

Gary Meggitt was admitted as a solicitor in England and Wales in 1993 and spent 12 years in practice with several leading UK law firms. He is also Called to the Bar in England and Wales. He has taught insurance law, civil litigation and professional conduct at the University of Hong Kong since 2007. He is the author of *Wilkinson's Professional Conduct of Lawyers in Hong Kong* (2022) and *Mediation and ADR Confidentiality in Hong Kong* (2019); a contributing author of *A Guide to Civil Procedure in Hong Kong* (2023); and has also contributed recently to *The Global Insurance Market and Change: Emerging Technologies, Risks and Legal Challenges* (2023) and *The Research Handbook on Marine Insurance Law* (2024).

Phillip Morgan

Professor of Private Law, University of York

Phillip Morgan is the Book Review and Review Article Editor of the *Journal of Professional Negligence*, and an Editor of the *Professional Negligence and Liability Reports*. He was formerly the Torts Subject Section Convenor for the Society of Legal Scholars. He has research interest in tort, contract and commercial law. He published in the *Cambridge Law Journal, Modern Law Review, Law Quarterly Review, Lloyd's Maritime* and *Commercial Law Quarterly, Legal Studies*, the *Journal of Professional Negligence*, and the *Torts Law Journal*, amongst others. He is a Council Member of the Society of Legal Scholars, a Member of the Society's Library Sub-Committee, and a Fellow of the Royal Society of Arts. He is also a Barrister. Phillip completed pupillage at Essex Court Chambers, (Commercial / Shipping / Civil Fraud / International Trade / Arbitration), where he mainly worked on large Commercial Court and Arbitral Tribunal cases, before moving to Crown Office Chambers, (Insurance / Personal Injury / Clinical Negligence / Construction), where he regularly appeared in trials and applications in the County Courts. He also appeared in the High Court, Companies Court, and in the Coroner's Court. He has also been Judicial Assistant to Lord Judge, The Lord Chief Justice, and also to Lord Carnwath, Justice of the Supreme Court, (then Senior President of Tribunals).

Livashnee Naidoo

Senior Lecturer in Commercial Law, School of Law, University of Glasgow

Dr Naidoo's primary research interests are in insurance law and shipping law. She is a former practising attorney and notary of the High Court of South Africa and currently lectures in commercial law and insurance law at the University of Glasgow. Dr Naidoo is a committee member of the British Insurance Law Association and is the Assistant Honorary Editor of the British Insurance Law Association's Journal. She has published widely on various topics in insurance law and theory and has had her interdisciplinary research funded both nationally and internationally. Her latest publications include contributions to the *Research Handbook on Marine Insurance Law* (EEP); *Regulating Risk in Trade, Maritime Transport and the Marine Environment* (Brill); *and the Research Handbook on International Commercial Contracts* (EEP). Dr Naidoo has been invited by several academic and industry bodies to present her research and has held visiting positions at the University of Cambridge, the University of Cape Town, and Tsinghua University

Rob Merkin KC

Professor of Commercial Law, University of Reading

Professor Merkin is Professor of Commercial Law at the University of Reading. He is honorary life president of the International Association of Insurance Law (AIDA) and past president of the British Insurance Law Association. He is the author of over 60 books on insurance, reinsurance and arbitration and numerous articles on these subjects. His writings have been cited as authoritative in courts worldwide on very many occasions. He is also the general editor of the Journal of Business Law and the Lloyd's Law Reports.

Professor Merkin is on international arbitration panels in Singapore, Hong Kong and New Zealand, and has sat as an arbitrator in England. He regularly acts as an expert witness in insurance and reinsurance disputes in overseas judicial and arbitral proceedings.

Jeffrey W Stempel

Doris S & Theodore B Lee Professor of Law, William S Boyd School of Law, University of Nevada, Las Vegas

Jeff Stempel is the Doris S & Theodore B Lee Professor of Law at UNLV, where he teaches Insurance, Civil Procedure, Contracts and Professional Responsibility. In addition to *General Liability Insurance Coverage: Key Issues in Every State* (5th ed, 2021), Professor Stempel is co-author of *Stempel and Knutsen on Insurance Coverage* (4th ed, 2016) as well as co-author of *Principles of Insurance Law* (5th ed, 2020), *Learning Civil Procedure* (4th ed. 2022); *Fundamentals of Pretrial Litigation* (11th ed, 2020) and *Motion Practice* (8th ed, 2020) as well as numerous articles. He is a member of the American College of Coverage Counsel, the American Law Institute, the European Law Institute, and the Project Group for Principles of Reinsurance Contract Law (PRICL). He received his BA degree from the University of Minnesota and his JD degree from Yale Law School and is admitted in Nevada and Minnesota.

Andrew Tettenborn

Member of the Institute of International Shipping and Trade Law, Swansea University

Professor Tettenborn has been attached to the IISTL at Swansea Law School since 2010, teaching international trade, banking and admiralty. He has also taught at the universities of Cambridge, Exeter and Geneva, and held visiting positions in Europe, Australia and the USA. He acts as general editor of *Marsden's Collisions at Sea* and *Clerk & Lindsell on Torts*, and also of the leading student textbook on commercial law (*Sealy & Hooley's Text, Cases and Materials*); and jointly with Professor Francis Rose authored *Admiralty Claims*.

He has authored numerous articles on commercial law and obligations, sits on the editorial boards of Lloyd's Maritime & Commercial Law Quarterly and the Journal of International Maritime Law, and has advised government departments and the Law Commission.

TABLE OF CASES

Australia

Germany

New Zealand

Singapore

United Kingdom

United States of America

TABLE OF LEGISLATION

Table of European and International Legislation

Australia

Denmark

European Union

France

Germany

International Conventions

Israel

New Zealand

United States of America

Table of Statutory Instruments and Regulations

Australia

European Union

Indonesia

New Zealand

United Kingdom

Introduction

Uncertainty is a reality of life and the fundamental justification (raison d'être) of insurance. However, there is no denying the fact that technological, geographical, political, sociological, and economic factors alter the world we live in constantly, resulting in an alteration in the nature and type of risks that most insurance products are designed to provide insurance cover for. Emerging risks are evolving all the time; and aided by actuarial studies (and most recently big data analytics), insurers aim to provide cover for emerging risks. However, they often face challenges in quantifying such risks, resulting in offering limited insurance cover or demanding excessive insurance premium, significantly reducing the value of insurance for individuals and corporations seeking such insurance cover. This results in people's very basic needs, such as obtaining house insurance against flood or fire, becoming unavailable or too expensive to afford. Occurrence of catastrophes (natural or human made) and significant losses that follow also bring to the fore the debate on whether certain losses are insurable in the open market. We witnessed such heated discussions emerging immediately after the terrorist attacks on the Twin Towers in 2001. In those days, several market participants and academics deliberated whether losses resulting from terrorist incidents are insurable at all in the market. In fact, many insurers and reinsurers withdrew their offers to insure terrorism, as a result of which governments had to intervene to encourage them to insure such risks through public–private partnerships. Similarly, in recent years, an increasing number of natural disasters, possibly resulting from climate change (eg, floods, earthquakes, hurricanes), have necessitated the need to resort to government-backed insurance and reinsurance covers. Therefore, it is becoming more apparent that standard insurance products and principles will have to be reconsidered in the context of insuring today's emerging risks.

The idea behind this book stems from workshops held at King's College London (November 2022) and Freie Universität Berlin (June 2023), which some of the contributors attended. Encouraged by the rigorous debates carried out during those workshops, the editors brought a team together composed of leading experts (experienced academics, solicitors, barristers) working in the fields of insurance and law of obligations to consider how insurance law and practice are dealing with emerging risks. In pursuing this goal, the contributors offer deliberations on the issue of insuring emerging risks from philosophical, economic and actuarial perspectives. They also engage on the question of how far existing private law rules can cope with emerging risks, and insofar as they cannot, how law should be developed by courts and lawmakers to deal with the emerging legal issues. Some of the contributions also offer an analysis as to how a balance could be best struck between the need to regulate and the needs of market participants.

The book is divided into three parts. The broad aim of **Part I** is to set the scene by focussing on theoretical, conceptual and market-related issues in the process of insuring emerging risks. This part also contains contributions elaborating how and under what conditions regulatory interference is required to ensure that insurance continues to deliver its primary function of providing protection against uncertainties. To this end, Chapter 1 (written by Professor Gürses) explores how the protection gap is addressed by nations in different parts of the World and reveals that overwhelmingly it is done through public–private partnerships (PPPs). Starting with some statistical information on the protection gap observed in several different countries, the chapter looks at whether such risks can be insured only with government involvement, and if so, what methods have been adopted. The chapter also examines the operation of those partnerships and their impact on policyholders, taxpayers, insurers, and governments. The chapter further refers to regional pools available in the world, and to the World Bank's involvement in supporting its members in enabling insurance for some certain types of risk.

In Chapter 2, Professors Knutsen and Stempel discuss why the insurance industry should give serious consideration to folding difficult/emerging risks into standard issue products made more comprehensive in their scope of coverage. They argue that segregation or use of broad exclusions, often employed by insurers, tends to produce insufficient coverage as well as increased operational costs for providing insurance.

The primary aim of Professor Soyer's contribution in Chapter 3 is to define the potential role and function of the 'solidarity principle' in the insurance context, considering more broadly the function of insurance in society and other fundamental values. Professor Soyer then attempts to devise fundamental principles that can guide attempts to develop insurance schemes, arguing that the suitability of the scheme employed will depend not only on these principles but also market conditions, political economic and socio-cultural factors.

In Chapter 4 Professor Brownsword, endorsing the call for regulatory control over AI, proposes an 'all-risks' approach to the governance of emerging technologies. While this approach assumes that regulators will continue to engage with their publics to identify a broad sweep of concerns about the risks presented by a particular technology, this is not its distinctive feature. Rather, it is an approach that accentuates the depth of human interests and the risks that emerging technologies might present to the viability of human communities. Having introduced the all-risks approach, and having considered how it relates to the concern that governance of AI should support an ecosystem of trust, this chapter discusses how it might be applied to the use of AI in the field of insurance – on the one side, to the use of AI by the providers of insurance and, on the other, by those who seek insurance (or who are insured).

Professor Tettenborn in Chapter 5 explores what can be done in the design of insurance policies to prevent overpriced insurance from strangling innovation, crippling liabilities hamstringing underwriters, or uninsured losses bankrupting innovators. The contribution suggests that the state might wish to play a role in providing insurance cover for emerging technologies in order to protect public interests.

In Chapter 6 Peter MacDonald Eggers, KC, noting that there is an obvious market appetite from the perspective of both insurers and insureds to provide cover for fines or penalties as part of some insurance policies (eg, cyber risks policies, directors and officers liability insurance policies, pollution policies, E&O policies, and protection and indemnity policies), elaborates public policy reasons for and against such cover. This contribution further explores the range of such cover, the breadth of the public policy concerns and the developing case law, and also considers the impact of such considerations on the validity of such insurance cover.

Parts II and **III** of the book move to consider the extent to which emerging risks insurance is available under the current practices and legal problems emerging with reference to the principles of insurance and the law of obligations. The contributions in **Part II** focus solely on risks associated with climate change. In Chapter 7, Professor Merkin focuses on the insurance of natural disasters in New Zealand. One of the oldest PPPs in the World, New Zealand sets a model where the government acts as the primary insurer for the nation for some certain risks. Although the system helped the nation greatly after the earthquakes in 2010–2011, it was by no means immune from any deficiencies. In 2020 the public inquiry report revealed the problematic areas of the then applicable regime, including the inability of both the government and the insurance industry to organise timely assessment and payment of the claims. Addressing the points raised in the report, New Zealand amended the system and moved to a new regime under the Natural Hazards Act 2023. Professor Merkin's chapter provides a broad chronological overview of the regime from its start after WWII to the present.

In Chapter 8 Fred Hawke analyses the Cyclone Reinsurance Scheme administrated by the Australian Reinsurance Pool Corporation (ARPC). After an extended review of many different types of PPPs adopted in the world by different nations, the Australian authorities opted for the compulsory reinsurance pool to enable affordable insurance of cyclones in high-risk areas, especially in northern Australia. Hawke examines in detail the challenges faced with insuring such risks, the work conducted by the authorities in amending the Terrorism Insurance Act 2003 (Cth) as the Terrorism and Cyclone Insurance Act 2003 (Cth), the risks falling under the new regime, and how the partnership between the Government and the reinsurance pool will be formed and operate. The chapter further discusses the implications of the cyclone reinsurance scheme for policyholders, insurers and ARPC.

In Chapter 9, Dr Naidoo examines the extent to which existing insurance and tort law doctrines and principles can accommodate climate litigation risks. The chapter explores the interaction between tort and insurance law whilst these two different areas are being developed in light of the emerging risks. It subsequently investigates whether climate litigation risk presents novel considerations for the intersection between tort law and liability insurance. Ultimately the chapter explores the role of insurance in balancing the value of liability insurance as a product against regulatory efforts.

In a similar vein, **Part III** focuses on the impact of AI and similar disruptive technologies on insurance cover and insurance law principles and doctrines. In Chapter 10, Professor Morgan discusses whether the Automated and Electric Vehicles Act 2018 is capable of solving the core problems raised by the interference of tort law with autonomy and concludes that the Act simply displaces these problems and places them onto insurers.

Gary Meggitt in Chapter 11 addresses the changing nature of the work, obligations and regulation of professionals by considering the possible changes in the same that may be brought about by AI and other technological aides. The contribution argues the need for insurers to remain familiar with these changes and to address them when it comes to underwriting and claims management in relation to professional indemnity cover and in the possible development of alternative forms of cover.

In Chapter 12, Professor Armbrüster notes that the use of nanotechnology affects various lines of insurance, yet how insurance can address nanotechnology is at its embryonic stage. The chapter attempts to clarify how such risks may be insurable by addressing the events insured against, the issues with the period of cover, and obligations the insurer would impose under such policies. The chapter also explores how insurance of nanotechnology can be supported by reinsurance, risk pooling, Alternative Risk Transfer (ART), statutory liability limits and compulsory insurance.

In Chapter 13, Professor Leloudas, after exploring the current legal and regulatory regime concerning Remotely Piloted Aircraft Systems (RPAS), elaborates whether the liability and insurance frameworks require adjustments, or whether a new, specialised regime to include product liability and insurance is necessary to accommodate the use of RPAS, especially in urban environments.

Reflecting on the contributions to this book, several conclusions can be drawn. First, despite posing actuarial challenges for the insurance market, there is certainly an appetite to offer cover for emerging risks. That said, insurers are naturally timid when dealing with risks associated with emerging technologies and often try to minimise their potential exposure by imposing significant restrictions in the shape of broad exclusions and limitations in cover. But as pointed out by several contributors, such limitations could be counterproductive and might lead to inefficiencies.

Another significant conclusion that emerges from several contributions is the need to find the right balance between regulation and innovation. Overregulating emerging technologies (especially AI-powered solutions) might not only hinder innovation but could also lead to economic inefficiencies due to the fact that producers, operators and manufacturers might still invest in liability insurance which will provide little benefit to them.

It is undeniable that insurance plays a crucial role in the economic wellbeing of nations. Several contributions demonstrate that some emerging risks, especially those closely associated with the climate change, might pose significant challenges for the insurance market. The main difficulty in this context will be addressing the issue of how necessary capital will be reserved to compensate the losses in case of occurrence of insured risks. The capital may be available through (i) private insurers and reinsurers, (ii) governments, or (iii) a partnership between the two. Considering the scale of the losses and unpredictable nature of the probability of some risks, option (i) appears to be out of the question. The biggest challenge both options (ii) and (iii) face is the initiation of the necessary action by the relevant bodies. This normally occurs, unfortunately, after mass losses are suffered by many and the public pressure reaches a level that is impossible to resist.

It will be an overstatement to suggest that this book provides answers to all the questions emerging. However, it is fair to say that contributions to the book have raised significant issues which market participants, policymakers and governments should be debating. Numerous interesting ideas and convincing recommendations that have been put forward by the contributors deserve further deliberation and will no doubt shape the direction of academic discourse in the field of insurance law, and more generally in law of obligations, in the years to come.

BS & OG
May 2024

PART I

Conceptual, Theoretical and Regulatory Issues

1

Public Private Partnerships: Providing Capital for Unaffordable Insurance Risks

ÖZLEM GÜRSES

I. Introduction

Insurance plays a major role in managing risks, whether it is an individual or a business who bears them. Whilst insurance coverage in principle may be obtained whenever a financial interest may be affected by a risk, it does not mean that any risk is insurable at the right price. In the case of systemic risks, for example, insurers and reinsurers may rapidly withdraw any coverage available in the market for such risks. Avoiding a non-profitable business is not a surprise for an industry driven by their profit-making capacity.

In disaster management, governments can play a strong enabling and guiding role. They can help improve the availability of insurance via many different channels. Through their regulatory authorities they may set up the framework for compulsory schemes which create sufficiently large risk communities and risk pools. As an insurance regulator, governments' relevant bodies may licence alternative risk transfers, such as parametric insurance, to provide timely compensation for frequently occurring losses. They can lead educational programmes which actively encourage risk prevention or minimisation efforts.

Most of these initiatives would materialise through public private partnerships (PPPs) so that uninsurable, or more precisely un-affordably insurable,[1] risks can be insured with accessible price. This paper will provide an overview of different examples of PPPs in the world and will discuss their impact on policyholders, insurers, and taxpayers.

[1] F Hawke, The Big Wind Blows: On Northern Australia, Chapter 8 of this work.

II. The Protection Gap

To an insurance lawyer, the words risk and insurance are so closely aligned that they are almost indivisible. Nevertheless, this does not mean that there will always be an insurance offer available for any risk. As a result, whilst the risks are inevitable and they have to be lived with,[2] there might not be any insurance coverage available to compensate the losses caused by them. This is named as the protection gap which is defined as 'The difference between the amount of insurance that is economically beneficial and the amount of coverage actually purchased'.[3] Such gaps occur with respect to many risks from terrorism to natural disasters. In the last decade the annual average of 180 natural disasters per year were recorded, yet many of the losses they caused were uninsured.[4] In 2019, the losses suffered amounted $232 bn, $71 bn of which was insured;[5] in 2022 the insured amount was 42% of the $313bn, and in 2023 it was 38% of $280bn.[6]

The report of the (Australian) Royal Commission into National Natural Disaster Arrangements highlighted that uninsured or underinsured households have reduced financial capability to recover from a natural disaster.[7] Undeniably, insurance is an important tool for households and businesses to manage financial risks. Lack of insurance coverage can increase costs and pressures for communities and for governments, through increased demand on health, emergency, and welfare systems. Protection gap therefore becomes an indication to assess how resilient societies and economies are to disasters.[8] Reducing the levels of underinsurance and non-insurance improves such resilience.[9]

Yet certain risks are considered uninsurable from a commercial viability point of view. For instance, prior to the 9/11 attacks on the World Trade Center and the Pentagon in 2001, terrorism coverage was usually included in general insurance policies without an additional cost to insureds. The 9/11 attacks were the most expensive terrorist incident in the US history with its cost of $47 billion to

[2] M Essen, S McCaffrey, J Abrams & T Paveglio, 'Improving Wildfire Management Outcomes: Shifting the Paradigm of wildfire from simple to complex risk' (2023) 66 *Journal of Environmental Planning and Management* 909–927.

[3] The Geneva Association, 'Understanding and Addressing Global Insurance Gaps' www.genevaassociation.org/sites/default/files/research-topics-document-type/pdf_public/understanding_and_addressing_global_insurance_protection_gaps.pdf 1.

[4] www.theinsurer.com/reinsurancemonth/the-worldwide-protection-gap-keeps-growing-what-can-insurers-do-about-it/.

[5] www.aon.com/protection-gap/default.jsp.

[6] www.theinsurer.com/reinsurancemonth/the-worldwide-protection-gap-keeps-growing-what-can-insurers-do-about-it/;https://www.swissre.com/risk-knowledge/mitigating-climate-risk/natcat-protection-gap-infographic.html#/country/UK/open.

[7] Explanatory Memorandum to Treasury Laws Amendment (Cyclone and Flood Damage Reinsurance Pool) Bill 2022, Attachment 1, Regulation Impact Statement, n7, 31–32.

[8] www.swissre.com/risk-knowledge/mitigating-climate-risk/natcat-protection-gap-infographic.html#/country/UK/open.

[9] www.oecd.org/fr/finances/assurances/33913415.pdf W Bugl 'Earthquake Risk Management Policy in Indonesia', a conference paper circulated at the Conference on Catastrophic Risks and Insurance, held in 2004 at the OECD, Paris.

the insurance industry. The losses included 33% for business interruption, 30% for property losses (the World Trade Center towers), and the rest was for workers' compensation, life, health, airline liability, and general liability insurance lines.

After the attacks, reinsurers severely cut back on their terrorism coverage or stopped offering it altogether.[10] The companies that continued to offer terrorism coverage charged exorbitant premiums, making terrorism insurance unaffordable and unattainable for many.[11] Similarly, extreme weather events are becoming uninsurable because they are incalculable, too catastrophic, and correlated to other risks.[12]

As Swiss Re reports,[13] it is not true that only developing economies face the largest gaps.[14] Swiss Re's research reveals the following country-specific information on protection gaps:

UK: 21% (not specified)

USA: 42% (flood and earthquake)

Australia 33% (not specified)

Canada: 41% (flood)

China: 94% (flood, typhoon, earthquake)

France: 46% (hail or windstorm)

Germany: 56% (flood and earthquake)

India: 91% (floods, landslides, tropical cyclones, earthquakes and tsunamis, and droughts)

Italy:80% (flood, landslides, earthquakes)

Japan: 55% (tsunami)

Mexico: 75% (earthquakes, tropical cyclones and floods)

South Africa: 71% (flood and cyclonic storms)

Switzerland: 28% (flood, windstorm and earthquake)

Many challenges are linked to the protection gap.[15] Transaction cost (high administrative and distribution fees, eg brokerage), institutional obstacles, a lack of

[10] iftrip.org/wp-content/uploads/2022/06/terrorism-pool-index-2022.pdf.

[11] As discussed below, terrorism insurance is currently provided through 'pools' in many different jurisdictions.

[12] www.theinsurer.com/reinsurancemonth/the-worldwide-protection-gap-keeps-growing-what-can-insurers-do-about-it/; F Arnold-Dwyer, *Insurance Climate Change and The Law*, (London, Informa, 2004).

[13] Ten-year totals between 2014–2023. www.swissre.com/risk-knowledge/mitigating-climate-risk/natcat-protection-gap-infographic.html#/country/UK/open.

[14] The Dashboard on Insurance Protection Gap for Natural Catastrophes in a Nutshell EIOPA-22/507 (2023) www.eiopa.europa.eu/document/download/bbdc653b-e335-41f0-8293-0d8280a09855_en?filename=EIOPA-BOS-23-418%20Dashboard%20on%20insurance%20protection%20gap%20in%20a%20nutshell.pdf.

[15] Understanding and Addressing Global Insurance Gaps n3, 2–3.

solvency margins, insufficient minimum capital requirements and a general lack of cohesion, transparency, consultation and implementation contribute to such gaps. Insurance is a regulated financial service in many jurisdictions. Institutional parameters, such as the legal and regulatory environment, are major determinants of insurance supply. Insurance gaps become unavoidable in places where the insurance business is not supported and supervised by an effective and sound regulatory framework.

Moreover, affordability, a lack of awareness, poor financial literacy or general education can be listed as main reasons for protection gap from policyholders' point of view. Product appeal, service quality, cultural and social factors including risk aversion can also be added to this list.[16]

Although it may depend on the maturity of insurance markets and the specific nature of protection gaps, it has been observed that a comprehensive and promising approach to narrowing insurance protection gaps can be enabled through multi-stakeholder efforts. Governments can address the protection gaps and improve insurance access and affordability, strengthen households and businesses resilience to certain risks including natural disasters, and reduce costs to governments due to pressure on many services and welfare systems.

General reliance on government aid as a substitute for insurance may be argued as another factor leading to protection gaps.[17] However, different levels of involvement may be considered for governments who may assume the role of a primary insurer or directly support policyholders by subsidising premiums, or they may initiate a reinsurance pool backed up by the government.

The table below summarises the options available for possible public private partnerships. The details of each option will be discussed in the following paragraphs.

	Residual Market Option	**Reinsurer Option**	**Pool Option**	**Open Market Option**
Primary Risk Taker(S)	Government	Private insurers	Private insurers	Private insurers
Secondary Risk Taker(S)	Reinsurers	Reinsurers	Government, reinsurers	Reinsurers

III. The Role of Governments as Primary Risk Takers

In order to prevent a protection gap the government may step in and act as a primary insurer who bears the risk. This is a more intrusive market intervention than establishing a government backed reinsurance pool.

[16] Understanding and Addressing Global Insurance Gaps n3, 2–3.
[17] Understanding and Addressing Global Insurance Gaps n3, 30.

As an example, the US Federal Government takes this role through the National Flood Insurance Program (NFIP),[18] under which it is compulsory to obtain flood insurance for properties that are in high-risk flood areas and that either have government-backed mortgages or have received federal disaster assistance previously.[19] A person can purchase an NFIP flood insurance policy, also known as the Standard Flood Insurance Policy (SFIP), either: (1) Directly from the federal government through a direct servicing agent, or (2) from a private insurance company.[20] The former is provided through NFIP Direct and the latter is available via around 50 insurance companies[21] who participate in the Write Your Own (WYO) programme.

Write Your Own is a public private partnership between the Federal Government and the insurers.[22] It has been in operation since 1983 and facilitates broad geographic distribution of policies. Through WYO, the NFIP has access to the expertise of private market insurers and agents that have broad access to millions of clients. It is the nation's largest single-line insurance programme, with more than five million policyholders nationwide, and nearly $1.3 trillion in coverage.

The insurance companies participating in the WYO can market, sell, and service NFIP policies under their own name in exchange for an administrative allowance from the NFIP.[23] When flood damage occurs, the participating company can process the claim. These are non-risk-bearing policies for the WYO companies, as any claims payments that are made by them are reimbursed by the NFIP.[24]

Insurance agents that do not conduct business with one of the WYO companies can still write flood insurance for their clients directly with the NFIP through the NFIP Direct programme. NFIP Direct is operated by a government contractor with no marketing component and performs the same basic functions as a WYO company.[25]

[18] Congress established the NFIP on August 1, 1968, with the passage of the National Flood Insurance Act (NFIA) of 1968, which has been modified over the years.

[19] The Flood Disaster Protection Act of 1973.

[20] www.marsh.com/content/dam/marsh/Documents/PDF/US-en/Reforming%20the%20National%20Flood%20Insurance%20Program.pdf.

[21] These insurance companies are selected based on their experience and expertise in the insurance industry, as well as their ability to provide quality customer service to policyholders. www.linkedin.com/pulse/what-nfips-write-your-own-program-rocket-mga?trk=article-ssr-frontend-pulse_more-articles_related-content-card.

[22] Under the National Flood Insurance Act of 1968 (NFIA), as amended (42 USC 4001 *et seq*) The Federal Emergency Management Agency (FEMA) may carry out the NFIP through the facilities of the Federal government, using, for the purposes of providing flood insurance coverage, insurance companies and other insurers, insurance agents and brokers, and insurance adjustment organizations, as fiscal agents of the United States. See 42 USC 4071.

[23] Companies retain a portion of the premiums they collect on behalf of the NFIP, and receive compensation for overseeing, administering, and paying claims. FEMA also provides for the possibility of a growth bonus the amount of which varies by the extent a WYO company meets certain marketing goals. www.federalregister.gov/documents/2019/07/08/2019-14343/national-flood-insurance-program-nfip-revisions-to-methodology-for-payments-to-write-your-own-wyo.

[24] The federal government who retains responsibility for underwriting losses reinsures the risks insured with private reinsurers.

[25] www.marsh.com/content/dam/marsh/Documents/PDF/US-en/Reforming%20the%20National%20Flood%20Insurance%20Program.pdf.

In order to qualify for flood insurance, the property must be in a community that has joined NFIP and agreed to adopt and enforce sound floodplain management regulations that meet or exceed the Federal Emergency Management Agency (FEMA) requirements to reduce the risk and consequences of serious flooding.[26]

The Federal Emergency Management Agency (FEMA)[27] manages WYO. FEMA establishes terms of insurance and rates, which are the same whether purchased directly from the NFIP or through the WYO programme.[28] The WYO strengthens the NFIP's competitive position and improves rates as the premium may fall due to competition from other non-WYO companies offering alternative private flood insurance at reduced rates.

FEMA has the dual functions of civil defence and emergency management. Before a disaster, FEMA's focus is to build a culture of national preparedness through active community engagement, trainings and education, and planning.[29] It works closely with the insurance industry to facilitate the sale and servicing of flood insurance policies. FEMA coordinates federal response efforts to stabilise communities after a disaster and support individuals and communities to build back and become more resilient than before. FEMA disaster assistance is only available when a federal disaster is declared by the president.

Some losses may not be covered by insurance. In order to receive any type of direct or indirect federal financial assistance either in the form of a grant, loan, or a subsidy, flood insurance is a pre-requisite for the properties in high-risk flood areas. Federal disaster assistance programmes are not designed to restore the property to its pre-disaster condition but, they aim to help the policyholders to get back on their feet. The assistance comes in two forms: a loan, which must be paid back with interest, or a FEMA disaster grant, which is about $5,000 on average per household.[30] By comparison, the average flood insurance claim in 2018 was more than $40,000. Grants provided by FEMA are therefore not always enough to cover all losses.

The New Zealand government provides a similar coverage[31] for earthquakes.[32] Having recognised that without state intervention there would be a big protection

[26] www.fema.gov/flood-insurance/work-with-nfip/community-status-book.

[27] The National Flood Insurance Act of 1968 (NFIA), as amended (42 USC 4001 *et seq*), authorizes the Administrator of the Federal Emergency Management Agency (FEMA) to establish and carry out the NFIP to enable interested persons to purchase insurance against loss resulting from physical damage to, or loss of, real or personal property arising from flood in the United States. See 42 USC 4011(a).

[28] The average annual premium for an NFIP policy is about $700.

[29] www.fema.gov/about/how-fema-works#FEMA-Before.

[30] FEMA grants do not have to be paid back. www.fema.gov/disaster/recover/faq.

[31] A thorough analysis of this public private partnership for natural disaster losses in New Zealand is covered by Prof Rob Merkin in Chapter 7 of this work. Here, in order not to duplicate, the New Zealand system will be mentioned briefly for comparison purposes only.

[32] New Zealand has experienced major earthquake losses through centuries. 'Major New Zealand Earthquakes since 1855 – New Zealand Parliament' www.parliament.nz.

gap, an Earthquake and War Damage Commission (EQC) was created in 1944[33] to provide primary layer coverage for domestic and commercial buildings. The excess coverage was provided by private market insurers. Later, storm, flood, tsunami and volcanic activity was included in this primary insurance and commercial properties were excluded.

The EQC was redesignated as a Crown entity in 1993[34] with the primary function of administering insurance against natural disaster damage. It was not regulated as an insurer, nor was it an insurer or in a contractual relationship with any claimant.[35] The EQC was funded by levies on insurance policies to be paid into a Natural Disaster Fund (NDF). EQC liabilities were subject to a Crown guarantee to which the NDF paid an annual levy, and which would meet losses if the NDF were to become exhausted. The EQC obtained reinsurance from the private insurance market.

The PPP reached between the insurers and the EQC provided a two-tier system: the EQC undertook to pay damage to residential buildings up to $100,000, plus 12.5% General Sales Tax (GST). This was available only where there was private insurance in place.

The earthquakes that occurred in 2010 and 2011 caused massive losses; close to 700,000 insurance claims were made, 168,000 of them involving private insurers. After another earthquake that hit Christchurch in 2016, the EQC and the majority of the private insurers piloted an agency model by which a private insurer acts as the EQC's agent to assess and settle claims made by their mutual customer.[36] On or about 13 December 2016, EQC entered into the memorandum of understanding relating to Kaikōura earthquake claims management with most (but not all) of the private insurers. Private insurers took over responsibility for assessing and settling on the EQC's behalf (and in some cases its own behalf) for dwelling claims. The EQC remained responsible for assessing and settling any claim for earthquake damage to residential land and any residential building where an EQC claim remained open for that building from a previous earthquake.[37] The EQC was then to reimburse the insurers for sums paid out by them under the cap and was to contribute pro rata to handling costs. This was such a success that 99% of building claims assessed and 95% of building claims received settlement by March 2018.

The report produced in March 2020[38] as a result of the Public Inquiry into the Earthquake Commission reflected the experiences with the earthquake claims

[33] Earlier, the War Damage Act 1941 had established the War Risks Commission.
[34] The Earthquake Commission Act 1993.
[35] *C & S Kelly Properties Ltd v Earthquake Commission* [2015] NZHC 1690.
[36] www.eqc.govt.nz/assets/Publications-Resources/11-v2.-The-Kaikoura-Earthquake.pdf 5.
[37] www.eqc.govt.nz/news/new-natural-disaster-response-model-to-improve-customer-experience-during-the-next-natural-disaster/.
[38] www.dpmc.govt.nz/sites/default/files/2021-01/report-of-the-public-inquiry-into-the-earthquake-commission.pdf.

made in the past decade: there was no formal co-operation between the EQC and private insurers in assessing claims and in sharing investigation costs; the cause (must be a natural catastrophe) and the amount of the damage (must exceed the EQC's retention) must be ascertained before an insurance claim is made. The sheer volume of claims had overwhelmed resources.

The Government and eight insurers reached the Natural Disaster Response Agreement (NDRA), which came into force on 30 June 2021.[39] The NDRA abolished the two-tier system in the claims stage that any person holding a property policy with one of the participating insurers and whose dwelling suffers natural catastrophe damage may claim only against his or her insurers.[40]

The Earthquake Commission Act 1993 was replaced by the Natural Hazards Act 2023, which came into force on 27 February 2024. The EQC was renamed the Natural Hazards Commission (NHC) Toka Tū Ake. Insured homeowners still have a single point of contact and are still able to lodge their claim directly through their private insurer. Insurers will act as agents of the NHC for all claims-handling purposes. The measure of indemnity for a building is, by ss 30 to 35, replacement cost, but NHC does not provide any additional funding for 'building back better' to improve a building's resilience to natural hazards. The sum recoverable is capped at $300,000 plus GST, with a deductible of $500, for each dwelling.

Moreover, in 2023 the Government established the New Zealand Claims Resolution Service to provide independent support to homeowners to resolve residential insurance issues resulting from natural disasters.[41]

IV. The Cost of Government Acting as an Insurer

The fact that the government steps in as a primary insurer addresses insurance affordability and strengthens the nation's resilience to certain risks. However, this type of PPP is not favoured universally due to its cost to the government.[42] Hurricanes Katrina, Rita, and Wilma in 2005 left the NFIP approximately $19 billion into debt. In 2012, Superstorm Sandy added $7 billion to NFIP's debt to the US Treasury.[43] The 2010 and 2011 earthquakes exceeded $21 billion in cost to the insurance industry,[44] which wiped out the $5.6 billion Natural Disaster Fund available to the EQC. Further earthquakes occurred in 2016, leading to

[39] www.icnz.org.nz/industry/media-releases/new-natural-disaster-response-model-to-improve-customer-experience-during-the-next-natural-disaster/.

[40] www.eqc.govt.nz/assets/Publications-Resources/EOM_Performance_Dashboard_Apr-22_Publication.pdf.

[41] 'Who we are: New Zealand Claims Resolution Service' nzcrs.govt.nz.

[42] Regulation impact statement (TI Act amendment) n7, 35; www.oecd.org/fr/finances/assurances/33913415.pdf.

[43] www.marsh.com/content/dam/marsh/Documents/PDF/US-en/Reforming%20the%20National%20Flood%20Insurance%20Program.pdf.

[44] www.icnz.org.nz/industry/canterbury-earthquakes/.

about 7000 claims in total, exhausting the Natural Disaster Fund, which received about $200 million from the Crown Guarantee. The US and New Zealand examples showed that governments would continue to bear increased costs after hurricanes and earthquakes for communities where there are high levels of underinsurance and no insurance.

Reinsuring the risk insured by the government would strengthen the financial capability of meeting catastrophic losses. However, still, the compliance rate to the insurance requirement is crucial in collecting the premiums. Subsidies can be considered to promote widespread access to and affordability of insurance.[45] However, such subsidies may negatively influence the programme's long-term ability to manage its financial obligations. They come at a fiscal cost each year, are often unsustainable as a long-term solution, and are difficult to withdraw.[46] Moreover, depending on the design of a subsidy, future price increases would either reduce the effectiveness of the subsidy or increase its cost to government.[47]

The worldwide experience is that reinsurance pools have been preferred over government acting as a primary insurer. Numerous different applications of such pools in the world rendered unaffordably expensive insurance coverage accessible for many. They demonstrated that over a period of time, the pools successfully collected the premium to fund their resources, which also led the rates being reduced.

V. Reinsurance Pools

Reinsurance is a safety net for private insurers through which the insurers secure their solvency and improve their capacity. Private reinsurers are commercial entities who diversify their exposure across many regions globally, ensuring that the prices they charge will allow them to remain solvent and profitable. Reinsurance cost to the insurers directly impact the premium charged by them under the primary insurance. Similarly, a lack of appetite amongst reinsurers to reinsure certain risks will reflect the insurer's behaviours towards insuring them.

Hence, although governments can purchase reinsurance for the coverage they undertake as a primary insurer,[48] reinsurance may not always be offered by the private market. Even if a reinsurance coverage was purchased, as observed by NFIP[49] and EQC,[50] it may be exhausted before the losses caused by a catastrophe

[45] NFIP subsidies about 20% of the premiums. www.marsh.com/content/dam/marsh/Documents/PDF/US-en/Reforming%20the%20National%20Flood%20Insurance%20Program.pdf.

[46] Regulation impact statement (TI Act amendment), n7, 35–36.

[47] Regulation impact statement (TI Act amendment), n7, 35.

[48] See NFIP and NHC above.

[49] NFIP has required additional funding on several occasions and since 2004 has borrowed $US39.4 billion from the federal government to pay out claims. Regulation impact statement (TI Act amendment), n7, 35.

[50] See Merkin, Chapter 7 of this work.

are fully compensated. As a result, rendering governments direct insurers might impose unjust and grave burden on taxpayers, or levies paid by the policyholders through the premium would have to be increased.[51]

Some nations therefore are of the view that a more balanced solution may be found encouraging private insurers and reinsurers to take certain risks and governments providing a guarantee for the loss exceeding the amount the pool bears.[52] A reinsurance pool has the potential to deliver premium reductions and promote competition through new entrants to the relevant insurance market.[53]

Although the reinsurance pools adopted by many nations worldwide have some common features, they are not identical to each other. They differ on how they are structured, how they are funded and how they approach setting premiums and paying claims. It is common for those pools to not set premiums at the true technical rate corresponding to the underlying risk, but instead they charge a flat rate fee, receive a levy from all insurers, set risk-based but discounted premiums, or implement a combination of these.

Most of such pools are backed by some form of a government guarantee which can be called on if claims exceed reserves. Where this is not the case, or where the guarantee is limited, the pool generally limits the claims it will pay in some way.

A. Natural Catastrophe Pools

Pool solutions are regarded as global best practice.[54] As an example of supporting insurance for natural catastrophes, the Florida Hurricane Catastrophe Fund (FHCF) was created in 1993. When Hurricane Andrew struck Florida in 1992, it caused $15 billion in insured losses and at least 11 insurer insolvencies. Having recognised that an unstable market for property insurance threatened the state's economy, the Florida legislature created the Florida Hurricane Catastrophe Fund (FHCF) in 1993.[55] The FHCF operates 'exclusively for the purpose of protecting and advancing the state's interest in maintaining insurance capacity' in Florida. Similar to private reinsurance, the FHCF aims to provide reimbursements to insurers for a portion of their catastrophic hurricane losses. Its cost is, however, significantly lower than purchasing a private reinsurance, as it does not include a profit factor or risk load in its rates, and it is exempt from federal taxes.

In general, the FHCF covers a percentage of the insurer's hurricane losses in excess of the insurer's retention. The FHCF's maximum potential obligation is capped at $17 billion for a single season. It charges each insurer for the coverage

[51] For the New Zealand earthquakes experience, see Merkin, Chapter 7 of this work.

[52] Regulation impact statement (TI Act amendment), n7, 33–38.

[53] Regulation impact statement (TI Act amendment), n7, 35.

[54] www.oecd.org/fr/finances/assurances/33913415.pdf 7.

[55] The Florida Legislature adopted the original FHCF statute, section 215.555. Since then, the Legislature has amended the FHCF statute many times. A summary of those changes can be seen on fhcf.sbafla.com/media/uvmnfyka/2022-fhcf-annual-report.pdf.

provided. Premiums, retentions, and coverage limits are based on each insurer's annual reporting of insured values by line of business, construction type, and zip code and on hurricane loss projection models found acceptable by the Florida Commission on Hurricane Loss Projection Methodology. In addition to premiums, other sources of liquidity to pay FHCF claims can include, when applicable, investment income, proceeds from pre-event bonding, recoveries from reinsurance and other risk transfer transactions, and proceeds from post-event revenue bonds. Participation in the FHCF is mandatory for Florida residential property insurers, except for insurers with Florida exposures below a de minimis threshold.

Such pools also support insurance of earthquake. In Indonesia it was made compulsory for general insurance and reinsurance companies to participate in the Indonesian Earthquake Pool.[56] The pool, operating since 2003, is a Special Risk Insurance Company which facilitates reinsurance protection at lower costs so that overreliance on the international reinsurance markets is prevented.

With an amendment to the Terrorism Insurance Act 2003, the Australian Government implemented a cyclone and related flood damage[57] reinsurance pool[58] to come into force on 1 July 2022.[59] Its core design is to provide mandatory[60] reinsurance for eligible cyclone risks held by insurance companies for the purposes of improving insurance access and affordability for households and small businesses in cyclone-prone areas.[61]

A reinsurance pool was selected over the Australian Government acting as a primary insurer as the former was found as a more balanced way that has the potential of increasing competition by encouraging greater insurer participation in cyclone-prone areas and support higher levels of insurance coverage by property owners.[62] Household property policies, strata policies, small business property policies, property policies for charities and not-for-profit entities and farm residential policies for loss of or damage to eligible property and associated business interruption or consequential losses are generally eligible under the cyclone reinsurance scheme.

[56] Government Regulation No 63 issued in 1999.

[57] Eligible cyclone related losses include damage caused by a cyclone that commences during a declared cyclone event, including any damage due to wind, rain, rainwater and rainwater run-off, storm surge and flooding, where these hazards are covered under the policyholder's choice of insurance cover.

[58] See Chapter 8 of this work.

[59] Insurers had until 31 December 2023 to reinsure all eligible cyclone insurance risks with the ARPC.

[60] Insurers that fail to participate in the scheme will be subject to a civil penalty which is 1,000 penalty units for every year (or part thereof) that the insurer fails to reinsure eligible cyclone risks with the ARPC. Some insurers are not required to participate in the cyclone reinsurance scheme. General insurers with minimum exposure to policies with eligible cyclone risks, if their total gross written premiums for a calendar year are below the threshold amount prescribed by the regulations (exempt general insurer); Lloyd's underwriters under the Insurance Act 1973; and unauthorised foreign insurers under the Insurance Regulations 2002.

[61] Explanatory memorandum, n7 [2.13].

[62] Explanatory memorandum, n7 [2.6].

The pool will cover all eligible claims above the policyholder's excess for cyclone events for the first three years. Thereafter, the pool will operate on a risk-sharing arrangement with insurers to allow a staged transition to a limited level of risk retention by insurers. The level of risk retention will be set by ministerial direction and will be informed by consultation with insurers. For example, the ARPC might pay up to a certain percentage of the eligible claim with a further cap to an insurer's annual liability thereafter. However, the pool is expected to continue to cover a significant proportion of eligible risks. In years where there are few or no claims on the pool the minister may also direct the ARPC to make payments to the Commonwealth's Consolidated Revenue Fund (with specific amounts to be set in ministerial determinations).

The cyclone reinsurance scheme is administered by the ARPC. The existing terrorism reinsurance scheme operates concurrently with the new cyclone reinsurance scheme. The Commonwealth guarantee for the cyclone reinsurance scheme is separated from the guarantee for the existing terrorism reinsurance scheme.

Insurers must obtain reinsurance for all eligible cyclone and related flood risks and must obtain it from the ARPC. The scheme aims for insurers to reinsure cyclone risks at a lower cost than in the private reinsurance market, as the scheme is designed to be cost-neutral to government over time and be backed by a Commonwealth guarantee.[63] It is funded by the insurers' premium payments to participate in the scheme. The premiums charged cover the long-term costs of insured risk in addition to expenses associated with operating the cyclone reinsurance scheme, including the pool's ongoing administration expenses. The cyclone reinsurance scheme to be backed by an annually reinstated $10 billion Commonwealth guarantee. High natural peril reinsurance costs have been a barrier to entry into the northern Australian market. By reducing reinsurance costs and sharing the risk of meeting cyclone damage claims in northern Australia, the pool is expected to encourage additional insurers to enter this market. With the stability and lower cost insurers are believed to manage their cyclone risk exposure.[64]

Participation is mandatory to maximise joining the insurers and to enable the greatest potential premium reductions. Moreover, with the diversification of risk for the reinsurance pool, mandatory participation negates the risk that insurers only pass on their 'worst' risks to the pool or that only insurers with the riskiest portfolios participate.[65]

Without minimum public standards of disaster awareness, education, information, monitoring, prediction, early warning, safety, prevention, alleviation, the insurance industry will not be encouraged to relieve the government and share the potential financial drain on fiscal resources.[66] Moreover, the mitigation activities

[63] Explanatory memorandum, n7 [2.18].
[64] Regulation impact statement (TI Act amendment), n7, 44.
[65] Regulation impact statement (TI Act amendment), n7, 40.
[66] www.oecd.org/fr/finances/assurances/33913415.pdf.

has the potential of sustainably reducing premiums.[67] In Australia the government has established the National Recovery and Resilience Agency (NRRA) following the 2020 Royal Commission into Natural Disaster Arrangements. In establishing the new agency, the Government provided $615.5 million for the Preparing Australia programme to provide grants for projects that support public and private disaster risk reduction and resilience.

B. Terrorism Pools

Reinsurance pools more often are available for insuring terrorism.[68] The pools were generally established through legislation. In Australia it is through the Terrorism Insurance Act 2003 (Cth) (TI Act); in France, the Code des Assurances article L126-2; in Israel, the Property Tax and Compensation Fund Law; in the USA, the Terrorism Risk Insurance Act of 2002 (TRIA); and in Denmark, it is the Danish Terrorism Insurance Act.

The pools were established as a result of the lack of insurance,[69] and reinsurance coverage for terrorism in the national and international insurance markets. Participation in the pools, in most countries, is voluntary for insurance buyers[70] but usually mandatory[71] for insurers. In the USA any insurer subject to TRIA must make the offer of terrorism risk insurance.

Usually, a scheme administers the collection of the fund and the payment of the claims.[72] In Australia, that is through the Australian Reinsurance Pool Corporation (ARPC), in the UK, it is through Pool Re.

Insurers are free to set their own terrorism premiums for the underlying policies to insurance buyers, according to normal commercial arrangements. In Spain there is a flat rate to extend the coverage for extraordinary risks, reflected in a surcharge payable by the policyholder when purchasing an in-scope policy.

The schemes are not usually extended to life, personal injury or workers compensation.

The coverage is primarily for property, including commercial and industrial buildings. In Israel homes are included.

Usually the coverage is provided in layers. The layers differ from country to country. A state guarantee is available in some but not in all. For instance, in most pools claims are covered by the insurers, and once insurers' retention is exhausted, claims are paid by the scheme. In Australia, for example, almost all commercial

[67] Regulation impact statement (TI Act amendment), n7, 36.

[68] Austria, Australia, Belgium, Denmak, France, Germany, India, Israel, Netherlands, South Africa, Spain, United Kingdom and USA. iftrip.org/wp-content/uploads/2022/06/terrorism-pool-index-2022.pdf.

[69] Except for South Africa and Israel.

[70] The uptake rate is about 95% (eg Belgium, Netherlands).

[71] Australia, South Africa, Denmark, France.

[72] www.oecd.org/daf/fin/insurance/Terrorism-Risk-Insurance-Country-Comparison.pdf.

property insurers choose to reinsure their risk with ARPC. Once ARPC's pool is exhausted, the retrocessionnaire will be called for. If the retrocession is exhausted, claims will continue to be met by the Commonwealth guarantee. Retrocession programme is sourced from the commercial reinsurance market. A similar system applies in Belgium, Netherlands and Germany except that there are three layers including the state guarantee.[73] In Germany EXTREMUS[74] is a company established by seventeen insurers and reinsurers, and it acts as a primary insurer, issuing the policies on its own paper. EXTREMUS buys reinsurance from its shareholders, from other companies active in the German market and from international reinsurers. Similarly, in South Africa, the South African government and the South African Insurance Association formed Sasria,[75] an insurance company focusing on political risk. Day-to-day administration of insurance contracts, and collection of premiums is undertaken by insurance companies, and Sasria only ever comes into direct contact with a client in the event of the settlement of a claim. Sasria's portfolio is protected by quota share and catastrophe reinsurance treaty underwritten by the global reinsurance market. Participation is compulsory for insurers.

In France[76] the state provides an unlimited backstop, but with the distinctive feature of the maximal use of private reinsurance to increase the limits covered by the market before state intervention.

In Austria all retention and reinsurance arrangements are on a non-state basis.[77] The private insurance market provides coverage structured in two layers; direct insurers, up to 100 million Euro; and, reinsurance by the international reinsurance market, 200 million. In India non-life insurers set up the Indian Market Terrorism Risk Insurance Pool (IMTRIP) in 2002. The participating insurers split shares and premiums based on the capacity they can provide.

The pool purchases reinsurance in most of these countries. In India members of the pool are responsible for reinsuring the entirety of terrorism risk on property insurance policies written by all companies.

Spain does not purchase reinsurance because a state-owned enterprise, Consorcio de Compensación de Seguros (CCS),[78] manages the Extraordinary Risks Insurance Scheme, which comprises natural (flood, windstorm, earthquake, tsunami, etc) and man-made risks, terrorism being included in the latter. In the event that these extraordinary risks (totally or partly) are not covered by the original issuer of the policy, CCS would automatically cover the damages for the same amounts and conditions in the original policy, provided that none of

[73] www.ecb.europa.eu/press/financial-stability-publications/fsr/focus/2007/pdf/ecb~7585877f4b.fsrbox200712_18.pdf.

[74] extremus.de/.

[75] www.sasria.co.za/.

[76] www.ccr.fr/en/l-entreprise-ccr.

[77] iftrip.org/wp-content/uploads/2022/06/terrorism-pool-index-2022.pdf.

[78] www.consorseguros.es/en/inicio.

these risks are expressly assumed by the insurer issuing the base policy. There is a state guarantee in case losses exceed CCS capacity.

The Dutch Terrorism Reinsurance Pool (NHT)[79] was founded in July 2003. Members include insurance and reinsurance companies, while international reinsurance companies and the Dutch government provide reinsurance. Insurers remain responsible for contact with the insured and handling of claims, but each member must implement the "NHT clause" in the policy wording, which makes the terrorism coverage and wording identical for all members. In Israel, where reinsurance coverage is not purchased for terrorism risk, compensation is paid by the state at a percentage of the purchase tax collections allocated to the fund each year and by the insurance industry.

In the UK Pool Re[80] was founded in 1993 by the insurance industry, in cooperation with Her Majesty's Treasury, to create a private-sector solution in support of a public policy objective. The scheme, which is owned by its members, is open to any authorised insurer. Pool Re's member are not only the UK companies. In total it has 149 members 84 of them from United Kingdom 25 of which are Lloyd's syndicates.[81] Pool Re's primary role is to enable the UK commercial market to underwrite the threat of terrorism to commercial property at affordable rates, by mitigating their exposure to the catastrophic losses associated with major attacks. It also undertakes risk mitigation initiatives in partnership with UK Government and the Counter Terrorism police.

At its inception the scheme only offered cover for fire and explosion, which was extended in 2003 to 'All-Risks' including CBRN and then widened further in 2018 to encompass damage caused by remote digital interference. The coverage was extended to non-damage business interruption losses in 2019. In the event of a certified act of terrorism, initial losses will be covered by member retentions; where the retention threshold is exceeded, the insurer can claim upon Pool Re's reserves. The scheme obtains reinsurance coverage on behalf of all its members from the professional reinsurance markets as part of a multi-layered programme. It has a Retrocession Agreement with HM Government under the terms of which HM Government will make funds available in circumstances where Pool Re's assets are insufficient to meet all claims.

Pool Re terrorism coverage can only be offered by members in conjunction with a commercial property policy. Where a member insurer provides property insurance in Great Britain, they must offer terrorism coverage upon request. They can provide coverage to all or any of their eligible policyholders who wish to buy terrorism coverage. All claims are handled by the underlying property insurer.

Pool Re's investment fund available in the event of an attack has been entirely built up by its members, and no public money has been involved. It has built an

[79] nht.vereende.nl/en/.
[80] www.poolre.co.uk/.
[81] www2.poolre.co.uk/membership/; assets.poolre.co.uk/sitefiles/2022/06/Pool-Re-Annual-Report-2021-FINAL.pdf 56.

investment fund valued at £6.9bn. A further £2.4bn of protection is provided under a commercial retrocession programme attaching above the first £0.4bn of the investment fund, with an additional £75m protection provided by the issuance of an Insurance Linked Security sitting within the first layer of the retrocession programme. Pool Re pays the Government each year for providing the backstop and in 2021, this amounted to £186m.[82]

Since its establishment in 1993, Pool Re has paid out a total of £635m for 13 certified terrorism events, without recourse to HM Government or the taxpayer.[83] The cost of reinsurance from Pool Re outside Central London was reduced by 20% from October 2022.[84]

Another example of a PPP to enable insurance of terrorism has been in place in the USA since the passing of the Terrorism Risk Insurance Act (TRIA) in 2002. Initially a temporary three-year federal programme was built with the objective of the federal government and the insurers to share monetary losses caused by a terrorist attack. TRIA since then has been renewed in 2005, 2007, 2015 and 2019. The current reauthorisation is valid until 31 December 2027. TRIA requires insurers to make terrorism coverage available to commercial policyholders, but it does not require insureds to purchase it. The US Government provides a backstop. The Treasury does not charge a premium to participating insurers for the protection provided by the programme. A mechanism, however, would operate in the event that federal payments are made to insurers under the programme, that the Secretary to recoup 'terrorism loss risk-spreading premiums' from insurers through surcharges imposed upon commercial policyholders.

C. Regional Pools

If a national pool on its own is not a feasible option, an alternative solution may lie in the establishment of a regional pool where different nations, developments agencies and external donors bring together their resources to be spent for a common good for all of them. This has been a practice especially in Africa, the Caribbean and the Pacific.

In 2007, the Caribbean Catastrophe Risk Insurance Facility (CCRIF)[85] was formed as the first multi-country risk pool in the world. The World Bank, with a grant from the Government of Japan, led the project developing CCRIF. The parametric policies developed by CCRIF are backed by capital markets including Canada, EU, UK, France, Ireland and Bermuda. It is owned, operated and registered in the Caribbean. A segregated portfolio company, SPC facilitate offering

[82] assets.poolre.co.uk/sitefiles/2022/06/Pool-Re-Annual-Report-2021-FINAL.pdf 2.

[83] assets.poolre.co.uk/sitefiles/2022/06/Pool-Re-Annual-Report-2021-FINAL.pdf.

[84] www2.poolre.co.uk/pool-re-reduces-overall-reinsurance-pricing/#:~:text=The%20reduction%20will%20come%20into,in%20many%20non%2Durban%20areas.

[85] www.ccrif.org/?language_content_entity=en.

CCRIF products which aim to provide a quick short-term liquidity when a policy is triggered for tropical cyclones, earthquakes and excess rainfall.

Throughout the policy year, CCRIF monitors and reports on tropical cyclone, earthquake, and excess rainfall events in the Caribbean Basin that have the potential to affect one or more of its members that have policies that are related to these events. Tropical cyclones are monitored to determine if any members' tropical cyclone or electric utilities policies or the Tropical Cyclone component of their COAST policies have been triggered. For policy year 2022/23, there were 55 tropical cyclone, excess rainfall, or earthquake events for which CCRIF prepared event briefing reports, which were disseminated to member countries and stakeholders. While some of the rainfall events were associated with tropical cyclones, some were unrelated to any cyclonic system, and one occurred outside the Atlantic Hurricane Season.[86]

The African Risk Capacity (ARC) Group was set up in 2012. ARC is led by 39 African Union Member States.[87] Its objective is to strengthen the continent's Disaster Risk Management systems through its capacity building and risk pooling services. Its activities include plan, prepare, and respond to natural disasters triggered by extreme weather events, as well as outbreaks and epidemics. ARC Ltd is the financial affiliate of the Group responsible for carrying out commercial insurance functions of risk pooling and risk transfer adopting parametric weather insurance. In Africa, considering the scale of the losses and the facilities available, natural disasters may cause a humanitarian crisis. ARC takes into account the diversification of weather risk across Africa and enables countries to manage their risk as a group in a financially efficient manner. With the ARC and parametric insurance, Africa's responses to natural disasters changed course from being post-disaster, reactive, and relying on international appeals to preventive long-term capacity-building to enable timely actions.

The ARC risk pool combines the risk of a disaster occurring across several countries to take advantage of the natural diversity of weather systems across Africa. ARC approached the market as a group rather than considering the risk profile of each individual country. A 50% reduction in the contingent funds needed if the risk is pooled among nations and managed as a group rather than borne by each country individually. Approaching the market as a group will therefore significantly reduce the individual premiums required to maintain the solvency of the facility.

Each member country pays a premium to ARC Ltd. When the rainfall deviation is sufficiently severe such that the estimated response costs cross a certain predefined threshold, qualifying risk pool members receive a payout within 2–4 weeks of the end of the rainfall season. Through such early intervention programmes, ARC prevents vulnerable populations from taking negative coping actions.

[86] www.ccrif.org/sites/default/files/publications/annualreports/CCRIFSPC-Annual-Report-2022-2023_lowres.pdf.

[87] For the list of ARC Member States, see www.arc.int/countries.

The Southeast Asia Disaster Risk Insurance Facility (SEADRIF) in Asia, although being a regional establishment, operates differently to the other regional regimes mentioned above. The SEADRIF is an insurance company incorporated in Singapore in April 2019 as fully owned by SEADRIF member countries.[88] The company provides disaster risk financing and insurance products to participating countries. The company is subject to the risk-based capital framework, with requirements for companies to put in place sufficient capital to ensure the ability to meet its liabilities and provide protection to the participating countries. It is monitored by the Monetary Authority of Singapore. As a whole, the SEADRIF Initiative is not managed for profit and any income or capital will be redeployed in ways that support its sole objective of providing protection to member countries.

The World Bank is not a member, but it has supported the SEADRIF initiative since inception, advancing the preparatory work for the region. Similar to CCRIF and ARC, SEADRIF provides insurance against natural disasters in the parametric and finite risk models. SEADRIF obtains reinsurance for the risks insured by it.

Parametric insurance follows a stepped payout structure based on fixed parameters that correspond to predefined levels of the modelled number of people affected by a disaster. In SEADRIF, for instance, the Flood Risk Monitoring Tool continuously monitor the situation on the ground, provides near real-time flood impact assessments like estimated water levels and determine whether a flood is occurring and, if so, how severe it is.

The tool combines various data sets to determine the severity of the event in terms of how likely it is to occur: 1 in 8 years (meaning, on average, an event with this severity or worse occurs every 8 years) for a medium-scale event or 1 in 20 years for severe events. This then determines whether the beneficiary will receive a 40% payout (for medium events) or 100% (for severe events). 40% of the policy limit is payable in the event of a 'medium' disaster, and 100% of the policy limit is payable in the case of a 'severe' disaster.

Unlike the ARC mentioned above, in SEADRIF each country's hydrological history and total population is taken into account so that event severity is calibrated to each country. The severity of an event is calculated based on the estimated number of people who live in areas flooded by at least 25 cm of water.

Triggers are set against a model or proxy which may not always fully reflect reality. For example, there can be instances when a payout is not made after a severe event despite relatively high losses. This is known as basis risk, which occurs when the index used as the basis for payouts does not fully correlate with the actual losses incurred. There may be cases when a payout is made following a minor event with relatively low losses (known as positive basis risk events). For the losses that do not fall under SEADRIF, the parametric component can be claimed under its finite component upon proof of the event that caused the loss.

[88] Cambodia, Indonesia, Lao PDR, Myanmar, Philippines, Singapore, Japan, Vietnam.

VI. Bonds

Catastrophe (CAT) bonds are financial instruments that use a process called securitisation to wrap natural disaster risk into a tradable format.[89] A CAT bond is defined as a security that pays the issuer when a disaster event meets certain pre-defined criteria, such as an earthquake reaching a magnitude of 7.0.[90] Entities exposed to natural disaster risk, such as insurers, state catastrophe funds, through CAT bonds, can transfer a portion of that risk from their balance sheet to bond investors.[91]

The sponsor, namely the entity exposed to the risk, enters into an insurance contract with a special-purpose vehicle (SPV) to act as a facilitator to transfer the catastrophe risk from the sponsor to the investors. As well as collecting the required risk capital by issuing the CAT bond to investors, the SPV grants reinsurance coverage or catastrophe swap protection to the sponsor.[92] Investors that purchased the bond collectively provide the sponsor with the capital to be used in case the insured risks take place and payouts become due. The SPV invests the cash raised by selling the bonds in highly rated securities that are held in a collateral trust. It has access to broader financial markets and may offer institutional investors, such as hedge funds, the opportunity to earn a return on investment in exchange for assuming catastrophe insurance risks.[93] The sponsor pays the premium which is paid to the investors as periodic coupons on the bonds.[94]

If a specified natural disaster occurs during the term of the bond, some or all of the assets held as collateral are liquidated and that money is paid to the sponsor as a pay-out under its insurance contract with the SPV. CAT bond payouts may be triggered on the basis of an actual loss (indemnity), or when the losses reach a certain aggregate (industry trigger), or through a parametric index.

In the event that no payouts had been necessary, the capital in proceeds would have been liquidated from the collateral account on the maturity date of the bonds and returned to investors. Investments through CAT bonds would be uncorrelated with the returns of other financial market instruments as the insured events; for example, hurricanes and tornadoes are largely unrelated to economic and financial activity.

Insurers may issue CAT bonds as describe above. Additionally, state catastrophe funds may transfer the risk from their balance sheet to investors. Florida Hurricane Catastrophe Fund (FHCF) mentioned above employs indemnity

[89] www.oecd-ilibrary.org/sites/99aa6fd8-en/index.html?itemId=/content/component/99aa6fd8-en.
[90] www.chicagofed.org/publications/chicago-fed-letter/2018/405.
[91] treasury.worldbank.org/en/about/unit/treasury/ibrd/ibrd-capital-at-risk-notes#3.
[92] www.oecd-ilibrary.org/sites/99aa6fd8-en/index.html?itemId=/content/component/99aa6fd8-en.
[93] www.chicagofed.org/publications/chicago-fed-letter/2018/405.
[94] A number of factors affect premiums, eg the number of perils covered in a CAT bond, time to maturity, the currency in which the bonds are denominated and the expected loss for investors, the estimation of which can be affected by the availability of robust, accurate and current data. www.oecd-ilibrary.org/sites/99aa6fd8-en/index.html?itemId=/content/component/99aa6fd8-en.

triggers as a way to ensure the risk coverage they receive from CAT bonds matches the losses in their portfolios. This risk-management strategy protects the long-run solvency of state funds by making sure that they have adequate resources to pay claims following a costly disaster.

FHCF's concern is to ensure a functioning insurance market. In developing nations governments may use CAT bonds with parametric triggers, so that they can establish multiyear access to insurance protection and quickly access disaster funds when their CAT bonds are triggered.

In this context the World Bank Treasury Disaster Risk Insurance Platform provides clients with advisory support and risk transfer solutions, including CAT bonds, against a wide range of shocks: droughts, floods, tropical cyclone, earthquake, tsunami, pandemic and other types of insurable perils.[95] The World Banks' Capital at Risk Notes can be used to transfer risks related to natural disasters and other risks from developing countries to the capital markets.[96] One of the CAT bonds issued by the World Bank's International Bank for Reconstruction and Development (IBRD) finances US$150 million of insurance coverage for the Government of Jamaica for tropical cyclone events.[97]

World Bank issued catastrophe bonds do not require an SPV. Instead, the sponsor (here Jamaica) enters into an insurance or derivative contract with the World Bank. The World Bank issues the bonds to investors, invests the proceeds, and manages payments to the sponsor and investors. Payouts to Jamaica will be triggered when a named storm event meets the criteria for location and severity set forth in the bond terms – on a parametric index base. The CAT bond attracted 15 global investors, providing the funding for catastrophe insurance to Jamaica for four hurricane seasons.[98]

Additionally, the Caribbean Catastrophe Risk Insurance Facility (CCRIF) – developed with the assistance of the World Bank – has used CAT bonds with parametric triggers to aid member states.[99]

Instead of reinsuring the risks, insurers may choose to transfer the risk to investors through CAT bonds. Alternative sources of capital attracted by CAT bonds may compete with reinsurers and exert downward pressure on reinsurance prices. CAT bonds may provide strong returns; however, investors will lose the

[95] treasury.worldbank.org/en/about/unit/treasury/ibrd-financial-products/disaster-risk-management#2.

[96] www.worldbank.org/en/news/press-release/2024/04/25/world-bank-returns-to-the-cat-bond-market-providing-financial-protection-to-jamaica.

[97] The CAT bond will be listed on the Hong Kong Exchange (HKEX), which is the second time the World Bank lists a CAT bond in Hong Kong. The first World Bank CAT bond listed on HKEX was for US$ 350 million providing the Government of Chile with financial protection against severe earthquake events for three years from 2023. www.worldbank.org/en/news/press-release/2023/03/28/world-bank-and-hong-kong-partner-on-a-350-million-cat-bond-for-chile#:~:text=This%20is%20the%20first%20World,country%20catastrophe%20risk%20transfer%20transaction.

[98] www.worldbank.org/en/news/press-release/2024/04/25/world-bank-returns-to-the-cat-bond-market-providing-financial-protection-to-jamaica.

[99] www.chicagofed.org/publications/chicago-fed-letter/2018/405.

total investment amount if a catastrophe arises. Although poor performance of other financial products may have no impact on CAT bonds, if a disaster occurs, the CAT bond investors will lose the total amount invested irrespective of the general performance of the financial markets.

VII. Insurance Buying Behaviour

In essence, the PPPs have emerged to manage the policyholder's buying behaviour as well as the accessibility and affordability of insurance.

Insurance affordability is one of the major factors in the availability and uptake of insurance coverage. Global consumer surveys suggest that about half of insurance buyers base their final purchasing decisions on price.[100] For many, the premium is a certain and near-term expense whereas the claim benefit is uncertain and distant and is therefore perceived as a potential loss.[101] Since individuals may be more sensitive to small losses than large gains, they may choose not to insure. Ease of purchase is also an important factor in insurance buying behaviour. Moreover, there is a correlation between risk awareness and insurance purchase and memory may fade quickly after a natural disaster that caused huge losses for the region or the nation.

The cost of high-risk insurance premiums was the largest barrier to adequate insurance coverage in northern Australia.[102] In 2018–2019, the average premium for combined home and contents insurance across the region was about $2,500 (in some parts $6,500) for homes and $13,400 for stratas, whilst the average premium for the rest of Australia was $1,400 for the former and $3300 for the latter.[103]

The challenge governments would face is therefore not only to ensure that insurance coverage is available but also affordable. It appears that the mandatory participation to the pool for the insurers targets premium reductions in high-risk areas without significantly affecting average premiums outside of those areas. The entry of additional insurers is expected to increase competition and place downward pressure on insurance premiums. The elimination of commercial profit margins through the mandatory participation of insurers and the government guarantee provides the premium reduction. The pool would not reduce the amount of private reinsurance coverage bought from the international reinsurance market, but it would reduce the price because there is less likelihood of claims.[104]

[100] Understanding and Addressing Global Insurance Gaps, n3, 25.
[101] Understanding and Addressing Global Insurance Gaps, n3, 7.
[102] Regulation impact statement (TI Act amendment), n7, 33.
[103] Regulation impact statement (TI Act amendment), n7, 30.
[104] Regulation impact statement (TI Act amendment), n7, 46.

Where the insurer's participation to the pool is voluntary, significant uncertainty may arise about the extent to which insurers choose to participate in the pool. The levels of savings could be further reduced by a lack of diversification of risk within the pool as insurers with higher-risk portfolios would cede to the pool, while insurers with lower-risk portfolios may not. Flood Re in the UK appears to apply a compromised solution between mandatory and voluntary participation to the pool. The Flood Re was established in 2016 with the objective of improving affordability for those households at highest risk of flooding and increase availability and choice of insurers for customers. The mandatory aspect of the Flood Re is that every insurer that offers home insurance in the UK must pay into the Flood Re scheme. This Levy raises £135m every year that is used to cover the flood risks in home insurance policies.[105] An insurer does not have to, but may, reinsure the flood risk with Flood Re, who then charges the insurer a fixed reinsurance premium. The reinsurance premium is tied to the insured home's council tax band, not the actual flood risk so that the overall price of the policy is low. Moreover, Flood Re's reinsurance is subject to £250 deductible for each policy.

A further benefit of a PPP is it improves the relationship between the policyholders and the insurers. Naturally, whether the insured risk will occur, and if it occurs, whether the loss will fall under the insurance coverage can only be found out after the policyholder suffers loss. A non-payment by the insurer, whether by a legitimate reason under the policy or not, would inevitably break the trust that a policyholder has towards the concept of insurance and the insurers. Governments' guarantees and the backing up claims for natural catastrophes may help build confidence in insurance. The joint work of the private insurers and the public bodies may provide more assurance for those who may be unsure about benefits of purchasing insurance coverage. This would then feed into the uptake of insurance and the collection of funds for the government's institutions or reinsurers through the premiums paid.

VIII. Concluding Remarks

When a risk is too great to be transferred to the insurance industry alone, it is also too great to be simply left uninsured and unmitigated on governments' balance sheets. Such risks cannot be simply left on individuals, insurers or governments alone. Through reinsurance pools uninsurable risks appears to be shared by all of these actors in a balanced way.

The insurance industry has the potential to shape behaviour and improve safety, security and resilience. Moreover, they have direct contact with the policyholders so that they can collect the premium, by which the reinsurance pools

[105] www.floodre.co.uk/how-flood-re-works/.

or governments guarantees supporting such pools will be funded. Insurers also have the expertise to assess and price risks and making insurance contracts and handling claims.

When the power that governments have meet the insurance companies' abilities to access policyholders, unaffordably insurable risks become insurable with accessible means and price for the interested parties.

It is true that governments have significant capacity for heavier involvement in insuring such risks. However, as observed in NFIP and EQC (now NHC), that might put an additional burden on the taxpayers. The methods followed by the reinsurance pools to collect and invest funds enlighten the burden on governments; they encourage competition amongst insurers and reinsurers and may improve the insurance price. Notably, FHCF appears to use CAT bonds as one of their risk transfer mechanisms.

As the risks are here and they have to be lived with, long-term solutions are desired. This is the case for every nation, irrespective of their economic strength. There is no one fit all approach, but in many different regions of the world, alternative risk transfer schemes are available, proving that so long as there is a will to cover so-called 'uninsurable' risks, a solution will be found. They may necessitate the government's intervention, whose choice will also determine whether it will act as a primary insurer, encourage either a compulsory or voluntary reinsurance pool, or sponsor a CAT bond issued by the World Bank. Currently reinsurance pools appear to be the most favoured approach worldwide.

Not surprisingly, the PPP models mentioned above commonly emphasise and somehow impacted by risk prevention and minimisation measures. Robust implementation of such measures inevitably renders insurance coverage, whether through the private market or PPPs, more accessible for policyholders.

2

Safety in Numbers: Towards More Comprehensive Approaches to Difficult Risks

JEFFREY W STEMPEL AND ERIK S KNUTSEN*

I. Introduction

Insurers and policymakers have tended to respond to difficult risks in suboptimal fashion because of undue fear, insufficient creativity, or unimaginative sales, underwriting, and pricing. We define difficult risks as those risks that, compared to 'normal' or 'ordinary' risks, are of greater magnitude or less predictability and resist sufficient market penetration and effective pricing by insurers.

This suboptimal or even counter-productive insurer response to difficult risks stems from a combination of cognitive distortion, business conservatism and undue industry attraction towards what might be termed 'à la carte' placement of coverage coupled with undue risk aversion.[1] This ethos tends to produce insufficient insurance coverage within a specific market as well as increased operational costs for providing insurance.

In our view, the response of disaggregating or fragmenting risk is incorrect and misguided because it overlooks or minimises the gains to be had from a comprehensive approach to risk that can provide both greater actuarial confidence and commercial advantage. Instead, we urge renewed commitment to insurer

* Thanks to Bill Boyd, Jay Feinman, the late Chris French, Leah Chan Grinvald, Dan Hamilton, Yong Han, Helmut Heiss, the late Doris Lee and Ted Lee, Randy Maniloff, David McClure, Ann McGinley, Lena Rieke, our colleagues of the American College of Coverage Counsel and the Project Group for the Principles of Reinsurance Law (PRICL), and the ALI Restatement of the Law, Liability Insurance process. The opinions expressed in this article are of course our own and should not be attributed to any of those we cite or thank.

[1] This is not to say that targeted insurance products are not apt in some circumstances. See generally H Weston, 'À la Carte Coverage: Unbundling Causes of Losses and Coverage Grants to Allow Consumer-Insured Selection' (2013) 11 *Rutgers Journal of Law and Public Policy* 39 (promoting this approach generally). Despite our enormous respect for Professor Weston, our view is generally to the contrary: more comprehensive insurance products should be the preferred option, with segmented coverage used only if absolutely compelled by the risks and circumstances presented.

bundling of risks, aided by improved sales, underwriting and pricing coupled with enhanced government efforts to encourage more comprehensive insurance industry embrace of risk.

Bucking the conventional wisdom, we urge serious insurance industry consideration of folding difficult risks into standard issue insurance products made more comprehensive in coverage. Assuming reasonable underwriting discipline, premiums charged, investment returns, and portfolio diversification, insurers can provide valuable protection to a wider range of policyholders with the protection of profit from more established predictable risks even when facing losses from difficult or emerging risks. In addition, insurers may well, in the end, reap substantial savings on the administrative costs of claims handling (not the least of which would be claims litigation). If past experience is any indicator, insurers are more than capable at earning money in the face of difficult risks – that is what they do.

II. The Problems of Retrenchment – For Policyholders

A common insurer response to difficult risks is segregation of the difficult risk or excluding it altogether from coverage. By segregation, we mean the separation of a particular risk from an insurance policy's overall scope through restrictive endorsements, sub-limits on coverage for the risk, or increased deductibles, retentions, or waiting periods imposed on the policyholder as a prerequisite for obtaining coverage (however otherwise limited) of the risk.

As an example, business interruption/business income coverage in property insurance policies often contain sub-limits that are dramatically lower than the overall policy limits as well as other restrictions such as a minimum waiting period before coverage incepts. For example, policies held by casinos, rodeos, and other entertainment venues that were affected by COVID-19 related closures in 2020 and 2021 had general policy limits of as much as $350 million but much lower sub-limits (eg $1.5 million or less) for losses tied to infectious disease. Although the better application of these sub-limits would grant the policyholder $1.5 million of coverage per location (rather than in the aggregate), this remains an enormous constriction in coverage even if not a 200 percent reduction in coverage.

While we understand the logic of restrictions on difficult risks and certainly prefer this approach to wholesale exclusion of such risks from coverage, these remain major constrictions on coverage that leave common entertainment venues highly vulnerable to difficult risks that ideally should be spread and can be done so to maintain both policyholder protection and insurer profit.

By exclusion, we mean the more straight-forward process of simply excluding the risk from a policy, often in overly broad language that, if taken literally, eliminates coverage for risks that were almost certainly in contemplation by the policyholder and insurer at the time the insurance contract was made and the insurance policy sold.

The mid-1980s revision of the standard form commercial general liability (CGL) policy in the United States took the exclusionary tack in response to increased exposure to asbestos liability and pollution claims (both policyholder liability and frequently successful efforts to obtain coverage for government-mandated clean-up of polluted property for which the policyholder was responsible – through either polluting conduct or even mere ownership of property polluted by a predecessor).[2]

The modern American CGL policy emerging from this major revision now contains a broadly worded exclusion from coverage for any claims arising out of or related to exposure to asbestos as well as an 'absolute' exclusion for claims involving the release or discharge of a pollutant (often sold in modified form as a 'total' pollution exclusion that contains an exception for smoke from a hostile fire) and with it a broad exclusion for government-mandated pollution remediation designed to avoid coverage for policyholder liability pursuant to the national Superfund law (Comprehensive Environmental Response Compensation and Liability Act or CERCLA).[3]

The definition of 'pollutant' (encompassing nearly 20 terms, including the immensely broad 'chemicals' as well as 'dust', 'irritant' and the like) is so broad that insurers have invoked the literal language of the exclusion in frequently successful attempts to avoid coverage in cases involving losses caused by activity normally not regarded as pollution, including carbon monoxide poisoning from an improperly installed or maintained furnace,[4] unsafe drinking water,[5] the wafting scent of Indian curry[6] and bat guano in an attic.[7]

To take a less well-known example of risk segretation in the wake of perceived difficult risks, liability insurers covering security services became concerned by suits alleging inappropriate behaviour by the night watchmen charged with protecting tenants and added versions of a sexual misconduct exclusion to their policies, often with wording so broad that if taken literally the policy would not only prevent coverage for insured-perpetrated crime but also insured failure to prevent or deter crime, which is presumably the core objective of a liability insurance policy sold to a private security company.

As these examples show, the use of broadly worded exclusions, even if in response to serious risk exposure, creates functional problems and openings for opportunism by insurers. The adage that the 'large print giveth and the small print taketh away' becomes less a cliché and more a trap for the unwary, particularly

[2] See J W Stempel and E S Knutsen, *Stempel & Knutsen on Insurance Coverage* §§14.01, 14.10 (Alphen aan den Rijn, WoltersKluwer, 2016); J W Stempel, E S Knutsen and P N Swisher, *Principles of Insurance Law*, Ch 11 (5th edn, Durham, Carolina Press, 2020).

[3] Stempel, Knutsen and Swisher, Ch 11.

[4] *Century Sur Co v Casino West, Inc*, 329 P.3d 614 (Nev 2018).

[5] *Village of Crestwood v Ironshore Specialty Ins Co*, 986 N.E.2d 678 (Ill. Ct. App. 2013).

[6] *Maxine Furs, Ins v Auto-Owners Ins Co*, 426 Fed. App'x 687 (11th Cir. 2011).

[7] *Hirschhorn v Auto-Owners Ins Co*, 809 N.W.2d 529 (Wis. 2012).

consumer and small business policyholders who often lack the time, expertise, or resources necessary to vet policy language for lurking or even hidden limitations on coverage.

Courts taking a more functional and less textually literal approach often reject aggressive insurer attempts to overuse a difficult risk exclusion, particularly if they remember the contract axiom that grants of coverage are to be broadly construed while exclusions are to be narrowly and strictly construed, with the insurer bearing the burden of persuasion and ambiguous language construed against the insurer that supplied the exclusionary language.[8] But many courts are not this sophisticatedly competent or improperly expand exclusions via textual literalism.[9]

The problem is only partially ameliorated where insurers are willing to offer the excluded coverage via endorsement (in return for increased premium) or sale of a separate stand-alone product such as an environmental impairment policy. While this may provide the insurer additional protection, it usually does so by undermining effective risk management in that the additional coverage is often limited (low policy limits, large retentions or deductibles), expensive (high premiums), or difficult to obtain if only offered by a limited number of carriers. As discussed below, the 'narrowcasting' of these coverages also inflicts economic detriment on insurers.

Other prominent examples of separation, segregation, or exclusion of risks include exclusions for flooding or water damage and earth movement in standard property policies. Cyber losses, losses from bacteria or viruses, and losses from government action are in the same vein. In addition to specific textual limitations contained in policy forms, insurers might also respond to difficult risks by taking a more resistant attitude towards claims through invocation of requirements that a loss be 'accidental' or adequately documented or sufficiently promptly reported (a claims restriction sometimes litigated with a vengeance by claims-made insurers).

Although insurers of course have the right to contest claims viewed as outside coverage, when one sees insurers claiming that liability incurred by commercial policyholders is not a sufficiently accidental occurrence because it arose from the volitional operation of the business or that the loss is excluded because the policyholder 'should have' anticipated the consequences of its alleged negligence, we wince as such defenses are so clearly frivolous and at odds with effective operation of insurance (which is designed to cover liability arising out of normal business operations, including the consequences of employee/agent negligence, which by definition is failure to anticipate what would have been reasonably foreseeable to a non-negligent actor).[10]

[8] *Stempel & Knutsen on Insurance Coverage*, §2.06.

[9] See eg J W Stempel and E S Knutsen, 'Rejecting Word Worship: An Integrative Approach to Judicial Interpretation of Insurance Policies' (2021) 90 *University of Cincinnati Law Review* 561 (detailing the problems created by courts applying a strictly literal approach to insurance policy construction).

[10] *Stempel & Knutsen on Insurance Coverage* §1.06.

III. The Undernourishment of the À la Carte Menu

Like the excessively broadly worded exclusion (eg, the pollution exclusion), unreasonable and overly aggressive resistance to claims (which can take the form of 'slow walking' insurer claims response, cutting investigative corners, and delaying resolution through 'lowball' settlement offers that prompt litigation and delay) seems to us an unfortunate consequence of the industry running away from difficult risks that it could instead embrace to its advantage.

Fear of excess obligation should be addressed not by segmenting or restricting coverage per se but through adequate retentions and limits as well as premiums charged and judicious decisions regarding time periods insured and triggers of coverage. Risk sharing above the retention also looms as an insufficiently explored source of protection for insurers willing to take on difficult risks. If these approaches prove insufficient to enable risk-taking by carriers, government support may be necessary and is in our view preferrable to undue Balkanisation of coverage or private sector refusal to provide coverage.

For many consumers, highly segmented, à la carte purchase of products is annoying. As this is being written, American television is awash in advertisements by the mobile phone provider AT&T in which it extolls the virtue of its comprehensive pricing by ridiculing the piecemeal pricing that dominates US airlines. The passengers on the aircraft successively find to their annoyance that the soft drinks, including water, require an additional payment made on board, as is the case for headphones necessary to enjoy the allegedly 'free' video entertainment promoted by the flight attendant.

Although the aggressive bundling done by US phone and cable companies may engender its own batch of criticism, the AT&T ads (presumably based on consumer research showing aversion to à la carte pricing and attraction to a single price) accord with our longstanding suspicion that consumers and even businesses hate the ticky-tack accumulation of additional fees, often undisclosed (or only weakly disclosed via fine print, densely packed disclaimers) until it is too late for an exercise of consumer choice. Particularised taxes (eg, for an obscure urban development district or infrastructure fund), user fees, resort fees, processing fees, and so on have become sufficiently annoyingly prominent in the US to have earned the moniker 'Junk Fees', and identified by President Joe Biden as a significant consumer protection issue.[11]

[11] See White House Press Release, 'Biden-Harris Administration Announces Broad New Actions to Protect Consumers From Billions in Junk Fees' (11 October 2023). www.whitehouse.gov/briefing-room/statements-releases/2023/10/11/biden-harris-administration-announces-broad-new-actions-to-protect-consumers-from-billions-in-junk-fees/#:~:text=Today%2C%20the%20Biden%2DHarris%20Administration,the%20full%20price%20up%20front. For analysis of a particular application of the FTC efforts and powerful political resistance from industry, see G Birenbaum, 'How Biden's Battle against Resort and Other "Junk" Dees Could Affect Las Vegas, Nevada Independent' (31 December 2023). thenevadaindependent.com/article/how-bidens-battle-against-resort-and-other-junk-fees-could-affect-las-vegas?utm_source=The+Nevada+Indepen

Although insurance typically lacks the point-of-sale drama and distress of extortionate food and drink policies imposed on a consumer trapped in an aluminum tube at 35,000 feet or the fait accompli of discovering that one's long weekend in Las Vegas will cost twice what it seemed on the booking website (because of a 'resort fee', and a local hotel tax and a high state sales tax), à la carte insurance pricing has many of the same undesirable traits – certainly for consumers.

À la carte pricing is less transparent and resists comparison shopping. Calculation of risk exposure, always a problem for prospective policyholders, is difficult. Even a diligent, rational individual or business will be hard-pressed to make an intelligent decision as to whether it is necessary to buy flood insurance, earthquake insurance, environmental impairment insurance, difference-in-conditions insurance, and so on.

Only the most sophisticated policyholder with substantial resources will be as well informed as insurers regarding their risk exposure. Historical fears about adverse selection and moral hazard, perhaps always inflated,[12] have become particularly weak concerns for insurers with extensive databases, computing power, and the ability to predict with considerable accuracy the proportion of a portfolio (eg, transatlantic shipping, business data processing) that will produce claims of a given range of magnitude over time.

So long as the insurer is not faced with an enormous volume of claims that must be paid with alacrity, the well-managed insurer can assemble sufficient capital to ride out rough spots and continue to thrive through prudent ongoing underwriting and sales while continuing to enjoy investment income. As discussed below, this provides insurers with an opportunity to combine risks on a more comprehensive basis – which in turn reduces the dangers of adverse selection and moral hazard even more by discouraging or even preventing targeted purchases of particularised insurance by prospective policyholders most likely to generate claims.

Fragmented coverage of risks is generally disadvantageous to policyholders because of their absolute and comparative informational disadvantages. As noted above, the traditional view that policyholders/applicants hold an informational edge over insurers needs serious rethinking in the modern information age. Put simply, the average insurer is more likely to make an accurate prediction about the policyholder's future risks of medical problems, disability, early death, liability, or displacement due to property damage than is the policyholder. In addition to the protections provided by an application form (over which insurers have exclusive content control) that can propound an enormous litany of questions (with answers lying in wait for a potential recission defence, insurers have access to enormous databases regarding probability.

dent&utm_campaign=5b2774397e-EMAIL_CAMPAIGN_2023_12_28_04_27&utm_medium=email&utm_term=0_-5b2774397e-%5BLIST_EMAIL_ID%5D. ('As FTC cracks down on junk fees, the state's largest industry pushes back, leaving Nevada's congressional delegation in an awkward position').

[12] See eg, P Siegelman, 'Adverse Selection in Insurance Markets: An Exaggerated Threat' (2004) 113 *Yale Law Journal* 1223.

Unless the policyholder has a particularly pronounced informational advantage that it manages to legitimately (eg, without fraud or material misrepresentation or intentional concealment that will result in loss of coverage) keep from the insurer (eg, the life insurance applicant who engages in cliff diving every day after work), insurers have the upper informational hand.

More prosaically, the typical individual policyholder and many commercial policyholders simply have no idea of the magnitude and frequency of the risks they face. The modal layperson/lay entity policyholder has a general sense that it exists in a world of risk and should have insurance but simply has no idea of the relative dangers posed by risks, many of which are unseen. Farmers and factory owners in 1975 understandably failed to foresee that the US would enact the CERCLA Superfund law in 1980. Utility companies and their vendors installing insulation in the 1950s did not anticipate that the asbestos used in insulation would lead to a rash of lawsuits and even company-ending liquidation bankruptcies. Refuse companies and municipalities using 'sanitary' landfills for waste disposal failed to foresee resulting groundwater contamination and eventual liability.

Simply put, the typical policyholder does not have anything near the 20–20 foresight required to assemble the optimal mix of targeted insurance policies necessary to weave a fully protective tapestry of risk protection. Better risk managers (eg, those earning 'Risk Manager of the Year' or similar accolades from the insurance trade press) may come close (or even succeed) in a given year but are unlikely to consistently make the right policy selection and assembly decisions year after year after year. To be sure, there may be some 'superstar' exceptions in this field, just as there are mutual fund or hedge fund managers that consistently beat the market – but they are exceptions. For every Ray Dalio[13] there are a thousand nameless fund managers or risk managers just muddling through.

Critics of our assessment of the realistic abilities of policyholders can of course point out that commercial policyholders commonly work with brokers, counsel, and consultants who have substantial expertise. Fair enough. But although these professionals may know more than a single insured, they logically continue to have the cognitive and informational disadvantages any human has in such situations. They also do not know the business or facts as well as the policyholder itself – they remain third-party advisors.

In addition, insurance brokers as a class have something of a systemic limitation in that despite legally being agents for the policyholder, they have tremendous practical allegiance to insurers that provide them with quotations, proposals, access to product and a large, often dominant portion of their compensation through commissions paid by the insurers that through the efforts of the broker make sales to the policyholders depending on the broker to protect their interests.

[13] Ray Dalio is a billionaire investor and founder of hedge fund Bridgewater Associates, considered the largest hedge fund in the world. He has crossed into popular culture with a series of books aimed at general business readership, most prominently *Principles: Life and Work* (New York, Simon & Schuster, 2017).

Further, policyholders (and their risk managers) and brokers do not operate in a vacuum. The real world of risk management and insurance purchase is one in which several factors work to impair the judgment of those buying insurance. People in the insurance arena frequently describe it as a 'relationship' business in which personal ties are important. But the human side of risk analysis is hardly an unalloyed benefit.

Although the friends-and-neighbors effect may open doors for purchase of otherwise unavailable product during hard insurance markets, it can also cloud the judgment of the participants. Is the broker suggesting purchase of X insurance product (eg, an infectious disease policy with a virus loss sublimit or government shutdown exclusion) from Y insurer because her independent judgment favors the product or because she likes the insurer's representative, enjoys all-expenses-paid conferences in the Caribbean, or simply has gotten lazy and fallen into a habit of accepting the insurer's contours of coverage uncritically?

In addition, structural factors operate to perhaps cloud judgment even more than personal ties. Commercial policyholders typically establish a budget for insurance premiums. Risk managers are rewarded for coming in under budget and may even be punished (through lost bonuses, lower salary, demotion or even discharge) for going over budget. When contingent risks emerge down the road and there is no coverage or an insurer unreasonably contests or minimises coverage, the risk manager who secured the low premium/low protection coverage often has left the company. Obtaining coverage at a later date becomes the problem of the policyholder's legal team doing battle with the insurer's claims department.

Even if our critics are correct that we are unduly pessimistic about the predictive power of commercial policyholders in assessing their insurance needs, their criticisms leave our concerns about individuals untouched. Absent enormous wealth (and according to economic theory, billionaires like the aforementioned Dalio and Jeff Bezos should simply self-insure or go bare rather than pay premiums), individuals purchase insurance in relative ignorance unaided by insurance professionals or counsel.

As a result, a world of fragmented or segmented risk insurance is one in which natural persons (and sole proprietors, small partnerships, mom-and-pop businesses) are unlikely to effectively gauge their insurance needs and assemble an appropriate quilt of coverage if required to do the assembly themselves.

And then there are the problems of cognitive error and limited means in the cost-benefit analysis of small policyholders. Even if they effectively calculate the necessary array of interlocking specific coverage necessary for effective protection, they may erroneously flinch at paying the required amount of premiums, even where more rational analysis augers in favour of the additional payments.

'Penny wise and pound foolish' may be a cliché, but it is one with meaning. Humans often make errors of cost-benefit analysis and even if arguably aware are tempted to tempt fate, at least for a policy period or two by forgoing coverage that should have been bought.[14] Alternatively (or perhaps relatedly), the small policyholder may be up against real limitations of capital or liquidity that prompts failure to pay the premiums required for adequate insurance or perhaps really does preclude purchase in order to instead pay the electric bill.

The net effect of all these factors is to disadvantage all but the most sophisticated (and lucky) policyholders in a world of fragmented, specialised insurance products. By contrast, more comprehensive bundling of insurance coverages both relieves the policyholder of search costs and is likely to save the policyholder from erroneous decisionmaking.

More comprehensive insurance policies will undoubtedly command higher premiums than less comprehensive policies, but so long as the additional coverage purchases are apt and not illusory, 'forcing' the policyholder to pay for adequate insurance is largely a good thing so long as not taken to extremes (eg, purchasing so much insurance that the policyholder is actually unable to pay the electric bill or mortgage).

A more comprehensive approach to insurance coverage is also likely to benefit the public and the economic system. When policyholders (both natural and artificial persons) are better insured, they are better equipped to survive physical and economic setbacks, resulting in fewer closures, bankruptcies, or relocations that reduce economic activity and can hollow out communities (eg, the rash of retail closures stemming from the COVID-19 pandemic). Public funds (assembled through taxation or debt) are far less likely to be required and in reduced amount if, in the aftermath of losses (to both isolated policyholders and the community as a whole), there is more insurance protection rather than less.

But in the absence of massive government insurance programs or a sea change of capitalism, more comprehensive insurance products benefitting policyholders and the public are unlikely to result unless insurers also have something to gain – a concern examined below.

IV. The Problems of Retrenchment – For Insurers – And the Corresponding Actuarial, Operational, and Civic Advantages of a Comprehensive Approach

Fortunately, there are in our view adequate incentives for insurers to reverse the recent ethos of segmented, à la carte, limited coverage in favour of a more comprehensive approach, one which insurers achieved in the past and can achieve again.

[14] See generally J K Robbenolt and J R Sternlight, *Psychology for Lawyers: Understanding the Human Factors in Negotiation, Litigation, and Decision Making* (2nd edn, Chicago, American Bar Association, 2021); D Kahneman, *Thinking Fast And Slow* (New York, Farrar, Straus and Giroux, 2011); R H Thaler and C R Sunstein, *Nudge: Improving Decisions About Health, Wealth & Happiness* (Yale, Yale University Press, 2008); A Tversky and D Kahneman, 'Judgment Under Uncertainty: Heuristics and Biases' (1974, Sept 27) *Science*.

Prior to the advent of the CGL policy in the late 1930s and early 1940s, basic liability insurance was highly segmented. Liability policies tended to be policies designed to provide liability coverage for a particular premises or operations hazard of the policyholder. For example, Employers Liability insurance was created to cover claims for work-related injuries and today continues but in modified form as an adjunct to workers compensation policies. Public Liability Insurance came into use and covered claims made against the policyholder by injured customers or passers-by, the type of classic 'slip and fall' claims that are staples of the first-year torts class. It was reasonably broad in scope but not as comprehensive as the modern CGL policy, discussed below.[15]

There also was Owners, Landlords, and Tenants Liability Insurance, Manufacturers' Public Liability Insurance, Contractor's Public Liability Insurance, as well as more narrow insurance products like Elevator Liability Insurance, Teams Liability Insurance, Contractual Liability Insurance, and Product Liability Insurance. Separate liability insurance for contractors and builders also developed during the first third of the twentieth century, usually denominated Owners' Protective Liability Insurance or Contractors' Protective Liability Insurance. The prudent commercial policyholder was required to assess various risks and sew together the cloak of coverage desired for liability protection.[16]

Liability insurers pivoted away from this separated coverage and produced the standard form CGL policy with a broad insuring agreement, a move driven by the industry's economic interests at least as much as by regard for consumers or sales initiative.[17] The arguable 'father' of the CGL, Elmer Sawyer (legal counsel and secretary to the National Bureau of Casualty and Surety Underwriters), viewed the collating of coverages as useful for discouraging adverse selection by customers seeking to purchase only the insurance they were most likely to need while avoiding premium payments for more distant risks. The bundled liability coverages of the CGL policy provided broader coverage but in return demanded higher premiums that could increase investment income while creating a larger pool of less correlated risks that would in turn allow actuarial calculation based on a larger, less volatile risk pool.[18]

Although the combining of risks under one costlier policy aided insurers in combatting adverse selection or possible purchase of insurance for known losses or losses in progress bordering on fraud, the new CGL product had

[15] See *Stempel & Knutsen on Insurance Coverage* §14.01[A] (4th edn, 2016).

[16] ibid.

[17] ibid. The first CGL policy resulted from the efforts of the National Bureau of Casualty and Surety Underwriters and the Mutual Casualty Insurance Rating Bureau and was issued in 1941, followed by a 1943 version that came into wide use. Particularly significant revisions of the policy took place in 1955, 1966, 1973 and 1986. The two rating bureaus merged in 1970 to become the Insurance Services Office (ISO) that continues to serve the industry through data collection and revision of standard form policies and endorsements.

[18] See E W Sawyer, *Comprehensive Liability Insurance* (Underwriter Printing and Publishing Co, 1943).

marketing advantages for insurers and was sold as a pro-policyholder development. It provided something close to 'one-stop shopping' for liability risks, lowered search and transaction costs, and shifted disputing burdens significantly in favour of policyholders.

As Sawyer put it: 'instead of insuring against only enumerated hazards, we now insure against all hazards not excluded'.[19] Even more sanguine was Travelers executive John Eglof, who gushed that:

> [with the CGL policy form, the] burden of determining what to insure and what not to insure is removed from the shoulders of the insured and placed squarely on the producer and the carrier. How much better it is to say—
>
> 'We cover *everything* except this and this and this—'
>
> instead of
>
> 'We cover *only* this and this and this.'
>
> No longer will an insured with Owners', Landlords' and Tenants' coverage in one company and Elevator coverage in another company take them both to court to prove where the claimant fell down.
>
> …
>
> Since a risk cannot choose the kind of accident that will give rise to the need for liability insurance, it is wise to be protected against all losses under one policy – *One policy – one premium and worry regarding liability insurance is off his mind.*[20]

One can of course make too much of the industry's move to the CGL (then expressly titled a 'Comprehensive' General Liability Policy; the industry later substituted 'Commercial' in hopes of discouraging courts from using the earlier nomenclature as a basis for resolving coverage disputes in favour of the policyholder). Although the insuring agreement is very broad, it nonetheless has limitations in that the policyholder's liability must be caused by a sufficiently fortuitous 'occurrence', which is defined as an 'accident, including continuous and repeated exposure to the same general circumstances'. And there are of course the exclusions – 15 or more in the typical CGL form, with additional exclusions or limitations often added by endorsement.

But one need not excessively lionise the CGL policy to appreciate its advantages for both policyholders and insurers and recognise its major industry shift towards wider coverage, a shift that has been successful for more than 80 years and continues to be successful. To be sure, the mass tort claims and subsequent coverage disputes regarding asbestos and pollution liability smudged some of the shine of the CGL product but hardly inflicted permanent tarnishing. One respected

[19] ibid, 11; J W Stempel, 'Rediscovering the Sawyer Solution: Bundling Risk for Protection and Profit' (2013) 11 *Rutgers Journal of Law and Public Policy* 170.

[20] J H Eglof, *Comprehensive Liability Insurance: The Outside*, Best's Ins. News (Fire & Cas Ed) Vol 42, No 1 (May 1941), 19 (emphasis in original). Mr Eglof was a Supervisor in the Agency Field Service of The Travelers Insurance Company.

consultant has estimated that the asbestos mass tort coverage battles beginning in earnest in the 1970s and continuing to this day created only a 1.5 percent diminishment of insurer earnings.[21]

If the asbestos liability wave, the largest mass tort in history, could do so little damage, the CGL and the insurance industry are indeed capable of successfully collating difficult risks, a hopeful sign for those of us urging use of the comprehensive approach for emerging difficult risks that may rival but are unlikely to exceed asbestos and pollution risks.

We are forced to acknowledge, of course, that the insurance industry response to these mega torts and mega risks was exclusion from coverage, leaving policyholders with such exposures to scramble for more specialised policies such as environmental impairment insurance or to go bare, as even limited stand-alone asbestos coverage appears effectively unavailable in the modern insurance market.

Although the 'lasering' exclusions of asbestos and pollution liability may have solved the drain on earnings presented by these risks, the problem could have been addressed through less drastic means that remained true to the comprehensive risk spreading ideal that animated the original CGL policy. For example, sub-limits could have been set on coverage for these risks. Or the insurer could charge an additional premium in return for removing or limiting the absolute exclusions by endorsement. Or the insurer could impose a higher deductible or retention or require a ratio of cost-sharing for losses similar to the 80 percent/20 percent ratio used for medical expense insurers. Or the exclusions could be narrowed to apply only to known risks of this type and not to all future asbestos or pollution liability that might emerge.

Our point is not that these methods would have been inevitably superior to the exclusionary strategy employed by the insurance industry but that alternative methods less at odds with the inclusive, comprehensive ideal are at least feasible and could have at least been tried before surrendering to the fragmented risk of the exclusionary approach.

Although the new/enhanced risks posed by climate degradation and cyber mischief-cum-warfare should not be easily dismissed or unduly minimised, neither are these risks likely to have the massive potential for loss posed by asbestos claims that the industry views as effectively uninsurable.[22] Rather, they are

[21] See J W Stempel, 'Assessing the Coverage Carnage: Asbestos Liability and Insurance After Three Decades of Dispute' (2005–2006) 12 *Connecticut Insurance Law Journal* 349, 363, n 34 (comments of V J Leary).

[22] Asbestos is a particularly difficult risk. As Professor Deborah Hensler observed, tort and insurance observers for years asked what type of mass tort might create the 'next asbestos', only to find that the next asbestos was composed of later waves of asbestos-related claims. S Kostal, 'Asbestos They Can?' (2005) 91 *ABA J ournal Accord*; C M Temple, 'The Ex Post Facto Effect: The U.S. Supreme Court's *DeVries* Decision and Asbestos Litigation in the United States' (April 18, 2019). www.foxrothschild.com/publications/the-ex-post-facto-effect-the-u-s-supreme-courts-devries-decision-and-asbestos-litigation-in-the-united-states (recent decision 'demonstrates why the tide of asbestos litigation is hardly receding. To the contrary, rulings such as the Court's rendition of current federal

more like pollution risks that may resist coverage at standard rates but are at least amenable to coverage through specialised policies, coverage that in our view could continue to be part of a broad-based CGL form or non-liability policy.

Opportunity exists for insurers in this regard because there remain significant opportunities for insurers to sell more comprehensive coverage that brings with it increased premium dollars for investment. There appears to be insufficient market penetration for insurance for risks in addition to those traditionally viewed as core general liability risks such as premises liability, product defect, and defective construction.

In particular, it appears that not enough prospective policyholders are purchasing enough cyber risk insurance. This is hardly surprising in view of the separation of this coverage from standard liability insurance and restrictions on first-party property insurance coverage for cyber-related losses. At the same time, in the absence of a sufficiently detailed exclusion for cyber risks, a CGL policy may result in 'silent cyber' coverage where cyber-related losses (by the policyholder or customers suing the policyholder over data breach) are deemed by courts to be sufficiently tangible to qualify for core CGL or property loss coverage.

Where cyber risk is sufficiently clearly excluded (as often explained by a broker or agent rather than through policyholder review of straightforward exclusionary policy language), the prospective policyholder seeking coverage will typically find coverage available only through stand-alone specialised policies with relatively low limits, high retentions, high premiums, or some combination thereof as well as normally being offered (for liability coverage) on a claims-made basis generally considered less advantageous to policyholders.[23]

maritime common law can reasonably be expected to energise a surge in claims in the [U.S.] national tort system').

And despite difficulties posed by the asbestos risk, it was not entirely too hot to handles for insurers. For example, billionaire investor Warren Buffet's Berkshire Hathaway was willing to acquire a large block of insurance facing asbestos-related claims, effectively betting that it could settle these claims for less than the massive amount of capital that came with the risky pipeline of asbestos exposure. P Olson, 'Buffett Bets on Asbestos' *Forbes* (23 October 2006). www.forbes.com/2006/10/23/buffett-lloyds-asbestos-face-cx_po_1020autofacescan01.html?sh=5890db1c1ab6 (Berkshire 'will be putting up $7 billion of reinsurance cover to cover Equitas, the unlisted company that took care of reinsuring Lloyd's liabilities before 1993'). Although access to proprietary data is limited, it appears to have been a profitable bet by Buffett. There have been no reports suggesting that the asbestos liabilities outpaced the cash and investment opportunity created by the acquisition. See also A R Sorkin, 'Buffett Buys Company Crippled by Asbestos Suits' *NY Times* (21 December 2000). www.nytimes.com/2000/12/21/business/buffett-buys-company-crippled-by-asbestos-suits.html.

If even these risks, where it has long been established that asbestos is a dangerous substance causing harm to those exposed, are not too hot to handle, one can justify optimism about insurance industry ability to include cyber and climate risks in broad general property, liability, life, health, and disability policies.

[23] General liability insurance typically has an occurrence-based trigger in which a policy is applicable if injury to the third-party claimant suing the policyholder took place during the policy period. Claims-made liability insurance, which is more prevalent in professional liability lines, is triggered if the claim (rather than the alleged injury) takes place during the policy period.

Although in theory, a claims-made trigger provides unlimited retroactive coverage, insurers typically include a retroactive date cutting off coverage and also require that the claim not only be made

Under these circumstances, it is not surprising that commercial policyholders are reluctant to make such separate purchase of an additional insurance policy. Like air travelers, vacationers, and airline passengers, policyholders find a litany of separate products or add-ons to be annoying as well as tiring. Worse yet from the insurer's marketing perspective is that the individual cost of a stand-alone cyber risk policy looks unduly large because of the cognitive biases afflicting human decisionmakers.

A separate significant premium added to the premium already paid for a basic policy looks like an expensive luxury that can be forgone in the service of other uses of the funds. By contrast, if the policyholder is paying a substantial premium for insurance coverage broadly defined, the separate premium costs of particular risks are to a degree hidden or viewed as part of an overall insurance purchase that the policyholder must make in any event.

When insurance purchases are viewed as a required cost of doing business, the policyholder is resigned to paying the premium. We posit that this effect increases in strength with the degree to which basic insurance coverage is seen as necessary. On one end of the continuum are policies formally legally required (eg, at least minimal automobile liability insurance; workers compensation insurance), followed by those uniformly contractually required (eg, homeowners insurance insisted upon by the bank as a condition of making a mortgage loan), followed by those widely viewed as minimally necessary for operation of a business or family (eg, general liability insurance, basic medical expense insurance, life insurance).

At the figurative end of the spectrum are policies seen more as luxuries than necessities, at least for policyholders without the ability to pay higher premiums. Sure, it would be nice for the average homeowner to also have additional insurance should the driveway crack or perhaps a home warranty policy (even though home warranty companies consistently and incorrectly contend they are not insurers). But most individual consumers and commercial policyholders are unlikely to see such policies as required, essential, or even standard operating procedure and will be willing to forgo coverage against future risks in return for immediate retention of funds that would otherwise be spend for yet another insurance premium.

Although the premium for broader basic coverage may be higher under our proposal because the policy provides more comprehensive protection (even if some of the coverages are constricted through sub-limits, retentions, joint financial responsibility, or temporal restrictions), the policyholder is less likely to balk and seek disaggregation of coverage. By contrast, the additional separate policy,

during the policy period but also reported during the policy period or an extended reporting period provided in the policy. Consequently, the temporal score of claims-made coverage is normally considerably shorter than that provided by an occurrence basis policy, which provides unlimited prospective coverage because an injury inflicted in the policy period triggers coverage even if suit over the injury does not take place until years or (as in the case of asbestos) decades later.

unless offered at only nominal cost,[24] looks more optional, less essential, and an opportunity for saving by spurning.

Offering insurance products on as broad a basis as possible can thus encourage more widespread purchase of the product at higher overall premiums, in turn providing the insurer with increased investment capital while simultaneously permitting more specific underwriting, another means of enhancing insurer revenue while simultaneously providing greater coverage for policyholders. Characterising coverage as broad, so long as not deceptive or misleading, legitimately markets the product as valuable to the policyholder because it reduces or even eliminates the search costs of à la carte shopping, The insurer also benefits through obtaining a higher volume of premium income.

Equally or more important, combining the risks insured in policies logically makes the insurer less vulnerable to specific instances of a particular narrower risk that may be less systemically and reliability predictable. Consider for example, a first-party property loss policy that by its terms covers physical injury or loss of property including loss due to cyber attacks or equipment malfunction, wildfires, flood, and earthquake. It of course takes on greater risk exposure than a policy that expressly excludes these hazards. But in return, the insurer receives more premium income and, importantly from an actuarial perspective, has received this increased premium for a variety of coverages representing a large risk pool that is likely to be less volatile than a small risk pool.

To illustrate: in a given policy period, the policyholder (and consequently the insurer) faces these risks and may find one or more might cause a covered loss. But it is unlikely that the policyholder will suffer injury from a cyber attack, wildfires, floods, and earthquake within the same confined period of time. With a larger, sufficiently varied risk pool, loss events during the policy period are more likely to adhere to long-term event risks profiles. While there can of course be any one of these losses in a policy year, the odds of multiple such losses are reduced as a matter of probability theory.[25]

[24] We posit two different worlds of additional cost and consumer reaction. When the additional costs are nominal and packaged as a convenience accommodation to the purchases, the customer often agrees to payment notwithstanding annoyance at 'junk fees'. The inertial path of least resistance is to simply accept the additional amount as something of a processing charge akin to the delivery fees of GrubHub or DoorDash.

But where the additional fees are substantial, or even significant, as are commercial insurance premiums, policyholders will experience at least a modicum of 'sticker shock' at the cost. When this is coupled with the policyholder's reasonable view that it has already paid for insurance through procurement of a generalised policy (first-party property or life/health/disability or third-party automobile or general liability), the stand-alone premium will appear comparatively more expensive and subject to avoidance by a policyholder who may already have 'overhead fatigue' from making other basic investments and expenditures related to the policyholder's business operations.

To a degree, this mirrors the tendency of individuals to see cash purchases as proportionally more burdensome than the credit purchases made in passing as part of establishing an office or business operation.

[25] See generally W von der Linden, V D and U von Toussaint, *Bayesian Probability Theory: Applications in the Physical Sciences* (Cambridge, Cambridge University Press, 2014); B A Olshausen, 'Bayesian Probability Theory' (1 March 2004). www.rctn.org/bruno/npb163/bayes.pdf.

To the extent one or more of the difficult risk losses take place, the insurer is protected to a degree by cross-subsidisation in that the profits from non-materialising losses operate as a de facto subsidy of materialising losses from the difficult risks. Although a given risk may cause more losses than predicted, through selling a more comprehensive and expensive product more widely adopted, the insurer is taking in sufficient additional premium to offset losses. In addition, the loss experience of the carrier, although worse than expected regarding Hazard A, will often be better than expected for Hazards B, C, D, etc.

In essence, we are promoting a type of forced portfolio diversification for insurers in which they offer broader coverages both as a form of risk management as well as sales and underwriting advantage. Broader insurance products can in turn demand higher premiums and spread risk more effectively while presenting marketing advantages that also tamp down whatever adverse selection advantages may still be retained by prospective policyholders.

V. Achieving More All-Encompassing Protection that Includes Difficult Risks

As outlined above, we contend a more comprehensive approach to underwriting risk will work in theory. But is it achievable in practice in light of the insurance industry's historically conservative pessimism[26] combined with the now nearly four-decade trend towards separation and exclusion or fragmentation of coverage? Perhaps not. But if our goal of more inclusive insurance products is to be realised, its implementation will look something like the following.

An enterprising insurer will need to emerge as one willing to pursue the comprehensive approach and seize on its marketing advantage, as did the industry when it launched and zealously marketed the CGL policy during the 1940–1960 period. Insurance sales personnel frequently describe themselves as operating in the 'peace of mind' business, providing a product best if never needed but at the ready to protect policyholders from the potential ravages of loss or liability exposure.

This sales tactic, however shopworn, remains prominent for a reason. It is effective, particularly for consumers and smaller commercial entities that lack the capacity for close calculation of their risks or alternative risk management arrangements such as self-insurance, risk retention groups, or catastrophe bonds.

The modal individual or small business policyholder wants to streamline and minimise the insurance purchasing process and is willing to pay for the convenience provided that the total premium, however high, appears to provide sufficient protection. In seeking one-stop shopping, it is willing to rely on those with greater

[26] See S M Fitzpatrick, 'Fear is the Key: A Behavioral Guide to Underwriting Cycles' (2004) 10 *Connecticut Insurance Law Journal* 255.

expertise, not only a broker or agent but on the insurer and the insurance industry generally as a cluster of people/entitities that 'knows' what insurance protection is needed and provides an apt product for the needs at a feasible price. Broader insurance products more broadly available fulfil this need.

For the insurer that seizes the marketing opportunity, there will be rewards. Insurers during the past 40 years, despite fears of being on the wrong side of a difficult risk, have frequently shown innovation and zeal in introducing new products. Insurance policies for employment practices liability, assisted living costs, home care costs, political risk, infectious disease, and loss of economic value are examples. But many of these products have been unpopular with consumers (eg, the assisted living expense policy that, through limiting language, results in narrow coverage despite decades of premium payment) or unprofitable for insurers (eg, assisted living policies again). We think a good deal of the unpopularity results from their stand-alone nature and the fragmented insurance market produced by à la carte marketing.

Employment Practices Liability insurance provides an illustration of this problem. As a stand-alone coverage, it has been expensive relative to the coverage and policy limits provided and lacked some of the benefits of other specialised coverages such as Boiler & Machinery insurance.[27] Although the EPL situation has improved with increased policy limits and comparatively lower premiums, the product has not achieved widespread market penetration in the manner of the CGL policy, property coverage, or medical expense insurance.

The EPL example highlights another factor likely necessary to spur movement towards more comprehensive insurance products: where possible, the economic and regulatory system should encourage or even require insurance of significant breadth. Automobile insurance is omnipresent not because drivers are uniformly concerned about self-protection or impose upon themselves a moral duty of ensuring that their victims will be adequately compensated. It is required by law. Homeowners insurance is in wide use not solely because owners prudently want to protect their largest asset but because mortgage lenders require it. Most US

[27] Boiler & Machinery insurance covers losses resulting from boiler explosions or similar mechanical malfunctions. A prime benefit of the coverage is not only the potential indemnity should there be catastrophic failure but also the underwriting process, which involves close inspection by expert engineers as a condition of obtaining coverage. The policyholder is alerted to problems requiring maintenance and must resolve those problems as a condition of obtaining the insurance. The process is widely credited with minimising losses for the benefit of workers and the public as well as policyholder companies obtaining the protection and insurers collecting and investing premiums on a book of business with comparatively few losses.

It appears that EPL insurance has not had the same impact. As a condition of policy placement or renewal, EPL insurers could audit policyholders regarding their personnel policies and could provide guidance and impose systems designed to reduce the risk of personnel decisions marred by race, gender, religious, or other biases. Although the modern human resources department of course engages in non-discrimination training (relatively poorly, in our view), this appears to have been driven by simple fears of liability unaided by insurer insistence or by rules established by policyholders or their parent entities (eg, a university system requiring such training on each campus in each department) rather than insurer initiatives or requirements for policy placement or renewal.

residents have at least some insurance coverage because of its popularity as an employment benefit and the national government's Obamacare nudging.[28]

Even among commercial interests that one might 'trust' to be wise enough to insure, much of market penetration takes place because of regulatory requirements. Would employers clammer for workers compensation insurance if it was not required by law? Perhaps, but the coldly calculating employer might rationally decide it is better off forgoing coverage or self-insuring.[29] So might a special purpose entity developing a shopping center, apartment complex, or casino.[30] Commercial entities are generally sufficiently aware of liability risks and likely to purchase CGL coverage, but it is often of insufficient amount unless subject to regulatory, contracting, lender, or other requirements.[31]

Even if effectively required to some degree, insurance is often insufficiently comprehensive in scope. Businesses frequently purchase commercial property insurance without also purchasing business income coverage (more commonly described as business interruption insurance), which can be fatal to a retail entity that loses its source of cash flow for weeks or months while waiting for repair or rebuilding of its facilities. And, as painfully demonstrated during the COVID-19 pandemic, even those entities buying such coverage found themselves out of luck when US courts overwhelmingly (and incorrectly in our view)[32] ruled that the

[28] On this issue, the Canadian situation diverges markedly from that in the US in that Canada has an extensive (if oft criticised because of waiting times) single payer system of medical coverage. But the point is the same: there exists widespread coverage because it is required, not because consumers went on a buying binge or because of aggressive marketing by medical expense insurers.

[29] Two strikingly different narratives dominate discussion of workers compensation in the US. Lawyers for injured workers complain that the schedule of benefits for injury is disproportionately low as compared to tort awards for comparable injuries and that this is not justified by the no-fault liability standards of workers compensation recovery. Employer lawyers complain that the automatic imposition of liability and difficulty policing the extent of injury and recovery efforts (or lack thereof) makes insurance costs for this coverage disproportionately high and imposes a major financial burden on insurers and commerce.

[30] Special purpose entities by their nature are separate legal entities designed for a particular purpose rather than ongoing business enterprises. In the US legal system that often de-emphasises financial responsibility (see eg, L M LoPucki, 'The Death of Liability' (1994) 80 *Virginia Law Review* 1887), they can be undercapitalised and ephemeral, disappearing shortly after completion of a project before problems are discovered and liability claims are made.

This was a particular problem in the construction industry in Sun Belt America during the late twentieth and early twenty-first centuries in which tract home neighborhoods were built by entities that were not merely undercapitalised but no longer in existence when construction defects were discovered and claims arose. Without the liability insurance policies purchased, often as a condition of obtaining building permits, there would effectively have been no source of compensation for injured buyers of homes with leaky roofs, shifting foundations, drainage problems and the like.

[31] In addition to whatever might be prompted by prudent risk management, business entities with property subject to loans are often effectively required by lenders or investors to insure to a minimum level of value and obtain a minimum amount of liability protection. For example, a large-scale commercial development such as a shopping center or casino/resort complex is often subject to an Owner Controlled Insurance Policy (OCIP) or 'wrap' policy that provides for minimum levels of general liability, professional liability, builder's risk, and commercial property coverage as well as protection as 'additional insureds' on the policies that subcontractors are required to purchase.

[32] See E S Knutsen and J W Stempel, 'Infected Judgment: Creating Conventional Wisdom and Insurance Coverage Denial in a Pandemic' (2020) 27 *Connecticut Insurance Law Journl* 185.

losses from the virus were not sufficiently physical or did not cause enough deprivation to qualify as covered loss.

Thus, despite considerable coverage-forcing by governments, contracting partners, and lenders, individuals and businesses tend to be insufficiently insured, both in scope and amount. The problem is exacerbated by claims-made and 'burning limits'[33] liability policies. The situation does not reflect failure of these approaches so much as it calls for increased use of these 'nudges' towards more comprehensive coverage that will bundle risks to achieve the benefits we posit for consumers *and* insurers *and* the public.

The risk management situation surrounding individual homeowners provides an example of both current deficiencies and the potential for relatively painless progress. Because most homes are purchased through a loan and lenders require protection, homeowner's insurance is ubiquitous (rental property is also widely insured for similar reasons or because the owner has requisite risk management acumen or sufficient capital). But the policy limits are often arguably too low or the policy lacks replacement coverage. More important, the typical policy excludes coverage for flood or earth movement[34] loss.

These difficult risks are not embraced by the insurance private sector. Although the option to purchase earthquake insurance by endorsement is often available, the additional premium is significant and, more important for homeowners with limited savings, the deductible is typically 10 to 20 percent of the value of the structure. A policyholder might pay additional premiums for years on her $500,000 house that is destroyed by an earthquake and yet still need to come up with $100,000 to facilitate replacement. As a result, purchase of additional insurance for earth movement is rare. And lenders tend not to require it.

In the US, flood insurance is typically available through the national government program but is undersold. Agents commonly tell homeowners that flood insurance is not needed unless the house is located in a designated flood zone based on maps widely regarded as antiquated in light of several decades' worth of climate change.[35] And, to perhaps state the obvious, one need not live in a designated flood zone to suffer water damage, not only through archetypical flood events such as a river overflowing its banks but also from sewer backup, heavy

[33] A 'burning limits' or eroding limits liability policy is one in which each dollar spent litigating the defence of the claim reduces the available policy limits. Yes, it's as bad for policyholders as it sounds. If unwise, over-aggressive, or greedy defence counsel over-litigates a case, there may be insufficient policy limits available for settling a claim, exposing the policyholder to risk of a judgment in excess of policy limits. Although the excess judgment risk is not eliminated with the typical CGL policy in which defence costs are 'outside limits' and do not reduce the funds available for settlement or judgment satisfaction, they present much less risk to policyholders and much less chance of what we deem litigation pathology.

[34] By earth movement coverage or exclusion, we mean not only earthquake-related damage but also injury from mudslide, soil settlement or erosion.

[35] See eg, J B Wriggins, 'In Deep: Dilemmas of Federal Flood Insurance Reform' (2015) 5 *University of California Irvine Law Review* 1443.

rains, or storm surge from a hurricane (which is not covered even if the policy generally provides windstorm coverage).

Professor Adam Scales proposed a rather elegant solution to this problem nearly 20 years ago that unfortunately has to date fallen on deaf ears.[36] Writing in the wake of Hurricane Kartrina, he urged that regulators require basic homeowners policies to contain flood coverage, a move that would force the design, marketing and sales of the type of insurance products we advocate. Going perhaps a step further, we also advocate that homeowners policies and their basic business equivalents also include earth movement and wildfire coverage and at least some cyber loss coverage (with sub-limits or a separate deductible if this proves the only way of inducing insurers to offer it).

The rationale of the Scales proposal, with which we agree, is that property insurers (both consumer and commercial) want to make money and, needing to sell product to make money, will then continue to operate and offer product subject to these strictures even if their preference would be to avoid including more difficult risks in the basic policy. If required to offer more comprehensive coverages as a condition of doing business, insurers will accept the strings attached by regulators, provided the market is otherwise sufficiently attractive and that they are permitted to charge actuarially sound premiums.[37] Those disputing this proposition can of course point to recent developments in California and the coverage experience in Florida over the past thirty years.

As to the latter, the destruction wrought by Hurricane Andrew in August 1992 sent a chill through the industry, leading to some withdrawals from the market or implementation of restrictions on the sale of new policies.[38] In response, Florida created Florida Citizens as an insurer of last resort where policyholders were not able to obtain coverage from private insurers. Over the next three decades, the number of policies placed with this government carrier increased substantially, aided in part by some bad hurricane years such as 2004, during which four major hurricanes made landfall in Florida.

[36] See A Scales, 'A Nation of Policyholders: Governmental and Market Failure in Flood Insurance' (2006–2007) 26 *Mississippi College Law Review* 3.

[37] The concerns of market attractiveness and adequate premium are intertwined, with the latter arguably the primary determinant of the former. As the saying goes, everything has its price. An insurer may understandably be reluctant to write windstorm and water damage coverage on coastal property or on a home perched on a cliff. But that reluctance should be overcome if the insurer is permitted to charge an appropriate premium across a book of business. Insurers providing coverage for difficult risks are (to use another saying-cum-cliché) not putting all of their risk eggs in a single basket (eg, insuring one home on a cliff or one luxury beach house in a hurricane zone). With even modest sales and underwriting acumen, they will have a relatively large risk pool that is sufficiently uncorrelated to permit relatively accurate loss prediction and charge premiums accordingly, even when constrained within a specific market (eg, hurricane-storm surge prone Florida). To the extent national or coordinated state regulation permits pooling over a wider geographic area, insurers should be able to make money even if grumbling about the required burdens of comprehensive coverage.

[38] Hurricane Andrew had particular impact because it hit the highly populated Miami metropolitan area, inflicting much higher cost than the typical hurricane that, however destructive, touches sparsely populated (eg, barrier islands) or less wealthy areas.

But the real culprit here seems not to be uninsurability per se but a tendency of agents to assign coverage to Florida Citizens (something over which they have considerable discretion) at the first sign of difficulty placing the risk in the private sector.[39] Louisiana, another state with significant hurricane exposure, has experienced similar problems, exacerbated by 2004's Hurricane Katrina, which brought considerable flooding, particularly in New Orleans when levees gave way.

Most recently, several insurers have announced restrictions on the sale of new policies in California due to wildfire loss in the state. Some have ceased sales of new policies. Others have excluded coverage for wildfire related loss.[40] Although we understand the insurer concern, we see no reason why it cannot be accommodated by more comprehensive product offerings and the ability to charge sufficient premiums for the coverage required by law or regulation. To the extent that regulators attempt to artificially suppress prices by fiat (a particular problem if an insurance regulator aspires to higher political office),[41] they do a disservice not only to insurers but to policyholders and the public. The problem is akin to rent control. In a short-term, superficial way, it looks like a win for

[39] An ever-present obstacle to risk management reform are the economic incentives and self-interest bearing upon those in the industry. Agents in Florida are well aware that most insurers in Florida would prefer a less risky pool of policies, which can be achieved if the larger risks are dispatched to Florida Citizens. The better to keep the agents' stock high with the private sector insurers they represent. So much of the Florida market has been shunted to Florida Citizens to suggest excessive shunting. But state insurance departments, perennially understaffed and underfunded, are unlikely to curb the problem.

Although the growth of Florida Citizens is consistently portrayed as a problem, it may in fact be a harbinger of a different approach to be implemented if the private sector continues to dodge difficult risks and sale of comprehensive policies. Although Florida Citizens is also portrayed as a consistent money loser, it need not be. All that is necessary is levying of sufficient premiums across a sufficiently large and varied risk pool. Even in Florida, this is achievable. Even in a terrible hurricane year like 2004, only relatively discreet portions of the state are afflicted (although some were hit twice that year). There is still relatively uncorrelated risk to be spread and a law of large numbers remaining in operation. Further, if the Scales proposal is adopted on a national basis, insurers doing business in different regions of the country can spread both risk and loss to a wide degree.

[40] See C Morris and A Botros, '4 More Insurers Are Leaving California After Allstate and State Farm Cut Back Due to Wildfire Risk' (31 October 2023) *Fortune*. fortune.com/2023/10/31/four-insurers-leave-california-wildfire-risk-allstate-state-farm/; L Griswold, E Lippiello, S Ebbs, K Livingston, A Pong and I Pereira, 'Fire Prone California Homeowners Left Behind as Insurance Companies Drop Coverage' (16 November 2023) *Associated Press*. abcnews.go.com/US/fire-prone-california-homeowners-left-insurance-companies-drop/story?id=104946925.

[41] In the US, insurance regulation is state-centered by law. See 15 USC §§1011–1105 (the McCarran-Ferguson Act), with state insurance commissioners selected by political appointment or statewide election. The law was rapidly enacted in 1945 to legislatively overrule a US Supreme Court decision subjecting insurers to national antitrust laws and to restore the traditional US practice of state-centered insurance regulation.

Although appointment of commissioners makes it less likely that the commissioner will have higher electoral ambitions for the future, the occupants of the post are often politically active and thus wish to be seen as consumer advocates and blunt criticism of industry capture. Those commissioners selected through outright election are by definition political enough to run for office and may be particularly interested in becoming a governor, lieutenant governor (eg, former California Insurance Commissioner John Garamendi), Senator (former Florida Insurance Commissioner Bill Nelson), or Congressperson (Garamendi again).

consumers because the next payment is lower. But in the long- or even medium-term, it causes more harm than good by discouraging new construction, new entrants into the building business, and adequate upkeep of existing properties while at the same time leading to wasteful and even deceitful behaviour.[42]

But our sympathy for insurers regarding the politics of regulation is largely limited to their often-legitimate complaints that they are too often prevented from charging an adequate premium for the risk assumed. Beyond this, much insurer resistance to regulation strikes us as posturing designed to defeat anything that might reduce profits rather than duly considered public policy assessments.[43]

[42] See R Diamond, 'What Does Economic Evidence Tell Us About the Effects of Rent Control?' *Brookings Institute* (18 October 2018). www.brookings.edu/articles/what-does-economic-evidence-tell-us-about-the-effects-of-rent-control/ (largely accepting anti-rent control economic arguments). But see M Paul, 'Economists Hate Rent Control. Here's Why They're Wrong' (15 May 2023) *American Prospect* (presenting counter-arguments).

[43] The insurance industry is an economic juggernaut. If it was a country, it would have the third or fourth largest economy in the world. See R Ericson, A Doyle and D Barry, *Insurance as Governance* 4 (2003). In the US in particular, it has significant political clout through lobbying, campaign contributions, public relations, and the grassroots network of retail insurance sales, comprising a significant portion of the prominent local business community, complete with sponsorship of Little League baseball teams and the like. See also A Tobias, *The Invisible Bankers* (1982) (describing invitations sent to insurer chief executives by then-President Jimmy Carter that was declined by roughly half the CEOs who were apparently 'too busy' to meet with the President or thought the snub would not cause appreciable damage to the industry's political agenda).

And a recurring tactic of insurers when faced with the prospect of adverse law, regulation, or judicial decision is some variant of Chicken-Little-Meets-Crocodile-Tears. For example, at the outset of the COVID-19 pandemic, insurer spokespersons predicted financial ruin of the industry should policyholders prevail in business interruption claims stemming from closures or limitations wrought by the virus, a tactic that we think aided the industry's remarkable win-loss record in such cases. See Stempel and Knuten, *Infected Judgment*. In any event, the pandemic did not result in significant injury to insurer fortunes.

More recently on a smaller scale, insurers in Nevada have voiced loud apocalyptic complaints when the state legislature passed a law forbidding the use of burning limits liability policies in which each dollar spent on litigating a liability defence reduced the policy limit, thereby shrinking the funds available for settling cases and paying judgments. The insurer claim is that the industry could not even write, under any circumstances, professional liability policies and certain other policies without the burning limits feature, a complaint that prompted state regulators to pass an administrative rule watering down the ban on burning limits.

We are, to put it mildly, highly skeptical of the extreme insurer claim that legal malpractice, medical malpractice, architect liability, account liability, directors and officers liability coverage and the like can not be written on a defence-outside-of-limits basis. Premiums might have to rise. Policy limits might be more constricted. The respective markets may become 'harder.' But the risks are hardly uninsurable without defence costs eroding limits.

Despite any such hardening of the market, a rational legislature might well find the ban on burning limits to be sound public policy. Erosion of indemnity coverage by defence expenditures creates a terrible incentive for insurers and panel counsel to delay evaluation of claims and engage in excessive litigation when matters could have been settled within limits for the net benefit of insurer and policyholder early on. But after years of litigation and depletion of the policy, fair resolution of the matter may be impossible and trial needlessly inevitable. In extreme cases, we have seen policy limits in meritorious cases depleted to almost nothing to the financial profit of lawyers engaging in borderline malpractice.

But regardless of whether a ban on burning limits is wise, it is enacted legislation that an insurance regulator should faithfully implement rather than bending to the complaints of insurers telling an unbelievable story of industry destruction or unavailability because of the new law.

Expressed insurer angst about writing wildfire risks is in this vein. California is a big state. Even in a terrible wildfire year, only a comparatively small portion of property will be injured by fire (including smoke damage). If insurers are collecting adequate premiums on a large enough pool of risk diversified properties, this risk is eminently insurable – even as a stand-alone risk. If wildfire coverage (which is really just the fire coverage insurers have been offering since the days of Benjamin Franklin, albeit with some greater risk of larger and more concentrated losses such as the San Francisco fire and earthquake of 1906) is bundled with other risks in comprehensive policies sold widely across a state or province or, better yet, an entire country, a coordination task that may be difficult in the state-centered regulatory framework of the US but not necessarily in Canada, the UK, or the EU, where regulatory efforts are more coordinated from region to region.

Rather than be unduly intimidated by insurer scare tactics of the 'we'll pull out' or 'we'll have to file for bankruptcy' variety, government regulators should force insurers to be if not their best selves, at least better selves. Notwithstanding industry resistance to change generally and occasional outright aversion to change advantageous to policyholders, insurers are in our view likely to benefit from this approach at least as much as policyholders.

Insurer resistance to providing greater coverage is reminiscent of the taxi industry in major cities. Until the 1990s or early 2000s, most cab fares were required to be paid in cash. Credit or debit cards were not accepted. But regulators to their credit (pardon the pun) persisted – and produced not only convenience for consumers but a benefit to cabbies as well. Once credit cards were accepted, the average tips increased because passenger tipping decisions were no longer constrained by the amount and denominations of cash on the person of the passenger. In the modern era, the passenger need only swipe and select a tip (often starting at a 20 percent option nudging the passenger not to undertip). We expect the economics of bundled risk to follow a similar pattern, provided that regulators do not unduly restrict premium charges.

The taxi example is also instructive in that industry resistance reflected a conservatism that invited market entry and exploitation by nimbler, more flexible, more creative entities. The advent of Uber and Lyft, which embraced technology for hailing a ride as well as paying for it provides a cautionary tale for insurers. If the industry resists change, it may prompt the government to not only impose more requirements of policy design and coverage but even to enter the field as what might be termed an insurer of next resort rather than one of last resort.

As discussed above, there is no reason that governments cannot operate insurance entities and that insurers such as Florida Citizens and Louisiana Citizens cannot profitably provide adequate coverage, perhaps with less combative claims policies than private sector insurers attempting to minimise claims payments and protect profits. The Troubled Asset Relief Program (TARP) enacted during the 2008 financial crisis in part because of the problems of AIG and other insurers involved short-term government subsidies but returned net profits to the US Treasury only a few years later. Although other government programs (eg, Social

Security, Medicare, Medicaid (social insurance programs), the Post Office) are typically characterised as money losers, this results not from any inherent limitation but from political constraints. Raising the social security payroll tax a half percent or continuing to collected it for high-wage earners would make the program more than solvent. Raising the price of stamps a nickel would do the same for the US Postal Service balance sheet.

Consequently, if private insurers are unwilling to take the strides necessary to ensure adequate coverage of both difficult risks and mundane dangers, lawmakers should consider not only prompting more effort through regulation but also government operation of risk spreading devices (whether formally labeled insurance or not). The US government is already in the flood insurance business and the crop insurance business (a risk made more difficult by climate degradation) and some state funds address earthquake exposure while all states have some form of guaranty fund that steps in to provide coverage (albeit sometimes limited) in the event of insurer insolvency. From here, it is only a small step to additional government operation of insurance programs covering difficult risks such as water damage, earth movement, or cyber loss.

As a condition of either regulation or operation, government activity in this area should not only force insurer adjustments but also prompt minimally acceptable consumer or commercial policy behaviour. If flood, earthquake, or cyber insurance is for sale, people should be required to buy it. If they fail to do so, they should be ineligible for disaster relief. For too long, at least in the US, the Federal Emergency Management Association (FEMA) has in the wake of catastrophes acted as a de facto property damage insurer that provides benefits to de facto policyholders that never paid a premium. By contrast, in Switzerland, policies comprehensively covering difficult risk perils are for sale. But if the property owner fails to buy the necessary policy, there is no post-catastrophe aid from the government as well as no insurance benefit.

One might deems such an approach harsh and argue that the 'premiums' on FEMA relief are paid in the taxes elicited from catastrophe victims. Perhaps. But it is an ineffective means of funding coverage in that there is no pre-loss calculation of the amounts that should be paid by the property that later requires 'coverage' in the form of post-disaster assistance. The greatest recipients of FEMA aid may well be those who paid comparatively little in taxation but presented substantial risk.[44]

[44] Alternatively, one could expand the FEMA model and acknowledge that it is something of a social welfare program in which some recipients receiving benefits are getting those benefits without regard to financial support of the program or risk at issue – that the government is subsidising victims of natural disaster with the tax dollars of citizens that have not suffered loss. Although this type of approach can be justified as a subsidy or welfare benefit for the needy, it also can disproportionally benefit wealthier citizens with beach houses hit by a storm surge or cliffside mansions subject to mudslide. More broadly, we prefer the government-as-insurer rather than government-as-benefit provider approach because it better links contribution and benefits and can be structured to fund itself rather than depend on the tax code and its attendant classifications and revisions.

As something of a middle ground when private sector forcing regulation fails, governments (state or national but hopefully extensive and consistent in authority and scope) can operate a reinsurance program or make available emergency funds (preferably by loan rather than grant) as an incentive for private carrier participation in a more comprehensive approach to risk. This is another area where the US Government has already done some of this, most prominently in the form of offering a reinsurance backstop for terrorism losses via TRIA (the Terrorism Risk Insurance Act of 2002).[45]

VI. Conclusion

Difficult risks cannot be wished away. But they can be more effectively addressed by insurers embracing them on a widespread basis that facilitates risk spreading, marketing, and overall profitability rather than retreating from those risks through narrower products that provide reduced protection for policyholders. If done effectively, such an approach can be financially sound for insurers as well as providing valuable risk management protection for the economy and public as a whole.

[45] See J W Stempel and E S Knutsen, *Stempel & Knutsen on Insurance Coverage* §24 (Alphen aan den Rijn, WoltersKluwer, 2016).

3

Going Beyond 'Risk Solidarity' in Private Insurance: The Changing Function of Insurance in Modern Times

BARIŞ SOYER

I. Introduction

In the private insurance sector, ensuring 'risk solidarity' – every member of the insurance pool paying a price (premium) in line with its risk level for the promise of indemnity from its insurer – has often been identified as the ultimate objective.[1] In this discourse 'risk classification' plays a vital role. As long as a risk presented to an insurer is correctly classified, solidarity amongst those participating in insurance is achieved, as those in the higher risk category pay more to the pool than those in the lower risk category, independently of who will receive future indemnities.[2] In this context, 'risk solidarity' has often been linked to notions of 'equality' and 'fairness' amongst pool members.[3]

Risk solidarity is distinct from other forms of solidarity (such as income or subsidising solidarity) that underpin social welfare systems. Social insurance schemes, for example, aim to equalise pool members' economic position in view of their income profiles. This effectively means that the well-to-do members of the society make a higher contribution to the pool in the shape of taxes and social insurance contributions even though they represent (in the actuarial sense at least) lower risks regarding health and unemployment, thus contributing to the welfare of the underprivileged in the society.[4] This kind of solidarity is imposed

[1] This is also referred to as 'actuarial fairness', particularly by those engaged in actuarial studies.

[2] See, T K Lehtonen and J. Liukko, 'Producing Solidarity, Inequality and Exclusion through Insurance' (2015) 21 *Res Publica* 155, and L Barry, 'Epidemic and Insurance – Two Forms of Solidarity' (2022) 39 *Theory, Culture & Society* 217.

[3] P S Harper, 'Insurance and Genetic Testing' (1993) 341 *The Lancet* 224–225.

[4] In the UK, for example, national insurance contributions are indexed to income so that higher-income households provide a level of coverage that lower-income ones could not otherwise afford. On the other hand, the benefits provided by the system are mostly flat rate.

by the power of the state and can only function by compulsion. It is, however, often justified on sentimental grounds such as the need for the members of such a pool to show mutual affection or identify with each other.[5]

At this stage, two significant observations are in order. First, although risk solidarity is omnipresent in the private insurance field, its role and function in facilitating mutuality should not be overstated. Risk solidarity is primarily dependent on the ability of insurers to be able to create accurate risk categories so that any distinction between the members of the class can be erased and homogeneity is achieved.[6] Although today the assessment process can be enhanced significantly with the advent of big data technologies and predictive analytics, it ultimately depends on the ability of insurers to be able to ask the relevant questions and utilise the data obtained in the process of refining risk categories. It has been suggested, for example, that although insurance companies might have access to more data, most of the data obtained from various sources is unstructured, and there likely will be difficulties in building such unstructured data in calculations[7] or utilising it effectively as part of current actuarial models.[8] Furthermore, working on the assumption that insurance creates a homogenous pool where assureds are divided into different categories and charged risk-related premiums for financing potential losses that pool members could suffer[9] is at odds with the mechanisms insurers in contemporary practice utilise to spread their potential losses. The portfolios of insurance companies are rarely (if ever) composed of homogenous risk pools. Most insurers opt to provide cover for a variety of risks, such as long-term business (eg, life insurance) and general business (eg, non-life) as well as emerging risks (such as cyber risk insurance); so they obtain premiums for different types of risk but equally minimise their exposure to heavy losses that might be suffered in one line of business in a given year. It is also worth noting that insurers invariably opt to reinsure their liabilities, hence spreading losses wider and further.[10]

Second, and perhaps most significant here, is that we are witnessing, particularly in the last few decades, the dividing line between different forms of solidarity being blurred in the private insurance field. Put differently, a

[5] T K Lehtonen and J Liukko, 'The Forms and Limits of Insurance Solidarity' (2011) 103 *Journal of Business Ethics* 33, 42.

[6] For an extensive debate on how the risk assessment process has evolved over the years, see, L Barry, 'Insurance, Big Data and Changing Conception of Fairness' (2020) 61 *European Journal of Sociology* 159.

[7] A E R Prince and D Schwarcz, 'Proxy Discrimination in the Age of Artificial Intelligence and Big Data' (2020) 105 *Iowa Law Review* 1257, 1273–74.

[8] L Moor and C Lury, 'Price and the Person: Markets, Discrimination, and Personhood' (2018) 11 *Journal of Cultural Economy* 501.

[9] K. Abraham, *Distributing Risk: Insurance, Legal Theory and Public Policy* (Yale, Yale University Press, 1986) at 64; J Stapleton, 'Tort, Insurance and Ideology' 58 (1995) *Modern Law Review* 820, 821–22.

[10] For a detailed analysis of how methods that insurance companies could employ to spread losses, see, R Merkin and J Steele, *Insurance and the Law of Obligations* (Oxford, Oxford University Press, 2013), 139–161.

deviation, often imposed by the authorities, from the premise of actuarial fairness is becoming more common. This is often associated with the protection of fundamental human rights.[11] For example, in the UK, insurers are not allowed to use data concerning protected characteristics of individuals (ie, age, disability, gender assignment, marriage or civil partnership, race, religion or belief, sex, and sexual orientation)[12] as part of the risk assessment process. In actuarial terms, this creates a redistribution of solidarity, as it is highly possible that high-risk individuals, who cannot be identified due to the limitation imposed by the anti-discrimination legislation, become subsidised by the other members of the insurance pool. We are also witnessing governmental interference in private insurance markets to ensure that insurers do not pull out of insuring certain risks based on their actuarial risk assessment highlighting high-risk levels. For example, in many countries, including the UK, schemes have been put in place to ensure that private insurers continue providing insurance coverage for properties that are highly exposed to natural disasters. Several commentators believe that defying risk solidarity and imposing a subsidised solidarity (akin to solidarity that underlines social welfare systems) in certain instances has become a fundamental right, perhaps even a democratic realisation of individual freedom.[13]

It is argued in this contribution that the trend of moving away from the paradigm of achieving actuarial fairness will continue and even accelerate in the light of several factors, such as climate change making natural disasters more common and unpredictable, and the use of big data analytics combined with advances in medical research (especially genomics) making it difficult or impossible for some individuals to obtain insurance. It will be argued here that private insurance (especially consumer insurance) will need to acquire a different role by adopting different solidarity principles. However, given that private insurers are commercial entities, it is inevitable that to expect them to play a different role in society, new schemes backed up by the state will need to be put in place. This contribution will deliberate the principles that need to guide any governmental interference in the market and the adjustments, particularly in the insurance products, that need to be made to achieve the most effective results for the assured, insurers and the society overall.

There is no doubt that the nature of interference in the market and the appropriate degree of subsidy in solidarity will depend on the risks emerging and the potential impact of such risks on individuals. To illustrate this, in Section III we shall consider the impact of risks emerging from climate change and discuss why interference is necessary, along with the form such interference should take. Similarly, in Section IV, the potential of advances in big data analytics and

[11] Y Tiery and C Van Schoubroeck, 'Fairness and Equality in Insurance Classification' (2006) 31 *Geneva Papers on Risk and Insurance* 190.

[12] Equality Act 2010, s 4–12.

[13] H Brunkhorst, *Solidarity: From Civic Friendship to a Global Legal Community* (Cambridge, MIT Press, 2005), 59–60. See also, D Parfit, 'Equality and Priority' (1997) 10 *Ratio* 202, at 213.

genomics in changing the landscape for life, critical illness, and income protection insurance products, and potential solutions to issues emerging, will be deliberated. However, before embarking upon an examination of how new solidarity principles will shape the nature of private insurance, it is necessary to clarify in Section II that occasional attempts of judges to disregard risk solidarity principles for the sake of protecting a group of individuals is a rather different notion than the one discussed here.

II. Judge Made Solidarity?

In recent times, we have witnessed occasionally judicial creativity coming into play to afford protection for a group of individuals perceived to be vulnerable. Two examples are sufficient to illustrate this point.

Towards the end of the last century, those who suffered from mesothelioma – a form of lung cancer that is commonly caused by the lodgement of asbestos fibres in the lungs following exposure to the substance – started bringing lawsuits to their previous employers (mainly those in the construction industry) for exposing them to the substance. Typically, an employee would work for different employers and would, therefore, be exposed to asbestos at different times. From a legal perspective, this creates a significant problem as it makes it impossible to determine which exposure had caused the disease. This legal difficulty in establishing causation was bypassed in *Fairchild* v *Glenhaven Funeral Services Ltd*[14] in a radical fashion. The House of Lords held that a liability case against an employer could be established merely by showing that, on the balance of probabilities, the risk of asbestos-related disease had been materially increased at the workplace at a certain time; and the claimant no longer had to show that but for that exposure, the liability would not have been occurred. Their Lordships did not engage in a debate as to the impact of various other factors, such as the claimant being a heavy smoker or suffering from other illnesses, potentially contributing to a claimant, who is exposed to asbestos at work, catching the disease. By imposing a less demanding causation test, the obvious objective of the judiciary was to enable those suffering from the disease to be able to bring action against their previous employers. The Parliament followed suit a few years later by introducing the Compensation Act 2006, which enables the victim of asbestos exposure to recover the full amount of damages from any employer responsible for any of the exposures if the victim can demonstrate that mesothelioma had been contracted by exposure to asbestos, the person sued faced liability in tort for the exposure, and medical science could not determine which exposure had led to the injury.[15] Effectively, this legislation allows the victim to bring a single

[14] [2002] UKHL 22; [2003] 1 AC 32.

[15] Section 3 of the Compensation Act 2006.

action for damages encompassing all periods of exposure, including those where the victim was responsible for their exposure, on the basis that each exposure is a tort, hence there is no need for the victim to demonstrate a causal link between any one exposure and the onset of the injury.[16]

More recently, a similar stance was taken by the Supreme Court when the Financial Conduct Authority (FCA) sponsored a test case[17] to clarify the position of some 370,000 affected business interruption insurance policyholders following the lockdowns and restrictions imposed by the government during the early days of the COVID-19 pandemic. Most of the claims that policyholders brought against insurers were denied on the premise that the wording used in such policies was not broad enough to cover the losses emanating. The FCA selected a representative sample of 21 types of policies issued by eight insurers for the test case. Objectively speaking, the legal battle was aimed at attempting to fit unanticipated events into contract wording that was never designed for that purpose.[18] However, the outcome was very much in favour of the assured business owners. For example, in a business interruption policy that provided indemnity for a 'disease or public health issues on, or the vicinity of the premises [sometimes specified as 25 miles], affecting the business conducted on the premises', it was held that the assured could recover as long as there was one case of illness caused by the disease within that radius.[19] Concerning policies that required 'closure or restrictions or loss of access ordered by public authorities by reason of disease' for indemnity, it was held that 'restrictions' did not need to be legally binding but could include instructions issued by authorities albeit not backed by force of law. Restrictions also included instructions or duties imposed upon the public and not necessarily on the business itself. In some other policies, a different wording (trigger) was used such as 'inability to use' or 'prevention of access' or 'interruption'. The Supreme Court was prepared to construe such triggers broadly too. For example, in policies where the insurance provided cover when there was 'inability to use' the premises, the Supreme Court was adamant that the requirement was satisfied if the policyholder was unable to use either the premises for a discrete part of its business

[16] Given that the liability under the Act is joint and several, the employer sued does have a right to seek contribution from others responsible for exposing the victim to asbestos under the Civil Liability (Contribution) Act 1978. In the following years, the courts also dealt with cases that concerned the liability of the insurers under the employer's liability and public liability policies (when the employer responsible tried to recover from its liability insurer following action from a successful previous employee) and reinsurance triggers: *Durham v BAI (Runoff) Ltd Employers' Liability Trigger Litigation* [2012] UKSC 14; [2012] 1 WLR 867 and *Zurich Insurance plc UK Branch v International Energy Group Ltd* [2015] UKSC 33; [2016] AC 509.

[17] *Financial Conduct Authority v Arch Insurance (UK) and Others* [2021] UKSC 1; [2021] AC 649.

[18] It is worth noting that in the insurance market after SARS in 2012 a specifically designed pandemic insurance policy was on offer but very few businesses opted for it.

[19] The Supreme Court by referring to the wording of the clause, especially the emphasis in the clause on 'any occurrence of a Notifiable disease', indicated that the wording of the clause is adequate to provide cover for the business interruption caused by any cases of illness resulting from COVID-19 that occurred within 25 miles of the business premises.

activities, or a discrete part of its premises for its business activities, as in both of these situations there was a complete inability to use.

Another legal point that was decided against the insurers was their argument that the 'causation test'[20] applied in insurance law should not be adopted as the appropriate test in the context of construing relevant provisions of business interruption policies. Instead, it was argued that it should be necessary to show, at a minimum, that the loss would not have been sustained 'but for' the occurrence of the insured peril. In their view, the business needed to show that the insured peril had operated to cause the loss; otherwise, due to the widespread nature of the pandemic, it would be very easy for holders of such policies to show business interruption losses even if the insured risk had not occurred. The obvious objective for developing this contention was to limit the scope of cover provided by such policies as otherwise (if the traditional causation rules were to apply in this context) businesses operating in locations that have no or few cases of the illness could still recover under the policy even though the loss in those instances was caused by disruption occurring outside the radius (or nationally). In developing their argument, insurers relied heavily on the decision in *Orient-Express Hotels Ltd v Assicurazioni General SpA*.[21] In that case, the claim was for business interruption losses caused by Hurricanes Katrina and Rita. The insured premises in question were a hotel in New Orleans. There was no dispute that the insured property suffered physical damage as a result of the hurricanes. When it came to the business interruption losses, however, insurers in *Orient-Express* case successfully argued that there was no cover because, even if the hotel had not been damaged, the devastation to the area around the hotel caused by the hurricanes was such that the business interruption losses would have been suffered in any event. Accordingly, the necessary causal test for the business interruption losses could not be met because the insured peril was the damage alone, and the event that caused the insured physical damage (the hurricanes) could be set up as a competing cause of the business interruption. The Supreme Court held that *Orient-Express* was wrongly decided and should be overruled. Analysing the facts of the *Orient-Express* case, the Supreme Court concluded that business interruption loss arose there both because of damage to the hotel and also damage to the surrounding area as a result of hurricanes. Therefore, two concurrent causes were in operation there, each of which was by itself sufficient to cause the relevant business interruption but neither of which satisfied the 'but for' test because of the existence of the other. In such a case, when both the insured peril and the uninsured peril that operates concurrently with it arise from the same underlying fortuity (ie, the hurricanes), then provided that damage proximately caused by the uninsured peril (ie, damage to the rest of the city) is not excluded, loss resulting from both causes operating

[20] *Leyland Shipping Co Ltd* v *Norwich Union Fire Insurance Sy Ltd* [1918] AC 350, 365 (per Lord Atkinson) and 369 (per Lord Shaw).

[21] [2010] EWHC 1186 (Comm); [2010] Lloyd's Rep IR 531.

concurrently is covered. Accordingly, the Supreme Court rejected the insurers' argument, holding that the traditional principles of causation should be applied. On this point, the Supreme Court concluded:[22]

> … there is nothing in principle or in the concept of causation which precludes an insured peril that in combination with many other similar uninsured events brings about a loss with a sufficient degree of inevitability from being regarded as a cause – indeed as a proximate cause – of the loss, even if the occurrence of the insured peril is neither necessary nor sufficient to bring about the loss by itself.

Applying the traditional proximity test essentially enables businesses to recover under such policies simply by proving a link between the local occurrences and the national reaction.

Given that in both instances discussed above the judicial intervention was value-laden and based on moral considerations (ie, to ensure that those who are deemed worthy of protection), one might be forgiven for thinking that these represent a trend within the judiciary to re-deign 'risk solidarity', which has underlined private insurance law. This would be, however, a misleading finding. The common feature of both interventions mentioned above is the fact that judges have creatively used causation and construction principles to achieve fairness as they deem appropriate in the circumstances. Both interventions are very much fact-specific, and there is no indication that the judiciary is developing a new line of thought when it comes to solidarity as perceived in insurance and what role it should play.

III. Risks Associated with Climate Change – The Need to 'Redefine' Scope of the Solidarity Principle

Scientists have been warning against the risk of natural disasters occurring more severely and frequently as a result of climate change. For example, under climate change scenarios forecasting a 2° C rise in global temperatures, it is predicted that the UK could see a 50 percent increase in expected annual damages to properties emanating from natural disasters and a 50 percent increase in the number of people living in properties which are at a high risk of flooding by 2080.[23] There is already ample evidence pointing out that the effect of climate change is being felt in communities worldwide in the form of extreme heat waves, severe flooding, and wind storms occurring more frequently.[24]

[22] [2021] UKSC 1; [2021] AC 649, [191].

[23] P B Sayers, M S Horritt, E Penning-Roswell and A Mckenzie, *Climate Change Risk Assessment 2017, Projections of Future Flood Risks in the UK* (2015) Report for the Committee on Climate Change. www.theccc.org.uk/wp-content/uploads/2015/10/CCRA-Future-Flooding-Main-Report-Final-06Oct2015.pdf.pdf.

[24] Intergovernmental Panel on Climate Change, (Sixth Assessment Report, 2021), *Climate Change 2021: The Physical Science Basis.*:www.ipcc.ch/report/ar6/wg1/.

Insurers, armed with increasingly sophisticated risk models, could easily pinpoint areas that are likely to be affected by more frequent extreme natural events, meaning that more and more properties will be falling into the 'high risk' category. Risk-reflective pricing would effectively mean that insurers will either decline insurance coverage to owners of properties in those areas, or the price of insurance will be prohibitively expensive. In the past, on several occasions, we have witnessed this happening in various insurance markets.[25] There is nothing extraordinary here. At the end of the day, insurers are driven by commercial considerations, and if risk solidarity is simply viewed as an exercise in achieving fairness and equality between pool members, private insurers are justified in taking this kind of stance. The main thrust of this part is to argue that solidarity provided by private insurance arrangements needs to be viewed in a different light, and the nature of private insurance must be altered to achieve this end. Accordingly, there will be a discussion as to why adopting a different solidarity approach is justified in this context as well as how it can be achieved. It will be also deliberated what kind of further alterations, beyond the compensation aspect of insurance, are needed to supplement a new insurance scheme.

A. The Continuing Role of Private Insurance

The ultimate question is whether there is still a role for private insurance to play in property insurance given that more properties will be exposed to increased levels of risk in the years to come as a result of climate change. One might be justified in suggesting that the state needs to step in if private insurers, based on actuarial risk assessment, are reluctant to offer insurance for the owners of properties in high-risk areas, or if the cover is made available at a very high premium making private insurance an unviable option for most. It is argued that there are several good reasons why private insurance should continue being part of any compensation regime available to members of society for uncertainties associated with such natural disasters, ideally under a tailor-made scheme supported by the state. It will be highlighted below why securing active participation of private insurance is vital.

First, there are sound economic reasons for this. If such losses are passed in their entirety to the state, this will effectively mean that more public funds need to be spent on disaster recovery, potentially leaving less funds available for other vital public expenditure (such as health or education). Another related issue,

[25] For example, in the USA private insurers ceased writing flood insurance in certain areas after the Great Mississippi Flood of 1926–7. Today in the USA, various federally backed schemes (eg, the National Flood Insurance Program) assist in the process of insuring properties in areas that could be affected by flooding. More recently, again in the USA private insurance market in Southeastern and Gulf states largely abandoned coastal wind coverage after an unprecedented sequence of four hurricanes swept the region in 2004.

at the macro-economic level, is that states that end up spending most of their resources on compensating individuals will not be able to raise sufficient capital to replace or repair damaged assets and restore livelihoods following major disasters.[26] This potentially represents a larger problem for developing economies, but even more developed economic systems are currently witnessing the adverse economic impact of excessive government borrowing at times of national emergency (eg, during the global pandemic, government borrowing in most developed economies increased significantly, creating inflationary trends and other adverse consequences on the economy in the aftermath).[27]

Apart from economic justifications, it can be argued that by providing victims of natural disasters security and thus reducing the burden on tax-funded benefits and compensation schemes, private insurance provides a wider social benefit.[28] Put differently, knowledge of the public that private insurance will be able to compensate their losses in the wake of such disasters would inspire confidence and thus reduce the negative impact of such events on the well-being of individuals. Hence, it can plausibly be argued that having the benefit of private insurance coverage helps to improve the condition of society as a whole.

Lastly, there are other social and ethical considerations at play here. It is likely that an area that is likely to be affected by natural disasters, such as a settlement near a riverbank prone to flooding, attracts those in the lower-income segment due to the lower value of housing in that area.[29] There can be an ethical argument that those are in need of protection most, as their decision to live and work in an area prone to natural disasters is not simply a matter of choice. If these people find themselves in a situation where they can no longer afford insurance and they need to rely on the state in case of a natural disaster for compensation, this could potentially lead to social unrest.

B. The Nature of Interaction between the State and Private Insurance Market

So far, we have established two important parameters on the debate. First, when it comes to insurance against risks caused by climate change, it is necessary to invoke a solidarity principle distinct from risk solidarity. Second, there is a significant benefit in keeping the private insurance sector involved as part of any system designed to provide compensation. The significant issue facing policymakers will

[26] See, J Linneroth-Bayer et al, 'Insurance, Developing Countries and Climate Change' (2009) 34 *The Geneva Papers on Risk and Insurance. Issues and Practice* 381, 382.

[27] Some of these issues have been deliberated by Professor Gurses in Chapter 1.

[28] R Avraham, 'The Economics of Insurance Law – A Primer' (2012) 19 *Connecticut Insurance Law Journal* 29, 41.

[29] For a more general debate on a similar theme, see E S Andreson, 'What is the Point of Equality?' (1999) 109 *Ethics* 287.

be determining the nature of governmental intervention and the shape of such a compensatory regime that brings public and private players together. Some influential commentators believe that providing premium subsidies is the best form of intervention to an insurance market, as this does not distort the price mechanism, leading to inefficiencies, and allows positive effects of premium differentiation to be maintained.[30] Assuming that those who own properties in high-risk areas are provided a premium subsidy, there are still missing parts of the jigsaw that need to be put together by policymakers. For example, a key consideration will be the source of such subsidies. Will the state underwrite such subsidies, or could they be shared by those who benefit generally from insurance arrangements (ie, the assureds)? Also, the relationship between private insurers and state resources needs to be settled, as it is very likely that private insurers would need to be assured that there will be a reliable mechanism (perhaps in the shape of a reinsurance scheme) that can help to redistribute and even absorb some of the losses, especially in cases where natural disasters of large magnitude occur.

The subsidy arrangements and state market relationship can be managed in different ways,[31] but one eye-catching arrangement that is currently in place is the UK's solution to insuring properties exposed to the risk of flooding. Flood Re Ltd is a not-for-profit company established by the Water Act 2014 with the mission to offer affordable insurance for properties that are facing serious risk of flooding. Flood Re performs several administrative functions as well as providing insurance capacity for the market. Its primary function is to provide reinsurance for insurers that offer personal property insurance to the extent that they are prepared to cede those risks to the Flood Re scheme.[32]

Flood Re's funding comes from two main sources. First, a levy is paid by all insurers offering home insurance in the UK (amounting to £135 million a year). Therefore, every person purchasing a home insurance policy, regardless of where their property is located, is expected to contribute to the pool as they will be charged by their insurer to cover this levy.[33] This effectively means that houses at significant risk of flooding are cross-subsidised by a levy on top of the premium on every household insurance policy. Technically, this subsidy is an application of the solidarity principle aiming to provide financial assistance and comfort to

[30] See C Kousky and H Kenreuther, 'Addressing Affordability in the National Flood Insurance Program' (2014) 1 *Journal of Extreme Events* 1450001.

[31] For example, under the threat of insurers withdrawing terrorism cover for commercial and other buildings following the IRA bombings in 1992, the Reinsurance (Act of Terrorism) Act 1993 established a state-backed reinsurer, Pool Re, which acts as a reinsurer, on commercial rates, of property insurers willing to underwrite terrorism risks. In Spain, a state-owned insurance company, the Consorcio de Compensaciõn de Seguros (CCS), covers extraordinary risks for the market. The cover is an add-on to property damage products. The CCS benefits from a state guarantee, although this has never been used in practice.

[32] Insurers are likely to cede policies that offer cover to properties located in high-risk areas for flooding.

[33] This notionally equates to roughly £10.50 in respect of each household purchasing home insurance in the UK.

those whose properties are at high risk of flooding. Second, Flood Re also charges a fixed premium to an insurer ceding risks to the scheme based on the Council Tax band, not the actuarial flood risk that the property in question poses. By using Council Tax bands to price its reinsurance premium, the scheme offers primary insurers cheaper reinsurance rates for high-risk properties than they could find with reinsurers basing their premium on an actuarial basis. The effect of this is that it enables insurers to charge lower premiums for those in the high-risk category.

In short, this scheme facilitates solidarity among all those who opt to purchase home insurance cover in the UK by ensuring that everyone contributes equally (regardless of their potential exposure to flood risks) to the funding of the reinsurance scheme operated by Flood Re. In return, the scheme not only ensures that there will be a viable reinsurance mechanism for insurers opting to write business in high-risk areas, but it also enables insurers to offer insurance cover to owners of properties in high-risk areas at a reasonable price by charging a flat rate for reinsurance premium regardless of the location of the property. As such, the scheme provides a market solution with little governmental interference and regulation to a specific problem. It is envisaged that the scheme will come to an end in 2039[34] and the market will return to risk-reflective pricing, on the assumption that this gives the local and central governments time to develop preventive measures against floods (eg, flood defences).

It is suggested that the Flood Re scheme could provide inspiration for developing a more embracing compensation scheme, one that puts solidarity at its heart, providing an effective mechanism to insure properties that might be exposed to additional risks caused by climate change. The remit of the current scheme, for example, could be expanded to include insurers providing cover for all risks caused by extreme natural events. Naturally, adjustments to the amount of levy and reinsurance premiums will be necessary considering the increased number of risks and potential losses,[35] but with the advances in predictive analytics and actuarial studies, this should not pose a significant problem. There are several good reasons why this recommendation deserves serious consideration. First, the Flood Re scheme provides a sound conceptual framework by utilising the idea of solidarity in a way that all those who benefit from the comfort that household insurance provides contribute to ensure that those living in high-risk areas can find insurance coverage at a reasonable price without being an additional burden to the state for premium subsidies. This potentially enables the state to put more resources into preventive measures such as flood defences. Given that climate change is likely to have an impact on the whole of the country, it certainly makes sense to

[34] 25 years from the date of Royal Assent to the Water Act 2014.

[35] It is projected that the total cost of climate change damages to the UK will increase from 1.1 percent of GDP at present to 3.3 percent of GDP by 2050 and 7.4 by 2010 (see, Grantham Research Institute on Climate Change and the Environment, *What Will Climate Change Cost to the UK? Risk Impacts and Migration for the Net-Zero Transition*, (2022), 2. www.lse.ac.uk/granthaminstitute/wp-content/uploads/2022/05/What-will-climate-change-cost-the-UK-risks-impacts-mitigation-1.pdf.

expect collective solidarity amongst policyholders to be developed to enable the state to focus on adjustments that can be made to prevent or mitigate adverse consequences of such extreme natural events. It should be also noted that since its inception in 2014, the Flood Re scheme worked rather well providing tangible benefits (especially in terms of affordability of insurance cover) for those living in areas that are prone to flooding.[36] With careful adjustments, under a new scheme, such benefits can be enjoyed by those whose properties will be under threat from the effects of climate change. Finally, one should not lose sight of the fact that the Flood Re scheme provides benefits beyond the insurance sector. For example, as financial institutions such as mortgage providers enjoy the benefits of the scheme and in the future, more and more properties face the risk of loss as a result of climate change-related events, the availability of insurance at a reasonable price will be important in those financial sectors.

That said, extending the remit of the Flood Re might pose some problems for the viability of the regime. For example, under the current scheme, there is no guarantee from the government that it would step in to pick up the tab for truly catastrophic risks if the funds available under the scheme were not adequate.[37] There has been no need for this so far but the situation can rapidly change if the scope of the scheme is extended or the effects of climate change lead to more severe losses in a shorter period than predicted. Of course, there could be market solutions, such as obtaining reinsurance cover (retrocession) for losses the scheme suffers over a limit, but the role of government backing must be specified, especially if the scheme will be extended to provide a market solution for the potential shortfall of insurance provision in the light of enhanced risks posed by climate change.

C. Insurance Supplementing Adaptive Measures Taken by Authorities

Adopting a different solidarity principle in this context symbolises a shift from individual responsibility to mutualisation. This is an important step, but risk transfer alone is not a sustainable solution in the long run. It needs to be supplemented with the development of precautionary principles in response to global threats such as climate change.[38] There are several adaptive measures governments could take to reduce the enhanced risks created by climate change. For example, there

[36] Since its inception, Flood Re backed insurance for more than 526,000 households (see Flood Re, *Our Call to Action – Transition Plan 2023–28* (2023) 15).

[37] Flood Re has the power to request further payment from the insurance industry either in the form of levy or by way of contribution if such is required for prudent management of the scheme or regulatory compliance.

[38] See S Surminski, 'Fit for Purpose and Fit for Future? An Evaluation of the UK's New Flood Reinsurance Pool' (2018) 21 *Risk Management and Insurance Review* 33, which develops coherent arguments that any compensation scheme needs to be supplemented by adaptive measures.

should be a serious consideration of the type of alterations in building regulations that can be made to ensure that new properties are better equipped for challenges posed by climate change. Similarly, risk profiles of different regions could be developed by utilising improved risk data and modelling, and these should play a vital role in determining in which areas new development will be allowed. It is beyond the scope of this contribution to evaluate which measures could be taken by governments and how effective their results could be,[39] but there are steps that the insurance industry could take to support the governments and policymakers in that regard by providing incentives for loss reduction. Some of these will be discussed next.

The nature of insurance is such that following a loss, indemnity is provided to restore the subject matter of insurance to its original condition. Therefore, if the assured chooses to make improvements to the subject matter, the additional cost required to make such improvements in the subject matter is to be deducted from the insured loss by reason of betterment.[40] This gives no incentive to an assured, whose property is damaged by extreme flooding, for example, to reinstate the property by using more resilient materials or building techniques. Insurers could support the resilient building standards that regulators are putting in place as part of adaptive measures to climate change by ensuring that terms in their contracts do not make any deduction when assureds choose to reinstate their properties to the more resilient standard. In any case, reinstating properties damaged because of enhanced risks associated with climate change in a more resilient manner is likely to benefit insurers in the long run by potentially reducing the risk of loss.

Furthermore, insurers could encourage their customers to put in place risk mitigation measures by offering incentives such as reduction in premiums. Such initiatives could be linked to the measures developed by authorities. For example, it has been already mooted in the context of the Flood Re scheme that a 'Flood Performance Certificate' is created, indicating the flood risk of a property and what flood resilience it has installed.[41] Expanding the scope of this initiative, the regulators could consider the development of a 'Climate Change Adaptation Certificate' similar to energy performance certificates, stating what resilience systems against climate change the property is equipped with. This would make it easier for insurers to offer responsive premiums if the relevant household were to install

[39] For an illuminating analysis on that point, see P Jarzabkowski, K Chalkias, D Clarke, E Iyahen, D Stadtmueller and A Zwick, *Insurance for Climate Adaptation: Opportunities and Limitations* (Rotterdam and Washington, DC, 2019). www.gca.org.

[40] See *Reynolds v Phoenix Assurance Co Ltd* [1978] 2 Lloyd's Rep 440, where Forbes, J, 453, explained the underlying basis of this principle in the following terms: '[T]he principle of betterment is too well established in the law of insurance to be departed from at this stage even though it may sometimes work hardship on the assured. It is simply that an allowance must be made because the assured is getting something new for something old'. The point has been reiterated more recently in *Sartex Quilts and Textiles Ltd v Endurance Corporate Capital Ltd* [2020] EWCA Civ 308; [2020] 2 All ER (Comm) 1050.

[41] Flood Re, *Our Call to Action – Transition Plan 2023–28* (2023) 69.

improved measures.[42] This will certainly eradicate the potential 'moral hazard' problem highlighted in some circles (the risk that having in place a comprehensive compensation scheme for losses emerging from climate change might remove incentives for policyholders to take preventive and adaptive measures).[43]

Finally, the insurance sector can play an important role in educating its customers and encouraging them to put preventive measures in place to prepare for natural disasters. This can be done by producing preparedness guidelines and checklists for their customers and making those available as part of the service they provide. Advances in technology and communication enable insurance companies to take additional steps to encourage their customers to take preventive measures. For example, in case of a storm alert customers may be warned to deploy shutters on their windows by mobile-text alerts or announcements through social media.

Obviously, for measures that insurance companies can take to be effective, they must dovetail with risk mitigation and climate adaptation measures developed by the state.[44] This requires the dialogue between policymakers and insurers to be strengthened and an integrated climate adaptation policy for any country to be developed considering specific climate change risks they face depending on their geography. However, the discussion above illustrates that private insurance can assist not only in terms of risk sharing but also in risk mitigation efforts.[45]

IV. Genetics and Potential Role of Data Analytics and Artificial Intelligence

The advances in genomics have brought to the fore the question of to what extent predictive genetic testing could be an effective way of determining insurance applicants' susceptibility to certain diseases. This could potentially be a game changer in some lines of business (eg, life insurance, critical illness insurance, and income protection insurance), as it could provide a valuable tool to insurance companies to demand prohibitive amounts of premium or even decline insurance for those

[42] Other schemes encourage similar initiatives. For example, under the US National Flood Insurance Programme, in order for their residents to benefit from subsidised policies, communities are required to put land-use and other mitigation measures in place.

[43] Moral hazard is a systemic risk faced by all insurers. It is essentially the risk of the assured taking less than optimal precautions against an insured risk after the attachment of the policy. This particular behaviour is commonly referred to as 'ex-ante' moral hazard. For more information on the subject, see R Avraham, 'The Law and Economics of Insurance Law – A Premier' (2012) 19 *Conn Insurance Law Journal* 28, 66.

[44] Some criticise Flood Re on the premise that it represents the UK government's reluctance to accept the need for long-term solutions beyond financial interventions such as reinsurance. See eg, B Christophers, 'The Allusive Market: Insurance of Flood Risks in Neoliberal Britain' (2018) 48 *Economy and Society* 1.

[45] For an interesting observation on this point see S Hampton and J Curtis, 'A Bridge over Troubled Water? Flood Insurance and the Governance of Climate Adaptation' (2022) 136 *Geoform* 80.

who are deemed to be high risk. This prompted the Council of Europe to introduce in 1997 a Convention on Human Rights and Biomedicine,[46] which prohibits the performance of genetic testing as a condition for entering into an insurance contract.[47] The UK has not ratified the Convention but the Association of British Insurers (ABI) in collaboration with the government imposed on its members[48] a voluntary agreement on the use of genetic testing.[49] This agreement, known as 'The Code on Genetic Testing and Insurance', is open-ended and reviewed every three years (last reviewed in 2022). The Code does not, however, impose a blanket ban on the use of genetic tests by insurers. It simply commits ABI member insurers not to require from their clients a predictive or diagnostic test as a condition for entering an insurance contract, but insurers could ask for such tests if the applicant is applying for life insurance over £500,000[50] (or critical illness or income protection insurance over £300,000). Insurers could also request the disclosure of the results of a predictive genetic test for Huntington's disease[51] in applications for life insurance cover over the financial limit of £500,000. It is worth noting that the agreement does not preclude an applicant from disclosing the results of a diagnostic genetic test already conducted – as such a test is treated in the same way as any other diagnostic medical test (such as a blood test).

The effect of these restrictions on genetic testing for insurance purposes is redefining the limits of solidarity in a fundamentally new way by increasing the role of subsidising risk solidarity in private insurance. Put differently, by controlling some risk factors (eg, the prospect of identifying genetic disposition to certain illnesses), those who have such genetic dispositions are enabled to obtain insurance cover without facing the risk of paying additional premiums or running the risk of their insurance applications being declined.

A. Use of Genetic Testing in Risk Assessment in Insurance

The debate surrounding the use of predictive genetic data as part of assessing insurance applications is ethically charged, and commentators often treat the stance taken by most governments on the matter as an open-and-shut case.

[46] As of 1 May 2024, thirty states have ratified this Convention: Albania, Andora, Bosnia & Herzegovina, Bulgaria, Croatia, Cyprus, Czech Republic, Denmark, Estonia, Finland, France, Georgia, Greece, Hungary, Iceland, Latvia, Lithuania, Montenegro, North Macedonia, Norway, Portugal, Republic of Moldova, Romania, San Marino, Serbia, Slovak Republic, Slovenia, Spain, Switzerland and Tűrkiye.

[47] Some countries have enacted much stricter prohibitions for insurers by restricting the use of preexisting test results (see eg, the Israeli Genetic Information Law 2000).

[48] Around 95 percent of insurance providers in the UK are ABI members.

[49] Some other European states, such as France, the Netherlands, and Finland, followed a similar path.

[50] 95 percent of life insurance policies issued by ABI members fall under this financial limit: *ABI Annual Report: Code on Genetic Testing and Insurance* (2022) 9.

[51] Huntington's disease is a condition that stops parts of the brain from working properly over time. It is inherited from a person's parents. It gets gradually worse over time and is usually fatal after a period of up to 20 years.

Admittedly, there are several sound reasons for redistributing solidarity among all holders of insurance products by preventing (voluntary or otherwise) insurance companies from taking into account predictive genetic data in the process of risk assessment.

It has been persuasively argued that no person should suffer from misfortunes for which he or she cannot be reasonably held responsible.[52] No one can choose his or her genetic constitution. It is, therefore, not fair that someone who has suffered ill fortune in the natural lottery by inheriting an increased susceptibility to disease should on this account suffer further from limited access or denial to insurance products.[53] This line of thinking links closely to another argument that private insurance should not be seen as a privilege but as a basic right.[54] Accordingly, everyone should enjoy the right to have access to a product (here insurance) that is for 'primary social good'.[55]

Two further right-based justifications have been put forward to lend support to the exclusion of genetic data from risk assessment in insurance. The first one is linked to the concept of individual freedom (or liberty) which is often identified as one of the prime values for human beings. People have a right to remain in ignorance of their genetic constitution,[56] hence it would be contrary to their fundamental right if insurance companies had a right to require predictive genetic testing as a condition of cover. The other justification is embedded in the right to privacy. Supporters of this view argue that the primary reason for protecting genetic information is to avoid the distress that would be felt if it were not protected given that genetic information is personal and private.[57]

Equally, there is no doubt that the matter is multidimensional, and several plausible practical and philosophical arguments could be advanced questioning the exclusion of genetic data from the risk assessment process in the context of insurance law. Judging from the perspective of insurance practice, one possible impact of sharing risk solidarity among policyholders widely is a potential increase in premium levels. If that increase is a sharp one, the market might get smaller (with fewer people seeking insurance) and that might lead to a potential collapse of the entire market. This risk is greater if, as is the case in some European countries, those

[52] R Dworkin, *A Matter of Principle* (Cambridge, Harvard University Press, 1985) 207.

[53] See J Rawls, *A Theory of Justice* (Oxford, Calerendon Press, 1972) 303. Some authors framed this argument in the context of the priority principle. D Partif, 'Equality and Priority' (1997) 10 *Ratio* 202, at 213, put it in the following manner: 'If people who already suffer from a natural disadvantage (the increased risk of developing diseases) are further burdened by reduced opportunities to insure themselves against this, this seems to be contrary to priority principle.'

[54] BM Knoppers, B Godard and Y Joly, 'A Comparative International Overview' in MA Rothstein (ed), *Genetics and Life Insurance: Medical Underwriting and Social Policy* (Cambridge, MIT Press, 2004) 173, 185.

[55] T McGleenan, 'Insurance, Genetics and the Law' in T McGleenan, U Wiesing and F Ewald (eds), *Genetics and Insurance* (London, Bioscientiofic, 1999) 75 at 80.

[56] P Sandberg, 'Genetic Information and Life Insurance: A Proposal for an Ethical European Policy' (1995) 40 *Social Sciences and Medicine* 1549, 1555.

[57] S Borna and S Avila, 'Genetic Information: Consumers' Right to Privacy versus Insurance Companies' Right to Know: A Public Opinion Survey' (1999) 19 *Journal of Business Ethics* 355, 357.

seeking insurance are not expected to disclose the results of diagnostic genetic tests that they already have,[58] which could create 'adverse selection' problems identified by law and economics scholars.[59] For example, those who are aware of the fact that they are predisposed to have certain genetic diseases could exploit insurers who do not possess that kind of information by choosing to purchase large amounts of insurance cover. As the theory goes, this would naturally increase the possibility of loss for certain types of insurers (particularly those providing insurance for life and critical illness). As a natural reaction, insurers might increase the premiums significantly. Consequently, assureds that possess lower risk (as they have better information themselves about their own risk) might find this average premium too high for their individual expected risk and as a result, drop out of the pool, leaving high-risk assureds in the pool with the prospect of premiums and losses going up further, thus making it impossible to buy insurance coverage for risks with a fair amount of premium for most of the assureds.[60] Faced with this kind of dilemma, another plausible cause of action for insurers could be introducing expansive exclusions into their policies, especially reducing the type and nature of treatments for some diseases.[61] There is no doubt that the incorporation of such exclusions would amount to a significant restriction on the utility that insurance policies provide.

Another challenging question that is worth exploring is why private insurance is expected to perform a redistributive function by achieving solidarity among the pool members simply by ignoring genetic data that can be critical for risk classification. Apart from those who might regard insurance as not the most efficient way of distributing resources,[62] some might also find it unjust if some individuals will have to pay a higher premium than is justified by the risk they represent.[63] This might be a legitimate function of a social insurance scheme, but it can be contended that it does not serve the notion of justice if people do not pay insurance premiums according to the actuarially accurate determination of their risk when purchasing private insurance. In a similar vein, libertarians would argue that each person (here insurers) is free to accept or reject the terms of the other party to the transaction,[64] and to be able to do that, they need to have all relevant information including the right to request genetic information from the other party.

[58] This is not the case in the UK under the Code on Genetic Testing and Insurance.

[59] G Akerlof, 'The Market for Lemons' (1970) 84 *Quarterly Journal of Economics* 488.

[60] S Shavell, 'On Moral Hazard and Insurance' (1979) 93 *Quarterly Journal of Economics* 541.

[61] A similar trend has been observed in cyber risk insurance. Those policies providing cover against cyber risks contain numerous exclusions due to moral hazard concerns of the insurers; see B Soyer, 'Cyber Risk Insurance – Developing A New Cover in the Market' in *Ship Operations: New Risks, Liabilities and Technologies in Maritime Sector* (Oxford, Informa Law, 2021) 109.

[62] See eg, J M Buchnan, 'Positive Economics, Welfare Economics and Political Economics' (1959) 2 *The Journal of Law and Economics* 124; H R Varian, 'Distributive Justice, Welfare Economics and the Theory of Fairness' (1975) 4 *Philosophy & Public Affairs* 223.

[63] N Daniels, 'Insurability and the HIV Epidemic: Ethical Issues in Underwriting' (1990) 68 *The Milbank Quarterly* 497, 500.

[64] R Nozick, *Anarchy, State and Utopia*, (New Jersey, Wiley-Blackwell, 2001) 151.

B. Are We at the Crossroads? The Impact of Advances in Science and Data Analysis

Despite its potential to disturb parameters relating to risk assessment in insurance, there are still question marks as to how many actuarially relevant and accurate genetic tests are available that can reliably inform insurers in that process. However, there is no denying the fact that extensive research has been undertaken in this field and there are some groundbreaking advances.[65] For example, genomic sequencing technology designed to speed up a patient's diagnosis and offer a tailored personalised treatment plan for various diseases (such as cancer) based on the genetic constitution of the patient, is becoming common. This will mean that going forward there is likely to be more reliable data that can be used for actuarial modelling purposes at the disposal of insurers. Also, as genetic testing becomes more incorporated into the health care systems, with eligibility criteria for genetic testing changing and a rapid increase in the number of private genetic testing companies, it is not fanciful to suggest that the number of individuals who have detailed information on their genetic attributes will correspondingly increase. These developments might lead insurers to question their present stance (in the UK), especially if actuarially they conclude that denying the use of genetic testing presents unacceptable risks for certain lines of business (eg, life insurance).

Also, assuming that predictive genetic test results could give insurance companies a more accurate picture of an individual developing a condition and the potential for managing its effects if it develops, there is the prospect of insurers utilising their enhanced understanding to their advantage. For example, insurance companies (if they know better what to look for and how they can identify a person carrying such genetic dispositions) might utilise data other than genetic data (proxies) to single out genetically high-risk individuals.[66] The problem becomes more pronounced in the era of big data analytics considering that algorithms at the disposal of insurers might be able to identify patterns in a vast amount of data sets available to them.[67] Thus, even though the algorithms are not programmed

[65] eg, as part of the Newborn Genomes Programme, scientists are exploring and making significant progress in better diagnosing rare genetic diseases, especially in babies to speed up diagnosis and access to treatment for affected children (see www.genomicsengland.co.uk/initiatives/newborns).

[66] This is not a new phenomenon. In the USA, when the use of HIV tests was prevented by regulators as a legitimate risk-assessment criteria, other medical tests (of T-cells) were used instead. When this was prohibited, insurance companies started using sexual orientation to identify the relevant high-risk population. When this was regulated insurance companies began to differentiate against occupations homosexuals were disproportionately represented. For an interesting analysis of how other proxies can be used by insurers, see M A Rothstein, *Genetic Secrets: Protecting Privacy and Confidentiality in the Genetic Era* (New Haven, Yale University Press, 1997) 471. See also M Radetzki, M Radetzki and N Juth, *Genes and Insurance – Ethical, Legal and Economic Issues* (Cambridge, Cambridge University Press, 2003).

[67] For a thorough discussion on the potential impact of the AI in insurance law and practice, see O Gűrses, 'Insurance Law and AI – Demystifying Insurtech' in E Lim and P Morgan (eds), *The Cambridge Handbook of Private Law and Artificial Intelligence* (Cambridge, Cambridge University Press, 2024) 534.

to take into account the genetic characteristics of individuals, they may find linkages between input data and target variables (ie, identifying those who are in a high-risk category), irrespective of the nature of these linkages. This is known as 'unintentional proxy discrimination' and is often identified as a potential problem of using algorithms as part of the risk assessment process.[68] It is also possible that unintended discrimination could creep in as a result of the data used to train algorithms not being sufficiently representative. Put differently, biased training data may lead to discriminatory models, either because the training data may view historical data influenced by prejudice as valid examples, or it may draw inferences based on a limited or biased sample of the population.[69]

This is a different problem than identified earlier (ie, insurers potentially changing their current stance on the use of genetic data). We shall deliberate that issue at the end of this section, after touching upon the safeguards that need to be put in place to ensure that algorithms used by insurers do not, unintentionally, find ways of utilising the genetic data of an individual as part of the risk assessment process – assuming, of course, the current stance of not using predictive genetic data (adopted by ABI) continues.

i. Potential Solution to Problems Created by Algorithms

Several options are open to regulators to eliminate unintended proxy discrimination (in this context using genetic data obtained through proxies as part of risk assessment) that can arise as a result of a high volume of data that can be analysed by algorithms. It needs to be stressed that the problem is not confined to genetic data, and this kind of discrimination could arise with regard to any of the protected characteristics (eg, race, sex, religion, etc). Perhaps the most straightforward solution to the problem of discrimination fuelled by big data analytics is allowing only certain preapproved variables, determined by regulators, to be used by algorithms in the risk assessment process. This might be easy to implement, but it will also remove most of the benefits that granular risk classification brings. Also, this solution does not tackle the problem of algorithms or data collection systems being adversely affected by human prejudice.

Another potential solution is to allow insurers to use any data legally available but require them to explain to regulators the impact of their algorithms on members of protected groups or attributes such as genetic data.[70] This might work

[68] J M Skopek, 'Big Data Epistemology and Its Implications for Precision Medicine and Privacy' in IG Chen et al (eds), *Big Data Health and Bioethics* (Cambridge, Cambridge University Press, 2008) 30; S Barocas and A D Selbst, 'Big Data's Disparate Impact' (2016) 104 *California Law Review* 671, 712; L Edwards and M Veale, 'Slave to the Algorithm? Why A "Right to Explanation" Is Probably Not the Remedy You Are Looking For' (2017) 16 *Duke Law and Technology Review* 18, 25.

[69] S Barocas and A D Selbst, 'Big Data's Disparate Impact' 680; see also The Geneva Association, 'Promoting Responsible Artificial Intelligence' 12–13.

[70] S Hoffmann, 'Big Data's New Discrimination Threats: Amending the Americans with Disabilities Act to Cover Discrimination Based on Data-driven Predictions of Future Disease' in G Cohen, H F Lynch and E Veyena (eds), *Big Data, Health Law, and Biometrics* (Cambridge, Cambridge University Press, 2018) 85.

if insurers can explain that a variable used in risk assessment and causally linked to the desired outcome (risk individualisation) is not acting as a proxy for a protected characteristic or attribute. Of course, showing a causal link in this context is not an easy task, but regulators could set the standard of proof low and expect a plausible causal link to be shown rather than requiring a definitive proof of causality.[71] The task is by no means a simple one, but it will certainly mean less interference from the regulators. The regulators will have to audit insurers' classification systems randomly looking at the data sets mined by algorithms as well as the source codes and programmers' notes describing the variables, correlations, and inferences embedded in the algorithm.[72] These audits should focus on whether the data are suggesting inappropriate correlative predictions. The insurance industry has never been a great admirer of regulation; but given the dangers algorithms pose, especially when used in risk assessment, the time is coming to consider regulatory interference.[73]

ii. Insurance Industry's Potential U-Turn on the Use of Genetic Data

In the light of the discussion above, it is not fanciful to suggest that a change in the UK insurance industry's stance about not seeking predictive genetic testing (unless the insurance is over a substantial amount) would leave high-risk individuals uninsured or in a vulnerable situation due to demands for a high insurance premium. Assuming that policymakers would in that situation opt to protect such individuals by reverting to a shared solidarity approach, difficult decisions will need to be taken.

One option, of course, is by law (not through voluntary industry agreement) to prevent insurance companies from relying on genetic data concerning any applicant as part of the risk assessment process. However, as discussed above, this can create significant adverse selection problems for the insurance sector and could potentially result in a collapse of the private insurance market. Any reduction in

[71] J Gaulding, 'Note, Race, Sex and Genetic Discrimination in Insurance: What's Fair?' (1995) 80 *Cornell Law Review* 1646, 1681.

[72] D K Citron and F Pasquale, 'The Scored Society: Due Process for Automated Predictions' (2014) 89 *Washington Law Review* 1, at 23.

[73] The need for insurance companies that utilise AI in the risk assessment process to ensure that the system in use does not inadvertently lead to discriminating outcomes has been amplified by the new Consumer Duty that has come into force for all retailers in the UK since 31 July 2023. This Duty has been introduced by the Financial Conduct Authority (FCA) with an amendment to existing Principles for Business (PRIN) and intends to impose a higher standard of behaviour for firms interacting directly or indirectly with retail customers. The scope of the duty has been extended to the regulated activities and ancillary activities of all firms authorised under the Financial Services and Markets Act 2000 (FSMA), the Payment Services Regulations 2017 (PSRs) and E-money Regulations 2011 (EMRs), and on that basis applies not only to insurers but also to insurance intermediaries (eg, insurance brokers). It is inevitable that to enforce this duty effectively regulators will need to start considering the suitability of the algorithms employed by insurers.

the availability of key insurance products (such as insurance for critical illness or life insurance) would leave individuals even more exposed and certainly does not accomplish the purported ethical objectives of such a regulatory stance.

Another, and perhaps more viable, option is to allow insurance companies to utilise fully any genetic data in assessing risks, and deal separately with the position of those who fail to obtain insurance cover or cover at a reasonable price from the market. For such individuals, it might be necessary to establish a subsidised risk pool. At first glance, this looks like an attractive proposition and a satisfactory way of subsidising high-risk individuals by expanding the boundaries of the solidarity principle. However, to put a scheme of this nature in place, policymakers need to deal with several challenging questions. The most difficult issue will be determining which individuals will be entitled to access to the pool and on what basis. The logical stance will be to make access possible for those failing to get adequate insurance on account of 'genetic circumstances'. However, given that our understanding of the genetic constitution and its potential links to different diseases are constantly evolving as a result of medical research, defining 'genetic circumstances' by legislation could pose significant challenges. Another issue will be determining the maximum compensation level that the pool can offer. This is a decision for public authorities to consider, but one would expect the benefits of such a scheme to be less than what private insurance could offer; so possibly it would correspond to what authorities consider to be necessary to ensure basic welfare.[74] Perhaps the most challenging question is how the scheme will be funded. Naturally, those on the scheme will be expected to make a basic contribution (perhaps a premium they would have been expected to pay if insurance was available with no consideration for their genetic circumstances). The scheme could be further funded with a levy collected from all individuals purchasing life and similar insurance products from the private market.[75] This will ensure the establishment of a mechanism whereby those vulnerable due to their genetic disposition are subsidised by others purchasing similar insurance products from the market. There might be a role for the private insurance market to play here especially if those in charge of the pool consider purchasing reinsurance for losses over a threshold (excess of loss).

It is not in the scope of this work to elaborate an economic and actuarial basis for the proposed solution, but three propositions can safely be made. First, as medical research advances and the implications of genetic composition on several diseases become more transparent, it will be highly unlikely that insurers will continue offering insurance products without seeking predictive genetic testing. Second, as increasingly sophisticated genetic tests are utilised by the insurance

[74] M E Broom 'Insurers and Genetic Testing: Shopping for that Perfect Pair of Genes' (1991) 40 *Drake Law Review* 121, at 146.

[75] Similar schemes are designed to protect those who are vulnerable. For example, the Motor Insurers' Bureau, funded by a levy on motor insurance policies, pays for any injury or damage sustained caused by an uninsured driver.

industry, it is highly likely that the access of genetically disadvantaged groups to insurance products will be significantly reduced. This will require a reconsideration of current private insurance arrangements and solutions that spread solidarity beyond its restricted meaning of risk solidarity. The scheme discussed above, or a variation of it, will certainly be vital, as it offers a solution to a particular problem on the horizon, by redefining the scope of solidarity in insurance law, without the need for substantial public financing. However, it is obvious that legislative interference will be required, and implications of different policy options need to be carefully considered.

V. Concluding Remarks

The main theme developed throughout this contribution is that in some lines of business it will not be possible to offer private insurance based on risk solidarity among the pool members in the future. In property insurance, for example, given that natural disasters will strike more severely and frequently in the light of climate change occurring, alternative arrangements distributing solidarity wider would become a necessity. A solution based on the philosophy underlying the Flood Re scheme has been identified as the main way forward in this contribution, but it has also been highlighted that measures beyond mere risk distribution should be considered as part of new insurance arrangements.

Similar difficulties might arise in the context of life, critical illness and income protection insurance, if genetic data of applicants are made available to insurers as part of the risk assessment process. This area is more complicated, as currently the use of such data (at least in the UK) is restricted, but problems might still surface given that insurers are increasingly using data analytics in risk assessment that might inadvertently detect those that have genetic predispositions to some illnesses through other means. It has been argued that, if the current position with regard to not using predictive genetic information continues, better control mechanisms should be developed to ensure that algorithms do not reach the same outcomes by making use of other data. If, however, the position of the insurance industry changes and use of genetic data becomes fair game for the purposes of risk assessment, arrangements need to be considered by policymakers to ensure that some individuals are not left without private insurance. Some suggestions in that regard have been put forward in this contribution. This area clearly needs careful deliberation since individuals who are genetically disposed to certain illnesses might have limited opportunity to take personal measures to protect themselves.

4

Regulating AI in Insurance: An 'All-Risks' Approach

ROGER BROWNSWORD

I. Introduction

Recently, in both Brussels and London, there has been intense political activity in relation to the governance of artificial intelligence (AI). In the EU, the final version of the Regulation on AI has been agreed,[1] and, in the United Kingdom, steps are being taken to implement the 'pro-innovation' approach that the government set out in its White Paper in Spring 2023.[2] While there are significant differences between the EU's hard law and the UK's soft law approach to the governance of AI, the common concern is to facilitate the beneficial applications of AI, to minimise the risks, and to instate an ecosystem of trust in relation to AI.[3]

Against this background, this chapter has three purposes. First, it proposes an 'all-risks' approach to the governance of new technologies such as AI. This approach demands not only responsiveness to risks that might impact on a broad range of human interests but also sensitivity to the *depth* and significance of those interests Secondly, it seeks to clarify the relationship between the proposed all-risks approach and the establishment of an ecosystem of trust in AI. Thirdly, it identifies issues that an all-risks approach might flag up where AI tools are used in the insurance sector, whether by insurers or by insured parties.

The chapter is in five principal parts. First, the context for proposing an all-risks approach, namely one of regulatory governance, is set. Secondly, the all-risks

[1] European Parliament Press Release, 'Artificial Intelligence Act: Deal on Comprehensive Rules for Trustworthy AI' (9 December 2023) www.europarl.europa.eu/news/en/press-room/20231206IPR15699/artificial-intelligence-act-deal-on-comprehensive-rules-for-trustworthy-ai. For the official text, see OJ L, 2024/1689, 12.7.2024.

[2] Department for Science, Innovation and Technology, *A Pro-innovation Approach to AI Regulation* (Cm No 815, 2023).

[3] Compare The Geneva Association, 'Regulation of Artificial Intelligence in Insurance: Balancing Consumer Protection and Innovation' (Research Summary, September 2023) www.genevaassociation.org/sites/default/files/2023-09/Regulation%20of%20AI%20summary_WEB.pdf where, at p 3, the 'key challenge for policymakers' is said to be 'to strike a balance between minimising AI risks to protect consumers and citizens, while also allowing enough room for innovation to benefit society at large'.

approach, highlighting three levels of human interests that might be threatened by AI, is introduced. Thirdly, the relationship between an ecosystem of trust in AI and an all-risks approach, is examined. Fourthly, turning specifically to insurance, the question is how the all-risks governance approach might be applied to the use of AI tools by providers of insurance. Finally, the question is how this approach might be applied to the use of AI-enabled devices by prospectively or actually insured parties.

Before working through this agenda, let me declare that I am writing this chapter, not as an expert on insurance law – no doubt, this will be all too apparent – but as someone with a general interest in law and technology. Accordingly, my focus is on bespoke governance of AI and possible risk questions as they might arise in relation to insurance and not on how current initiatives in AI governance fit in the already heavily regulated European insurance markets.

II. The Context: Regulatory Governance

Before getting to the proposed all-risks approach, I should state three assumptions that I am making: first, that the political branch increasingly bears the burden of responsibility for the governance of technologies such as AI; secondly, that both lawyers and ethicists, nevertheless, have a role to play in the broad enterprise of governance; and, thirdly, that the all-risks approach is relevant to the thinking of all parties who aspire to good governance.

These remarks invite several questions. Here, I will speak to the following three matters: (i) the relationship between law and governance; (ii) the nature of good governance; and (iii) regulatory governance and politics.

A. Law and Governance

Famously, Lon Fuller characterised law as the enterprise of subjecting human conduct to the governance of rules.[4] This chimed in with the widely held view that law is an affair of *rules* and that legal concepts are to be understood in the context of systems of *rules*;[5] it enabled Fuller to develop his ideal of legality around the commitment to governance by *rules*. However, if we focus on 'governance', we can differentiate between governance in a broad and functional sense and governance in a narrow sense. In the narrow sense, governance is to be contrasted with law – for example, by reference to its lesser formality, or lesser institutionalisation, or its less top-down nature, or its non-governmental or transnational or technological characteristics, and so on.[6] For the purposes of the present chapter, it is

[4] L L Fuller, *The Morality of Law* (New Haven, Yale University Press, 1969).

[5] H L A Hart, *The Concept of Law* (Oxford, The Clarendon Press, 1961).

[6] See, eg, R Brownsword and M Goodwin, *Law and the Technologies of the Twenty-First Century* (Cambridge, Cambridge University Press, 2012).

not necessary to comment on whatever competing conceptions of governance in the narrow sense might be up for debate; for present purposes, it is the idea of governance in the broad and functional sense that is being assumed.

Taking this broad and functional meaning, law is one, but by no means the only, mode of governance. Functionally, governance identifies a range of matters that need to be agreed by groups of humans if they are to form viable communities. Following Karl Llewellyn,[7] we can say that, if members of groups are to interact and transact, if they are to act in the collective interest, if they are to manage conflicts and disputes, and so on, they need governance. The group needs a basic code of conduct to channel behaviour, to stabilise expectations, and to coordinate actions; it needs mechanisms to settle disputes; it needs to have a sense of direction or common purpose; and it needs to allocate authority to group members for drafting the code, settling disputes, and maintaining the direction of the group.

So much for governance in the broad sense; however, if law's governance simply connotes rule-guided order, and if the function of governance is to ensure that a particular group of humans is viable as a group, what do we make of 'good governance'?

B. Good Governance

Recognising that good governance is a contested matter,[8] let me nevertheless suggest that the core idea is that of (i) the enterprise of instating and maintaining order in the group, (ii) where those who govern act with integrity, and (iii) where they strive to govern in the interests of the group. Elaborating this idea, 'good governance' entails more than mere viability of a particular group, more than calculable order, more than the predictable application and enforcement of published rules, more than effective, economical, and efficient ordering of community life. Good governance, as governance that is in the interests of the group, should also be both acceptable and legitimate. If challenged about a particular position that has been taken, those who govern should be able to defend that position, and they should be able to defend it relative to the interests of the members of the group viewed as members of a particular community and viewed simply as humans.[9] That said, there is a good deal more work to do in unpacking the idea of the interests of the group and this is to be picked up in a later part of the chapter when the 'all-risks' approach is outlined.

[7] K N Llewellyn, 'The Normative, the Legal and the Law Jobs: The Problem of Juristic Method' (1940) 49 *Yale Law Journal* 1355.

[8] See, eg, H Addink, *Good Governance* (Oxford, Oxford University Press, 2019).

[9] For good governance in the context of public health screening, see R Brownsword and C Joynson, 'Good Governance and the Development of an Ethical Framework for the UK National Screening Committee' (2023) 23 *Medical Law International* 271.

C. Regulatory Governance and Politics

Elsewhere, I have drawn a distinction between traditional doctrinal legal thinking and regulatory thinking, labelling the former mode 'Law 1.0' and the latter 'Law 2.0'.[10] In both cases, law continues to be viewed as an enterprise of governance by rules (together with standards and principles). However, these are fundamentally different modes of legal thought. Thinking in a Law 1.0 way, lawyers are guided by the historic general principles that are the foundations of their body of legal doctrine and by the jurisprudence in an attempt to maintain an overall coherence and integrity in the law. The question of whether the rules and principles are fit for purpose simply does not arise. By contrast, thinking in a Law 2.0 way, lawyers are guided by specified policies and the leading question is whether the existing rules are fit for purpose in serving those policies. So, Law 2.0 is a mode of thinking that is less concerned with consistency and coherence and is focused instead on putting in place rules that work, that are instrumentally effective.

It is important to understand that Law 2.0 does not eclipse Law 1.0. Rather, as legal systems evolve, we begin to see that while Law 1.0, but not Law 2.0, reasoning is for the judicial branch and for the courtroom, policy and Law 2.0 reasoning is for the political branch.[11] So, today, in the EU and the UK, we assume that the governance frameworks for new technologies, like AI, will be put in a legislative form and that the legislation will reflect a regulatory deal that is negotiated amongst stakeholders.

In line with this assumption, we see that, in many parts of the world, the political branch is actively engaged with the governance of AI. Here, politicians have to address questions of both policy and strategy. The policy questions include whether the priority is to build the consumer market for AI-enabled goods and services or to put in place a regulatory environment that is supportive of AI innovation, and whether the priority is to capture the benefits of AI or manage and minimise the risks; which then lead to strategic questions about whether to rely on ex ante risk assessment or ex post compensation and correction, and whether and when to articulate hard-wired law or softer and more agile governance. This is not to say that the political branch will achieve competent let alone good governance, but, in both the EU and the UK, the policy and strategic questions are simply not ones that the judicial branch has either the mandate or the resources to engage with.

[10] R Brownsword, *Law 3.0* (Abingdon, Routledge, 2020). It should be noted that, in the present account, I am omitting to discuss a further mode of legal thinking, Law 3.0, which is also regulatory, but which asks whether reliance on rules and on humans is the best way of serving regulatory policies and objectives.

[11] See, further, R Brownsword, 'Private Law, Technology, and Governance' in D Clifford, K H Lau, and J M Paterson (eds), *Data Rights and Private Law* (Oxford, Hart, 2023) 19.

With the political branch now playing a leading role in setting the terms and conditions for the application of new technologies, ethics has a significant supporting role to play. Indeed, the first step taken by the EU in its governance of AI was to appoint a High-Level Expert Group to advise on the ethical issues. It was through the work of this group that the demand crystallised that all applications of AI should be human-centric.[12] For the Commission, this might be viewed as a reminder that governance of AI should ensure that human rights (and human dignity) are respected but it might also point to deeper human interests. This takes us to the next part of the chapter.

III. An All-Risks Approach

An all-risks approach assumes that regulators will engage with their publics to gather a broad sweep of concerns.[13] However, the main idea of the approach is that we need to cultivate a new awareness of the dimension of *depth* alongside our attention to the *breadth* of our human interests. Without doing this, there is a danger that we will flatten human interests and lose sight of what really matters to humans.

A. The Breadth of Concerns

Without consulting people about their particular concerns in relation to some new technology, we can assume that humans have an interest in life, in their physical and mental well-being, in their property, in their economic well-being, in their various personality interests, and in their freedom; we can expect that there will be resistance to technologies that are perceived to threaten these interests (especially threats to human health and safety); and we know that the law already has these interests on its governance radar. However, before politicians lay down the ground rules for the governance of a new technology, they will check that they have the full sweep of challenges and concerns on board.

For example, the House of Commons Science, Innovation and Technology Committee, reviewing the governance of AI, has identified twelve governance challenges that need to be addressed.[14] Some of these challenges relate directly to risks to interests that we assume humans will have. In this category, we can

[12] See, European Commission, digital-strategy.ec.europa.eu/en/policies/expert-group-ai.

[13] See R Brownsword, 'AI and Fundamental Rights: the People, the Conversations, and the Governance Challenges' in D M Vicente, S de Vasconcelos Casimiro, and C Chen (eds), *The Legal Challenges of the Fourth Industrial Revolution* (Cham, Springer, 2023) 335.

[14] House of Commons, Science, Innovation and Technology Committee, 'The Governance of Artificial Intelligence: Interim Report', Ninth Report of Session 2022–23, HC 1769.

place the challenges of bias (which might have negative consequences for individual freedom, economic well-being, and esteem), privacy (and fair collection and processing of personal data), resolving questions about IP and copyright, changing patterns of employment (which might have negative economic consequences for some individuals), and last but not least existential threats. We also have closely related challenges, such as the black box features of AI decision-making (which might inhibit appeals against AI-enabled decisions), agreeing liability in the event of harm being done (who is to be treated as liable and on what terms), misrepresentation (and, we can add, disinformation which might impact on physical and mental well-being as well as inhibiting informed choice), agreeing on the extent of open source AI (the more open, the greater the chance of beneficial innovation and use but also the greater the risk of abuse), and the need for international coordination (without which any response to existential threats will be inadequate).

The Committee also identifies two challenges – one having access to large volumes of training data and the other having access to powerful computing facilities – without which the research and development of potentially beneficial AI is likely to be slowed down. For some individuals, these might be important considerations, but, as presented by the Committee, these are challenges that relate more to the benefit rather than to the risk side of the regulatory equation.

Although these remarks suggest that modern governance is pretty good at detecting a breadth of risks, some might dissent from this view, arguing that we have a blind spot in relation to risks that relate to groups and to society.[15] To the extent that this is saying that we are not so good at recognising the depth of particular human interests and the significance of the risks, then this precisely my point. To the extent that something different is being said – for example, that harm to groups should not be reduced to harm to so many individuals, or that there is a material difference between discriminating against a particular individual on the basis that they have certain characteristics and discriminating against them as a member of a group by reference to features which it is inferred the individual has – then there is certainly something to discuss but I will not enter into debates about such matters here.[16]

B. The Depth of Human Interests

As is well-known, the EU Regulation on AI is organised around categories of risk: some risks (and applications) are treated as unacceptable and are categorically

[15] Compare, eg, L Edwards, *Regulating AI in Europe: Four Problems and Four Solutions* (London, Ada Lovelace Institute, 2022) (critiquing the draft EU Regulation).

[16] See, eg, L Taylor, Luciano Floridi, and Bart van der Sloot (eds), *Group Privacy: New Challenges of Data Technologies* (Dordrecht, Springer, 2017); M Taylor, 'Group Privacy? A Further Question for our Information Societies' in M Borghi and R Brownsword (eds), *Law, Regulation and Governance in the Information Society* (Abingdon, Routledge, 2023) 367.

prohibited; other risks are treated as acceptable provided that they are appropriately characterised and managed. Within the category of acceptable AI, those systems that are 'high risk' (posing significant risks to human health or safety or fundamental rights) will attract the most intense ex ante scrutiny and then there will be less demanding requirements in the case of 'limited' and 'minimal' risk applications. This regulatory regime reflects a sense of proportionality, and it might be taken as implying a grasp of the relative depth of human interests. But, of course, this is governance for the EU and the framing of risk reflects EU values and an EU perception of risk. To have an all-risks approach, we have to look beyond the EU, or the UK, or any other particular governance regime.

In order to structure our all-risks thinking, it is proposed that we adopt a three-level 'layered' idea of human social orders. We can start with the basic idea, then speak to the deepest interests that humans have simply by virtue of being humans, and then to the interests that humans have as members of particular communities.[17]

i. The Basic Idea

The basic idea is that we should place human interests in three tiers, reflecting their depth and importance to humans as humans, and then to humans as members of particular communities. At the deepest level, all humans *in all communities* have a common infrastructural interest in what we can call the global commons; the interest here is in maintaining the (generic) conditions that underpin the viability of human communities. In their own *particular communities*, members have an interest in the fundamental values to which they have committed, for example, to respect for human rights and human dignity. And, as members of *particular pluralistic communities*, humans have an interest in having their preferences, priorities, and principles taken into account by regulators in their attempt to reach an acceptable accommodation of the various interests that members have.

As a corollary, it is proposed that regulators should only permit technological applications that meet the terms of a 'triple licence'.[18] This comprises a global licence (the application being compatible with the maintenance of the global commons), a community licence (the application being compatible with the fundamental values of a particular community), and a social licence (confirming that, within a particular community, the application is in line with an acceptable accommodation of members' interests).

While the regulatory responsibilities at the first level are cosmopolitan and non-negotiable, the responsibilities at the second and third layers are contingent,

[17] This draws on R Brownsword, 'Informational Wrongs and Our Deepest Interests' in Borghi and Brownsword (n 16) 199.

[18] As sketched in Brownsword (n 10) 85–86.

depending on the fundamental values and the interests recognised in each particular community. Any conflicts between these responsibilities are to be resolved by reference to the levels of importance: responsibilities relating to a deeper layer always outrank those relating to other layers.

ii. The Global Commons

As the essential infrastructure or platform for human communities, the global commons commands the utmost respect and gives rise to three imperatives as follows:[19] first, humans must respect the planetary boundaries and its resources lest human existence on Earth is no longer sustainable;[20] secondly, despite their conflicting and competing values, priorities, and interests, humans must observe the conditions for peaceful co-existence, both within a particular community and between communities; and, thirdly, humans must respect the conditions that support their agency and autonomy.

Quite simply, the biological characteristics of the *human* species limit our options for settlement and survival. Most planets, it seems, will not support *human* life. While some planets are too hot for humans, others are too cold. As James Lovelock has explained, the conditions on planet Earth are specially suited to *humans* with their particular biology – but the fragility of these conditions and, concomitantly, the vulnerability of humans is all too apparent.[21]

At the same time, it is characteristic of human *agents* that they have the capacity to pursue various projects and plans whether as individuals, in partnerships, in groups, or in whole communities. Sometimes, the various projects and plans that they pursue will be harmonious, but often they will not. In the event of disharmony and conflict, there needs to be a process for resolution that maintains peaceful co-existence.

Prior to either harmony or disharmony, there needs to be a context in which the exercise of agency (understood as self-directed purposive activity) is possible. This context is not one that privileges a particular articulation of agency; it is generic, and it is a condition precedent for, and entirely neutral between, the particular plans and projects that agents individually favour.

In sum, there is a deep and fundamental critical infrastructure, a commons, for any community of human agents. From any practical viewpoint, *prudential or moral*, that of regulator or regulatee, the protection of the commons must be the highest priority.

[19] As specified in R Brownsword, *Technology, Humans and Discontent with Law* (Abingdon, Routledge, 2024) Ch 16.

[20] Seminally, see Johan Rockström, et al, 'Planetary Boundaries: Exploring the Safe Operating Space for Humanity' (2009) 14 *Ecology and Society* 32; www.ecologyandsociety.org/vol14/iss2/art32/.

[21] See, eg, James Lovelock, *Novacene* (London, Allen Lane, 2019); and, noting the significance of the Anthropocene, see R Brownsword and H Somsen, 'Law, Innovation and Technology: Fast Forward to 2021' (2021) 13 *Law, Innovation and Technology* 1.

iii. Interests within Each Community

Within a particular community, those who govern have a responsibility to ensure that its constitutive values are respected. Just as each individual human agent has the capacity to develop their own distinctive identity, the same is true if we scale this up to communities of human agents. At this level, we can have a plurality of views both between communities and within a particular community where the distinctive values are contested. For example, while one community might be committed to liberal human rights, another might be committed to conservative dignitarian principles, and in each community, there is more than one view about the interpretation or application of these distinctive values.

It is, of course, essential that whatever the fundamental values to which a particular community commits itself they should be consistent with (or cohere with) the commons' conditions. It is the commons that sets the stage (or the platform) for community life, and then, without compromising that stage, particular communities form and self-identify with their own distinctive values.

Beyond this, there will be many debates about questions that do not implicate either the global imperatives or the community's particular fundamental values. Judgments about benefits and risks, and about the distribution of benefits and risks, might be varied and conflictual. Inevitably, whether one favours seeking consensus or sharpening difference, dealing with a plurality of competing and conflicting views will be messy.

At this level, the responsibility of regulators is to seek out an acceptable accommodation between the competing and conflicting interests of individuals and groups that are members of the community. Where the issues are both widely and deeply contested, the accommodation will be unlikely to satisfy everyone. There is no right answer as such, and, because the balancing exercise allows a broad margin for 'acceptable' accommodation, there are likely to be several regulatory positions that can claim to be reasonable while, conversely, we have no compelling reason to favour one such reasonable accommodation over another.

These difficulties and contingencies notwithstanding, those who have governance responsibilities should act in good faith, both in reaching the accommodation and in keeping the position under review, and, correlatively, members of the community will have a responsibility to respond in ways that are compatible with both the fundamental values of their community and the maintenance of the commons' conditions.[22] Good governance is not a one-way street: it implies reciprocal responsibilities.

[22] See, further, R Brownsword, *Technology, Governance and Respect for Law* (Abingdon, Routledge, 2023).

IV. An All-Risks Approach and Trust in AI

While both the EU and the UK are signatories to the Bletchley Declaration on AI Safety,[23] we should not expect their respective governance of AI to be identical. At first blush, whereas the EU's priority is to identify and manage risks and to ensure that applications of AI are 'human-centric', the UK's priority (at any rate, in the White Paper) is not to miss out on the benefits and opportunities that innovative AI will offer. Nevertheless, it is common ground not only that AI should be 'safe' but also that an eco-system of trust for AI should be established. This invites questions about both how we should understand an ecosystem of trust and how it relates to the proposed all-risks approach to governance.

We can respond to these question by proceeding as follows: (i) by identifying three deliberative judgments of trust (featuring a moral, a prudential, or a technical judgment); (ii) by distinguishing such judgments from unreflective and non-deliberative trusting dispositions or a lack of trust; (iii) by taking stock of what this analysis means for the relationship between the all-risks approach and trust; and (iv) by exploring what the EU and the UK might have in mind when they envisage an eco-system of trust in AI.

A. Three Deliberative Judgments of Trust

If we pause to ask whether we trust another human, or some technology, we are making a deliberative judgment, but the nature of our judgment might be moral, prudential, or technical.

i. Trust and Moral Judgment

To judge another person to be morally trustworthy is to say something about how we judge the character of that other person, and to judge that we trust that person in a particular situation is to confirm our belief that they will try to do the right thing. Moreover, when we trust other persons in this *moral* sense – whether we trust them to honour their promises or to respect our privacy or whatever – we do so without the need for checking, certification, or any other kind of assurance that would be characteristic of governance that addresses *prudential* concerns and reservations about AI. Of course, we might be let down in which case we will feel that our trust has been betrayed.

Where our reservation is moral, we might express this by saying that we do not trust someone to do the right thing (or, at any rate, to try to do the right thing) –

[23] www.gov.uk/government/publications/ai-safety-summit-2023-the-bletchley-declaration/the-bletchley-declaration-by-countries-attending-the-ai-safety-summit-1-2-november-2023.

for example, that we do not trust those who are responsible for the governance of AI, or those who are associated with the research, design, promotion, production, or application of AI, or, of course, insurance companies that offer AI-enabled services.[24] Alternatively, our moral reservation might be directed at the AI itself in that we do not trust its operation to be fair or otherwise morally defensible.[25]

ii. Trust and Prudential Judgment

Where our practical reason is of a prudential nature, to say that we trust another person or thing is not so much to speak to the character of that person or thing, as it is to judge how reliance on that other person or thing will serve our interests. Trust here is a proxy for our self-serving willingness to rely on another person or thing.[26]

If we judge that our self-interest will not be served by relying on AI where it is used by others or by ourselves, then this might be an all things considered prudential judgment weighing both possible benefits and risks, or it might be simply a one-sided judgment about the risks. In the latter case, we reject AI on the grounds that we believe that it will be harmful to our own interests, physical, psychological, economic, reputational or whatever; the higher the perceived risk to our interests, the greater the regulatory management of risk will need to be if it is to assuage our prudential concerns – which is very much the pattern of risk regulation of the kind that the EU is pioneering in its governance of AI.

Our lack of trust in a prudential sense might be directed at both human beings and tools or machines. For example, we might say that we do not trust a person whom we judge to lack the necessary expertise to operate the AI (as when we decline a medical procedure that involves a human being working with an AI tool). Alternatively, our distrust might be directed at the tool itself (as when we decline a ride in a fully autonomous AI-enabled vehicle on the ground that we do not believe it is safe).

[24] Interestingly, in the Geneva Association report (n3) at 4, we read:

> Insurers also have a major role to play in building trust around the responsible use of AI. They should take the concerns that exist around the use of AI seriously; for example, by embracing transparency and by clearly communicating the way AI is used in consumer-facing areas of their business such as underwriting and claims handling. In addition, it is important for insurers to monitor the outcomes of AI models. While it is currently challenging to test outcomes for bias, insurers could work with stakeholders such as regulators, supervisors and consumer organisations to develop testing methods and address broader concerns related to the use of AI in insurance.

[25] Of course, in saying this, we do not necessarily suppose that AI reasons in the way that humans reason.

[26] On the distinction between mere reliance and trust-based reliance, see C Kletzer, 'Law, Disintermediation and the Future of Trust' in L A DiMatteo, A Janssen, P Ortolani, F de Elizalde, M Cannarsa, and M Durovic (eds), *The Cambridge Handbook of Lawyering in the Digital Age* (Cambridge, Cambridge University Press, 2021) 312.

iii. Trust and Technical Judgment

There is also the possibility that our reservation is of a technical nature, which is exemplified when we say that we do not trust an AI tool to work in accordance with its technical specification. Even if we are not AI experts, we might say that we do not trust autonomous AI tools always to function in ways that their designers intended or reasonably foresaw.

B. Unreflective Trust and Lack of Trust

All of the expressions of trust or a lack of trust that we have so far considered are based on a degree of deliberation. However, we also need to recognise that some attitudes of trust or distrust might not result from deliberation of any kind. Given that we cannot trust no-one and check everything,[27] and if we are surrounded by technologies that we do not really understand but which we routinely rely on, what should we do? Should we be 'philosophical', give the matter no thought and simply default to an unreflective trust? Perhaps, we might differentiate between technologies with which we are familiar and those that are new to us, trusting the former but not the latter. But we might not so differentiate, always being disposed to go with the technological flow and passively trust AI without giving it a moment's thought.

C. An All-Risks Approach and Trust

Where governance follows an all-risks approach to the governance of AI, what follows in relation to trust?

First, where we trust those who have governance responsibilities in a moral sense, and where they assure us that they have given full consideration to all risks and taken whatever protective measures are required, then we should have no concern on the risk side of the equation. However, it does not follow that we will make use of AI tools, not because we have residual risk reservations but because we do not see the benefit. So, even if we trust those who govern, even if we think that they act with integrity, we might judge that, from a prudential point of view, there is no case for using AI.

Secondly, although a lack of trust – especially a lack of trust in a prudential sense – will often signal a need for further assurance or security (as is the case, for example, in international trade), it does not follow that the take-up of AI will be delayed or deterred because these various expressions of a lack of trust are in circulation. In pluralistic communities, there will be many different views. In particular,

[27] Compare M Power, *The Audit Society* (Oxford, Oxford University Press, 1997).

some people will be more risk-averse than others and, while some will be late-adopters, others will be early adopters (keen to use new technologies).

Thirdly, even those who express a lack of trust might be willing to use AI. For example, we might have moral reservations about the use of AI in insurance (believing, for instance, that AI-enabled dynamic pricing of insurance is unfair) but, because automated insurance is so convenient, we will use it anyway.

This said, recalling the push-back by European consumers against GM,[28] even with sustained assurances about safety, if we do not trust the technology or its promoters on *prudential* grounds, there will be major work for governance to do in assuaging our concerns (which the UK government now seems to be realising). However, if our lack of trust is *moral* and it is the promoters of the technology whom we do not trust, then (as with both GM and current accusations of ethics-washing[29]) it might not be possible to restore damaged corporate reputations.

Fourthly, where humans have a disposition to trust AI, their conduct is unlikely to be affected by whether those who govern do or do not use an all-risks approach. However, if governance does not adopt an all-risks approach, humans who are disposed to trust AI might be in for a catastrophic shock.

In short, governance that adopts an all-risks approach gives AI every chance of being adopted and accepted, but it does not guarantee it. On the other hand, if those who govern do not adopt an all-risks approach, they expose those who are governed in a way that might undermine confidence in AI and, indeed, result in unacceptable harm to the governed. But, in the final analysis, what the all-risks approach is designed to do is minimise the risk of catastrophic harm to humans not to persuade humans that they should trust AI.

D. An Eco-System of Trust

How should we envisage an ecosystem of trust for AI? In principle, and in the light of the foregoing, its complexion might reflect a mix of many kinds of judgment. Moreover, we should distinguish between the process of building trust and the ecosystem of trust that is the outcome of the process.

For both the EU and the UK, it might be the case that the desired *outcome* is that consumers and others will not say that they do not trust AI or, as the Minister put it when introducing the UK White Paper, that they are 'nervous about adopting [AI]'.[30] However, when it comes to the *process*, we might detect a difference.

[28] See R Brownsword and M Goodwin, *Law and the Technologies of the Twenty-First Century* (Cambridge, Cambridge University Press, 2012) 15–18.

[29] See eg, B Wagner, 'Ethics as an Escape from Regulation. From "Ethics Washing" to Ethics-shopping?' in E Bayamlioğlu, I Baraliuc, L Janssens, and M Hildebrandt (eds), *Being Profiled: Cogitas Ergo Sum. 10 Years of 'Profiling the European Citizen'* (Amsterdam, Amsterdam University Press, 2018) 84–88.

[30] Department for Science, Innovation and Technology (n2), Ministerial Foreword.

We might wonder whether for the UK, the process is simply about doing what is required to put in place an ecosystem that is fit for purpose. By contrast, in the EU, we might sense that – at any rate for the Parliament – the process has an integrity that is to be valued in its own right. On this view, the job of governance is to work with the community so that a depth and breadth of trust is cultivated. EU citizens should fully buy into AI, their concerns being comprehensively addressed.[31]

So, while it might be right to say that in both the UK and the EU, the desired ecosystem of trust is about keeping people onside with AI, this ignores some rather different views about the kind of trust that matters and about the importance of process. To repeat, while we might treat those who commit to all-risks governance as trustworthy, this is not its purpose, and to this we can add that in some places, the ecosystem of trust might be valued for its own sake.

V. AI-Enabled Insurers

We can now apply our all-risks approach to the particular case of insurance, looking first at the use of AI by insurers. A quick surf on the Web takes us to sites that advertise the benefits of AI, mainly efficiency benefits to insurers but also potentially benefits to customers as the service becomes more personalised.[32] However, our interest here is in the risks.

Applying an all-risks approach, we start by asking whether AI-enabled insurance provision might compromise the generic conditions or present an existential threat to our well-being and agency. Then, we can think about the kind of fundamental community values that might be engaged before discussing the social acceptability of A1-enabled insurance provision.

A. Risk and the Generic Conditions

Famously, Stephen Hawking said that, 'the advent of super-intelligent AI would be either the best or the worst thing ever to happen to humanity'.[33] More recently, we have heard a number of concerned voices in Silicon Vally worrying that generative AI might present existential threats.[34] Clearly, there are some serious risks in

[31] Compare M Findlay, 'Disruptive Regulation' in M Findlay, J Seah, and W Wong, *AI and Big Data: Disruptive Regulation* (Cheltenham, Elgar, 2023) 1.

[32] See eg, The Geneva Association (n3); R Balasubramanian, A Libarikian, and D McElhaney, 'Insurance 2030 – The Impact of AI on the Future of Insurance' (McKinsey and Company, 12 March 2021) www.mckinsey.com/industries/financial-services/our-insights/insurance-2030-the-impact-of-ai-on-the-future-of-insurance.

[33] S Hawking, *Brief Answers to the Big Questions* (London, John Murray, 2018) 188.

[34] See, eg, the open letter signed by Elon Musk and others arguing that there should be a pause in uncontrolled AI development. futureoflife.org/open-letter/pause-giant-ai-experiments/.

contemplation, and, without joining debates about just how bad it would be if AI were to lead to the end of humanity or how likely it is to eventuate, we can take it that it would be catastrophic and that nothing else would be as bad.

That said, the use of AI by the insurance industry – which, after all, is in the business of risk management – is not the obvious place to be looking for catastrophic threats such as the extinction of humanity. To be sure, AI might have some impact on the patterns of employment in insurance, but this is true of many sectors and it is characteristic of all automating technologies. If not in insurance, then where is AI going to be most dangerous? The obvious answer is that the most serious risks will be in the military where WMDs are AI-enabled. If humans recognised the need for peaceful co-existence, we should not find ourselves in such a situation, but international relations are not what they should be,[35] and there is no denying that we live in dangerous times. On the face of it, though, the use of AI in insurance is not one of the Horsemen of the Apocalypse and it is not going to either increase or reduce this kind of risk.

If AI in insurance is not going to kill us, might it compromise the conditions for the development of agency? This is a possibility to the extent that humans in the insurance sector become so reliant on AI that they lose some key skills (skills that humans previously had) and, crucially, they lose the capacity for self-direction. But, if it is only in insurance that this dependence exists, it should not be a serious problem. If, on the other hand, reliance on digital assistants and delegation of tasks to machines is pervasive, the context might inhibit human agency and the development of autonomy, and it might be difficult to know where the tipping points lie.[36] This is a matter to which we will return in the final part of the chapter.

B. Risk and Compatibility with Fundamental Community Values

Whether or not the use of AI by insurers raises questions about compatibility with a community's fundamental values will depend on which values a particular community recognises as constitutive. It is unlikely that any of the community's fundamental values will speak explicitly to insurance (or to AI in insurance) but there might well be flexible concepts – notably, privacy and dignity, and now human-centricity – that invite interpretation and application to concerns about AI and insurance.

[35] Compare Robert Skidelsky, *The Machine Age* (London, Allen Lane, 2023) 257: 'Following the Russian invasion of Ukraine, the idea that it may be possible for different cultures and value systems to coexist peacefully in a multipolar world has virtually lost all traction with western strategic analysts and their journalistic camp followers'.

[36] Compare R Brownsword, 'Lost in Translation: Legality, Regulatory Margins, and Technological Management' (2011) 26 *Berkeley Technology Law Journal* 1321.

Here, we can sketch three potential conversations that raise the question of whether AI in insurance is compatible with fundamental values. These relate to: (i) profiling and discrimination; (ii) privacy and data protection; and (iii) human dignity and human centricity.

i. Profiling and Discrimination

To the extent that AI tools enable insurers to discriminate in a fine-grained way between applicants and insured persons as well as to offer insurance to individuals on a basis that aligns with their risk profile, this will be seen as a benefit where a community is fundamentally committed to individualistic values but it is likely to be seen as problematic where values such as solidarity, vulnerability and dignity are constitutive.

In this context, we might recall that, at the time of the sequencing of the human genome, there were concerns about the use that insurers might make of genetic information about individuals, leading to various degrees of prohibition and restriction – such as prohibitions on requiring genetic tests to be taken, or on requiring disclosure of results, or on acting on test results.[37] To the extent that these concerns reflected a commitment to solidarity as a fundamental community value, or to respect for humans as persons not as profiles, then AI profiling might be seen as no different to genetic profiling. However, if the concern about genetic profiling rests on the idea that it would be unfair to discriminate against persons on the basis of their having genetic characteristics over which they have no control and for which they are not responsible, then a distinction might be drawn between genetic profiling and AI profiling. In that case, whether or not the latter would invite unfair discrimination by insurers would depend on whether the data points were within the control of the person and within their sphere of responsibility. Given the range of data that might be collected for AI profiling purposes, governance might start by building on clear cases while leaving more difficult cases to be individually assessed.

ii. Privacy and Data Protection

Picking up the last point, in the world of connected cars and, more generally, the Internet of Things, there will be an abundance of data that indicates how careful an individual is as a driver and about their health and lifestyles.[38] If insurers access and act on this data, there are likely to be concerns about both privacy and data protection. While many simply elide privacy and data protection, the

[37] See Brownsword and Goodwin (n28) 286–289; M Radetski, M Radetski, and N Juth, *Genes and Insurance* (Cambridge, Cambridge University Press, 2003).

[38] See eg, F van den Boon, 'Informational Rights, Informational Wrongs: Regulating Connected Car Data Access and Use for Telematics Insurance in Europe' in Borghi and Brownsword (n16) 307.

EU Charter recognises two distinct fundamental rights: Article 7 recognises the right to private and family life, and Article 8 recognises a right to the protection of personal data.[39] Whereas a claim-right to privacy places others under a duty not to try to access private information and gives the rights holder control over who may access information covered by this right, the right to protection of personal data relates more to the way in which, and the purposes for which, personal data is processed. In other words, the latter assumes that personal data will be available and that the rights will relate to the processing and securing of that data.

In practice, there is a great deal of confusion about these rights and about the role of consent, but, in principle, if privacy is a fundamental right it might stand in the way of insurers accessing AI-derived data. That said, if individuals rely on connected data-gathering goods and services, this might be viewed as weakening the argument that the data that is collected is private, or that data derived from the collected data is covered by a privacy right.

iii. Human Dignity and Human-Centricity

As we have said, in the EU, it now seems to be accepted that applications of AI should always be human-centric, but how should we understand this limitation? For example, we might consider that, in limiting AI to human-centric applications, AI would not kill, injure, or otherwise harm humans; AI would not degrade, or de-centre humans; AI would be 'human compatible' in the sense that it would align with human purposes and values;[40] and humans would remain in control and have the final word on AI applications.

Articulating and elaborating such a multi-pronged idea of human-centricity invites a jurisprudence that connects with human rights and human dignity, and, in so doing, we will no doubt find that liberal readings of human dignity come into tension with more conservative dignitarian readings.[41] The jurisprudence also should address to what extent the default should be for humans to remain in, on, or over the loop of insurance decision-making as well as how consent, opt-in, and opt-outs might work in a world where humans have different preferences about the use or non-use of AI tools by insurers.[42]

C. Risk and Social Acceptability

In pluralistic societies, where members have different dispositions and prudential views as well as different personal values, it will not be easy to instate socially

[39] Charter of Fundamental Right of the European Union (2016/C 202/02).

[40] See eg, S Russell, *Human Compatible* (London, Penguin, 2020); B Christian, *The Alignment Problem* (London: Atlantic Books, 2021).

[41] See D Beyleveld and R Brownsword, *Human Dignity in Bioethics and Biolaw* (Oxford, Oxford University Press, 2001).

[42] On consent, see D Beyleveld and R Brownsword, *Consent in the Law* (Oxford, Hart, 2007).

acceptable governance of AI-enabled insurance provision. Consider the following three uses of AI tools by insurers: detection of fraudulent claims; settlement of claims; and dynamic and differential pricing.

i. Fraudulent Claim Detection

On the face of it, it is in no-one's interest that insurers pay out on fraudulent claims. In the long run, this will increase the cost of insurance for everyone. Accordingly, if AI tools are used to flag up possibly fraudulent claims, and if this means that the humans to whom these claims are referred for a hard look do then succeed in reducing the number of fraudulent claims that get through the net, then this should be welcomed – and, all the better if the number of fraudulent claims that are made is reduced because it is known that AI will be used to detect fraud.

So far so acceptable. But, we also want non-fraudulent claims to be paid and to be paid promptly. If the use of AI tools throws up a significant number of false positives or causes significant delay, there is a downside to their use. Having humans in or on the loop might do something to reduce the false positives but the more careful the human review the longer the process will take.

Clearly, any discussion about the social acceptability of using (or not using) AI tools to detect fraud will need to take into account both the upsides and the downsides. In a community where, say, the Revenue makes use of AI tools to detect tax fraud, or where government uses these tools to detect fraudulent claims for welfare benefits, it might be thought that the burden is on those who oppose the use of these tools by insurers to show why fraud in the insurance sector should be treated differently. On the other hand, if these has been a scandal in the use of such tools by public bodies who are trying to identify fraudulent returns or claims, then this might well set back the acceptability of AI for some time.[43]

ii. Claims Settlement

Would it be socially acceptable for insurers to use AI tools in the settlement of claims? If humans are still in the loop in signing off on settlements or if there is an appeal to a human against an otherwise automated AI decision, this might be acceptable but, if there is a concern about the time that it takes to agree on a settlement, then leaving it to the AI might be a way of speeding things up.

If, in the event of a dispute about a settlement, the case is processed online and arbitrated by AI, the fact that the insurers have used AI would seem to be in line

[43] Compare AI scandals of this kind in Australia and the Netherlands. For the Dutch benefits' fraud scandal, see M Heikkilä, 'Dutch Scandal Serves as a Warning for Europe over Risks of Using Algorithms' *Politico* (29 March 2022) www.politico.eu/article/dutch-scandal-serves-as-a-warning-for-europe-over-risks-of-using-algorithms/; for the Australian Robodebt scandal, see Seb Starcevic, 'Australian Robodebt Scandal Shows the Risk of Rule by Algorithm' *Reuters* (15 December 2022) www.reuters.com/article/australia-tech-ai/feature-australian-robodebt-scandal-shows-the-risk-of-rule-by-algorithm-idINL8N3340SN/.

with general practice. Moreover, for users who have seen how many disputes can be disposed of on eBay and how quickly this is done, it might be easy to accept that insurers will also use these tools to settle claims – or, at any rate, low-value claims.

Of course, some might jib at the opacity of the process. If the AI simply hands down a ruling for or against the insurer, and if the decision goes against the insured, then the latter might want to be given some reasons for this. In some cases, the insured might be satisfied if there is confirmation that the AI has operated in accordance with its technical specification and has not been hacked or corrupted. But, if the insured wants a justification for the ruling, the technical explanation will not do. Possibly, another kind of AI tool will be able to draw on a database of similar claims and give reasons that show the instant ruling as consistent with the rulings given in similar cases. This might or might not satisfy the demand for reasoned decisions, and, if more is required, then the question will be whether it will be possible to develop AI tools that can meet this demand and overcome barriers to social acceptability.

iii. Dynamic and Differential Pricing

In the context of claims settlement, the opacity of AI left a question about whether like cases were treated alike. The same question might be posed where AI sets a different price for insured party A and insured party B when the material facts associated with insuring A and B seem to be the same, and, similarly, the same question might be asked where A is quoted different premiums for the same policy at different times of the day. Without transparency, in the sense of justificatory reasons being given, this is likely to be perceived as unfair – indeed, as a reason for withholding trust – and as socially unacceptable.

Responding to this objection, the insurers might argue that the technical specification of the AI is such that, overall, customers get their insurance at the lowest possible rates, that any change will increase the cost. If this is the case, then the question is whether the community is prepared to pay the price for transparency (and justified reasons) or for eliminating differential or dynamic pricing. In some communities, the utility of the AI might carry the day, but, in others, the price will need to be paid if the tools are to be socially acceptable.

VI. AI-Enabled Insured

Finally, we can turn to consider the use of AI tools by those who seek insurance cover or who are already insured – for example, guiding the former towards the best deals in the marketplace or alerting them to unusual terms and conditions in policies, and so on.[44]

[44] For a future imaginary, see Balasubramanian et al (n32).

In a world of smart phones and devices, it is easy to imagine that our digital assistants might prompt us to renew an insurance cover that we have and still need; that the assistant not only prompts us but also presents us with some options or even a recommendation; that the assistant arranges the renewal of cover but checks back with us for authorisation to proceed; or that the assistant simply proceeds with the renewal. We can imagine a similar story of progressive reliance on, and handover to, digital assistants for other aspects of insurance such as negotiating the original cover and making claims.[45]

If we start with our digital assistants doing no more than reminding us that our cover will soon expire, each step from there on is potentially significant but just how significant these steps are perceived to be will vary from one person to another. Some insured might view each step as a big one; others might think that it is only when they drop out of the loop (all the transactional work being done by the digital assistant) that there is a step change in the process, and, while some might see each step as an inevitable slide down a slippery slope, others might be perfectly comfortable with the move towards full automation. Quite simply, humans will have different preferences and expectations about the practice.

If the challenge for governance is to accommodate the different preferences of insured persons, and if the test of good governance is that the arrangements should be socially acceptable, then, broadly speaking, there are three options. First, governance might try to superimpose a normative pattern of prohibitions, permissions, and requirement onto what seem to be the community's views about the acceptability of using digital assistants. Secondly, governance might leave it to the market (largely to insurers) to respond to different demands and preferences. Or, thirdly, governance might leave it to the market but take steps to ensure that minority preferences that would otherwise be ignored are provided for.

However, adopting an all-risks approach, those who govern should do more than try to accommodate the different preferences and priorities of the members of their particular community. They should also ask whether the use of AI-enabled digital assistants would be compatible with the fundamental values of their community and, most importantly, whether their use has any negative impact on the global commons.

With regard to fundamental values, it is possible that some communities might identify themselves with their eschewal of modern technologies, including digital assistants. If so, it is the responsibility of those who govern to maintain the integrity of the community's constitutive commitments whether we think that the fundamental values rest on a collective prudential judgment or on a sense

[45] Compare R Brownsword, 'Autonomy, Delegation, and Responsibility: Agents in Autonomic Computing Environments' in M Hildebrandt and A Rouvroy (eds), *Autonomic Computing and Transformations of Human Agency* (London, Routledge, 2011) 64.

of what is morally right. For example, if a community adopts 'human-centricity' as one of its identifying values, then there are several readings of this idea that would militate against the use of digital assistants by insured, including that humans should not be de-centred. As Henry Kissinger, Eric Schmidt, and Daniel Huttenlocher put it, humans still want to place 'themselves at the center of the story'.[46]

That said, the different preferences of members of the community might develop into opposed readings of 'human-centricity'. On the one side, some might argue that members have a *duty* not to act in ways that de-centre humans; on the other side, those who want to use digital assistants might argue that 'human-centricity' is a fundamental *right* which means that it is for individuals to make their own choices about how far they rely on digital devices and AI.

This leaves the question of whether the use of AI-enabled digital assistants might compromise the global commons. On the face of it, this might seem implausible. However, those who govern need to think about the environmental costs of servicing the technology, and, as we mentioned earlier when discussing the use of digital assistants by insurers, they need to ask whether the use of digital assistants has implications for the human development of agency and autonomy. Possibly, to cover this latter risk, humans need at some point to exercise their agency and autonomy in making a decision to opt-in to insurance that, until further notice, takes them out of the loop. That said, we should recognise that this is just the start of a complex conversation: assessing risk relative to the agency and autonomy elements of the global commons is perhaps the most challenging aspect of good governance.

VII. Concluding Remarks

In this chapter, I have proposed that an all-risks approach to governance should be adopted so that we appreciate the depth of human interests that might be impacted by the use of new technologies such as AI. No doubt, there is much devil in the detail of all-risks governance. However, unless the governance of AI is guided by this approach, we should be careful about who or what we trust; an ecosystem of misplaced trust might prove extremely costly. Existential risks are not to be taken lightly;[47] governance of AI needs to anticipate and prevent potentially catastrophic applications.

To be sure, the use of AI in the insurance sector – even the prospect of generative AI drafting insurance contracts – does not look like the most obvious source of existential threats to humanity. Nevertheless, even if an all-risks

[46] H Kissinger, E Schmidt, and D Huttenlocher, *The Age of AI* (London, John Murray, 2022) 179.
[47] See eg, T Ord, *The Precipice* (London, Bloomsbury, 2020); R Skidelsky (n35).

assessment does not indicate such foundational risks, it matters that AI applications are compatible with the fundamental values of our particular communities (whether these are the fundamental values of the EU or of post-Brexit UK), so that where applications in insurance are incompatible, they need to be corrected and constrained. Even though this is not always straightforward, particularly where members of the relevant community have many different preferences and priorities, governance should aspire to channel insurance practice in ways that are socially acceptable.

5

Insuring the Uninsurable, Or the Nearly Uninsurable

ANDREW TETTENBORN

I. Introduction

If you ask an insurance professional about what is meant by uninsurable risks, they will very often roll off a list of categories dinned into them during training some time ago. Traditionally, these are reputational, regulatory, trade secret theft, political and pandemic risks.[1] In fact, however, all this is fairly out-of-date. Regulatory risks are admittedly difficult, but none of the risks just mentioned is strictly uninsurable. In all of them, at least as regards some losses resulting can be covered.

The kind of uninsurability this paper seeks to deal with is more subtle. It relates not so much to types of risk as to risks with particular features, and not to uninsurability but to the practicality of obtaining cover at a reasonable price.

II. Factors Tending against Practical Insurability

Insurance is essentially a matter of division of risk. What makes most established types of insurance work, and work effectively, is a combination of two things: the predictability of events of a given description in terms of probability, and fairly accurate means of assessing the magnitude of their consequences. Where these factors are present, they allow for pretty efficient risk-pooling and the setting of reasonable premiums in most cases, even if there are problems at the edges, either because of the sheer frequency of events makes them virtual certainties rather than contingencies (for example, hurricanes in Florida, or inundations in English floodplains, both now difficult to insure at a reasonable price), or because the likely

[1] eg, A Freedman, 'Top Five Uninsurable Risks' (2 September 2014) *Risk and Insurance*.

losses vary stochastically and unpredictably between zero and the incalculable (for example, terrorism).[2]

Unfortunately, with some risks (which we can call problematic emerging risks) this easy solution does not apply because the above factors are often not present. Particularly with new or fast-developing technologies, there is typically a lack of adequate past data and also of knowledge of likely effects when something goes wrong. This makes things much more difficult. We do not yet have easy or entirely reliable means of estimating the likelihood of, or the seriousness of the losses likely to be caused by (say) cyber-attacks on a large company.[3] And much the same, at least for a few years, is likely to go goes for accidents involving autonomous vehicles or ships, or for mishaps concerning AI-controlled machinery. In all these cases, the chances of particular casualties may remain difficult to calculate, thus making the task of providing cover at anything like a reasonable premium hard.

This matters. Innovators, and more importantly industrialists and others making use of state-of-the-art inventions, need the ability to protect themselves against ruinous losses and unpredictable liabilities. If insurers, ever careful of their solvency ratios, keep out of areas like this because they might get their fingers burnt badly (or offer cover but are so risk-averse that this comes only at a premium that soaks up most of an innovator's profit), innovation will flounder. Indeed, the need to avoid this also arises from another factor: given the need as far as possible to avoid a situation of near-monopoly and a resultant upward drift in insurance costs it is important to have not simply some insurers, but as many players as possible, in this market.

III. Extra-Legal Solutions

What can the insurance industry do about this? To some extent the answer lies in extra-legal measures. One such would be by using the tried technique of piggybacking on administrative, industry or professional regulation,[4] and possibly seeking to influence its content. On the assumption that state or professional regulation of this sort is likely to aimed at requiring a degree of responsibility in carrying on a commercial activity, there is much to be said for insurers limiting their services

[2] Giving rise in this latter case to complex matters such as extreme value theory in the determination of probabilities: eg, P Embrechts and H Schmidli, 'Modelling of extremal events in insurance' (1994) 39 *ZOR – Mathematical Methods of Operational Research* 1.

[3] A point made in J Scheuermann, 'Cyber Risks, Systemic Risks and Cyber Insurance' (2018) 122 *Penn State Law Review* 613.

[4] In the case of AI, this is now at an advanced state of planning. In the UK, see the White Paper of March 2023, *A Pro-Innovation Approach to AI Regulation* (Cm 815). For the EU, see the planned AI Act (Regulation laying down harmonised rules on artificial intelligence and amending certain Union legislative acts, 2021/0106 (COD)), agreed in principle in December 2023. As regards autonomous vehicles, see s 1 of the UK's Automated and Electric Vehicles Act 2018.

to customers who are subject to an active regulator and are in good standing with it, and providing for curtailment of cover if they cease to be in that state.

Another well-established extra-legal technique involves taking steps in concert with the assured to encourage risk avoidance and reduction. Both insurers and clients have an interest in measures aimed at preventing insurable losses happening and mitigating the damage done when they do. As regards insurers, the costs saved by not having to pay and administer claims are likely to exceed any reduction in premium income, while the reputational gain arising from safety-consciousness may also be worth having. For insureds, even without the deductibles that are now almost universal, in practice any casualty inevitably leaves some losses not made good; furthermore, they too may make reputational gains both from publicising their commitment to safety, and also from avoiding embarrassing events that harm third parties. Not surprisingly, both sides are aware of these points. Larger insurers, indeed, spend considerable resources in collaborating with clients to reduce the incidence of casualties in the first place.

IV. Legal Answers

Extra-legal measures are all very well, but a good deal can also be done within insurance law, especially by insurers when it comes to the drafting of policies for problematic emerging risks. This can take a number of forms, but I will concentrate on four: the partitioning of cover, the drafting of apt exclusions, the judicious use of warranties, and carefully drawn limitations on the extent of ant liability for losses.

A. The Partitioning of Cover

Partitioning of cover is an old phenomenon. If a household policy covers public liability, it will exclude areas of greater hazard traditionally subject to specialist cover, such as motor vehicle or professional liability. Marine hull cover has long excluded war risks, leaving owners to obtain separate cover.[5] As terrorism became depressingly quotidian, property damage policies similarly began to exclude it,[6] and so on. So too, this is an obvious way forward for modern 'problematic emerging risk' fields of cover, such as cyber risks or AI-caused problems.

The point is this. With what we can call 'ordinary' cover, for example a standard business property or BI policy, the setting of premiums, policy terms and limits of recovery is likely to be relatively straightforward. Indeed, the issue and pricing of such policies is becoming almost automatic and industrial, a little like the

[5] eg, ITCH 95, Cl 24.

[6] And so too with related policies, such as marine hull policies: eg, ITCH 95, Cl 25.2.

essentially computerised process used by consumer insurers to provide buildings or motor insurance on the spot to those whose requirements are boring but orthodox and who do not admit to any unusual or awkward circumstances.

By contrast, things are very different with cover dealing with new technology and other awkward areas. There is likely to be a need for a very precise description of the risks and losses covered, for carefully drafted limits on losses claimable and perhaps continuing warranties, and doubtless much more substantial deductibles. And even before the contract is entered into, there may equally be a requirement for a great deal more information provided by the assured, either generally as part of the duty of fair presentation under s 3 of the Insurance Act 2015, or by specific demand on any proposal form.[7] From all this it follows that it will nearly always be in insurers' interest to separate such things from ordinary insurance, since different considerations apply to each. (It is also likely to be in the interest of many assureds, if only because it gives them more scope to pick and choose between which particular types of cover they want or are prepared to pay for.)

All the more reason to separate the risks. Unfortunately, without careful drafting this will not necessarily happen. True, an ordinary business damage or BI policy will not respond to a simple loss of profits due to a disastrous malfunction of AI or a cyber-attack, since for any insurance to respond the loss must be tied to a particular insured peril and this is unlikely to qualify. But things are different where the effects of a malfunction of new technology are mediated through a type of damage that is already covered in principle, since here the problem of 'silent cover' manifests itself. Imagine, for example, damage to premises caused by a disastrous glitch in the AI controlling machinery in them which causes the machinery to go haywire, or a fire that rages out of control owing to a cyber-attack on a sophisticated fire control system. Both these will, it is suggested, be covered, in the same way as a general pre-COVID prevention of access cover aimed at fairly short-term emergency restrictions such as those involving nearby gas leaks was construed as covering the compulsory closure of premises due to a prolonged and universal coronavirus pandemic.[8]

To prevent this there would be a need for a positive exclusion of the type of liability in question so as to override the generality of the damage cover.[9] Insurers will be well aware of this. In future we are likely, it is suggested, to see added to the standard exceptions for war, terrorism and the like a fairly long list of exclusions

[7] This latter is likely to be more important and to pre empt the general duty. In the absence of a great deal of necessary background knowledge of, and experience with, new technology, it is a brave insurer who will rely on having to show that a given piece of information was in the abstract a 'material circumstance' within s 3(4) of the 2015 Act. For an example of the necessary extensiveness of such questions as regards cyber risk, see C de Azevedo, *Cyber Risks Insurance: Law and Practice* (2nd edn, London, Sweet & Maxwell, 2022), para. 1-008 onwards.

[8] *Financial Conduct Authority v Arch Insurance (UK) Ltd* [2021] UKSC 1; [2021] AC 649. This phenomenon is sometimes referred to as 'silent cover'.

[9] Under the principle in *Leyland Shipping Co Ltd v Norwich Union Fire Insurance Society Ltd* [1918] AC 350. A well-known example is the Institute Cyber Attack Exclusion Clause – CL380.

from ordinary business and BI policies of various kinds of high-tech causes, together with matters whose long-tail effects are effectively unknowable, such as the effects of COVID-style contagions.

B. Exclusions

Exclusions are not only necessary for standard policies for risk separation purposes. Having separated out the effects of new technologies from standard policies, insurers will have to think carefully what cover they are prepared to offer in respect of high security risks. This will not necessarily be easy: to do it they may need to draft exclusions carefully and, in addition, would be well advised to offer cover not generally, but for a limited list of eventualities.[10] For example, providers of cyber insurance may well baulk at the idea of indemnifying an insured for the consequences of any form of unauthorised access whatever, and instead list in detail the forms of interference included; in addition they may regard deliberate employee misconduct as simply too likely to occur to make it a realistic subject of insurance, and demand that this risk be borne by the employer itself. Again, where AI malfunctions are involved there will have to be a careful definition of precisely what amounts such a malfunction in order to be covered; and with pandemic cover, they may well wish to tighten the parameters considerably in order to avoid having to indemnify for consequences of a universal shutdown on the basis of a single person being taken ill within a radius of a given number of miles.[11]

Insurers may also need to consider what kinds of loss they are prepared to cover in this connection. For example, if giving cover for AI malfunctions, how far should this include the effects of business interruption? After all, cover would not normally be available for loss of profits due to a bad business decision, nor yet for the effects of incompetence in a human accounting division; there seems no reason to do anything different in either case merely because the decision is taken by AI. They may consider that any liability should be limited to, say, remediation and liability costs, with possibly the addition of physical property damage.

C. Terms of Cover

We have already hinted at one matter that may be important to insurers wishing to take advantage of regulatory requirements as a means of limiting the risk.

[10] For an example of the latter, see the RSA standard cyber liability policy terms, available at static.rsagroup.com/rsa/commercial-insurance-products/cyber/cyber-risk-insurance-policy-wording.pdf, listing the eventualities covered and then following them with a long list of exclusions. See too the fairly similar Hiscox Cyber Clear Policy, available as Appendix 1 to C de Azevedo, *Cyber Risks Insurance: Law and Practice* (2nd edn, London, Sweet & Maxwell, 2022).

[11] As again was held to be the case in *Financial Conduct Authority v Arch Insurance (UK) Ltd* [2021] UKSC 1; [2021] AC 649.

Such an insurer will naturally wish that its insured, in carrying on a high-tech business involving problematic risk and which is subject to regulation, is at all times not only covered by the regulatory scheme but also in good standing with its regulator. In order to ensure this, there may well be inserted into the policy, whether as a warranty or a condition precedent to cover, a strict requirement that this remains the case.

Nor is this the only clause of this type that might appear. The insurer may well also be concerned to hold the assured to some further technical standard, or to an obligation to submit to some kind of periodic inspection.

There are also other protections an insurer might wish to insert. For example, given the feature of problematic risks that it is nearly always hard to predict the amount of third-party liability when things go wrong, they might wish to make cover conditional on all services being rendered subject to terms limiting the assured's liability to third parties.

One point needs to be noted about such clauses: Certainly in the case of the first two,[12] they are probably subject to the causation rules in s 11 of the Insurance Act 2015. This means that even if they are broken, if the insured can show that non-compliance with their requirements could not have increased the loss that actually occurred, then they cannot be relied on to negative any liability to indemnify.[13] In practice, however, the prospect of s 11 applying here may be largely theoretical. With most losses arising from problematic risks, it will be hard to show that failure to observe regulatory or technical requirements *could* not[14] have contributed to the risk of the loss that occurred.

D. Limitations in the Amount of Cover

In addition to the above, the fact that losses likely to result from problematic risks may be difficult to quantify in terms of amount and probability may well lead

[12] The third, requiring the use of a limitation clause, is more problematic. It is submitted that it would not be subject to s 11 because compliance with it would not tend to reduce the risk of loss of a particular kind, location or time within s 11(1). Compliance would, it is true, tend to reduce the *amount* of the loss suffered by the assured, and it would certainly reduce the risk of the insurer having to pay it. But neither of those is the same thing.

[13] It could just be argued that such a term, if suitably drafted, could count as a term 'defining the risk as a whole' within s 11(1) and therefore outside the section; in other words, as showing that the insurance itself applied only to regulated operators in good standing and nobody else. But this seems unlikely; compare *Maxwell v Highway Hauliers Pty Ltd* [2014] HCA 33; (2014) 312 ALR 530, a case on s 84 of the Australian Insurance Contracts Act 1984 deciding that a limit of cover to insureds with a particular qualification did not go to delimit the risk as a whole. For more detailed discussion on this matter, see B Soyer 'Risk Control Clauses in Insurance Law: Law Reform and The Future' (2016) *Connecticut Law Journal* 109, 119–122.

[14] The use of the phrase "could not" is here very suggestive. However easy it might be to suggest that a breach of an insurance term did not affect what actually happened, it will be much harder to demonstrate a positive impossibility that it might nevertheless have contributed to the risk of it taking place.

insurers to impose fairly low limits of liability, and possibly impose fairly high deductibles. This may well be particularly true in regard to matters outside the direct control of the assured, such as the amount of any third-party liabilities.

V. Other Approaches

So far we have concentrated on simple matters of the drafting of insurance policies, mainly with the aim of reducing the exposure of the insurer so as to make premiums at least potentially affordable. But the limitations of this need to be borne in mind. While some cover is better than none, all limitations on the cover available to an assured increase the risks faced by that assured without the prospect of protection.[15] To that extent the mischief referred to at the start of this paper remains: absent arrangements for adequate protection from risk, innovative technology may remain stunted, or be transferred from the United Kingdom to places with better protections. This, however, raises a further point: there may be a role for the state if we see this as a matter involving not merely private, but public, interests.

The British state has in the past not shied away from itself intervening in the insurance of particular risks where it has seen this as promoting the public interest. In both world wars, for example, it acted as reinsurer of last resort for marine war risks, on the basis that the unavailability of such insurance would be catastrophic fort the war effort.[16] Since 1993[17] it has acted similarly as regards terrorism; the state organisation Pool Re[18] allows commercial insurers to cover terrorist property damage and business interruption by backing them with reinsurance and ultimately with a state guarantee.[19] Flood Re followed in 2016, following a similar scheme and essentially allowing homeowners in flood-prone regions to insure against flooding at a reasonable rate;[20] and during COVID temporary

[15] And, of course, any curtailment of an assured's or insurer's liability to third parties pro tanto transfers substantial risks directly to the latter, which itself may be controversial.

[16] For the First World War see G Richard, 'War Damage and Reparation During World War I in Europe: Between Individual Rights and State Interventionism' in C Bond (ed), *Law and War* (2021) 11–13; N Hill, 'State Insurance against War Risks at Sea' in N Hill et al (eds), *War and Insurance* (1927) 1. During the Second World War analogous arrangements were made under the War Risks Insurance Act 1939. The UK government retains the power to reinsure war risks in times of war affecting the UK; see now the Marine and Aviation Insurance (War Risks) Act 1952. Unsurprisingly it and the fund it sets up are currently dormant. See HM Government, *Marine and Aviation Insurance (War Risks) Fund Account 2022–23*, HC 1728.

[17] Following the Fenians' Bishopsgate bombing in April of that year.

[18] See S Atkins, 'The Pool Re Scheme in the United Kingdom' in S Atkins (ed), *The Future of Terrorism Risk Insurance* (2005) 191–200. The statutory backing comes in the Reinsurance (Acts of Terrorism) Act 1993.

[19] The organisation recently had reserves of some £11.2 billion, besides its premium income, before it had to call on the Treasury: OBR, *Fiscal Risks and Sustainability* (July 2022) (Cm 702) 52–53.

[20] It is funded by all insurers issuing home policies, its powers to demand such funds coming from the Flood Reinsurance (Scheme Funding and Administration) Regulations, SI 2015/1902.

arrangements were made to back trade credit insurance,[21] and also the entertainment industry.[22]

It would certainly be possible for some kind of similar scheme to be set up for problematic risks in the area of innovative technology. (Indeed, the Pool Re scheme mentioned above has already dipped its toe in the water by extending its reinsurance coverage to cover terrorist cyber-attacks in so far as they cause property damage.) It all depends on how important the maintenance of adequate insurance coverage is seen to be by the government, and on the attitude of the Treasury to the creation of yet another contingent liability.

But one thing is clear. The uninsurable is rapidly becoming insurable, if only you know how to go about it.

[21] 'Trade Credit Insurance Backed by £10 Billion Guarantee' (HM Government Press Release, June 4, 2020).

[22] 'Government-Backed Insurance Scheme to Give Boost to Events Industry' (HM Government Press Release, 5 August 2021). See generally P Tereszkiewicz, 'Business Interruption Insurance as a Means of Spreading Pandemic-Related Losses' (2023) 48 *The Geneva Papers on Risk and Insurance – Issues and Practice* 714.

6

The Insurability of Fines

PETER MacDONALD EGGERS KC

I. Introduction

The insurability of fines is an important issue for many commercial concerns. Fines are imposed for many reasons. They can be imposed as a punishment for a criminal, administrative or civil offence. They can also be payable for infringement of regulatory offences or breach of other types of regulations. Fines can be very substantial in amount and can be assessed by reference to the revenue or turnover of an insured company or organisation.

It is not surprising therefore that an insured may wish to insure against the risk of a fine being imposed; without such insurance, the fine may have a substantial impact on the insured's business. Many insurance policies contain provisions which purport to provide an indemnity against fines, for example directors and officers liability policies, media risk or cyber risk policies, professional indemnity or errors and omissions policies, and protection and indemnity policies. In some cases, such insurance policies provide cover against fines, subject to the requirement that such fines are insurable as a matter of law.

On the other hand, fines can be levied to penalise an insured for wrongful or unlawful conduct, and it might be thought that the ability of the insured to recover an indemnity for a fine would render the purpose of the fine futile in that the pain, discomfort or lesson intended to be inflicted by the fine will have been diminished by a successful insurance recovery.

For this reason, the question whether fines are insurable engages questions of public policy, in particular the illegality doctrine, which if applied may well disable the insured from recovering an indemnity against a fine, even if the policy makes provision for such an indemnity. The illegality doctrine has developed over the years. It found early expression in Lord Mansfield's Court in 1775.[1] The doctrine was developed by the Courts slowly and surely. In recent years, there have been several signal steps towards the formulation and effect of the doctrine. The first

[1] *Holman v Johnson* (1775) 1 Cowp 341.

was the House of Lords' decision in *Tinsley v Milligan*,[2] where it was held that if a claimant sought to rely on its own unlawful conduct in support of a claim for civil relief, the Court should disable the claimant from succeeding in the claim. The House of Lords disavowed any 'public conscience' test, whereby a claim would be debarred if its enforcement would be an affront to the public conscience), which had been applied by the Court of Appeal in a series of decisions beforehand.

However, the decision in *Tinsley v Milligan* was overruled by the Supreme Court in *Patel v Mirza*,[3] by holding that in determining the impact of illegality on a claimant's right to sue, the Court should adopt a more open-textured approach (a policy-based approach) to determine what is or is not in the public interest and whether the enforcement of the claim would or would not be in accordance with that public interest. This bears echoes of the public conscience test disavowed by the House of Lords in *Tinsley v Milligan*, albeit in a more structured form. The pendulum has shifted (a little) again with the Supreme Court's decision in *Henderson v Dorset Healthcare University NHS Foundation Trust*,[4] in holding that *Patel v Mirza* is not to be regarded as 'year zero' and accordingly earlier decisions of the Court remain of precedential value unless they are not compatible with the decision in *Patel v Mirza*.

With this changing approach to public policy and the consequences of illegality, the question inevitably arises what is the effect of illegality on a claim under an insurance policy? In order to consider this question, this paper will reflect the development of the doctrine of illegality and then apply that doctrine to claims under insurance contracts.

II. Public Policy

The doctrine of illegality is underpinned by considerations of public policy or the 'public interest'. In applying public policy, the Courts have been alert to their role and that of the legislature, recognising that they should allow public policy to intervene in a civil claim where there is clarity in the existence and extent of that public policy. If there were doubt in the application of public policy, then the Court should eschew the temptation to rely on what it might consider to be in the public interest.

In *Fender v St John Mildmay*,[5] Lord Atkin said that the public policy 'doctrine should only be invoked in clear cases in which the harm to the public is substantially incontestable, and does not depend upon the idiosyncratic inferences of a few judicial minds'. Similarly, in *McLoughlin v O'Brian*,[6] Lord Edmund-Davies

[2] [1994] AC 340.
[3] [2016] UKSC 42; [2016] 3 WLR 399.
[4] [2020] UKSC 43; [2021] AC 563.
[5] [1938] AC 1, 12.
[6] [1983] 1 AC 410, 426, 428.

stated that 'any invocation of public policy calls for the closest scrutiny' and will have to meet the standards of 'clarity and cogency'.[7]

Where that clarity and cogency is absent, even if there are strong hints of it, the Court should step back. Thus, in *Masefield AG v Amlin Corporate Member Ltd*,[8] Rix, LJ referred to the need for a clear public interest which requires protection and where there was a clash of interests, the rule of public policy was not generally to be invoked. Thus, in considering whether there was a public policy against the payment of ransoms to pirates, Rix, LJ said:

> In these morally muddied waters, there is no universally recognised principle of morality, no clearly identified public policy, no substantially incontestable public interest, which could lead the courts, as matters stand at present, to state that the payment of ransom should be regarded as a matter which stands beyond the pale, without any legitimate recognition. There are only elements of conflicting public interests, which push and pull in different directions, and have yet to be resolved in any legal enactments or international consensus as to a solution, save that of wary watchfulness, the deployment of naval resources as a form of law enforcement or policing operation, and a regard for a comprehensive approach, seeking to address political, economic and security aspects of the crisis in a holistic way.

The importance of these pre-conditions for formulating a new rule of public policy is that what is in the interests of the public is ordinarily a matter for Parliament, not for individual judges. So, Parke B, in *Egerton v Brownlow*,[9] observed that '[i]t is the province of the statesman, and not the lawyer, to discuss, and of the Legislature to determine, what is best for the public good, and to provide for it by proper enactments'.

Parliament is best suited to deal with such issues, not least because there may be two or more different approaches to any issue falling within the scope of public policy, and Parliament is much better place to determine which of contrasting views should be upheld. Thus, in *Johnstone v Bloomsbury Health Authority*,[10] Stuart-Smith, LJ said that where there were two bona fide views on a particular issue, it would be unwise for the Court to apply any public policy considerations.

Naturally, this approach to public policy is chiefly concerned with the development of new rules of public policy. The doctrine of illegality, however, has been applied since the eighteenth century, although the boundaries of that doctrine are now being tested and debated. It is perhaps when dealing with the doctrine's boundaries that this approach to public policy comes to the fore; the clarity and urgency of the public interest should be invoked not to challenge the illegality doctrine itself, but its boundaries. The approach adopted by the Supreme Court in

[7] See also *D v National Society for the Prevention of Cruelty to Children* [1978] 1 AC 171, 233–235.
[8] [2011] EWCA Civ 24; [2011] Lloyd's Rep IR 338, at [71].
[9] (1853) 4 HLC 1.
[10] [1992] 1 QB 333, 346–347.

Patel v Mirza presupposes, or should presuppose, that the Court is in a position to identify, with certainty, the public interest in a particular case, having regard to a particular statute or legal principle. Where however the public interest is not self-evident, the question arises how the illegality doctrine should be applied. Should it be applied as the Courts have applied it prior to *Patel v Mirza*, unless the public interest clearly requires otherwise, or should it be applied only if the Court is clear in its own mind that there is a public interest to protect?

III. Doctrine of Illegality

The public policy doctrine of illegality – or the *ex turpi causa* principle – was classically stated by Lord Mansfield CJ in his oft-quoted dictum in *Holman v Johnson*:[11]

> No court will lend its aid to a man who founds his cause of action on an immoral or an illegal act. If, from the plaintiff's own stating or otherwise, the cause of action appears to arise *ex turpi causa*, or the transgression of a positive law of this country, there the court says that he has no right to be assisted. It is on that ground the court goes; not for the sake of the defendant, but because they will not lend their aid to such a plaintiff …

This principle recognises that a claim will be disabled where there is a sufficient causal relationship between the illegality and the claim.

Traditionally, there were two relevant rules of public policy which evolved from the *ex turpi causa* principle which would deprive a claimant, of the right to enforce an otherwise valid claim:[12]

i) A party may not rely on its own fraud or illegality in order to found a claim.[13] This is sometimes called the *Bowmakers* principle.[14]
ii) A claimant is not permitted to benefit or profit from the commission of a crime; in other words, a claimant will not be entitled to sue for the benefits or proceeds of its crime. This principle is sometimes referred to as the *Beresford* principle.[15]

However, the law has developed substantially since that traditional approach, with the decisions of the Supreme Court in *Patel v Mirza*,[16] and *Henderson v Dorset Healthcare University NHS Foundation Trust*.[17]

[11] (1775) I Cowp 341, 343. See also *Les Laboratoires Servier v Apotex Inc* [2014] UKSC 55; [2015] AC 430, at [13]; *Patel v Mirza* [2016] UKSC 42; [2016] 3 WLR 399, at [1].

[12] *Royal Boskalis Westminster NV v Mountain* [1997] LRLR 523, 574–577; *Sea Glory Maritime Co v Al Sagr National Insurance Co* [2013] EWHC 2116; [2014] 1 Lloyd's Rep 14, at [298].

[13] *Tribe v Tribe* [1996] Ch 107, 124.

[14] *Bowmakers Ltd v Barnet Instruments Ltd* [1945] KB 65.

[15] *Beresford v Royal Insurance Co Ltd* [1937] 2 KB 197; [1938] AC 586.

[16] [2016] UKSC 42; [2016] 3 WLR 399.

[17] [2020] UKSC 43; [2021] AC 563.

In *Patel v Mirza*, the claimant paid a large sum of money to the defendant pursuant to an agreement that he would use it to bet on the movement of shares on the basis of inside information. The agreement contravened the prohibition on insider dealing in section 52 of the Criminal Justice Act 1993. In the event the agreement could not be carried out because the expected inside information was not forthcoming. The claimant brought a claim against the defendant for the repayment of the money. The Supreme Court held that a person who satisfied the ordinary requirements of a claim in unjust enrichment should be entitled to the return of his money or property and such a person should not prima facie be debarred from recovering money paid or property transferred by reason of the fact that the consideration which had failed in whole or in part was an unlawful consideration; and that, since an order for restitution of the money paid by the claimant to the defendant would merely return the parties to their previous position before the conclusion of the illegal contract and prevent the defendant gaining by unjust enrichment, such an order should be made.

The majority of the Supreme Court's decision was expressed in Lord Toulson's judgment. His Lordship summarised the principles of public policy as follows:[18]

> Looking behind the maxims, there are two broad discernible policy reasons for the common law doctrine of illegality as a defence to a civil claim. One is that a person should not be allowed to profit from his own wrongdoing. The other, linked, consideration is that the law should be coherent and not self-defeating, condoning illegality by giving with the left hand what it takes with the right hand.

Lord Toulson further explained:[19]

> The essential rationale of the illegality doctrine is that it would be contrary to the public interest to enforce a claim if to do so would be harmful to the integrity of the legal system (or, possibly, certain aspects of public morality, the boundaries of which have never been made entirely clear and which do not arise for consideration in this case). In assessing whether the public interest would be harmed in that way, it is necessary (a) to consider the underlying purpose of the prohibition which has been transgressed and whether that purpose will be enhanced by denial of the claim, (b) to consider any other relevant public policy on which the denial of the claim may have an impact and (c) to consider whether denial of the claim would be a proportionate response to the illegality, bearing in mind that punishment is a matter for the criminal courts. Within that framework, various factors may be relevant, but it would be a mistake to suggest that the court is free to decide a case in an undisciplined way. The public interest is best served by a principled and transparent assessment of the considerations identified, rather by than the application of a formal approach capable of producing results which may appear arbitrary, unjust or disproportionate.

[18] [2016] UKSC 42; [2016] 3 WLR 399, at [99].

[19] [2016] UKSC 42; [2016] 3 WLR 399, at [120].

In essence, the Court said that it would undertake a balancing approach to determining the public interest. Many have applauded this decision.[20] However, there are two disadvantages to this approach. The first is that in many cases the identification of the public interest may not be clear, especially where there are competing public positions.

The second disadvantage with this approach is that the clearly stated rules – the *Bowmakers* and *Beresford* principles – which were of a readily understandable application had become, with a balancing approach, uncertain. This has the disadvantage of rendering the parties' rights uncertain in the face of an allegation of illegality. In some respects, although the Supreme Court spoke against an 'undisciplined' assessment, this was redolent of the 'public conscience' test which the House of Lords disavowed in *Tinsley v Millgan*.[21] In that case, Lord Goff said that 'It is very difficult to reconcile such a test with the principle of policy stated by Lord Mansfield C.J.'. Lord Goff, dissenting in the application of the doctrine to the facts of the case, stated that the public conscience test was inconsistent with authority,[22] but then considered whether it was desirable to adopt this test in any event. Lord Goff answered this question as follows:[23]

> the adoption of the public conscience test, as stated by Nicholls L.J., would constitute a revolution in this branch of the law, under which what is in effect a discretion would become vested in the court to deal with the matter by the process of a balancing operation, in place of a system of rules, ultimately derived from the principle of public policy enunciated by Lord Mansfield C.J. in Holman v. Johnson, 1 Cowp. 341, which lies at the root of the law relating to claims which are, in one way or another, tainted by illegality. Furthermore, the principle of public policy so stated by Lord Mansfield cannot be disregarded as having no basis in principle. In his dissenting judgment in the present case Ralph Gibson L.J. pointed out [1992] Ch. 310, 334:
>
> > 'In so far as the basis of the ex turpi causa defence, as founded on public policy, is directed at deterrence it seems to me that the force of the deterrent effect is in the existence of the known rule and in its stern application. Lawyers have long known of the rule and must have advised many people of its existence. It does not stop people making arrangements to defraud creditors, or the revenue, or the D.S.S. Such arrangements as are under consideration in this case are usually made between married couples as in Tinker v. Tinker, or between unmarried lovers as in this case or in Cantor v. Cox, 239 E.G. 121. If they do not fall out, no one will know. If they do fall out, one side may reveal the fraud. It is an ugly situation when that is done. I think that the law has upheld the principle on the simple ground that, ugly though its working may be, it is better than permitting the fraudulent an avenue of escape if the fraud is revealed.'

[20] A Burrows, 'A New Dawn for the Law of Illegality' in S Green and A Bogg (ed), *Illegality after Patel v Mirza* (Oxford, Hart, 2018) Ch 2. See *RO v Gray* [2021] EWHC 2770 (QB); [2022] 1 WLR 1484, at [129].

[21] [1994] AC 340.

[22] [1994] AC 340, 358–359.

[23] [1994] AC 340, 363.

> I recognise, of course, the hardship which the application of the present law imposes upon the respondent in this case; and I do not disguise my own unhappiness at the result. But, bearing in mind the passage from the judgment of Ralph Gibson L.J. which I have just quoted, I have to say that it is by no means self-evident that the public conscience text is preferable to the present strict rules. Certainly, I do not feel able to say that it would be appropriate for your Lordships House, in the face of a long line of unbroken authority stretching back over 200 years, now by judicial decision to replace the principles established in those authorities by a wholly different discretionary system.

Lord Browne-Wilkinson, in the majority, agreed with Lord Goff's assessment of the public conscience test:[24]

> I agree with the speech of my noble and learned friend, Lord Goff of Chieveley, that the consequences of being a party to an illegal transaction cannot depend, as the majority in the Court of Appeal held, on such an imponderable factor as the extent to which the public conscience would be affronted by recognising rights created by illegal transactions.

Perhaps because of this, the Supreme Court, in *Henderson v Dorset Healthcare University NHS Foundation Trust*,[25] stated that the decision in *Patel v Mirza* was not the revolution in the doctrine of illegality as had originally been thought, holding that *Patel v Mirza* is not to be regarded as 'year zero' and accordingly earlier decisions of the Court remain of precedential value unless they are not compatible with the decision in *Patel v Mirza*.[26] Nonetheless, the principle applies across the civil law.[27]

The inconsistency principle is a relevant consideration. Lord Hamblen stated that 'For one branch of the law to enable a person to profit from behaviour which another branch of the law treats as being criminal or otherwise unlawful would tend to produce inconsistency and disharmony in the law, and so cause damage to the integrity of the legal system, as is recognised in Patel (at paras 99 to 101). In cases where it features, it too is a factor to be taken into account, even though it may not reflect the purpose of the prohibition transgressed'.[28]

The centrality of the illegality to the relevant transaction is also a relevant consideration. Lord Hamblen said:

> The closer that connection is, the greater and more obvious may be the inconsistency and consequent risk of harm to the integrity of the legal system. The rejection by the majority in Patel of reliance as the test of illegality did not mean that reliance was thereby rendered irrelevant to the policy-based approach. It may not provide a satisfactory test of illegality, but it will often be a relevant factor" and "When considering the

[24] [1994] AC 340, 369.

[25] [2020] UKSC 43; [2021] AC 563, at [76–77], [119–120], [124]. See further *Energizer Supermarket Ltd v Holiday Snacks Ltd* [2022] UKPC 16; [2023] 2 P & CR 9 (Trinidad and Tobago).

[26] *Lewis-Ranwell v G4S Health Services (UK) Ltd* [2024] EWCA Civ 138; [2024] 2 WLR 1377, at [30–31].

[27] It also applies to foreign illegality: *Magdeev v Tsvetkov* [2020] EWHC 887 (Comm) (Cockerill, J) and *Haddad v Rostamani* [2021] EWHC 1892 (Ch) (Zacaroli, J).

[28] *Day v Womble Bond Dickinson (UK) LLP* [2020] EWCA Civ 447; [2020] PNLR 19, at [41–43].

> circumstances relating to the illegality, whether there is a causal link between the illegality and the claim, and the closeness of that causal connection, will often be important considerations.[29]

Therefore, the principles developed in numerous decisions before *Patel v Mirza* remain relevant, even if they are not as determinative as they had previously been. By the authorities, the Courts have established a number of principles over the years.

A. The Two Versions of the Doctrine

There is a wider and narrower form of the doctrine of illegality (public policy / *ex turpi causa*). In *Gray v Thames Trains Ltd*,[30] a decision which was held to remain binding following *Patel v Mirza*,[31] the claimant was a passenger on a train which crashed due to the negligence of the defendants, which were the operator of the train and the entity responsible for the rail infrastructure. As a result of the crash, the claimant suffered psychiatric injury in the form of PTSD, depression and substantial personality change. Two years after the accident and while under medical treatment, the claimant killed a man who had stepped in front of his car. He pleaded guilty to manslaughter on the ground of diminished responsibility. He was ordered to be detained in a hospital. The claimant brought proceedings in negligence against the defendants and claimed general damages for his detention, conviction, feelings of guilt and remorse and damage to reputation and an indemnity against any claims which might be brought by dependents of the person he killed. Lord Hoffmann said:

> My Lords, the question in this case is in my opinion whether the intervention of Mr Gray's criminal act in the causal relationship between the defendants' breaches of duty and the damage of which he complains prevents him from recovering that part of his loss caused by the criminal act … [The appellants'] principal argument invokes a special rule of public policy. In its wider form, it is that you cannot recover compensation for loss which you have suffered in consequence of your own criminal act. In its narrower and more specific form, it is that you cannot recover for damage which flows from loss of liberty, a fine or other punishment lawfully imposed upon you in consequence of your own unlawful act. In such a case it is the law which, as a matter of penal policy, causes the damage and it would be inconsistent for the law to require you to be

[29] In *Stoffel v Grondona* [2020] UKSC 42; [2021] AC 540, at [43] the Supreme Court stated: 'As a result of the change in the law brought about by Patel v Mirza, the question whether a claimant must rely upon illegal conduct to establish a cause of action is no longer determinative of an illegality defence. Nevertheless, the question of reliance may have a bearing on the issue of centrality'. See also *Day v Womble Bond Dickinson (UK) LLP* [2020] EWCA Civ 447; [2020] PNLR 19, at [28–34].

[30] [2009] UKHL 33; [2009] AC 1339, at [27, 29, 32, 35, 51–53]. See also *Safeway Stores Ltd v Twigger* [2010] EWCA Civ 1472; [2011] 1 Lloyd's Rep 462, at [16]; *D Geddes (Contractors) Ltd v Neil Johnson Health & Safety Services Ltd*, [2017] CSOH 42; [2018] Lloyd's Rep IR 264, at [17].

[31] *Henderson v Dorset Healthcare University NHS Foundation Trust* [2020] UKSC 43; [2021] AC 563, at [64–65, 91].

> compensated for that damage … The particular rule for which the appellants contend may, as I said, be stated in a wider or a narrow form. The wider and simpler version is that which was applied by Flaux J: you cannot recover for damage which is the consequence of your own criminal act. … The leading English authority is the decision of the Court of Appeal in Clunis v Camden and Islington Health Authority [1998] QB 978 … the health authority relied upon the wider version of the rule. Beldam LJ, who gave the judgment of the court, accepted this submission. He said, at pp 989–990:
>
> > 'In the present case the plaintiff has been convicted of a serious criminal offence. In such a case public policy would in our judgment preclude the court from entertaining the plaintiff's claim unless it could be said that he did not know the nature and quality of his act or that what he was doing was wrong … The court ought not to allow itself to be made an instrument to enforce obligations alleged to arise out of the plaintiff's own criminal act and we would therefore allow the appeal on this ground.'
>
> … I must therefore examine a wider version of the rule, which was applied by Flaux J. This has the support of the reasoning of the Court of Appeal in Clunis's case [1998] QB 978 as well as other authorities … The wider principle was applied by the Court of Appeal in Vellino v Chief Constable of the Greater Manchester Police [2002] 1 WLR 218 … This decision seems to me based upon sound common sense.

The wider doctrine is therefore that a claimant cannot recover compensation for loss which it has suffered in consequence of its own criminal act.[32]

The narrower doctrine is that a claimant cannot recover for damage which flows from loss of liberty, a fine or other punishment lawfully imposed upon the claimant in consequence of its own unlawful act. The justification for this narrower rule is that the punishment inflicted on the claimant should operate as both deterrent and punishment.[33] Further, the rationale is said to be the need for the criminal courts and the civil courts to speak with a consistent voice, given that it would be inconsistent for a claimant to be criminally and personally liable (or liable to pay penalties to a regulator) but for the same claimant to say to a civil court that he or she should be compensated or indemnified against the consequences of such conduct or that he or she is not personally answerable for that conduct.[34] In other words, as Lord Toulson said in *Patel v Mirza*,[35] 'the law should be coherent and not self-defeating, condoning illegality by giving with the left hand what it takes with the right hand'. Thus, it has been said that the public interest may be more likely to require the application of the illegality doctrine to disable a claim.[36]

[32] There must, however, be a criminal act; where a defendant is acquitted on grounds of insanity, there is no criminal conduct to attract the illegality doctrine: *Lewis-Ranwell v G4S Health Services (UK) Ltd* [2022] EWHC 1213 (QB); [2023] QB 229; [2024] EWCA Civ 138; [2024] 2 WLR 1377.

[33] *Askey v Golden Wine Co Ltd* [1948] 2 All ER 35, 38-39; *Safeway Stores Ltd v Twigger* [2010] EWHC 11 (Comm); [2010] Bus LR 974, at [39] (Flaux, J); *Gujra v Roath* [2018] EWHC 854 (QB); [2018] 1 WLR 3208, at [30]; *Khan v Hussain* [2019] CSOH 11; 2019 SLT 319, at [27–40].

[34] *Gray v Thames Trains Ltd* [2009] UKHL 33; [2009] AC 1339, at [29]; *Safeway Stores Ltd v Twigger* [2010] EWCA Civ 1472; [2011] 1 Lloyd's Rep 462, at [16]; *Day v Womble Bond Dickinson (UK) LLP* [2020] EWCA Civ 447; [2020] PNLR 19, at [28–34].

[35] [2016] UKSC 42; [2016] 3 WLR 399, at [99].

[36] *Owadally v Planology Ltd* [2023] EWHC 339 (KB); [2023] PNLR 17, at [86–87].

B. The Relevance of Moral Turpitude

The illegality doctrine applies especially to criminal acts, but it also applies to conduct attracting civil or administrative penalties and serious, that is, dishonest or torts.[37]

The application of the doctrine depends on there being a sufficient level of moral turpitude or responsibility for the offence or prohibited conduct.[38] Such moral turpitude plainly exists in cases of fraud, dishonesty or deliberate misconduct.[39] The principle was explained by Lord Denning, MR in *Hardy v Motor Insurers' Bureau*:[40]

> no person can claim reparation or indemnity for the consequences of a criminal offence where his own wicked and deliberate intent is an essential ingredient in it … This rule is not rested on an implied exception in the policy of insurance. It is based on the broad rule of public policy that no person can claim indemnity or reparation for his own wilful and culpable crime.

On the other hand, it seems that strict liability for a criminal offence would not, or would not necessarily, be sufficient to engage the illegality doctrine insofar as the offence was perpetrated innocently, meaning neither deliberately nor negligently.[41] However, this is not certain in light of the decision in *Patel v Mirza*, because whatever is found to be in the public interest is the determinant.[42]

It is less clear whether negligence on the part of the claimant provides the necessary level of moral blameworthiness or turpitude in the context of a criminal offence.[43] However, the Courts have also indicated that if negligence is sufficiently serious, it may attract the doctrine, for example if the negligence is such 'the legislature considered so serious that it should be regarded as a crime'.

[37] *Les Laboratoires Servier v Apotex Inc* [2014] UKSC 55; [2015] AC 430, at [25, 28].

[38] *Stone & Rolls Ltd v Moore Stephens* [2009] 1 AC 1391, at [24]; *Safeway Stores Ltd v Twigger* [2010] EWHC 11 (Comm); [2010] Bus LR 974, at [26] (Flaux, J); *Les Laboratoires Servier v Apotex Inc* [2014] UKSC 55; [2015] AC 430; *McCracken v Smith* [2015] EWCA Civ 380; [2015] PIQR P19; *Sainsbury's Supermarkets Ltd v Mastercard Incorporated* [2018] EWCA Civ 1536; [2019] Bus LR 198, at [42] (CA); *Clark v Farley* [2018] EWHC 1007 (QB); [2019] RTR 21.

[39] *Burrows v Rhodes* [1899] 1 QB 816, 828–830; *Hardy v Motor Insurers' Bureau* [1964] QB 745, at 760; *Sea Glory Maritime Co v Al Sagr National Insurance Co* [2013] EWHC 2116; [2014] 1 Lloyd's Rep 14, at [298–303].

[40] [1964] QB 745, 760. See also the judgments of Pearson, LJ (at 762) and Diplock, LJ (at 769). See further *Charlton v Fisher* [2001] EWCA Civ 112; [2001] Lloyd's Rep IR 387, at [24, 35]. *Cf. Lancashire County Council v Municipal Mutual Insurance Ltd* [1996] 3 All ER 545, 554.

[41] *Griffin v UHY Hacker Young & Partners* [2010] EWHC 146 (Ch); [2010] PNLR 20, at [47, 60]; *Les Laboratoires Servier v Apotex Inc* [2014] UKSC 55; [2015] AC 430, at [29]; *Khan v Hussein* [2019] CSOH 11; 2019 SLT 319; *cf. Safeway Stores Ltd v Twigger* [2010] EWCA Civ 1472; [2011] 1 Lloyd's Rep 462, at, [18].

[42] *Owadally v Planology Ltd* [2023] EWHC 339 (KB); [2023] PNLR 17, at [79–85].

[43] J Birds, B Lynch, and S Paul, *MacGillivray on Insurance Law* (15th ed, London, Sweet & Maxwell, 2022), at para 14-052: 'we do not believe that it is now possible to state a simple distinction between a loss intentionally caused by a criminal act in respect of which no indemnity is permitted, and a loss caused by a negligent act of the insured, also criminal, in respect of which a claim is maintainable. The distinction should be sought in terms of the requirements of public policy'.

In *Askey v Golden Wine Co Ltd*,[44] the plaintiff was convicted of selling cocktails unfit for human consumption and was fined £316. The plaintiff had been supplied by the defendants with liquor which had been contaminated with methylated spirits. The defendants had earlier been convicted and were fined and sentenced to terms of imprisonment. After the defendants' conviction, the plaintiff was assured by the defendants that the conviction had nothing to do with the liquor they manufactured for him. The plaintiff went on selling the cocktails and was then convicted and fined. The plaintiff sought to recover the fine and damages from the defendants. The Court dismissed the claim. Denning, J said:

> It is, I think, a principle of our law that the punishment inflicted by a criminal court is personal to the offender, and that the civil courts will not entertain an action by the offender to recover an indemnity against the consequences of that punishment. In every criminal court the punishment is fixed having regard to the personal responsibility of the offender in respect of the offence, to the necessity for deterring him and others from doing the same thing again, to reform him, and, in cases such as the present, to make him and others more careful in their dealings, to make him choose with more discrimination his suppliers or his servants, and to make him more exact and scrupulous in his supervision of the matters for which he is responsible.

Denning, J then proceeded to deal with the more general claim for damages and said that the claim was:

> due to his own criminality, not in the sense of a positively wicked mind, but in the sense of a grossly negligent one negligence which the legislature considered so serious that it should be regarded as a crime. Does that debar him from claiming damages from those guilty of the contamination? I think it does. Speaking generally, public policy requires that no right of indemnity or contribution or damages should be enforced in respect of expenses which the plaintiff has incurred by reason of being compelled to make reparation for his own crime. That principle is to be gathered from *Haseldine v Hosken* and *Beresford v Royal Insurance Co Ltd*. This case comes within that principle.

Thus, Denning, J was prepared to accept that 'gross negligence' could engage the public interest in disabling the claim. Similarly, in *Osman v J Ralph Moss Ltd*,[45] the plaintiff instructed the defendant insurance brokers to effect a policy of motor insurance for him, which they did, but the insurer subsequently became insolvent, of which the plaintiff was unaware; he had a motor accident and was fined £25 for driving without insurance for breach of section 201 of the Road Traffic Act, 1960; the plaintiff sought to recover the fine as damages from the defendants. The Court of Appeal allowed the plaintiff's claim. Sachs, LJ said:[46]

[44] [1948] 2 All ER 35, 38–39.

[45] [1970] 1 Lloyd's Rep 313, 316, 318, 319–320. See also *Strongman (1945) Ltd v Sincock* [1955] 2 QB 525, 535–536.

[46] *ibid*, 316.

> Next I turn to the fine of £25. Having examined the authorities as to cases where the person fined was under an absolute liability, it appears that such fine can be recovered in circumstances such as the present as damages unless it is shown that there was on the part of the person fined a degree of mens rea or of culpable negligence in the matter which resulted in the fine. The onus in cases such as the present is on the defendants, who were the true cause of the sequence of events leading to the fine, to show that there are circumstances which make that fine irrecoverable as damages by the plaintiff.

Edmund Davies, LJ added:[47]

> As to the prosecution, Mr. Cheyne submits on the authority of Mr. Justice Denning's decision in *Askey v. Golden Wine Co. Ltd. and Others*, [1948] 2 All E.R. 35, that neither the fine of £25 for driving without being insured, nor any part of Mr. Osman's own £31 10s. costs are recoverable. But in Askey's case the plaintiff had himself been guilty of gross negligence. Mr. Cheyne has very properly drawn our attention to the comments on that case made by Lord Justice Denning (as he had then become) in *Strongman (1945) Ltd. v. Sincock*, [1955] 3 All E.R. 90 … The facts of Askey's case were thus widely different from those with which this Court is now concerned for this plaintiff was, in my judgment, entirely free of culpable negligence. I am aware that as to the recoverability of a fine in civil proceedings there are conflicting decisions. Thus, in *Cointat v. Myham & Son*, [1913] 2 K.B. 220, both fine and costs were held recoverable, while in *R. Leslie Ltd. v. Reliable Advertising and Addressing Agency Ltd.*, [1915] 1 K.B. 652, a similar claim was held not maintainable. But they turned on different facts, and I regard the former as preferable and certainly more applicable to the circumstances of the present case. As to the amount of the fine, no material has been placed before us from which it would be proper to infer that in imposing a fine of £25 the Magistrates were influenced by any particularly aggravating feature in the plaintiff's conduct and for all we know to the contrary it was not an unusually heavy fine in such circumstances. I see no reason why the plaintiff should not recover it in full from the defendants.

Phillimore, LJ also commented:[48]

> I would add one word on the item of £25, the fine for driving while uninsured. As I see it, the law is accurately summarized in *Mayne and McGregor on Damages*, 12th ed. (1961), at p. 313. There after referring to the judgment of Mr. Justice Denning (as he then was) in *Askey v. Golden Wine Co.*, sup., the position is summarized thus:
>
> > … Thus the cases all agree that where the now plaintiff's conviction has involved mens rea he cannot recover as damages the fine which he has been ordered to pay …
>
> They then go on to suggest that where there is no mens rea, the law is not settled and to suggest that the Courts ought to follow the reasoning of Mr. Justice Rowlatt in *R. Leslie Ltd. v. Reliable Advertising and Addressing Agency Ltd.*, [1915] 1 K.B. 652, and prefer the broad ground of public policy to the suggestion that where there is no mens rea and no personal negligence the now plaintiff should be able to recover the fine. The Court

[47] *ibid*, 318.
[48] *ibid*, 319–320.

> has not had a very full argument on this particular problem, but it seems to me that the argument of Mr. Justice Denning in the case referred to, and his observations, to which my Lord, Lord Justice Edmund Davies has already alluded, in *Strongman (1945) Ltd. v. Sincock*, [1955] 3 All E.R. 90, at p. 93, are sound and for myself, certainly in the circumstances of the present case, I should prefer them. Here is a case of absolute liability. This man incurred that liability through no fault, no negligence or dishonesty on his part. He incurred it because he was grossly misled by the insurance brokers whose duty it was to advise him. It would, as I think, be quite wrong in such circumstances if he was not able to recover the amount of this fine as a just debt.

Thus, gross or culpable negligence may be sufficient grounds to invoke the rule of public policy. However, it is difficult to define what constitutes gross or culpable negligence.[49] Thus, in *Griffin v UHY Hacker Young & Partners*, Vos, J said:[50]

> I agree with Flaux J. that the use of the epithets 'gross', 'culpable' or 'crass' to describe negligence are unhelpful in this, as in many other, contexts. Negligence is a well understood concept, but negligence characterised by one of these epithets is not. Moreover, in my judgment, the use of these epithets in some of the cases, seems to me to belie the fact that the court was searching for some ill-defined element of culpability beyond negligence. Whether that be recklessness or some other higher level of blameworthiness, it seems to me that it could at least be argued that negligence would not be sufficient to deprive a claimant guilty of some, at least, strict liability offences of a remedy against a defendant guilty of professional negligence.

That said, ordinary negligence has also been referred to as providing a sufficient degree of moral turpitude to justify the application of the illegality doctrine.[51] In other cases, it has not been regarded as sufficient.[52]

It is also unclear to what extent the level of moral turpitude required for the application of the illegality doctrine varies depending on whether the wider or narrower form of the doctrine applies, though in *Safeway Stores Ltd v Twigger*,[53] Longmore, LJ considered that the main difference between the two forms of the doctrine was the question of causation, but made no reference to the question of turpitude in this context. In one reading of the Scottish Court's decision in *D Geddes (Contractors) Ltd v Neil Johnson Health & Safety Services Ltd*,[54] there was no difference as to moral turpitude between the two versions of the doctrine.

[49] *Safeway Stores Ltd v Twigger* [2010] EWHC 11 (Comm); [2010] Bus LR 974, at [99] (Flaux, J). Nevertheless, 'gross negligence' has been defined by the Courts when necessary: see eg, *Red Sea Tankers Ltd v Papachristidis* [1997] 2 Lloyd's Rep 547, 586.

[50] [2010] EWHC 146 (Ch); [2010] PNLR 20, at [60(ii)].

[51] *Osman v J Ralph Moss Ltd* [1970] 1 Lloyd's Rep 313, 319–320 (Phillimore, LJ)); *Safeway Stores Ltd v Twigger* [2010] EWHC 11 (Comm), at [99] (Flaux, J); [2010] Bus LR 974; [2010] EWCA Civ 1472; [2011] 1 Lloyd's Rep 462, at [18, 23] (Longmore, LJ); *D Geddes (Contractors) Ltd v Neil Johnson Health & Safety Services Ltd* [2017] CSOH 42; [2018] Lloyd's Rep IR 264, at [18–19].

[52] *James v British General Insurance Company Ltd* [1927] 2 KB 311, 323; *Wallett v Vickers* [2018] EWHC 3088 (QB); [2019] Lloyd's Rep IR 205, at [38]. *Cf. Sainsbury's Supermarkets Ltd v Mastercard Incorporated* [2016] CAT 11; [2016] Comp AR 33, at [307] (CAT).

[53] [2010] EWCA Civ 1472; [2011] 1 Lloyd's Rep 462, at [16].

[54] [2017] CSOH 42; [2018] Lloyd's Rep IR 264, at [17–19].

In that case, a lorry driver was killed while tipping a load of materials into a feed hopper at a quarry owned by the claimant, who was the employer of the driver. At the edge of the raised area above the hopper there was a stop block, whose purpose was to prevent lorries from reversing over the edge. As the driver went to tip his load, he reversed his lorry over the stop block into the hopper and was killed. The claimant was charged with a breach of Regulation 6 of the Quarries Regulations, which required a quarry operator to take the necessary measures to ensure, so far as was reasonably practicable, that the quarry and its plant were designed, constructed, equipped, commissioned, operated and maintained in such a way that persons at work could perform their work safely. The claimant pleaded guilty and was convicted and fined £200,000. The claimant sued the defendant, who was a health and safety advisor with regard to the operation of the quarry, for the recovery of the £200,000 fine on the grounds of the defendant's negligence in failing to advise that the stop block was lower than the minimum height required. The defendant denied negligence and also argued that the claimant should not be permitted to recover damages in respect of the fine which was levied for the claimant's own criminal act.

The defendant applied to strike out the claimant's action on the latter ground (*ex turpi causa*). The Scottish Court refused to grant the application, because it was unclear whether the conduct of the claimant justified the application of *ex turpi causa* principle. The Court reviewed the relevant authorities and concluded that there is no authority for the proposition that recovery of a criminal penalty is necessarily excluded by reason of the illegality (*ex turpi causa*) doctrine; where there are authorities against such recovery, they are cases 'in the context of a claimant who was, or was at least presumed to have been, aware of what he was doing when he committed the offence'; where however the claimant has committed a criminal offence unwittingly, different policy considerations arise. That said, the Court stated that the doctrine will apply to exclude recovery not only in cases of intentional wrongdoing, but in cases where the claimant is legally responsible, for example in cases of negligence; therefore, if negligence is the cause of penalty, the doctrine excludes the claimant's right to recover that penalty from a third party.

Thus, the Court appears to have focussed not on moral turpitude as the justification for the application of the illegality doctrine, but the existence of legal responsibility for intentional or negligent unlawful conduct. Moral turpitude is a clear and understandable basis for the rationale of the illegality doctrine, but a criminal offence based on negligence, which certainly engages questions of legal responsibility, rather than moral responsibility (at least in some cases), is a technical reason for denying a claimant a right of recourse for the consequences of its negligence. Of course, there may be cases where this accords with the public policy, but there may be many cases where it does not.

That all said, ultimately, there are no inflexible rules or automatic bars to recovery simply because, a claimant has to rely on its own illegality to found its claim or the claim made falls within the narrow form of the *ex turpi causa* principle.

The Court should consider the public policy and apply the doctrine flexibly after consideration of: (a) the underlying purpose of the prohibition which has been transgressed and whether that purpose will be enhanced by denial of the claim, (b) any other relevant public policy on which the denial of the claim may have an impact and (c) whether denial of the claim would be a proportionate response to the illegality.[55] That is, the mere fact that the claimant has committed an illegal act, even deliberately, does not mean that the *ex turpi causa* doctrine will automatically debar the claim.[56] However, as matters stand, these considerations have not overruled the law set out in *Gray v Thames Trains Ltd*.[57]

This issue was discussed recently by the Court of Appeal, in *Lewis-Ranwell v G4S Health Services (UK) Ltd*,[58] in its consideration of the application of the illegality doctrine to a claim made by a person who suffered from mental health problems and who had killed three men against his healthcare providers. The defendants argued that the claim should not be allowed on the grounds of illegality. However, the claimant had been found not guilty of murder by reason of insanity. In those circumstances, the Court of Appeal held that the illegality doctrine did not undermine the claim. The Court of Appeal, however, took the opportunity to comment on the role of moral turpitude in the application of the doctrine.

Underhill, LJ commented as follows:

> 32. … there is one aspect of the general law of illegality which, as will appear, is relevant to the analysis. There are a number of authorities which hold that the *ex turpi causa* principle has no application where the claimant was unaware of the unlawfulness in question. Two older cases in particular – *Adamson v Jarvis* (1827) 4 Bing 66, and *Burrows v Rhodes* [1899] 1 QB 816 – are regularly cited, but we were also referred to the judgment of Lord Sumption JSC in *Les Laboratoires Servier v Apotex Inc* [2015] AC 430 and to some observations by Lord Toulson JSC in Patel v Mirza …
>
> 36. In *Les Laboratoires Servier* the issue was whether the *ex turpi causa* defence could apply where the claim was based on a civil wrong. Lord Sumption JSC, with whom the majority agreed, held that it could not. Although that is a long way from the issue with which we are concerned in this case, we were referred to two passages in Lord Sumption JSC's judgment.
>
> 37. The first is at para 25, where he says (I omit some parts in the interests of brevity):
>
> > 'The *ex turpi causa* principle is concerned with claims founded on acts which are contrary to the public law of the state and engage the public interest. The paradigm

[55] *Hounga v Allen* [2014] UKSC 47; [2014] 1 WLR 2889, at [42, 55]; *Patel v Mirza* [2016] UKSC 42; [2016] 3 WLR 399; *Sainsbury's Supermarkets Ltd v Mastercard Incorporated* [2018] EWCA Civ 1536; [2019] Bus LR 198; *Wallett v Vickers* [2018] EWHC 3088 (QB); [2019] Lloyd's Rep IR 205, at [35–37]; *Khan v Hussein* [2019] CSOH 11; 2019 SLT 319.

[56] For an example of cases where illegality did not debar the claim, see *Barrowfen Properties Limited v Patel* [2021] EWHC 2055 (Ch), at [337–340, 695–696]; *RO v Gray* [2021] EWHC 2770 (QB); [2022] 1 WLR 1484.

[57] [2009] UKHL 33; [2009] AC 1339.

[58] [2024] EWCA Civ 138; [2024] 2 WLR 1377, at [30–39].

> case is, as I have said, a criminal act. In addition, it is concerned with a limited category of acts which, while not necessarily criminal, can conveniently be described as "quasi-criminal" because they engage the public interest in the same way … this additional category of non-criminal acts giving rise to the defence includes cases of dishonesty or corruption … …'

The defendants sought to apply the terminology of 'engagement of the public interest' and 'quasi-criminality' to cases like the present where a criminal act is done albeit that the actor had no criminal responsibility. But Lord Sumption JSC was not concerned in this passage with the issue of culpability. He was deploying those terms in order to make clear that the availability of the defence was limited to acts which were crimes, or which engaged the public interest in the same way as a crime, and did not therefore extend to civil wrongs. In fact all his examples of 'quasi-criminality' involve conscious wrongdoing.

38. Lord Sumption JSC does, however, address the question of unwitting wrongdoing in para 29 of his judgment, where he considers 'exceptional cases where even criminal and quasi-criminal acts will not constitute turpitude for the purposes of the illegality defence'. One such class of case is where the acts in question are trivial and would not normally be regarded as morally culpable. More pertinently for our purposes, he observes that where the relevant unlawful act is an offence of strict liability 'the fact that … the claimant was not aware of the facts making his conduct unlawful may provide a reason for holding that it is not turpitude at all' because it lacked the necessary 'moral culpability'. That is in line with the older cases referred to above, and in fact he cites *Burrows v Rhodes*.

39. As for *Patel v Mirza*, the defendants point out that in para 93 of his judgment Lord Toulson JSC set out a list of factors suggested by Professor Burrows as potentially relevant if a policy-based approach were adopted, and that these included, as (b), 'whether the party seeking enforcement knew of, or intended, the conduct'. At para 107 Lord Toulson JSC described that list as 'helpful' but continued:

> 'I would not attempt to lay down a prescriptive or definitive list because of the infinite possible variety of cases. Potentially relevant factors include the seriousness of the conduct, its centrality to the contract, *whether it was intentional* and whether there was marked disparity in the parties' respective culpability'. (Emphasis supplied.)

The defendants argue that that shows that knowledge or intentionality of wrongdoing on the part of the claimant is not to be regarded as a prerequisite for the operation of the illegality defence but simply as a factor to be taken into account. That is correct as far as it goes, but Lord Toulson JSC himself emphasised that he was speaking at a level of extreme generality. What he says is not inconsistent with the usual position being in accordance with the cases identified above, and the reference to intentionality may well be directed principally to cases of the kind referred to by Lord Sumption JSC in *Les Laboratoires Servier*. In any event, it is important to bear in mind the point made at para 31 above: we are not starting from a clean slate …

The Court of Appeal therefore appeared to consider that the fact that the relevant unlawful conduct was intentional is not of itself sufficient to disengage the illegality doctrine, but it is a highly material circumstance on which to justify the application of the doctrine.

IV. The Illegality Doctrine Applied to Fines

There are a number of decisions which deal with the recoverability of a fine by way of damages or indemnity. In cases where the fine is imposed as a penalty for a criminal offence,[59] the Court has held that the fine is irrecoverable by reason of the *ex turpi causa* doctrine,[60] unless perhaps where there has been no intentional or criminally negligent conduct.[61]

There is one case where a civil or administrative penalty was treated as attracting the *ex turpi causa* doctrine. In *Safeway Stores Ltd v Twigger*,[62] the claimant companies participated in commercial initiatives which resulted in an increase in the selling price of milk and other dairy products. The claimants admitted that they had thus breached section 2(1) of the Competition Act 1998 and they became liable to pay a penalty to the Office of Fair Trading under section 36 of the 1998 Act. The claimants sought to recover an indemnity for the penalty from the defendant employees and directors of the claimants, who had been responsible for the claimants' participation in the initiatives. At first instance, Flaux, J held that the illegality defence could extend to anti-competitive acts. In considering the argument that the doctrine applies only to cases of moral turpitude, Flaux, J said:

> 26. … I accept the underlying principle enunciated in *United Project Consultants Pte Ltd v Leong Kwok Onn* [2005] 4 SLR 214, that before the *ex turpi causa* rule can apply, there must be an element of moral turpitude or moral reprehensibility involved in the relevant conduct …
>
> 28. In my judgment, anti-competitive acts in breach of the prohibition in Chapter I of the Competition Act 1998 do involve the necessary element of moral reprehensibility or turpitude and are sufficiently serious to engage the *ex turpi causa* rule in principle. I have reached this conclusion for a number of reasons.
>
> 29. First, it has been held by the Court of Appeal in the context of what is now article 81 of the EC Treaty, which is in almost identical terms to section 2 of the Competition Act 1998, that an agreement which is in breach of the prohibition in that article is an illegal agreement and that a party to such an agreement cannot claim damages for loss caused by being a party to the illegal agreement …

[59] In *United Project Consultants Pte Ltd v Leong Kwok Onn*, the penalty was imposed for breach of the Singaporean revenue laws; it is unclear if the penalty was criminal or administrative in nature.

[60] *Askey v Golden Wine Co Ltd* [1948] 2 All ER 35, 38–39; *Osman v J Ralph Moss Ltd* [1970] 1 Lloyd's Rep 313, 316–320; *Griffin v UHY Hacker Young & Partners* [2010] EWHC 146 (Ch); [2010] PNLR 20, at [47, 59–60].

[61] *Osman v J Ralph Moss Ltd* [1970] 1 Lloyd's Rep 313.

[62] [2010] EWHC 11 (Comm); [2010] Bus LR 974, at [26–43, 99–105] (Flaux, J); [2010] EWCA Civ 1472; [2011] 1 Lloyd's Rep 462, at [16–18, 23, 26, 44] (CA).

> 32. The second reason why the acts of the defendants for which the claimants are responsible under the Competition Act 1998 are sufficiently serious to engage the *ex turpi causa* rule in principle is that, whilst proceedings brought by the OFT which result in the imposition of a penalty are not criminal, this is essentially so that domestic law under the statute is in line with European law under the Treaty or Directives, as expressly provided for by section 60 of the Act. The penalties which the European Commission can impose for anti-competitive acts are regarded as of an 'administrative' nature, so as to avoid legal and political arguments relating to sovereignty which might arise if the Commission had power to impose criminal sanctions …
>
> 36. The third reason is that, although the penalty which the OFT may impose is a civil or administrative penalty, it has many of the characteristics of a fine imposed for commission of a criminal offence. …
>
> 39. The purpose of the penalty, as with a fine, is twofold: punishment and deterrence, but not compensation. As with fines, any penalty is paid into the Consolidated Fund. That the purpose is punishment and deterrence is clear from the OFT's guidance as to the appropriate amount of a penalty (December 2004). This states, in Part 1 at para 1.4, that the twin objectives of the policy of the OFT on penalties are to impose penalties on infringing undertakings which reflect the seriousness of the infringement and to ensure that the threat of penalties will deter undertakings from anti-competitive practices …
>
> 43. In all the circumstances, I accept the defendants' submissions that (i) an infringement of the Chapter I prohibition is a sufficiently serious wrongful act to engage the *ex turpi causa* rule in principle and (ii) a penalty imposed by the OFT under section 36 of the Competition Act 1998 is akin to a fine. It follows that the authorities dealing with the recoverability or otherwise of fines in civil proceedings are relevant and applicable by analogy.

Flaux, J then went on to consider the relevant authorities and concluded:

> 99. I agree with Mr Mitchell that the *Cointat* case [1913] 2 KB 220 is a somewhat unsafe foundation for the principle which the Court of Appeal was enunciating but, none the less, the *Osman* case [1970] 1 Lloyd's Rep 313 is clear authority for the principle that a fine or penalty will be recoverable where the claimant was not negligent or otherwise personally at fault, nor do I consider that the application of the principle is limited to strict liability offences properly so called. I should add in parenthesis that the cases refer to gross or culpable or crass negligence. I accept Mr Mitchell's submission that these are no more than epithets and that on analysis, none of the cases is suggesting that something more than negligence would have to be shown before recovery of a fine was precluded on the grounds of public policy …

Flaux, J refused summary judgment because whether the claimant was personally or vicariously liable was a triable issue. The Court of Appeal reversed the ultimate decision of Flaux, J and held that that public policy (the *ex turpi causa maxim* principle) operated as a defence where the claimant was directly at fault and that the claimants' liability to pay a penalty under section 36 of the 1998 Act was not vicarious but was personal because the penalty could only be imposed on them if they had intentionally or negligently infringed section 2(1) of the Act; that it would be inconsistent with that liability for the claimants to be able to recover the amount of the penalty in the civil courts from the defendants. Longmore, LJ described the illegality doctrine as follows:

> 16. Although the maxim goes back at least as far as the judgment of Lord Mansfield CJ in *Holman v Johnson* (1775) 1 Cowp 341 its modern application dates from *Tinsley v Milligan* [1994] AC 340, which held, overruling *Euro-Diam Ltd v Bathurst* [1990] 1 QB 1, that the courts had no discretion in relation to the maxim. The modern law has now culminated in *Gray v Thames Trains Ltd* [2009] AC 1339 when Lord Hoffmann said, at para 30, that it expressed not so much a principle as a policy, and at para 32, that it was a rule which may be stated in a narrower form and a wider form. In its narrower form it is that a claimant cannot recover for damage which is the consequence of a sentence imposed upon him for a criminal act; in its wider version it is that a claimant may not recover for damage which is the consequence of his own criminal act. Both versions of the rule are often in play, as they are in the present case because it is said that recovery of the penalty likely to be imposed by the OFT is recovery for the consequence of a sentence for the criminal (or quasi-criminal) act of entering into an illegal agreement, whereas recovery of the costs of the OFT investigation is recovery for the consequences of making the illegal agreement. The main difference between the application of the two forms of the rule appears to be that there is no question of any causation problem in the application of the narrower version, whereas difficult problems of causation may (in theory) arise if it is only the broader version of the rule on which reliance can be placed: see *Gray*'s case [2009] AC 1339, para 51. The rationale of the maxim is the need for the criminal courts and the civil courts to speak with a consistent voice. It would be inconsistent for a claimant to be criminally and personally liable (or liable to pay penalties to a regulator such as the OFT) but for the same claimant to say to a civil court that he is not personally answerable for that conduct.
>
> 17. Most of the cases in which the maxim has been applied to criminal or illegal acts and their consequences have been cases in which the crime or other illegal act has involved a mental element …
>
> 18. It has not been expressly decided whether the maxim (in either its narrower or wider version) applies where the criminal act is one of strict liability and the claimant may not have been at fault at all. The closest case is *Askey v Golden Wine Co Ltd* [1948] 2 All ER 35, in which Mr Askey had been convicted of offences under the then applicable Food and Drugs legislation and was held to be unable to recover an indemnity for the consequences of his punishment, but it was clear that Mr Askey had in fact acted intentionally or in a criminally negligent way. The problem of strict liability offences need not, however, concern the court in this case because section 36(3) of the 1998 Act makes it clear that the OFT may only impose a penalty if it is satisfied that the infringement 'has been committed intentionally or negligently by the undertaking'. We must therefore proceed on the basis that the claimants are attempting to recover damages for the consequences of an infringement committed intentionally or negligently.

It was argued that the claimant companies were not personally at fault, instead their employees were at fault. Longmore, LJ rejected this submission, stating that:

> This submission misunderstands or misapplies the use of the word 'personally' as applied in the requirement for the claimant to be 'personally' at fault. No one is liable

> for the penalty imposed by the 1998 Act except the relevant undertaking. The liability is therefore personal to the undertaking. If there is a liability it cannot be imposed on any person other than the undertaking, and the undertaking is personally liable for the infringement. If a penalty is imposed it will only be because the undertaking itself has intentionally or negligently committed the infringement. In those circumstances it is the undertaking which is personally at fault (there can be no one else who is), and once the maxim is engaged the undertaking cannot say that it was not personally at fault in order to defeat the application of the maxim. The whole hypothesis of the undertaking's liability is that it is personally at fault.

Pill, LJ also held that the policy of the 1998 Act is to protect the public and that the policy of the statute would be undermined if the claimants were entitled to pass on the liability to others, including employees or their insurers. The Court left open the question whether the principle applies where the liability of the company is personal but the offence is one of strict liability so there has been no intention or negligence on the part of any person.

Thus, in *Safeway Stores Ltd v Twigger*, the issue concerned the penalties imposed under section 36 of the Competition Act 1998 and Flaux, J said that for the illegality doctrine to apply 'there must be an element of moral turpitude or moral reprehensibility involved in the relevant conduct', but considered that a penalty for anti-competitive acts, whether deliberate or negligent, was sufficient to attract the doctrine; the judge equated this particular (competition law) administrative penalty with a criminal sanction.[63] The Court of Appeal, however, considered that where negligence is the foundation of the unlawful conduct, that may well be sufficient to engage the illegality doctrine.[64]

In *Khan v Hussain*,[65] the Scottish Court accepted that the principle applied to regulatory fines. However, in *Stone & Rolls Ltd v Moore Stephens*,[66] Lord Walker said that: '… it seems unlikely that such a regulatory breach, not involving dishonesty, would bring the *ex turpi causa* principle into play'. On the other hand, in *Les Laboratoires Servier v Apotex Inc*,[67] Lord Sumption considered that the public interest (in the form of this doctrine) can be engaged in cases where there has been 'the infringement of statutory rules enacted for the protection of the public interest and attracting civil sanctions of a penal character, such as the competition law', but otherwise breaches of a statutory duty giving rise to private law claims require dishonesty to engage the doctrine.

[63] See also *Sainsbury's Supermarkets Ltd v Mastercard Incorporated* [2016] CAT 11; [2016] Comp AR 33 (CAT), at [307, 327, 333–335]; [2018] EWCA Civ 1536; [2019] Bus LR 198 (CA), at [42]; *D Geddes (Contractors) Ltd v Neil Johnson Health & Safety Services Ltd* [2017] CSOH 42; [2018] Lloyd's Rep IR 264, at [19].

[64] This is consistent with the approach adopted in *D Geddes (Contractors) Ltd v Neil Johnson Health & Safety Services Ltd* [2017] CSOH 42; [2018] Lloyd's Rep IR 264, at [17–19].

[65] [2019] CSOH 11; 2019 SLT 319, at [27–40].

[66] [2009] 1 AC 1391, at [179].

[67] [2014] UKSC 55; [2015] 1 AC 430.

V. The Illegality Doctrine as applied to Insurance Contracts

The question arises how the illegality doctrine should be applied to insurance claims in cases of fines levied for unlawful conduct, where the conduct was itself not deliberate or wilful. It should be observed that few of the authorities considered above are insurance cases.[68]

The traditional rules developed in respect of the doctrine illegality – the *Bowmakers* and *Beresford* rules – have generally been applied to insurance claims.[69] Thus, in *Sea Glory Maritime Co v Al Sagr National Insurance Co*,[70] the Court summarised the principles as follows:

> … the court may refuse to enforce a claim on a policy where the assured, in order to advance it, has to rely on ('plead and prove') his own unlawful conduct (*Bowmakers Ltd v Barnet Instruments Ltd* [1945] KB 65), at least in the case of major transgressions … Similarly, a claim under a contract of insurance will not be enforced where the effect of enforcing the claim would be to enable the assured to profit from his own crime and/or to be indemnified against the adverse consequences of his own wrongdoing (*Beresford v Royal Insurance Co Ltd* [1938] AC 586).

In most cases, it is the dishonesty or deliberate conduct of the claimant which has a disabling effect on its claim. Thus, in *Charlton v Fisher*,[71] Rix, LJ said:

> 51. It is a basic rule of insurance law that a contract of insurance does not cover an assured against his deliberate or wilful infliction of loss, at any rate in the absence of express stipulation or necessary implication. This is a matter of construction, quite apart from public policy …
>
> 82. In this connection, *Hardy v MIB* and *Gardner v Moore* are authorities binding on this court to the effect that an insured cannot recover under his motor policy, even if it would otherwise cover the risk, where he claims in respect of a liability which he has incurred as a result of his deliberate and wilful criminal act of intentional damage or injury.

This explains why, at least prior to *Patel v Mirza*,[72] any illegality doctrine might be alleviated, in claims for restitution, where the claimant repents by voluntarily withdrawing from the illegal conduct before it is completed.[73] If the relevant conduct is

[68] The insurance cases include *James v British General Insurance Co Ltd* [1927] 2 KB 311; *Hardy v Motor Insurers Bureau* [1964] QB 745; *Osman v J Ralph Moss Ltd* [1970] 1 Lloyd's Rep 313; *Sea Glory Maritime Co v Al Sagr National Insurance Co* [2013] EWHC 2116; [2014] 1 Lloyd's Rep 14; *Clark v Farley* [2018] EWHC 1007 (QB); [2019] RTR 21.

[69] See eg, *MacGillivray on Insurance Law* (15th ed, London, Sweet & Maxwell, 2022), at para 14-002.

[70] [2013] EWHC 2116; [2014] 1 Lloyd's Rep 14, at [298].

[71] [2001] EWCA Civ 112; [2001] Lloyd's Rep IR 387, at [51, 82].

[72] H Beale (ed), *Chitty on Contracts* (35th ed, London, Sweet & Maxwell, 2023) para 19–188, 19–193.

[73] The claimant is said to be allowed a '*locus poenitentiae*'. See *Tribe v Tribe* [1996] Ch 107, 135; *Collier v Collier* [2002] EWCA Civ 1095, at [107–112]; *21st Century Logistic Solutions Limited (in liquidation) v Madysen Limited* [2004] EWHC 231 (QB); [2004] 2 Lloyd's Rep 92 at [23].

less than deliberate misconduct, for example negligence, the claimant will not have that opportunity (because it might not realise that there was any illegal or immoral conduct to purge), and paradoxically would be worse off (as far as its claim is concerned) than a dishonest claimant.

To repeat, the question arises whether, in the context of an insurance claim, the illegality doctrine should be applied to disable the claim under a policy only where there is wilful or deliberate unlawful conduct or other conduct which clearly and cogently engages the public interest (eg, unlawful discrimination under the Equality Act 2010),[74] or whether the doctrine should extend to other instances of unlawful conduct, based on negligence.[75]

In *Lewis-Ranwell v G4S Health Services (UK) Ltd*,[76] the Court of Appeal alluded to this issue:

> I should add that there are many other decisions, particularly in the context of claims under an insurance policy or the like, in which the *ex turpi causa* rule has been formulated by the court in terms that refer explicitly to knowing wrongdoing. Examples are *Hardy v Motor Insurers' Bureau* [1964] 2 QB 745, 760, where Lord Denning MR refers to the conduct necessary to attract the defence as 'wilful and culpable', and *Gray v Barr* [1971] 2 QB 554, where he uses the same phrase (p 568H).

The Courts appear to recognise the application of the doctrine to administrative penalties imposed by reason of regulatory breaches, such as here, given that there is a relevant public interest. There is much to be said in favour of the view that the denial of a claim would not harm the public interest and would not be proportionate. This is because the obtaining of insurance against the civil consequences of one's negligence is well understood and is an endemic feature of commercial life (indeed, it is a mandatory legal or regulatory requirement in some cases). There is no public policy objection to the recovery of damages or claims for contribution or an indemnity based on the claimant's own negligence.[77] The indemnification of a civil or administrative fine, imposed by reason of negligence, is not meaningfully different. Further, such indemnification is not at odds with the punishment of negligent conduct. The existence of such insurance further ensures that any

[74] There are additional considerations, in particular whether there is a regulatory requirement that an insurer not provide insurance cover against or pay a claim in respect of regulatory breaches. The FCA Handbook, by General Provision 6 ('Insurance against financial penalties') (*Colinvaux and Merkin's Insurance Contract Law* (London, Sweet & Maxwell, 2024) para B-0505). provides that no firm may enter into, arrange, claim on or make a payment under a contract of insurance that is intended to have, or has or would have, the effect of indemnifying any person against all or part of a financial penalty (rule 6.1.5). There is a similar prohibition in respect of insurance contracts placed at Lloyd's (rule 6.1.6). However, these prohibitions relate only to 'a financial penalty that the FCA has imposed, or may impose, under the Act. It does not include a financial penalty imposed by any other body' (rule 6.1.4).

[75] *Chitty on Contracts*, para 19-083.

[76] [2024] EWCA Civ 138; [2024] 2 WLR 1377 at [35].

[77] See *James v British General Insurance Company Ltd* [1927] 2 KB 311 and *Wallett v Vickers* [2018] EWHC 3088 (QB); [2019] Lloyd's Rep IR 205.

penalties imposed by a regulator or any liability to a third party will be met, if the insured is financially incapable of honouring such liability.

Moreover, it is well accepted that in general a claimant can insure against the adverse financial consequences of its own negligent conduct, such as its liability to pay damages to a third party, but not the adverse consequences of its fraudulent or dishonest conduct. Unless the negligence amounted to criminal negligence (ie, a criminal offence), it is difficult to justify a distinction between debarring a claim for an indemnity for an administrative penalty and allowing a claim for an indemnity for damages to a third party, where the same civil negligence gives rise to both liabilities. The most obvious ground of distinction lies in the policy of deterrence, but the very exercise and publicity associated with the levying of a fine and the impact of such a fine on the cost of insurance makes this distinction less convincing.[78]

It might be that the recoverability of an indemnity under an insurance policy attracts different considerations of public policy than a claim for an indemnity against a non-insurer third party.[79] There is some support amongst commentators on this approach.[80]

In an extra-judicial speech, 'Insurance Law – A View from the Bench', on 19th September 2013, the Chief Justice of New South Wales said:[81]

> 40. Moving away from the criminal realm the next obvious question in relation to penalties imposed on directors is whether the public policy exception for intentional criminal conduct should be extended to prevent recovery for civil penalty provisions under the Corporations Act, for example a penalty imposed for failure to act in the best interests of the company. A related issue is whether directors should be able to recover for loss of income incurred due to being subject to a disqualification order under s 206C of the Corporations Act, consequent on breaching a civil penalty provision.
>
> 41. At the moment, I would suggest, it is widely accepted that directors can indemnify themselves in such circumstances. While some D&O insurance policies have an unqualified exclusion on fines and penalties, others provide for some cover for 'pecuniary penalties' and I am aware of cases where such insurance has been available and utilised.

[78] In *Pecuniary Penalties – Guidance for Legislative Design*, Report no 133 (Aug 2014), the New Zealand Law Commission set out as Guideline G16 (page 149) in designing legislation on this issue: 'The deterrent effect of the penalty. Would the availability of indemnification significantly dilute the deterrent effect of a pecuniary penalty provision? Or does the disciplinary effect of indemnification and insurance contribute to the deterrence objectives of the pecuniary penalty regime? Similarly, would those insured prefer to allow the breach and recover under their insurance policies rather than to avoid the breach altogether?'.

[79] Note the lack of restriction in connection with the obtaining of D&O insurance in sect 233 of the Companies Act 2006, and the restriction placed upon other forms of indemnity where the director is liable to pay a regulatory fine or penalty under sect. 234 of the 2006 Act.

[80] See eg, J Goudkamp, '*Ex Turpi Causa* and Immoral Behaviour in the Tort Context' (2011) 127 *Law Quarterly Review* 354.

[81] See also New Zealand Law Commission, *Pecuniary Penalties – Guidance for Legislative Design*, Report no 133 (Aug 2014) Ch 15.

> 42. The question of whether indemnity should be available for civil penalties, or for the personal financial consequences of breaching a civil penalty provision is a difficult one.
>
> 43. On the one hand allowing insurance in such circumstances tends to negate, or at least significantly undermine the deterrent and punitive goals that underlie the imposition of such penalties …
>
> 44. Further, civil penalties, although not criminal in nature, nonetheless occupy a somewhat 'hybrid position' between the civil and criminal law …
>
> 46. The factors I have outlined tend to point away from insurance being available, at least in relation to civil penalties. Nonetheless, I am wary of the public policy exception for criminal penalties being extended in this way. To my mind, excluding indemnity for civil penalty provisions would be at odds with the general acceptance that insurance is available for the civil consequences of negligent behaviour. Breaches amounting to civil penalty provisions may often be the result of honest but careless behaviour …
>
> 47. No doubt, the exclusion of indemnity in these circumstances would also cause great consternation in boardrooms across the country, and justifiably so. Because companies are incapable of indemnifying directors for civil penalties pursuant to section 199A of the Corporations Act,[82] the availability of directors and officers insurance may be the only thing standing between a director and personal bankruptcy …
>
> 48. It must be remembered that there are ever increasing obligations on company directors and advisors, in particular auditors … it does not seem to me unreasonable that directors should be able to protect themselves from liability for civil penalties as well as liability to third parties …

That all said, there are powerful arguments to be made to the contrary and that a claim for the recovery of a fine is to be denied by reason of the illegality doctrine, because:

i) Denying recovery of the fine under an insurance policy would fall within the narrower form of the doctrine and would in effect condone wrongful behaviour which should be punished.
ii) There is a deterrent element to be respected and that deterrent element might be dulled by allowing the insurance claim.[83]
iii) There are a number of decisions of the Courts where mere negligence is said to justify the application of the doctrine to any claim for the recovery of an administrative penalty. The decision in *Safeway Stores Ltd v Twigger* is the most significant in this context.[84]
iv) Some commentators have supported this contrary view.[85]

[82] The restriction is qualified in the United Kingdom: ss.232-234 of the Companies Act 2006.

[83] *Askey v Golden Wine Co Ltd* [1948] 2 All ER 35, 38; *Safeway Stores Ltd v Twigger* [2010] EWHC 11 (Comm); [2010] Bus LR 974, at [39] (Flaux, J); *Gujra v Roath* [2018] EWHC 854 (QB); [2018] 1 WLR 3208, at [30]; *Khan v Hussain* [2019] CSOH 11; 2019 SLT 319.

[84] [2010] EWHC 11 (Comm); [2010] Bus LR 974, at [99]. See also *D Geddes (Contractors) Ltd v Neil Johnson Health & Safety Services Ltd* [2017] CSOH 42; [2018] Lloyd's Rep IR 264.

[85] See eg, Milligan, 'Can You Recover a Criminal Penalty in Criminal Proceedings?' (2017) 136 *Reparation Bulletin* 2–4.

That said, if the fine is imposed upon an employer or principal for the deliberate or negligent conduct of its employee or agent, there may be no public policy to protect and the insurance of such liability for the fine may be insurable,[86] although questions may arise as to whether the conduct of the employee or agent is to be attributed to the employer or principal as their own conduct or whether the liability is merely vicarious.[87] Similarly, it has been said that if the insured's rights have been transferred to a third party by statute, such as under the Third Parties (Rights against Insurers) Act 2010, public policy will not prevent the claim being made by the third party (so long as that third party has not been privy to any disqualifying illegal conduct).[88] This is because the illegality doctrine attaches itself to the claimant as a personal disability, as opposed to the claim itself. However, such an assertion ignores the derivative nature of the third party's title to sue by reason of a statutory assignment.[89]

VI. Conclusion

The doctrine of illegality which, if applied, disables a civil claim on the grounds that the claimant must rely on its own unlawful conduct is a doctrine to be considered by the Court in its application in the round, having regard to the public interest. The difficulty in many cases is knowing with sufficient clarity what that public interest is. It is at its most clear, it is suggested, where the conduct is deliberate or wilful and therefore there may be said to be moral turpitude. However, there are many circumstances where a claimant will have suffered loss, including having been punished by a criminal, administrative or regulatory fine, in circumstances where the claimant's conduct was neither deliberate nor wilful. In those circumstances, the question arises whether the public interest should disqualify the claim. It is difficult to see why it should do so, if the conduct is simply that of negligence or less egregious conduct (for example in the case of a strict liability defence).

[86] *Lancashire County Council v Municipal Mutual Insurance Ltd* [1996] 3 All ER 545. See eg, P Watts, 'Illegality and Agency Law: Authorising Illegal Action' (2011) *Journal of Business Law* 213.

[87] *Safeway Stores Ltd v Twigger* [2010] EWCA Civ 1472; [2011] 1 Lloyd's Rep 462, at [16–18, 23, 44] (CA).

[88] *Total Graphics Ltd v AGF Insurance Ltd* [1997] 1 Lloyd's Rep 599, 606; *Charlton v Fisher* [2001] EWCA Civ 112; [2001] Lloyd's Rep IR 387, at [83–84].

[89] *Charlton v Fisher* [2002] QB 578, [92]–[97].

PART II

Insuring Various Emerging Risks: Environmental Risks

7

The New Zealand Experience of Insuring against Natural Catastrophes

ROB MERKIN KC*

I. Introduction[1]

New Zealand has some of the most spectacular scenery on the planet. But all good things come at a price, and for New Zealand that price is geological instability. The country straddles the Australian and Pacific Tectonic Plates and is riddled with fault lines. The result is an average of some 14,000 earthquakes per year, although no more than 200 are of sufficient size to be felt. In 2018 Lloyd's of London estimated that earthquakes and other natural catastrophes cost New Zealand 0.66% of its annual Gross Domestic Product, second in the world only to Bangladesh at 0.83%.[2] It is disconcerting to relax on a beautiful New Zealand beach under to a sign declaring it to be a Tsunami Emergency Evacuation Point.

The history of recorded significant earthquakes in New Zealand was published in a Parliamentary Research Paper on 17 February 2021.[3] This document provides details of the earthquakes on: 23 January 1855 (magnitude of 8.2, the most powerful to date, Wellington); 1 September 1888 (North Canterbury); 16 November 1901 (Canterbury and Christchurch); 9 March 1929 (Arthur's Pass); 17 June 1929 (Murchison); 3 and 13 February 1931 (Hawke's Bay, with at least 256 fatalities); 5 March 1934 (Hawke's Bay again); and 24 June and 2 August 1942 (Wellington).

The early earthquakes led to revisions to safety codes on the construction of buildings, and ad hoc compensation had been provided by the Government. In particular, the 1929 and 1931 earthquakes triggered financial assistance payments, taxation relief and loans to local authorities. The 1942 earthquakes prompted more

* The author is grateful to Franziska Arnold-Dwyer and Sophie Hudson for their comments on an earlier draft of this paper.

[1] J McLean, *The Legal Framework for Emergencies in Aotearoa New Zealand* [2022] NZLC SP23.

[2] *A World at Risk: Closing the Insurance Gap*. pdf-lloyds-underinsurance-report-final.pdf.

[3] Major New Zealand earthquakes since 1855 – New Zealand Parliament. www.parliament.nz; G Belton-Brown, 'Revolution or Evolution? The Response of the Law to Earthquakes in New Zealand 1848–1948' (2012) 18 *Canterbury Law Review* 213.

generalised action in the form of the Earthquake and War Damage Act 1944, which came into force in 1945.[4] The most serious earthquake activity was confined to the South Island and to the south of the North Island, but it was nevertheless thought appropriate 'to work out a principle under which the whole loss is deemed to be a national loss, and under which those people who might be affected will subscribe towards a fund to meet losses which may come to any of them'.[5] The 1944 Act built upon the model established by the War Damage Act 1941 which had established the War Risks Commission to provide compensation from a national fund in the event of war damage, although fortunately there was never a need for it to be called upon to respond.

The 1944 Act created a single Earthquake and War Damage Commission. It was funded by levies on insurance policies on domestic and commercial buildings and provided primary layer cover for insured losses with the private market operating as excess layer insurers. The thinking behind this structure was that, without state intervention, many owners would be uninsured or underinsured, thereby requiring the state to intervene with ad hoc support. It was also thought that a national body would find it easier to seek reinsurance in international markets, thereby spreading the risks of earthquake losses away from the domestic market. The Act was subsequently amended to offer insurance for the land itself, which was, and remains, not covered by property policies sold by private insurers.[6] Further amendments brought in other natural catastrophes, including storm, flood, tsunami and volcanic activity. The extension of perils covered provided something of a national balance, given that the vast majority of volcanoes – many of which are active or at least dormant – are located on the North Island.[7] Auckland itself has been built in an earthquake field consisting of 53 dormant volcanoes.

Major earthquake incidents continued – notably on 24 May 1968 near Westport and on 2 March 1987 in the Bay of Plenty – and, after a series of inquiries and reports, a revised measure, the Earthquake Commission Act 1993, was introduced. This Act established the Earthquake Commission (EQC) in succession to the previous body. This measure was pressed into use sporadically, notably after an earthquake in Gisborne on 20 December 2007, which generated in excess of 3,000 claims against the EQC. Its most severe test was the Canterbury earthquake sequence. The first struck on 4 September 2010. The intensity was only 6.3, but its

[4] *Initial Briefing for the Purposes of the Inquiry.* eqc.govt.nz. This document contains much of the detailed statistical information set out in this chapter.

[5] Walter Nash MP, Minister of Finance, New Zealand Parliament, 28 September 1944.

[6] *Bakerland Pty Ltd v Coleridge* [2002] NSWCA 30; *Southern Response Earthquake Services Ltd v Shirley Investments Ltd* [2017] NZHC 3190.

[7] The most recent was the devastating eruption on White Island (Whakaari) on 9 December 2019, killing 22 of the 47 tourists and guides present and leading to both civil and criminal proceedings against tour operators for allegedly ignoring seismological warnings. The present author's attempt in 2013 to conquer the 20km Tongariro Crossing was thwarted at the halfway point by the earlier eruption of Mount Tongariro, coupled with rumblings from Mount Ngauruhoe famous for its casting as Mount Doom in the film adaptation of Tolkien's *Lord of the Rings* trilogy.

most harmful feature was the shallow depth of 10km, which disturbed subsurface water and by the process of liquefaction turned much of the land into unstable mud. This was followed by a series of over 11,200 aftershocks. The most intense were on 22 February 2011, which claimed 185 lives, on 13 June 2011 (twice) and on 23 December 2011. Much of Christchurch was flattened, and the city centre was left little more than a collection of piles of rubble with virtually all landmark buildings destroyed. Much of the iconic Cathedral, completed in 1865 and which had suffered damage to the spire in the 1901earthquake, collapsed.[8]

This chapter discusses the response of the insurance industry and the EQC to the Christchurch earthquakes, highlighting the deficiencies in the regime that became apparent when claims fell to be settled. The chapter considers also the interim Governmental responses and, finally, the adoption of a much-reformed scheme in the Natural Hazards Act 2023.

II. The Earthquake Commission Act 1993

The 1993 Act redesignated EQC as a Crown entity from its previous status as a body corporate. It was managed by a board. EQC was held by the courts not to be an insurer or in a contractual relationship with any claimant,[9] and so it was not bound by the various pieces of legislation applicable to insurance contracts, most importantly the Insurance Law Reform Act 1977 under which breaches of policy terms are excused in the absence of prejudice to the insurers.[10] EQC was not regulated as an insurer, although it was subject to ministerial direction. EQC's primary function was to administer insurance against natural disaster damage. Natural disasters were defined by s 2 as: earthquake, natural landslip, volcanic eruption, hydrothermal activity, tsunami and fire following a natural disaster. Much of the detail of the scheme was contained in the Earthquake Commission Regulations 1993. The insurance was to consist of three separate strands.

First, damage to residential buildings, capped at $100,000,[11] plus 12.5% General Sales Tax (GST).[12] That figure was chosen because at the time some 75% of New Zealand homes were valued at no more than $85,000, so a cap of $100,000

[8] It was originally thought to be damaged beyond repair and was to be demolished, but it was reprieved after judicial review proceedings – *Great Christchurch Buildings Trust v Church Property Trustees* [2013] NZCA 331 – and is now undergoing repairs, with full restoration scheduled for the end of 2027. A temporary replacement 'Cardboard Cathedral' was erected in 2013 on the nearby site of a destroyed church, and it has now been decided to retain this as a permanent (subject to its projected 50-year life) structure.

[9] *C & S Kelly Properties Ltd v Earthquake Commission* [2015] NZHC 1690.

[10] *AMP Fire & General Insurance Co (NZ) Ltd v Earthquake and War Damage Commission* [1983] 2 ANZ Ins Cas 60-529; *Earthquake and War Damage Commission v Waitaki International Ltd* [1992] 1 NZLR 513.

[11] All references to $ in this chapter are to NZ$.

[12] There were variations up to the cap, depending upon whether the policy specified a replacement sum: see *AD Ltd v Earthquake Commission* [2019] NZCEIT 6.

was thought to be sufficient to rebuild the vast majority of homes if they were destroyed by earthquakes or natural disasters. Top-up insurance would therefore normally not be required, or if in place would not to be called upon to respond.

'Residential buildings' were in essence private dwellings, including individual apartments within a single building and boarding houses.[13] Garages were covered. There was no cover for fences, driveways, pavings and swimming pools,[14] and buildings erected in breach of planning or other regulatory laws were ineligible. Commercial properties were excluded, and in the same way, financial loss caused by interruption to a business operated from a residential building was outside the scope of the EQC. A building that had suffered previous damage for which the EQC had paid but in respect of which repairs had not been effected could not be the subject of a further payment in the event of a second natural catastrophe. Cover could be withdrawn from a building in imminent danger of natural catastrophe damage.

Second, damage to contents was capped at $20,000. Intangible property, motor vehicles, vessels, plants, animals, jewellery, works of art, documents and money were excluded.

Thirdly, damage to residential land was capped at the value of the land, and for the purpose of this cover, only the insured perils were extended to storm and flood.

In all cases, fraudulent claims could be refused.[15]

The Act contemplated that EQC cover could – depending on the wording of private insurance – be either top-up cover sitting above the private insurance, or primary layer insurance with private policies acting as the excess layer. In practice all private policies are expressly stated to be excess layer. EQC protection was offered only where there is private insurance in place: this was referred to as 'fire insurance', but the definition meant that the policy could cover other risks as well as fire. Provision was made for direct insurance with EQC, to cover cases where private insurance was unobtainable.

EQC was to pay for the losses by way of a levy on premiums of 5% the sum insured under the policy.[16] Those were to be paid into a Natural Disaster Fund established for the purpose. EQC liabilities were subject to a Crown guarantee – funded by an annual levy on the Fund – to meet losses if the Fund were to become exhausted.[17] EQC was empowered to obtain reinsurance in the private market. The sum reinsured is currently $7 billion for aggregate losses in excess of $1.75 billion.

[13] *Morley v Earthquake Commission* [2013] NZHC 230.

[14] Although these are covered by some private insurance policies with extended definitions of 'house'.

[15] *LL v Earthquake Commission* [2021] NZCEIT 11; *LTL v Earthquake Commission* [2022] NZCEIT 38.

[16] This formulation was held to mean that the sum insured was the aggregate limit, whereas if there was no aggregate limit then the sum insured was the maximum liability that the insurers could face under the policy: *Earthquake and War Damage Commission v Waitaki International Ltd* [1992] 1 NZLR 513; *Earthquake Commission v Cigna Insurance New Zealand Ltd* 1998, unreported.

[17] As occurred in 2018.

The Act contained detailed provisions on claims and settlements, including limiting claimants to persons with insurable interest and requiring all claims to be reported to EQC within 30 days of the occurrence of natural disaster damage. Settlements could be made by way of reinstatement or cash.

The requirement for the claimant to have taken out a property policy created difficulties where the claimant was uninsured for reasons beyond his control. In *Marchand v Jackson*[18] the claimant instructed his broker to effect property insurance. The broker neglected to do so, and when telephoned by the claimant's wife to ensure that cover was in place the broker fraudulently stated that the insurance had been effected. The claimant suffered losses in the Christchurch earthquakes, but the broker's breach of duty deprived him both of insurance cover and of EQC cover.[19] The unfortunate sequel was that the broker's professional indemnity insurers successfully persuaded the Court of Appeal that the proximate cause of the claimant's loss was not the broker's negligent failure to arrange insurance but rather his fraudulent cover-up in the conversation with the claimant's wife.[20] Such are the dangers of follow-up phone calls. EQC had a discretion to pay despite the absence of insurance, but it is not known whether that discretion was exercised in this case.

III. The 1993 Act and the Canterbury Earthquakes

It was unfortunate that the first serious test of the EQC structure was for New Zealand an unprecedented calamity with which any compensation regime would have seriously struggled. Within days of the 4 September 2010 earthquake, over 185,000 EQC claims had been made, and to accommodate them, the statutory time for notification was extended from 30 days to three months.[21] The 22 February 2011 earthquake both exacerbated existing damage and created far more in its own right, and the death blows were inflicted on 13 June and 23 December. One insurer, AMI, became insolvent almost immediately, and had to be rescued by a government package that involved transferring AMI's business to a state-owned entity, Southern Response.[22] The Insurance Council of New Zealand reported in 2022[23] that the Canterbury earthquakes were the fourth most expensive global

[18] [2012] NZHC 2893.

[19] The broker's defence that the claimant was uninsurable by reason of previous convictions, so that the claimant had suffered no loss, was rejected.

[20] [2013] NZCA 302.

[21] Earthquake Commission Amendment Regulations 2010.

[22] In *Ruscoe and Thorn v Canterbury Policy Holders* [2012] 17 ANZ Ins Cas 61–921 it was decided that s 9(1) of the Law Reform Act 1936, under which a statutory charge is imposed on the proceeds of a liability policy for the benefit of a third-party claimant against the assured as from the date of the wrongful act, in principle extended to reinsurance. That gave policyholders a direct claim against AMI's reinsurers. No thought appears to be given as to how the process might have worked in practice, but the matter appears to have gone no further. The Insurance Contracts Bill 2024 removes reinsurance from the new cut-through provisions that replace the statutory charge.

[23] https://www.icnz.org.nz/industry/canterbury-earthquakes/.

natural catastrophe ever to occur. Ultimately, close to 700,000 insurance claims were made, 168,000 of them involving private insurers. The cost to the insurance industry exceeded $21 billion and it has been estimated by ICNZ that at current premium rates it would have taken some 40 years for private insurers to meet the sums paid out. The Natural Disaster Fund available to EQC stood at $5.6 billion before 2010 and was wiped out by the Christchurch earthquakes. The sum paid out by the EQC was around $10 billion, some $4 billion of which was recovered from reinsurers. In 2012 the EQC levy on premiums was trebled to 15% to assist with the shortfall. Knock-on economic losses have been estimated at a further $10 billion.[24]

The Canterbury earthquakes exposed three key difficulties for the system when faced with major catastrophe.

First, while many of the claims for property damage and business interruption were relatively straightforward and raised issues of quantum only, others produced novel and complex legal issues.[25] Policy wordings in 2010 were of some antiquity and had not contemplated the knotty problems posed by an earthquake sequence. The matters requiring resolution have included: the measure of indemnity and the standard of repair required, particularly where local laws have dictated enhanced earthquake protection for rebuilds;[26] the prospects for recovery where a building has been left uninhabitable but undamaged;[27] recovery for losses from successive earthquakes in the same policy period where repairs had not been effected or only partially effected between aftershocks, a problem exacerbated by the fact that many policyholders were underinsured so that two or more claims were necessary to make good the actual losses;[28] the operation of aggregation provisions where there was a single limit of indemnity for a 'series' of events;[29] and the assignability of insurance claims along with the sale of damaged property.[30] As an aside, and welcomed at least by lawyers, the cases on

[24] Further detail can be found in the EQC's Annual Reports, published online.

[25] See the author's anticipatory piece, 'The Christchurch Earthquakes: Insurance and Reinsurance Issues' (2012) 18 *Canterbury Law Review* 119.

[26] See, most recently: *Fitzgerald v IAG New Zealand Ltd* [2018] NZHC 3447; *Body Corporate 328564 v Vero Insurance New Zealand Ltd* [2022] NZHC 2716.

[27] *Kraal v Earthquake Commission* [2015] NZCA 13: no recovery. This case has proved important for business interruption claims arising from enforced closures after COVID-19, in that inability to use premises does not mean that they have suffered 'damage', which is the primary trigger for cover under such policies.

[28] *Ridgecrest NZ Ltd v IAG New Zealand Ltd* [2014] NZSC 117, in which the Supreme Court failed to appreciate the distinction between the date on which a cause of action accrues and the date of the right to seek payment if repairs are not carried out. This was put right very soon afterwards by the Court of Appeal in *QBE Insurance (International) Ltd v Wild South Holdings Ltd* [2015] NZCA 246.

[29] *Moore v IAG New Zealand Ltd* [2020] NZCA 319.

[30] *Xu v IAG New Zealand Ltd* [2019] NZSC 68, holding that if a damaged house was sold for full repaired value, accompanied by an assignment of the insurance claim in respect of the damage, the claim was still that of the original owner but there was no loss and thus no insurance claim because of the price received for the sale. Lawyers soon found a way round this: the purchase price was allocated to the land, with only $1 for the house itself, so that the insured loss remained unsatisfied by the proceeds of sale.

property insurance decided by the New Zealand courts since the earthquakes have made a substantial contribution to the jurisprudence on the subject, not the least in clarifying the scope of the principle of utmost good faith in the claims process and introducing into the common law the concept of damages for late payment.[31]

Secondly, the volume of claims was quite simply well beyond the capacity of the national infrastructure. A country with a population of just over 4 million necessarily has a limited supply of insurance assessors, structural engineers, surveyors and builders. The sheer scale of the task in adjusting claims and then effecting the necessary repairs was, to say the least, daunting. Policyholders in urgent need of money took quick settlements, normally without legal advice, and signed waivers with private insurers, and in some cases with the EQC,[32] whereby they accepted the agreed amount in full and final settlement of all claims known and unknown and irrespective of any mistake of fact or law. However, once judicial decisions on standard wordings and common law principles began to appear it became obvious that many of the settlements excluded legitimate heads of claim and were otherwise far short of what the law demanded. Settlements were successfully attacked on the ground of misrepresentation despite the fierce settlement wording,[33] and in 2022 EQC reported that there were some 1,361 reopened claims following 'missed damage, poor workmanship, faulty or inappropriate materials, or inappropriate or poorly lasting repairs'.[34] It is noteworthy that in December 2021 Southern Response settled a class action brought by 3,000 policyholders for some $400 million, based on undervalued early settlements,[35] although other class actions remain pending.[36] A further consequence of the extent of the damage was that poorly qualified builders were let loose on damaged houses, with the inevitable botching of repairs. Insurers who had themselves instructed builders as their agents were obviously contractually liable to put matters right under policy reinstatement clauses, but it took the High Court in *Sleight v Beckia Holdings Ltd*[37] to confirm[38] that even where

[31] *Young v Tower Insurance* [2016] NZHC 2956; *Southern Response Earthquake Insurance Services Ltd v Dodds* [2020] NZCA 395.

[32] There has to be a doubt whether such waivers are valid, because EQC has a statutory duty to pay up to cap and it surely cannot be open to EQC to attempt to contract out of that liability where its full extent became apparent after settlement. The point has not been tested.

[33] *Southern Response Earthquake Services Ltd v Dodds* [2020] NZCA 395.

[34] EQC Annual Report for 2022, p 80. See eg, *Ideal Investments Ltd v Earthquake Commission* [2022] NZHC 400.

[35] See *Southern Response Earthquake Services v Southern Response Unresolved Claims Group* [2017] NZCA 489; *Ross v Southern Response Earthquake Services* [2019] NZCA 431.

[36] *Sneesby v Southern Response Earthquake Services* [2023] NZHC 346; *Ressels v Southern Response Earthquake Services Ltd* [2023] NZCA 3344.

[37] [2020] NZHC 2851, and subsequent proceedings against the repairers, *IAG New Zealand Ltd v QBE Insurance (Australia) Ltd* [2022] NZCA 208. See also *Davern v QBE Insurance (Australia) Ltd* [2023] NZHC 2146.

[38] The Australian courts have followed suit: *Baralaba Coal Co Pty Ltd v AAI Ltd* [2024] FCA 532. The present author had previously taken a contrary view: 'Insurers' Liability for Defective Repairs' (2019) 25 *New Zealand Business Law Quarterly* 133.

insurers had simply made cash settlements so that policyholders themselves paid the builders the insurers remained liable under standard policy wordings to make good the defective work because an indemnity had not been provided. In practice, insurers released funds for repairs only if the assured appointed the insurers' nominated builder, so there is much to be said for a consistent outcome, and insurers were greatly relieved that *Sleight* classified the additional liability as contractual rather than extra-contractual, because the liability then fell within the scope of any reinsurance.

Thirdly, and most importantly for present purposes, was the relationship between EQC and insurers. EQC was initially unprepared to deal with a widespread catastrophe in terms of capacity, experience and liaison with insurers. As an emergency measure, a number of loss adjusters from overseas were brought in by EQC. In the aftermath of the 2010 earthquake the Government established the Canterbury Earthquake Recovery Authority (CERA), the powers of which were extended after the February 2011 earthquake.[39] CERA worked with EQC to put in place a programme of emergency repairs. EQC took it upon itself to effect those repairs rather than to make cash settlements and a deal was entered into with Fletcher Construction, one of the largest firms of its type in New Zealand, to undertake project management and to effect the necessary works. CERA was also responsible for introducing a traffic-light zoning system under which red zones became no-go areas. In April 2012 the one-year time limit for EQC to settle a claim was scrapped.[40]

But what really mattered was how all of this fitted in with EQC's role as a primary layer insurer. The $100,000 cap was based on 1992 house values so that by the time of the earthquakes the assumption made by the 1993 Act that private insurance would be called upon only in a small minority of cases had ceased to be true. The two-tier approach to domestic property damage meant that victims had to make separate claims, against the EQC up to cap, and against private insurers for the excess. In practice victims would not know whether their losses exceeded the cap, and it was necessary on a precautionary basis for claims to be made against both EQC and insurers.[41] Those claims clearly below the $100,000 dwellings cap and the $20,000 contents cap, along with all land damage losses, were of concern only for EQC and many were settled quickly: by the end of November 2011 EQC had resolved 84,965 dwelling claims, 15,439 land claims and 106,455 contents claims. A protocol between EQC and insurers agreed in November 2011 provided that if EQC via Fletcher undertook repair work on damage thought to be under cap, but later proving not to be so, EQC would

[39] The current legislation is the Greater Christchurch Regeneration Act 2016.

[40] Canterbury Earthquake (Earthquake Commission Act) Order 2012.

[41] The risk of a claim against an insurer being denied for being out of time has been all but removed in New Zealand by s 9 of the Insurance Law Reform Act 1977, which permits reliance on a time limit only in cases of demonstrable prejudice to the insurers. Because EQC is not an 'insurer', the section has no application to late EQC claims. But note the amendments of the 1993 Act in 2019, which extended time limits to up to two years.

nevertheless carry out the full repair and later seek reimbursement. However, wider agreement was not possible, despite government attempts in June 2011 to broker a generalised claims settlement approach.

In many cases it was unclear from the outset whether the damage was sufficiently substantial to engage the private insurers, and accordingly those insurers could do little in respect of any individual claim until EQC had concluded whether it was above or below cap.[42] A below cap determination by EQC was not of course conclusive, and it was open to a policyholder to contend that the loss exceeded the cap, so private insurers could well be required to reach their own assessment of the amount of damage. If EQC and insurers reached a different conclusion on cap, there was no agreed mechanism for resolving the dispute between them, let alone a process for joint claims-handling, and the only victim could be the policyholder anxious for payment.

Even where it was clear that a claim was above cap, the EQC and the insurers could well disagree as to whether there was coverage under the policy or whether there was an available defence. That problem was potentially limited by the fact that many policies simply shadowed the wording of the 1993 Act, but there remained plenty of room for disagreement on their application.

Factors other than coverage and quantum also gave rise to disputes. EQC insured both land and buildings, whereas insurers covered only buildings. Assume a building whose foundations were damaged by land erosion. Was that a problem that could be fixed by strengthened pilings or was it also necessary for repairs to be effected to the land? If both were required in a single operation, how were the costs to be allocated between EQC and insurers? In early declaratory proceedings, *Earthquake Commission v Insurance Council of New Zealand*,[43] the High Court established that EQC could be liable for land damage where there was increased flooding vulnerability by reason of the movement of tectonic plates during an earthquake. A further, and in practice highly significant, problem was the allocation of losses where the successive earthquakes had occurred in different policy years, particularly where the policy had renewed between any two of the earthquakes. There were reinsurance implications. EQC was reinsured under an excess of loss reinsurance treaty subscribed to by London market reinsurers whereby cover was obtained once aggregate losses (the ultimate net loss) in a policy year reached the then deductible of $1.5 billion. It favoured EQC to treat losses as falling within a single policy year so that the ultimate net loss was exceeded, and for that reason it made very little effort to allocate losses as between successive earthquakes and simply lumped them together without further investigation. Insurers, by contrast, had their own reinsurances which required proper analysis of the matter, and disputes inevitably arose.

[42] As in *W v SR* [2020] NZCEIT 20.

[43] [2014] NZHC 3138. See also: *G v Earthquake Commission* [2020] NZCEIT 10; *Freer v Earthquake Commission* [2023] NZHC 3662, where the High Court authorised a class action based on potential losses from liquefaction.

The overlapping roles of EQC and private insurers resulted in delays, disputes and also duplication of investigation costs. There was in 2017 also a major 'wash up' dispute relating to the Christchurch earthquakes between EQC and private insurers. Some private insurers had in 2011 and 2012 paid their own losses and also EQC losses on the assumption that there would be indemnification on the ordinary restitutionary principle of agreed payment of another's debt.[44] Insurers proceeded on the basis that the earthquakes were separate insured perils. They then sought indemnification from EQC for a cap payment for each earthquake, based on an early test case, Re Earthquake Commission,[45] where it was decided that by the clear terms of the 1993 Act, EQC cover reinstated for repaired damage after each earthquake. EQC insisted that in many of the cases where multiple claims had been paid by the insurers, only one cap payment was due either because there was only one loss unaffected by later quakes,[46] or because the initial earthquake had rendered the buildings total losses so that there could be no future liability. After some years of negotiation, the EQC was able to report in 2022 that agreement had been reached with the four largest insurers.[47] However, individual disputes still linger, and at time of writing there are pending proceedings on the question whether a settlement entered into by EQC on the basis that the cost of repairs was below the cap is binding and can be relied on by private insurers.[48]

By way of ironic twist, the insurers' arguments in the 'wash up' dispute came back to bite them in *Moore v IAG New Zealand Ltd*.[49] The Court of Appeal here held that a per event limit of indemnity of $2.5 million applied separately to each of the earthquakes in February and June 2011 so that two payments were required, the very opposite of what they had hoped for. In the Court's view, the use of the word 'series' in the aggregating provision, whereby an event was defined as 'a single event or series of events which have the same cause', referred to 'a linked sequence of losses occurring proximately in time', which could not be said of the earthquakes. It is perhaps little comfort to the insurers to know that, despite the Supreme Court refusing permission to appeal, the decision is out of line with authority from England and Australia which suggests that a 'series' is simply a sequence and that any required connection is to be found in any additional words in the aggregation clause, for example, 'series of related'[50] or 'series of similar'.[51]

[44] It was disputed whether there was ever a formal agreement to that effect despite Government participation in the negotiations. Note that this was not a contribution issue, as that principle applies only where there is joint liability for the same debt, whereas the sums owed by EQC and private insurers were quite separate: cf *Limit (No.3) Ltd v ACE Insurance Ltd* [2009] NSWSC 514.

[45] [2011] 3 NZLR 695.

[46] Which was certainly true in some cases: *He v Earthquake Commission* [2019] NZSC 149.

[47] EQC Annual Report 2022, p 80.

[48] *CM Trust v Tower Insurance Ltd* [2019] NZCEIT 12; *RT v IAG New Zealand* [2023] NZCEIT 3.

[49] [2020] NZCA 319.

[50] *Lord Bishop of Leeds v Dixon Coles and Gill* [2020] EWHC 2809 (Ch), affirmed without reference to this point *Baines v Dixon Coles & Gill* [2021] EWCA Civ 1211; *Distillers Co Bio-Chemicals (Aust) Pty Ltd v Ajax Insurance Co Ltd* (1974) 130 CLR 1; *Bank of Queensland Ltd v AIG Australia Ltd* [2019] NSWCA 190.

[51] *Axis Specialty Europe SE v Discovery Land Company LLC* [2024] EWCA Civ 7, where the focus was on 'similar' and not 'series'.

The potential conflicts between EQC and insurers required expert reports not just from them but also from policyholders. An unfortunate thread running through the whole claims settlement process in Christchurch was the complete unreliability of a minority of experts, many of whom seemed to forget that their overriding duty was to the court and not to the appointing party.[52] A few were 'hired guns' whose objectivity was sacrificed on the altar of money: sadly, they were associated with a small number of lawyers who secured business by promising unrealistic levels of recovery and hiring supportive experts. Others relied on modelling of the date and extent of loss, and courts were from time to time required to choose between wildly conflicting models.[53] Some experts peddled pet theories that were plainly at odds with reality. In one case it was proposed to use an untested procedure involving in effect towing a house back up a slope after it had slipped down in the earthquakes: even if this had been vaguely feasible, the policy itself demanded that only established and proven means of repairs were permissible. Disputes between reputable experts were readily resolved by the generalised use of joint reports or, in judicial proceedings themselves, by 'hot-tubbing',[54] but the evidence of others had to be carefully unpicked.

As of 30 June 2017, there were 209 outstanding claims against the EQC arising out of the Christchurch earthquakes and filed with the New Zealand courts. These relate primarily to defective repairs and underpayment.[55] Such was the volume of outstanding matters against both private insurers and EQC that in 2019 the Government passed the Canterbury Earthquakes Insurance Tribunal Act, which established a Tribunal to determine claims by householders arising from the earthquakes. This is a free service designed to produce speedy resolution, although lawyers are invariably involved and costs can be awarded where unmeritorious matters are raised.[56] Provision was made for the transfer of cases from the High Court to the Tribunal.[57] Most claims are resolved at preliminary case management conferences and mediation, and the Tribunal appoints its own experts where necessary.[58] A binding decision has been required, very often on preliminary issues of law,[59] in a few situations where the parties or their experts could not agree.[60] By September 2023 there had been 160 applications,

[52] See *Prendeville v Earthquake Commission* [2016] NZHC 3207.

[53] On modelling generally, see *Vero Insurance New Zealand v Morrison* [2015] NZCA 246.

[54] Concurrent – rather than consecutive – cross-examination of experts.

[55] Eg: *B v Earthquake Commission* [2019] NZCEIT 21; *Goodier v Earthquake Commission* [2019] NZHC 2176; *CW v Earthquake Commission* [2020] NZCEIT 39; *DW v Earthquake Commission* [2021] NZCEIT 10; *Mathias v Earthquake Commission* [2023] NZHC 705.

[56] *IAG New Zealand Ltd v Dewes* [2022] NZHC 3555; *RM v Earthquake Commission* [2023] NZCEIT 1. In *LS v Medical Insurance Society Ltd* [2021] NZCEIT 2 it was noted that claimants made use of litigation funding services.

[57] *Busby v IAG New Zealand Ltd* [2019] NZHC 1852; *Pinot Properties Ltd v Vero Insurance New Zealand Ltd* [2019] NZHC 2244; *Bolstad v Earthquake Commission* [2019] NZHC 3283.

[58] *E v IAG New Zealand Ltd* [2020] NZCEIT 24, where the Tribunal dismissed a challenge to an expert on the ground of apparent bias.

[59] The Tribunal has power to refer preliminary issues of law to the High Court. See eg, *Evans v IAG New Zealand Ltd* [2020] NZHC 1326.

[60] eg, *AG v Earthquake Commission* [2019] NZCEIT 59; *BRL v Earthquake Commission* [2019] NZCEIT 51; *BD v Southern Response Earthquake Services Ltd* [2020] NZCEIT 15; *PFWE v IAG*

149 of which were accepted as falling with the Tribunal's jurisdiction.[61] This number may not sound substantial until it is remembered that the claims arose from events occurring a dozen years earlier.

IV. Kaikoura and Moves Towards Reform

From 2012 onwards, there were numerous investigations into the performance of EQC in its response to the Canterbury earthquakes, covering matters such as the operation of the repair programme, the speed of its response for information requests, customer satisfaction and the impact on human rights. In 2013 the Government established the Residential Advisory Service, which offered free legal advice to earthquake victims with unresolved claims. In July 2015 the Treasury published a discussion document on possible changes to the 1993 Act.[62] This put out for consultation a series of proposals: (1) All claims would be lodged with private insurers rather than the EQC and (subject to the agreement between the parties) managed by them. This was an aspirational proposal, designed to foster agreements between EQC and the insurance industry. (2) Buildings cover would be extended to additional siteworks such as installation of retaining walls, thereby removing the often unworkable distinction between buildings and land damage. (3) The cap for buildings damage would be increased to $200,000. That move would ensure that private top up insurance remained affordable and would also serve to reduce the number of overlapping claims, that is, over cap claims, by about two-thirds. (4) Land damage would be paid only where rebuilding was not practicable, thereby removing claims for land where the dwelling itself was not damaged. (5) Terms and conditions would be aligned with those of private insurers, to remove friction. (6) A standard excess of $2,000 per building claim would be imposed. (7) Contents insurance by EQC would be discontinued, thereby eliminating overlap and allowing EQC to focus on buildings. (8) Premium levy rates would be reviewed at least every five years. (9) The funding model for EQC including the Natural Disaster Fund and the Crown guarantee would be retained.

Before any action could be taken to implement the proposals, further earthquakes intervened. On 14 and 29 February 2016 earthquakes rocked the Christchurch district, giving rise to some 30,000 claims. Echoing the Treasury

New Zealand Ltd [2022] NZCEIT 13; *WD v IAG New Zealand Ltd* [2022] NZCEIT 14; *PJ v Holloway Builders Ltd* [2022] NZCEIT 68.

[61] See the presentation by the Tribunal's chair, Christopher Boys, at the New Zealand Insurance Law Association Annual Conference in Wellington in September 2023: 'The Canterbury Earthquake Insurance Tribunal' nzila.org. The author is grateful to Mr Boys for detailed information on the Tribunal's operations, although less so for misconceived views on the merits of West Ham over Tottenham.

[62] 'New Zealand's Future Natural Disaster Insurance Scheme – Proposed changes to the Earthquake Commission Act 1993'.

proposal, EQC entered into an agreement with Vero, one of the leading insurers, to delegate claims-handling to Vero for its customers, and EQC's liabilities were satisfied by cash payments rather than repairs.

Much more significantly, on 14 November 2016 there was a 7.8 magnitude earthquake near the tourist town of Kaikoura, 180 km north of Christchurch and notorious for the sight of fur seals sleeping on the bonnets of cars in the seafront carpark. The earthquake caused substantial damage, resulted in 40,000 claims and two fatalities, and captured the attention of much the world's media with iconic footage showing the successful rescue of two cows and a calf stranded on the seaward side of a crack in the land opened up by the force of the quake. These additional losses again impacted the Natural Disaster Fund, and in November 2018 it proved necessary for the first time for the Fund to call upon the Crown Guarantee, from which the Fund received some $200 million.

Both EQC and private insurers were acutely aware of the relationship issues that had bedevilled Christchurch, and the partial solution to them developed early in 2016. In December 2016, again in line with the Treasury recommendation of the previous year, EQC and eight private insurers – although not NZ's largest insurer – entered into a Memorandum of Understanding (MOU) under which EQC appointed the insurers as agents to settle claims made by the insurers' policyholders. EQC was then to reimburse the insurers for sums paid out by them under the cap and was to contribute pro rata to handling costs. Land damage remained the responsibility of EQC, as did claims made against EQC where the insurers were not signatories to the MOU.

The Kaikoura experiment was a great success. Within a year 90% of the claims for which EQC was responsible had been settled,[63] and 54% of those claims for which the insurers were responsible had been settled. By June 2018 only 2% of claims remained unresolved. This prompted renewed pressure for reform. The Greater Christchurch Claims Resolution Service, established in 2018, expanded the work of the earlier Residential Advisory Service. The 1993 Act was amended by the Earthquake Commission Amendment Act 2019, which partially implanted the 2015 Treasury consultation proposals: the cap for damage to buildings was raised to $150,000, less than recommended in 2015 but nevertheless one that eliminated many over cap disputes; the per claim deductible was raised from $1,000 to $2,500; liability for contents damage was eliminated; the time limit for making claims was increased from three months to two years in cases where the damage was not reasonably have been discovered or there was some incapacity affecting the claimant's ability to give due notice; and EQC was empowered to collect information for in support of its functions under the Act and for facilitating natural disaster preparedness.

[63] EQC Annual Report for 2022, p 83, noted that the total losses did not exceed the reinsurance deductible, so there were no reinsurance recoveries for the Kaikoura event.

There remained public disquiet over the performance of EQC and the insurance industry in settling Christchurch claims in particular. With effect from 1 January 2016 the Insurance Council of New Zealand, the membership of which includes most of New Zealand's leading insurers, brought into effect a revised Fair Insurance Code which set a target of 10 days for determination of whether or not a claim should be accepted. Specific provision is made for large events:

> 37. When a catastrophe or disaster strikes we may receive a large number of claims, and we may be especially reliant on third parties. This means we may not be able to meet the timeframes set by this Code.
>
> 38. However, when a catastrophe or disaster strikes, we will: use our best efforts to meet all of our commitments in this Code; respond as quickly as possible and in a professional, practical and compassionate manner; update you at least once every 20 business days, or another such interval as we may agree with you, until your claim is resolved; and prioritise our service for our most vulnerable customers.

The Code is not legally binding, does not take effect as an implied term in contracts with ICNZ insurers[64] and does not itself contain provisions for redress, but there is a complaints procedure built into the Code.

Stuart Smith MP, a member of the then National Party, introduced the Insurance (Prompt Settlement of Claims for Uninhabitable Residential Property) Bill in 2018. This provided that an insurer (although not the EQC) that received a claim in respect of a residential property that had become uninhabitable was to take all reasonably practicable steps to ensure that the claim was processed as promptly as possible, with determination within six months of receiving the claim. The Bill was adopted for Committee consideration in 2020 but was then withdrawn on the Government's assurances that other measures were in contemplation.

There was indeed a separate response to the declining image of the insurance industry. In November 2019 the Ministry of Business, Innovation and Employment (MBIE) initiated an insurance contract law review[65] which has led to a number of consultation documents and, in 2023, the publication of a draft bill which to a large extent aligns with the law of the UK and Australia substantive New Zealand law on, most importantly, pre-contract presentation of the risk, policy terms and third party rights on insurer insolvency.[66] Although the Bill was in part prompted by the volume of complaints arising out of the Christchurch catastrophe, somewhat ironically nothing in the Bill touches upon any of the legal disputes generated by it.

By far the most important initiative post Christchurch and Kaikoura was the Government's appointment in November 2018 of a Public Inquiry into

[64] *Domenico Trustee Ltd v Tower Insurance Ltd* [2015] NZHC 981; *Kristinsson v Southern Response Earthquake Services Ltd* [2018] NZHC 2863.

[65] https://www.mbie.govt.nz/business-and-employment/business/financial-markets-regulation/insurance-contract-law-review/.

[66] The change of government following the September 2023 general election has left the fate of the Bill uncertain.

the Earthquake Commission. This was chaired by the inestimable Dame Silvia Cartwright, previously a High Court Judge and from 2001 to 2006 Governor General of New Zealand. The terms of reference were 'to investigate and report on the lessons that can be learned from the application of the EQC's operational practices and the EQC's approaches to claims outcomes in relation to the Canterbury earthquake events and subsequent events. It will make recommendations to improve the EQC's readiness to respond to future events'. The Royal Commission reported in March 2020[67] and the Report was laid before Parliament on 9 April 2020.

The Inquiry was concerned in particular to consider the experiences of customers and insurers in claims handling. To that end, the Inquiry received written evidence, held public forums and conducted interviews. By way of supplement to the Report, a separate document entitled *What We Heard*, containing feedback gathered during the investigation process, was also published.[68] The Report highlighted the demarcation disputes between insurers and the EQC. It found that there had been no formal co-operation between the EQC and private insurers in assessing claims and in sharing investigation costs. Insurance could not kick in until it had been ascertained both that the damage was caused by a natural catastrophe and that the amount of damage exceeded the cap. The EQC and insurers could take their own views on these matters, leading both to delay and also to inconsistent views. The Inquiry noted also that the structure had given rise to disagreement on coverage issues, particularly on identifying the policy year into which loss fell, whether there was one or multiple losses and whether the damage was to the land (covered only by the EQC) or also the dwelling. Finally, the sheer volume of claims had overwhelmed resources. The delays involved had damaged the reputations of the EQC and private insurers alike.

The findings of the Report were both positive and negative. The EQC was praised for its response to an unparalleled disaster, in particular for its attempts to disseminate information and engage with the public. However, the Report highlighted a number of serious defects, not just in its dealings with the private insurance market and in its claims-handling procedure but also with regard to wider structural issues. The Report found that there was in the period up to the Canterbury Earthquakes 'little or no thinking about how to manage land damage and to repair a vast swathe of urban housing', repairs were effected before proper loss assessments had been made and there was also a failure of co-ordination between the Government and the EQC in disaster-management planning. The Report also criticised the EQC for its claims-handling procedures, including unwillingness to provide data to clients and inadequate damage assessment mechanisms.

[67] Department of the Prime Minister and Cabinet (DPMC), 'Inquiry into the EQC'.

[68] 'Report: What We Heard: Summary of Feedback from the Inquiry's Public Engagement (9 April 2020) – EQC Inquiry'. dpmc.govt.nz.

The Report made a series of important recommendations. At a wider level, the EQC was urged to plan for future mass disasters, by increasing its access to data as to how natural catastrophes affect land and by research into the implications of climate change. No provision was made for this under the 1993 Act. At the claims-handling level, the concern of claimants and private insurers alike, the EQC was urged to commit to a set of principles which ensure: fairness and balance; competence; clear and transparent processes; and respect for claimants. The Report endorsed the creation of the Canterbury Earthquakes Insurance Tribunal and suggested a need for a more structured step-by-step approach to dispute resolution, involving expert determination and mediation.

Finally, the Report addressed the future of the Earthquake Commission Act 1993 suggesting:

> inserting a clear purpose statement into the EQC Act; clarifying the extent of EQC cover and key definitions (such as the reinstatement standard, apportionment and the treatment of residential areas in multi-unit buildings); giving EQC the ability to call on assistance from other state agencies; ensuring that any new functions assigned to EQC do not detract from its core responsibilities; and enabling a comprehensive and enforceable information-sharing regime that is both flexible and effective. In addition, providing EQC a more formal role in land-use planning might be worthwhile.

Of equal significance was the operation of the cap. The Report recognised that the cap was the source of much of the disagreement between the EQC and the private insurance market, giving rise to delay, and suggested that the figure should be 'sufficient to enable the average homeowner to rebuild – as was the initial intent of the cap in 1993'. That suggests a cap of an entirely different scale to the 2019 revised figure of $150,000.

In summary, the recommendations, most of which are aimed at the Government, were as follows:

(1) clarification of the EQC's role, including co-ordinating its response with that of the insurance industry and clarifying expectations about land remediation following a natural catastrophe;
(2) amending the 1993 Act to include a statement of purpose and principles;
(3) reviewing the legislative framework to resolve many of the issues that had arisen in the courts, including the meaning of phrases such as "when new" and "reinstatement";
(4) greater co-operation between Government and EQC;
(5) review of the cap of $150,000;
(6) review legislation on the standard of repairs;
(7) in the case of a multi-occupied building, clarification of the responsibilities of the EQC and private insurers to the various parts of the building;
(8) in handling claims, the EQC should be required to treat claimants with dignity, share information with claimants, provide community advice, develop clear guidelines as to how assessments were to be carried out, put in place quality assurance programmes in respect of repairs and develop policies as to reinstatement and to the making of cash payments;

(9) consideration of the adoption of a legislative requirement for private insurers to advise the EQC at least annually of their residential policyholders' location and property ownership; and

(10) in terms of dispute resolution, (i) develop a standing dispute resolution mechanism that was robust, accessible, timely and responsive to complainants, drawing on the experience of the Canterbury earthquakes, including the experiences of EQC and claimants, if necessary backed by legislation, (ii) supporting and ensuring adequate resourcing of a community law service that provided free or low-cost legal advice to assist claimants in the event of dispute with EQC, and (iii) consideration of the regulation of insurance advocates or those providing related services to claimants to secure assurance and clarity for claimants and to avoid predatory behaviour.

The Report had an immediate effect that did not require legislation. The agreements reached in 2016 between EQC and Vero, and after Kaikoura between EQC and other leading insurers, proved to be the model for game-changing measures that have all but eliminated demarcation disputes. That model was used again in July 2020 in response to flooding in Whangarei 162km north of Auckland following what was described as a once in 500-year storm.[69] Implementing in full the 2015 Treasury proposals and the Public Inquiry proposals, the Natural Disaster Response Agreement (NDRA) was entered into in 2020 between EQC and eight insurers constituting the vast bulk of the domestic property market. The Agreement came into force on 30 June 2021. Heralded as the first of its type in the world, the Agreement provides that any person holding a property policy with one of the participating insurers and whose dwelling suffers natural catastrophe damage may claim only against his or her insurers. The days of dual claiming are gone, and there is no longer any separate claim against EQC. The insurers themselves are required to manage and settle claims on behalf of themselves and EQC, so that any determination as to the operation of the cap will not require separate adjudication. Further, insurers now handle land damage claims for EQC even though they fall outside the scope of private policies.

In 2023 the Government established the New Zealand Claims Resolution Service, in succession to the Residential Advisory Service and the Greater Christchurch Claims Resolution Service. Its stated function is to provide independent support to homeowners to resolve residential insurance issues resulting from natural disasters.[70]

[69] 500 years passes quickly. Cyclone Gabrielle in February 2023 caused 11 fatalities and obliterated pretty much the whole of the Esk Valley, close to Napier. There were further catastrophic floods across the nation in July 2022 and then in Auckland and the North Island in January and May 2023. The January 2023 flood resulted in four fatalities and generated some 8,000 claims. In 2021–2022 EQC reported that 76% of claims against it were for landslip, storm and flood damage to land, the result of the increasing number of weather events.

[70] New Zealand Claims Resolution Service, 'Who We Are'. nzcrs.govt.nz.

V. The Natural Hazards Insurance Act 2023

It remains to consider the terms of the Natural Hazards Act 2023, the second offspring of Dame Silvia's Report. The 2023 Act came into force on 27 February 2024 and is in many respects far more detailed than its predecessor, making express provision for the various practical issues encountered by EQC in handling claims. Further detail will be included in Regulations, not available at the time of writing but proposals were published in draft form in October 2023.[71]

EQC has been replaced by the Natural Hazards Commission (NHC).[72] The 1993 funding model is retained. The Natural Disaster Fund has been renamed the Natural Hazard Fund and, as before, receives its revenues from the premium levy, investment earnings and state support where necessary (ss 108–115). The levy is to be set out in the Regulations. The Act does not formalise the NDRA, but it is integral to its operation. It is intended that insurers will act as agents of NHC for all claims-handling purposes, and the regulations are likely to provide that a claim may be made either to NHC or the insurer, but that claims may be made against, and handled by, the insurer whether or not it is a party to the NDRA. As is stated in the commentary to the draft regulations:[73]

> Providing in regulations for claims under the NHI Act to be able to be lodged with insurers whether or not insurers participate in the [Natural Disaster Response Model] provides certainty for insured persons who may not know whether their insurer participates in the NDRM. This will avoid confusion caused by having to lodge two separate claims and reduce the risk of late claim lodgement. This regulation will further strengthen processes and procedures associated with notification of natural hazard damage and enable the homeowner to enter into the claim process faster providing a better overall experience.

Section 3, which has no 1993 equivalent, defines the purposes of the Act, which are, in summary: (a) to reduce the impact of natural hazards on people, property, and the community; (b) to contribute to the management of the financial risk to the Crown of providing natural hazard cover; (c) to enable NHC to facilitate the Crown arranging reinsurance or other risk transfer products in respect of Crown risks beyond those covered in this Act, and (d) to improve awareness and understanding of matters relating to natural hazards, improving natural hazard risk management, and improving resilience to natural hazards. The last mentioned is an important innovation because it takes the NHC's remit beyond indemnification and arguably makes it responsible for risk management and loss prevention. Contents are outside the legislation and are covered, if at all, only by private insurance. The Act applies only to land and buildings in New Zealand.

[71] Cabinet Paper DEV-23-SUB-0185: Natural Hazards Insurance Act: Proposed Regulations – 23 August 2023 treasury.govt.nz.

[72] Toka Tū Ake.

[73] Para 33. Para 32 acknowledges that the NDRA could for one or other reason be terminated but does not suggest what action would be taken if that occurred.

Turning first to buildings cover, as under the 1993 Act only 'residential buildings' are protected: commercial properties remain excluded. The 1993 definitions of the meaning of this phrase have been greatly expanded and explained with a series of illustrations. A residential building is a 'dwelling', defined as any self-contained premises which are a home or holiday home and include the facilities necessary for day-to-day living on an indefinite basis, including somewhere to cook, sleep, live, wash, and use a toilet.[74] This includes long-term accommodation for the elderly. A building remains a dwelling even if it is used to provide temporary accommodation, or if it becomes temporarily unoccupied (as where it is undergoing repairs). Movable facilities, including a boat, vehicle or aircraft, are not dwellings, although a fixed caravan qualifies. Buildings used for large scale occupations, including dormitories, hostels and university halls of residence, are not dwellings.

Special provision is made for apartment blocks, which may contain multiple dwellings but with shared joint property (eg, roof, elevator, etc) and also for buildings providing both residential and business accommodation (eg, a shop): in the case of a mixed use building, the residential percentage (based on floor area, etc) must be 50% or more for the Act to apply, and there are complex provisions relating to "common property" excluding such areas from the percentage calculation As under the 1993 Act, any claimant must have 'insurable interest' in any part of a building for which a claim is made,[75] and that concept is to be defined by the Regulations to take account of the various complex arrangements that may be adopted in respect of ownership

As far as land is concerned, s 16 of the 2023 Act provides separate cover for 'all the land that the estates and interest that make up the land holding within which a residential building is situated relate to'. There must, however, be a proprietary interest: a mere right to use land does not suffice. Land includes retaining walls, bridges and culverts necessary for the residential building or residential land located within 60 metres of the building.

Cover under the 2023 Act is available only where, under s 21, there is a fire policy in place, although the right of a person to apply directly to NHC for natural hazard cover – typically, where insurance is unobtainable – is retained by s 48. As in 1993, a fire policy means a contract of insurance (but not reinsurance) providing insurance against a dwelling in respect of fire and other perils. The insured natural hazards are: earthquake, hydrothermal activity, landslide, tsunami, volcanic activity, flood, storm, and natural hazard fire. Flood and storm cover is confined to land. The normal action of the wind or water causing gradual erosion (including, for example, coastal erosion, bank erosion, and sheet erosion) is not a natural hazard. Insurance is by s 24 triggered by physical loss or damage to a residential building or residential land is natural hazard damage

[74] Even if located in an outbuilding.

[75] Note that insurable interest for private insurance on property was abolished by the Insurance Law Reform Act 1985, s 7.

either occurring as a direct result of a natural hazard or damage is imminent (ie, that it is more likely than not that there will be damage within 12 months unless remedial action is not taken). This is much the same as in the 1993 Act and does not reverse the decisions holding that a building that is uninhabitable but neither damaged nor at risk of imminent harm is not insured. There is nevertheless some clarification of the allocation of costs to buildings and land cover where such action is necessary.

The measure of indemnity for a building is, by ss 30 to 35, replacement cost, defined as 'the total cost that would reasonably be incurred to replace or reinstate the damaged parts of the building to a condition substantially the same as, but not better or more extensive than, their condition when they were new', with an uplift where it is necessary to modify the building to comply with any building code. However, NHC does not provide any additional funding for 'building back better' to improve a building's resilience to natural hazards. The provisions are far clearer than the 1993 Act on costs such as fees, and specifically excludes claims handling costs and any allowance for contingencies. The sum recoverable is capped at $300,000 plus GST, with a deductible of $500, for each dwelling. The measure of indemnity for land is indemnity, which generally means the cost of repairs or value where repair is not possible. One important feature of the bill is the improvement of cover for retaining walls, now paid for by reference to undepreciated value but capped at $50,000. Express provision is made for consecutive losses, setting out exactly when subsequent loss is to be treated as part of an earlier peril (48 hours, or seven days for volcanic activity). The Act also deals with cases where the insured person has to be relocated[76] and how the moneys payable are to be allocated by persons with different or overlapping interests.

The claims procedures set out in the Act specify the details to be provided. There is a time limit of three months from the date of the damage, although that varies as between the various perils, and time is extended for up to two years in the case of hidden damage or incapacity affecting the claimant,[77] although a time bar can now be relied upon only if the delay is prejudicial, in line with the position applicable to insurance contracts (ss 54 and 68). The statutory responsibility for receiving, assessing and settling claims is borne by NHC (ss 57–66). The exclusion for preventable repeat damage to a building from a landslide or to land from landslide, storm or flood is as before (s 50), and claims may be declined for fraud and for damage caused by failure to comply with legal requirements or substandard construction (ss 75 and 76). Crucially, and unlike the common law, claims can be assigned to a purchaser of the building or land.

There are some important innovations in the 2023 Act. There is to be a Code of Insured Persons' Rights under which claims are to be managed and settled in a fair and timely manner. The Code must impose rights on insured persons

[76] In which case NDC has rights of salvage over the site, as under the 1993 Act.

[77] This period may be extended under the Regulations.

and obligations on the Commission, there are to be remedies for breach and a complaints procedure. The Code is in addition to any other rights open to insured persons and is to be implemented by regulation (ss 88–91). There are to be independent reviewers of Commission decisions to ensure that the Code has been complied with (ss 92–100). Unlike the Fair Insurance Code, this is an official legislative measure. To date, no drafts of the Code have appeared, but it will doubtless work alongside the voluntary Fair Insurance Code. There is also to be a dispute resolution scheme which is accessible, independent, fair, accountable, efficient and effective (ss 101–107). This will doubtless work along the same lines as the Canterbury Earthquakes Insurance Tribunal, ensuring that claims are kept out of the ordinary courts so far as is possible.

VI. Comment

The New Zealand approach of the state acting as primary layer insurer is something of an outlier. The underlying philosophy of state provision aligns with the Accident Compensation Corporation (ACC) Scheme, in force since 1972 and codified in the Accident Compensation Act 2001. ACC pays compensation for personal injury suffered in New Zealand, however caused, although ACC assessments and claims are handled by the state and not by the private market.[78] Personal injury suits have been all but eliminated. Top-up insurance, particularly for loss of earnings or complex medical treatment is necessary for many, but the principle remains that the state is the provider.

Other nations have adopted other techniques for providing cover for risks that are uninsurable at any price or at least unaffordable to those who need protection most.[79] The most common alternative model is for the state to leave insurance to the private market but instead to provide the necessary security for insurers by reinsurance. That is the technique used in the UK under the Reinsurance (Acts of Terrorism) Act 1993, a measure passed to prevent the exodus of foreign banks from the City of London in the light terror attacks on commercial buildings by the Irish Republican Army following which private insurers simply withdrew terrorism cover. There is no compulsion on the market to offer this form of insurance, but it is now widely available. Similarly, flood cover in the UK was at one time unavailable or unaffordable for areas prone to flooding, the result of building residential properties on flood plains. That matter has been addressed by the Water Act 2014, which established the Flood Reinsurance Scheme pursuant to which flood insurance cover is bundled into all residential property insurance policies. The Flood Re Scheme is exclusively financed from policyholder premiums and an insurance industry levy and without any contribution

[78] A brief dalliance with privatisation from 1998 was rapidly abandoned.
[79] F Arnold-Dwyer, *Insurance, Climate Change and the Law* (Abingdon, Routledge, 2024) Ch 9.

from the UK Government. Those insurers willing to offer cover for flood have the benefit of reinsurance. As Fred Hawke's chapter in this work shows,[80] Australia has similar measures in place.

At the end of 2023 Italy adopted a compulsory scheme for catastrophe risks.[81] Companies established and operating in Italy are required to purchase insurance for buildings and commercial assets, and Italian insurers are required to offer that insurance. Once again, the market is protected by a state reinsurance scheme.

What is unique about the New Zealand scheme is that – given the new enhanced cap – pretty much the entire risk of catastrophe cover for domestic dwellings and domestic land is borne by the state on statutory terms, funded by levies on private insurance premiums. Catastrophe cover in New Zealand is thus a state responsibility, but the effect of the 2023 Act is to 'privatise' claims handling by leaving it in the hands of the insurance market. Whether the funding structure can refill the depleted Natural Disaster Fund sufficiently remains to be seen. It is to be hoped that the new legislation never has to undergo the tests posed by Christchurch in 2010 and 2011, and it is readily apparent that many of the problems that have and continue to bedevil that process are a thing of the past.

[80] See Chapter 08.

[81] Law no 213 of 30 December 2023.

8

The Big Wind Blows: On Northern Australia

FRED HAWKE*

I. Introduction

The Cyclone Reinsurance Scheme is designed to lower insurance premiums for households and small businesses with high cyclone and related flood damage risk by reducing the cost of reinsurance, which is a significant cost component of premiums for these policies. The Scheme would allow insurers to reinsure cyclone risks at a lower cost than in the private reinsurance market as it is designed to be cost neutral to the Government over time and be backed by a Commonwealth guarantee. The Scheme is expected to improve insurance access and affordability in cyclone-prone areas. The Scheme is also expected to increase competition by encouraging greater insurer participation in cyclone-prone areas and support higher levels of insurance coverage by property owners.[1]

The establishment in 2003 of the Australian Reinsurance Pool Corporation (ARPC), to provide backstop reinsurance against terrorism-related losses which local property and liability carriers were prohibited from excluding,[2] and the extension in 2022 of its remit to include weather damage losses in the same classes,[3] represents the latest recognition of the practical limitations of commercial, open-market insurance as a means of distributing and mitigating societally-significant and emergent risks. Contrary to popular belief, it has never been the case that everything is insurable at the right price. Since the advent of premium-based underwriting for profit, in the latter half of the seventeenth century, it has been

* The helpful suggestions of Dr Ian Enright and Mr David Abell with respect to the content of this Chapter are acknowledged. Any errors are the author's sole responsibility.

[1] Explanatory Memorandum to the Treasury Laws Amendment (Cyclone and Flood Damage) Reinsurance Pool Bill 2022 (Explanatory Memorandum), paras 1.7–1.9.

[2] By section 8 of what was the then Terrorism Insurance Act 2003 (Cth), Act Number 43 of 2003 (Terrorism Insurance Act 2003).

[3] By the Treasury Laws Amendment (Cyclone and Flood Damage Reinsurance Pool) Act 2022 (Cth), Act Number 13 of 2022. Henceforth the Terrorism Insurance Act 2003 was renamed the Terrorism and Cyclone Insurance Act 2003 (The Act).

recognised that for certain categories of risk exposure, the combined effects of correlation, frequency and magnitude render them commercially uninsurable, at least at the local market level.[4]

Such risks fall into two principal divisions. There are novel risks, where the lack of sufficient data as to frequency and magnitude of occurrence means that they cannot properly be rated using the insurance industry's traditional underwriting tools. Then there are known risks where because of environmental or demographic factors, application of those tools now results in a premium cost that is too large to be borne by the affected populace. In the former case, Bayesian heuristics may be resorted to in order to kickstart the premium underwriting process.[5] In the latter, the only alternative to allowing losses to lie where they fall is effectively to deepen the premium pool, by widening the population of contributors from whom it is drawn. The simplest and most obvious way of achieving that is for society at large, through the medium of Government, to become the ultimate underwriter.

This is not unprecedented. For many years in Australia health insurance has been what is known as 'community-rated', meaning that premiums are regulated according to health insurers' overall portfolio claims experience. They are not permitted to 'load' or vary premiums based on individual characteristics of age, gender, health status or other variables. Under the Private Health Insurance Act 2007 (Cth), all proposed premium increases require approval of the Commonwealth Minister for Health, who must balance the competing social objectives of keeping the cost of private health cover as low as possible, while maintaining the prudential regulatory compliance and commercial viability of its providers. Such a system, however, carries the risk of impairing the effectiveness of the price signal, which also is one of the key functions of insurance in the context of long-term risk management.[6] As the authors of the recent report of the United Nations University Institute for Environment and Human Security put the matter:[7]

> While efforts to address the issue of un-insurability have traditionally looked to economic solutions, such as government subsidies, to support affordability, relatively little attention has been given to reducing the underlying risks that have been escalating unchecked. Insurance can be a valuable tool to manage our risk when hazards strike, however, it has limits when the risks are too high. As such, insurance is most

[4] For the most recent appreciation of this perennial issue see C Eberle, J O'Connor, L Narvaez, M Mena Benavides and Z Sebesvari, 'Interconnected Disaster Risks 2023: Risk Tipping Points. United Nations University – Institute for Environment and Human Security 23 October 2023' (Interconnected Disaster Risk 2023). collections.unu.edu/eserv/UNU:9288/UNU_Tipping-Points_231017_no-watermark.pdf, and the references there cited.

[5] As was the case with statutory Workers' Compensation benefit insurance, when first envisaged.

[6] Interconnected Disaster Risk 2023: Risk Tipping Points, (n5) above, at 40–42.

[7] ibid, 43. The conclusion stated is that 'Increasingly severe hazards drive up the costs of insurance until it is no longer accessible or affordable. Once this point is passed, people are left without an economic safety net when disasters strike, opening the door to cascading socio-economic impacts in high-risk areas'.

> useful when used in combination with other risk reduction measures, and should not be perceived as a licence to live in hazardous situations. Transformative approaches to tackle the underlying social and environmental drivers of risk are needed before we lose access to a valuable safety net when we need it most.

When it comes to determining whether a known risk has become uninsurable due to changes in frequency, magnitude or both, reinsurance pricing is the canary in the coal mine. It is not necessary to subscribe to the more alarmist speculations concerning the consequences of climate change in order to understand the rationale for this most recent expansion of the ARPC's operations, the Cyclone and Related Flood Damage Reinsurance Pool. A question that remains to be considered, however, is whether, in creating it, the Australian Federal Government has achieved a genuine mitigation of the risks that cyclones and attendant flooding pose to property and economic welfare, in affected parts of the country, or has merely succeeded in evolving a tougher and more resilient breed of canary.

This chapter will examine the structure and manner of operation of Australia's Cyclone and Related Flood Damage Reinsurance Pool, in the context of the earlier, terrorism-related legislation onto which it is grafted, and assess the extent to which it dispenses with and potentially erodes the insurance industry's traditional role in the evaluation and pricing of risk. It will consider whether and to what extent the assumptions and rules governing orthodox contracts of insurance, in the commercial as well as the personal lines, may be rendered unfit for purpose or otiose in light of changes in society's awareness and management of risk. In particular, the implications for conventional underwriting practice of risk transfer that previously was regarded as facultative instead being treated as a social imperative, leading to mandatory pooling and parametric triggers, will be scrutinised and evaluated.

II. Genesis of the Scheme

The Australian Federal Government's first major engagement with the problem of uninsurable risk took place in 2003, leading to enactment of the Terrorism Insurance Act 2003 (Cth). It established the ARPC as a government-guaranteed reinsurer of last resort against terrorism risk to commercial property and related legal liabilities, in response to market failure in the aftermath of 9/11. Consideration of the Terrorism Reinsurance Pool, its legislative framework and manner of operation are outside the scope of this chapter, however, it appears to be functioning as intended to mitigate the impact on Property and Casualty insurance of Declared Terrorism Incidents on Australian soil. At the time of writing there has been just one declared terrorist incident under the scheme, involving 92 reinsurance claims totalling AUD2.3 million from 20 insurers.[8]

[8] This was the Lindt Café siege on 15–16 December 2014 when a lone gunman held hostage 18 people, two of whom were killed, in a café in the Sydney central business district. See www.theguardian.

The proposal to expand the government-sponsored reinsurance scheme for designated terrorism risks, by creating a second pool to reinsure cyclone and resultant flooding coverage under property policies in specified parts of the country, was first announced on 4 May 2021 in the context of the Mid-Year Economic and Fiscal Outlook for 2021–22. A consultation paper on the Commonwealth Treasury website was open for comment from 21 May until 18 June 2021 and received 64 submissions from 'a broad range of industry and community stakeholders'.[9]

The Treasury Laws Amendment (Cyclone and Flood Damage Reinsurance Pool) Bill 2022 was subsequently introduced to Federal Parliament. That the Government was well aware of the desirability of minimising the scheme's impact on the insurance price signal and wider, socio-environmental management of the relevant risks, is apparent from various passages in the Bill's Explanatory Memorandum:

> The mandatory nature of the Cyclone Reinsurance Scheme is consistent with the intention to improve insurance accessibility and affordability for households and small businesses in cyclone-prone areas. For the scheme to achieve the maximum reductions in insurance premiums in cyclone-prone areas, insurers holding eligible cyclone risks must participate.[10]
>
> The ARPC and reviewing actuary must seek to ensure the premiums are kept as low as possible for insurance contracts that involve medium to high levels of exposure to eligible cyclone losses, while maintaining incentives for risk reduction and encouraging cyclone and flood-related mitigation over time.[11]
>
> As the risk rating for pricing properties covered by the pool develops, the pool will also incorporate discounts for properties where the risk of cyclone and related flood has been mitigated. In addition to encouraging policyholders to engage in strategies to mitigate cyclone and related flooding risks, the discounts will help to improve the affordability and sustainability of property insurance over time.[12]

There also is an expectation, which may or may not be justified in the event, that the availability of guaranteed reinsurance at a competitive price coupled with more effective risk mitigation at the environmental, planning and building regulatory

com/australia-news/2014/dec/20/sydney-siege-timeline-how-a-day-and-night-of-terror-unfolded-at-the-lindt-cafe. Whilst the Minister's declaration of a terrorist incident had the effect, under then the Act, of negating terrorism exclusions in Property and Liability insurance contracts and allowing the affected policyholders to claim their otherwise covered losses, the consequence of triggering similar exclusions under travel insurance or other classes unaffected by the Act was not evaluated.

[9] Explanatory Memorandum (n2), 5 Consultation: These included 38 from community and consumer advocates and 15 from insurance industry participants comprising insurers, reinsurers, insurance brokers and their respective representative organizations. There were two public and two standing roundtables, the latter consisting of an Industry Advisory Panel and a North Queensland Consultant Panel, comprised of actuaries, insurance and reinsurance underwriters and other persons with 'significant, deep experience' and local knowledge, established to assist the design process. There also was 'targeted consultation' with a wide range of persons considered to possess specific expertise such as existing reinsurance pool operators, catastrophe modelers, meteorologists and other scientists.

[10] Explanatory Memorandum (n2), para 1.14.

[11] ibid, para 1.87.

[12] ibid, para 1.88.

level, will entice commercial and domestic property insurers to retain more of the relevant risk over time:

> The pool will cover all eligible claims above the policyholder's excess for cyclone events for the first 3 years. Thereafter, the pool will operate on a risk-sharing arrangement with insurers to allow a staged transition to a limited level of risk retention by insurers.[13]

The rationale for the scheme is made clear in the Memorandum's Regulation Impact Statement:

> Due to the greater risk of extreme weather events, including cyclones, insurance premiums are significantly more expensive in northern Australia. While there are legitimate reasons for this, including the greater cost to insurers to provide property insurance in northern Australia, this has led to cover becoming less affordable and accessible for consumers and small businesses in the region …
>
> Technology and greater granularity in the pricing of cyclone and flood risks is also contributing to rising insurance premiums in northern Australia. Since 2013, insurers have moved towards address level pricing for cyclone risk, which makes up a large part of premiums. The use of these technologies has led to premium increases in Far North Queensland and the Northern Territory, while average premiums did not experience large changes at national level. **Address level pricing allows insurers to more directly align premiums paid to the level of risk and minimise potential over-pricing of low-risk policies – reducing the extent of risk pooling through insurance.** However, in some cases, this change has resulted in very large increases to premiums for consumers most vulnerable to cyclone risk, exacerbating affordability issues. For example, a consumer's target premium increased by 70%, from about $3,000 to $5,000, following the adoption by the insurer of address level pricing for cyclone risks leading to cyclone component changes across the insurer's portfolio …
>
> Claims are on average larger and more frequent in northern Australia compared with the rest of Australia. Higher claim costs are due primarily to the frequency and scale of natural disasters experienced in northern Australia. … The Australian Competition and Consumer Commission found that risk is the largest deterrent of new insurers from entering northern Australia.
>
> In the short to medium-term, the insurance market is unlikely to unilaterally assist with these premiums, **given that higher premiums reflect the level of natural disaster risk in northern Australia.**[14] (Emphasis added.)

III. The Problem of Uninsurable Risk

What is being described above is not 'market failure', the politicians' usual pretext for market intervention, but a market functioning as expected to deliver efficient pricing of risk. It is not a case of the relevant market's inability to determine a

[13] Ibid, para 1.91.

[14] Explanatory Memorandum (n2), Attachment 1 Regulation Impact Statement, pp 29–34.

proper price for the risks of cyclones and attendant flooding over the geographical areas in question, as might be the case with a novel or emergent risk. Nor is it a situation in which the frequency and/or magnitude of potential losses is beyond the capacity of that market to absorb and distribute, given the ability to charge premiums commensurate with the cost of available reinsurance. This point is developed further below, in the penultimate section of this chapter.

Rather, it is a case of the community at risk simply not being able to afford to transfer that risk to insurers at the market price, and the economic, social and political consequences to which that situation gives rise. That government has a legitimate role to play in remedying this situation is not seriously disputed, since, as the United Nations University study cited in the Introduction makes clear, in the developed world at least insurance, if not precisely a human right, is generally acknowledged to be an essential service.

> Due to the greater risk of extreme weather events in cyclone-prone areas, insurance premiums are significantly more expensive. This has led to cover becoming less accessible and affordable for households and small businesses in these regions. Households that are underinsured or have no insurance have reduced financial capacity to recover from a natural disaster or other event. Poor insurance coverage can exacerbate costs and pressures for communities and for governments, through increased pressure on health, emergency and welfare systems. It can slow the economic recovery of a region following a disaster.[15]

What remains to be seen is whether the measure chosen – establishment of a compulsory, government-guaranteed reinsurer operating on a cost-neutral basis to compete with the international reinsurance markets for northern Australian risks – represents the optimal solution.

The most significant statement in the extract above, perhaps in the entire document, is 'Address level pricing allows insurers to more directly align premiums paid to the level of risk … **reducing the extent of risk pooling through insurance**'[16] (emphasis added). But risk pooling is the very essence of insurance. 'The premiums of the many support the losses of the few'.[17] Risks must still be 'cross-subsidised' (ie, shared), just through the medium of a state mechanism rather than a private one. Public capital is put up in the form of a Commonwealth guarantee, in lieu of the private capital of open market reinsurers. More will be said on this in the section dealing with the implications of the scheme.

IV. Prior Analysis

The emergence of uninsurable weather risks to property, following the traditional ones of war, civil war, quarantined disease, strikes riots, civil commotion etc. and

[15] Explanatory Memorandum (n2), Statement of Compatibility with Human Rights, para 2.4.
[16] Explanatory Memorandum (n2), Attachment 1 Regulation Impact Statement, p 31.
[17] Attributed to Warren Tickle, former Australian Insurance Commissioner and insurance lecturer.

the more recent one of terrorism, is not a novel phenomenon. The ARPC's working party responsible for development of the Cyclone and Related Flood Damage Reinsurance Pool carried out extensive review and analysis of recent investigations into the issue, notably:

(a) the 2011 Natural Disaster Insurance Review;
(b) the 2015 Northern Australia Insurance Premiums Taskforce Report;
(c) the 2020 Royal Commission into Natural Disaster Arrangements; and
(d) the Australian Competition and Consumer Commission's Northern Australia Insurance Inquiry.

The experience of other countries with natural disaster insurance pools designed to 'smooth risk' across regions was also considered, specifically that of Japan, France, the United Kingdom and Indonesia. Various options for structuring and funding the proposed pool were canvassed and rejected by the task force before settling on the mandatory participation model. An interesting observation from the Explanatory Memorandum is that:

> Most (state-sponsored) reinsurance pools do not set premiums at the true technical rate corresponding to the underlying risk. Most charge a flat fee, receive a levy from all insurers, set risk-based but discounted premiums, or a combination of these.[18]

But in underwriting theory, the 'technical rate corresponding to the underlying risk' is not just a function of the frequency and magnitude of losses. It also is influenced by how widely the risk is spread – a function of the breadth and depth of the premium pool. The ultimate premium pool, of course, is the polity of Australian tax-paying citizens through their contributions to Commonwealth consolidated revenue.

It was further observed that:

> Reinsurance pools are often backed by some form of government guarantee which can be called on if claims exceed reserves. Where this is not the case, or where the guarantee is limited, the pool generally limits the claims it will pay in some way.[19]

The legislation under consideration for amendment – the Terrorism Insurance Act 2003 (Cth) – already incorporated such a limiting mechanism in the form of section 6, which remains in place but applies only with respect to the Terrorism Reinsurance Pool. That section provides that in case of a declared terrorist incident the total potential cost of which exceeds the applicable AUD10 billion Commonwealth guarantee, the responsible Minister must declare a 'reduction percentage'. This is essentially a proportionate write-down of pool-participating insurers' ceded policy liabilities, so that the ARPC's total reinsurance liability arising from the incident does not exceed the limit of the guarantee.

[18] Explanatory Memorandum (n2), Attachment 1 Regulation Impact Statement, International Comparison, p 49.

[19] ibid.

A reduction percentage once declared cannot be increased but may be reduced, should the incident's consequences prove less costly than initially anticipated. Given the inherent difficulty, if not impossibility, of estimating with any degree of accuracy at the outset of a terrorist incident what its eventual total cost is likely to be, a prudent Federal Treasurer therefore can be expected to pitch the reduction percentage at its highest credible level and hope to work downward. Be that as it may, the critical point is that under this mechanism, the risk of the total losses from a declared terrorist incident exceeding the amount of the relevant, state-sponsored reinsurance pool's resources, rests with the community of affected policyholders.

This is understandable, given that the effect of the Terrorism Insurance Act 2003 (Cth) on the operation of underlying insurances in the event of a declared terrorist incident is limited to the commercial property and liability classes. In the wake of 9/11, in order to preserve the value of commercial property, in which Australian pension and superannuation funds are substantially invested, it was essential to maintain its insurability. In the case of declared cyclone events a different imperative applies, that of preserving the economic viability of the entire community, and so the Commonwealth Government has chosen not to impose any limits on the applicable Commonwealth guarantees. This will be discussed further in the relevant section below.

V. The Intervention Model Selected

The options under consideration eventually boiled down to three:

i) maintain the status quo and hope that the normal, cyclical operation of the insurance and reinsurance markets, would eventually distribute sufficient capital to the relevant property insurance portfolios to alleviate the cost of the insurance to consumers, before the affected communities sustained permanent damage;
ii) establish a compulsory, government administered and guaranteed reinsurance pool; or
iii) establish an optional, government operated and guaranteed reinsurance pool.

The clear conclusion reached was that the second option, creation of a Federal Government-backed reinsurance pool to which insurers underwriting property cover in the affected regions must cede 100% of prescribed risks, offered the best prospects of an effective solution. According to the Explanatory Memorandum, the second option was preferred, as:

> On the basis of a mixture of quantitative and qualitative analysis, Option 2 has the highest net benefits. It would maximise the pool's ability to improve the affordability of insurance for household, strata and small business property policies in

> northern Australia, and this benefit outweighs the estimated additional regulatory impact over Option 3.[20]

The options of the Commonwealth assuming the role of a primary insurer, or directly supporting policyholders by subsidising premiums, were both considered and rejected. The first, because it would be likely to crowd out private competition and result in an effective state monopoly; the insurer of last resort instead becoming the default option. The second, because it would dilute more severely the impact of the insurance price signal on risk management, having the potential also to become open-ended and politically difficult to withdraw. There was acute awareness of the risk of major increases in the costs associated with either form of direct market intervention, as well as possible unintended consequences in the form of continued unsustainable coastal development. The Explanatory Memorandum considered that:

> Direct subsidies are only likely to temporarily reduce the issues of affordability, without making any lasting improvements to insurance affordability because the underlying issues will remain unchanged and, unless designed carefully, subsidies could facilitate inappropriate development in high-risk areas.[21]

It can be argued of course that by artificially reducing the cost of a key insurance input through direct participation in the reinsurance market, the Commonwealth Government is risking the same adverse consequences. Nevertheless, terminal economic decline and eventual depopulation of large areas of northern Australia also are unacceptable risks and the insurance availability crisis had to be addressed, in order to ensure the continued viability of established regional communities.

It was decided that intervention in the reinsurance market, one degree removed so to speak from the underlying value at risk, achieves the right balance between the immediate imperative to reduce the up-front cost of insurance to consumers and the medium to long term requirement of maintaining incentives to risk management and mitigation at the community level. The ARPC's Cyclone and Flood Reinsurance Pool may be viewed, in this light, as part of the Commonwealth Government's contribution to mitigating the effects of climate change and a paradigm example of how polities may adjust to it.

Mandatory participation was seen as essential in order to avoid adverse selection and maximise the flow of reinsurance premium to the pool, both of which are vital if it is to achieve the greatest possible premium savings for primary policyholders and operate cost-neutrally over time. The major impact is through elimination of reinsurance profit margins from the class. Reduction in the transactional costs of reinsurance placement is also expected to contribute to the overall benefit of the scheme, as:

> The savings arise from the elimination of commercial profit margins through the mandatory participation of insurers and is (sic) also supported by the government

[20] Explanatory Memorandum (n2), Best option of those considered, p 64.
[21] Ibid, Attachment 1 Regulation Impact Statement, p 35.

> guarantee. The discounts available to consumers are greatest under a reinsurance pool with mandatory participation.[22]

Ousting the private market from a substantial field of business, using the advantage of a lower cost base (in terms of the capital required to support the guarantee) backed up by legislative fiat, is not something to be done lightly. This is especially so in a country which relies, as does Australia, on the international insurance and reinsurance markets for placement of the greater part of its insurable infrastructure risk. Since, however, the relevant business is unprofitable or at best barely profitable or the need for such a step would not exist, it would seem to be an economically efficient approach to the problem and is not expected to contribute to unfavourable perceptions of Australia's sovereign risk. Moreover, allowance is made for the possibility of the Pool outwardly retroceding some of the relevant risk over time, should suitable commercial market conditions emerge.

> Given the global scale and competitive nature of the reinsurance market, as well as the material proportion of Australian natural disaster loss exposure that the reinsurance pool would leave unaffected, it is not expected that reinsurers would attempt to "penalise" Australian insurers to any significant degree for any loss of profit margins due to the transfer of cyclone risk to the reinsurance pool.
>
> … There would be an estimated $0.44 million average annual regulatory cost on the insurance industry to support a benefit for properties in high-risk cyclone areas.[23]

VI. The Scheme's Manner of Operation

The key terms which direct the operation of Part 2A of the Terrorism and Cyclone Insurance Act (Cth),[24] under which the Australian Reinsurance Pool Corporation's Cyclone and Related Flood Damage Reinsurance Pool is established, are 'pool insurance contract', 'eligible property', 'eligible cyclone loss', 'cyclone event' and 'declared claims period'. If a general insurer undertakes liability under pool insurance contracts in respect of eligible cyclone losses, it must enter into contracts of reinsurance with the ARPC that:

A. cover the insurer's liability, under all pool insurance contracts that it enters into, in respect of all eligible cyclone losses; and
B. insure against 100% of the insurer's liability, under each of those pool insurance contracts, in respect of all eligible cyclone losses.[25]

[22] Explanatory Memorandum (n2), p 43.
[23] ibid, pp 46–47.
[24] Terrorism and Cyclone Insurance Act 2003 (Cth) (the Act). Which is the original Terrorism Insurance Act 2003 (Cth), as amended by the Treasury Laws Amendment Act (Cyclone and Flood Damage Reinsurance Pool) Act 2022 (Cth) (No 13 of 2022).
[25] Terrorism and Cyclone Insurance Act 2003 (Cth) s 8A (1).

A 'pool insurance contract' is one which insures against loss of or damage to 'eligible property' owned by the insured, including resultant business interruption and other consequential loss arising from loss of or damage to or inability to use eligible property owned or occupied by the insured. 'Eligible property' includes domestic buildings and their contents, residential strata or community title properties,[26] where 50% or more of the floor space is used for residential purposes and commercial properties with less than AUD5 million total sum insured, including business interruption.[27]

All these terms are defined consistently with their meanings under other Australian consumer legislation, as well as the Insurance Contracts Act 1984 (Cth) which is the country's principal Federal statute governing the operation of insurance policies. A pool insurance contract can also include any other insurance 'in respect of' a building and/or its contents where the sum insured does not exceed the amount prescribed by regulation.[28]

The following are not pool insurance contracts:

i) contracts of insurance covering buildings and/or contents owned and managed by governments or their instrumentalities, Commonwealth, State, Territory or Local;
ii) contracts of insurance over other buildings and/or contents where the sum insured exceeds the amount prescribed by regulation under subsection 8B (3) (d) (ii);
iii) contracts of reinsurance;
iv) farm insurance contracts, except for home building and contents;
v) any other insurances specifically excluded by regulation; or
vi) State insurances, not extending beyond the limits of the State concerned.

'Eligible cyclone loss' is defined, essentially, as a loss which arises:

i) from a weather system which is designated by the Bureau of Meteorology as a cyclone event; or
ii) from wind, rain, rainwater, rainwater run-off, storm surge or flood caused by that weather system;

and commences during the 'declared claims period' for that cyclone event.

The Bureau of Meteorology (BOM) decides at what point a weather system is designated a cyclone event, whether it has dropped below the requisite level of intensity for that classification and if and when it has re-intensified.[29] The BOM must promptly inform the ARPC of such events, specifying dates and times[30]

[26] Defined in Reg 4A of the Terrorism and Cyclone Insurance Regulations 2003.

[27] Terrorism and Cyclone Insurance Act 2003 (Cth) ss 8B (1)–(4).

[28] Terrorism and Cyclone Insurance Act 2003 (Cth) s 8B (3) (d) (ii).

[29] Terrorism and Cyclone Insurance Act 2003 (Cth) s 8C. This does not mean though that the BOM has an unfettered discretion. *Cyclone, cyclone end and re-intensify* have been defined by Regulation in consultation with the Bureau's scientists. See Reg 3A.

[30] Terrorism and Cyclone Insurance Act 2003 (Cth) s 8E.

and the ARPC then must declare a claims period in respect of that cyclone event[31] as soon as practicable and in any event within 24 hours.[32] Such declaration is by notifiable instrument, which cannot be revoked or varied, published on the ARPC's website again as soon as possible and in any case within 24 hours. The ARPC's Cyclone Pool reinsurance contracts are triggered by the claims period declaration and respond to covered losses commencing after the cyclone event and within 48 hours of its end. The 48-hour deadline is for losses to occur, not for claims to be made or reported in respect of them, but has already given rise to some controversy among local insurers due to its comparative brevity.[33]

VII. Inception of the Scheme

The scheme became fully operational from 1 July 2022 but is subject to a gradual uptake process:

> Large insurers have until 31 December 2023 to join the scheme, at which point they must have obtained reinsurance for all their eligible cyclone risks with the ARPC.[34]

A 'large insurer' is any primary property carrier whose Gross Written Premium (GWP), in the classes now designated pool insurance contracts, equals or exceeds AUD300 million per annum. Small insurers, meaning those with GWP less than that amount, have until 31 December 2024 to engage fully with the scheme.[35]

Exempt general insurers, being those whose relevant GWP in the prior financial year fell below AUD10 million, Lloyds underwriters authorised under the Insurance Act 1973 (Cth) and Direct Offshore Foreign Insurers are not required to join it at all, on the basis that the Scheme is intended primarily for the benefit of APRA-authorised and regulated local carriers. The presence of DOFIs is not essential to keep the local market competitive and Underwriters at Lloyds have access to their own, specialised reinsurance facilities. Should any of them choose to do so, however, then like all other participants they must reinsure 100% of their

[31] Terrorism and Cyclone Insurance Act 2003 (Cth) s 8F.

[32] As to what happens if it is not practicable to make such a declaration within 24 hours, the Act is silent, but the contingency probably is remote.

[33] According to a report in the Australian Financial Review of 20 December 2023, in the wake of Cyclone Jasper, open market reinsurance contracts in the class commonly provide a seven-day run-off period for resultant damage to occur.

[34] Explanatory Memorandum (n2), para 1.13.

[35] GWP is defined in accordance with the Financial Sector (Collection of Data) (reporting standard) Determination 18 of 2013 and the relevant business classes under the Australian Prudential Regulation Authority's General Prudential Standard (GPS) 001. The ARPC has power under section 8A (7) of the Terrorism and Cyclone Insurance Act 2003 (Cth), to issue Determinations in the form of notifiable instruments prescribing the details of the Act's operation. The Terrorism and Cyclone Insurance (Areas of Negligible Cyclone Risk) Determination 2023 contains a list of postcodes where the risk of eligible cyclone losses is considered so small as to be negligible, within which premiums may be excluded from the calculation: ARPC, 'Insurer Onboarding', *Reinsurance Pools* (1 December 2023) arpc.gov.au/reinsurance-pools/cyclone/insurer-onboarding/.

liabilities under pool insurance contracts, in respect of eligible cyclone losses.[36] The principle of 'one in, all in' applies across the board to pool contract liabilities, for the reasons referred to above, irrespective of whether there is any other reinsurance applicable to the policy in question. However, private reinsurance of risks other than cyclone and related flood damage, which may be covered under the same policies, is not precluded.

VIII. Commonwealth Guarantees

The Commonwealth of Australia guarantees all of the ARPC's cyclone and related flood damage loss reinsurance liabilities, and its allocated expense commitments in relation to them.[37] The guarantee is notionally set at AUD10 billion for cyclone loss liabilities but may be revised upward if necessary.[38] The way this works is that should the ARPC at any time consider that it might not be able to discharge all its cyclone loss liabilities, even with the existing guarantee, it must give the responsible Minister a notice to that effect.[39] The Minister must consult with the Treasurer, the Finance Minister and the Prime Minister and determine, again by notifiable instrument which cannot be revoked, a financial year amount which, in his or her opinion, will enable the ARPC to meet all its cyclone loss liabilities. The cap on the guarantee then is raised to that amount.[40]

The operation of these provisions may be contrasted with the 'reduction percentage' mechanism which the Act applies, with respect to the corresponding guarantee of the ARPC's liabilities under Terrorism Pool reinsurance contracts.[41] The effect of the latter is to revise the cedants' policy liabilities, toward their original insureds, downward, limiting the ARPC's and by extension the Commonwealth's ultimate exposure to relevant loss.[42] In the case of cyclones and related flooding, the Act effects a total transfer of the risk in the prescribed locations, from the original insureds by way of the private insurance market to the Commonwealth.

IX. Premium Setting

How does the ARPC set its rates for Cyclone and Flood Damage reinsurance in the areas where it now has a statutory monopoly? Well, basically the same way in

[36] Terrorism and Cyclone Insurance Act 2003 (Cth) ss 8(5)–8(6). This is subject to any direction from the Minister to the ARPC under sub-section 38 (2) (e), regarding risk-retention by reinsured.

[37] Terrorism and Cyclone Insurance Act 2003 (Cth) ss 35 and 35A. The Consolidated Revenue Fund is appropriated for the purpose by section 37 (b).

[38] Terrorism and Cyclone Insurance Act 2003 (Cth) s 35A (4).

[39] Terrorism and Cyclone Insurance Act 2003 (Cth) s 35A (3). More than one notice may be given, if required.

[40] Through the operation of sub-section 35A (2) (b).

[41] Terrorism and Cyclone Insurance Act 2003 (Cth) s 6 (7).

[42] See discussion above in the section entitled Prior Analysis.

which porcupines are said to make love: with great care and precision. A critical consideration throughout the process of establishment of the Pool was the problem for the ARPC's actuaries of calculating an appropriate rate table. The ARPC is required to set its rates so as to ensure that 'over the longer term', premiums collected are sufficient to cover or offset amounts paid out under Pool reinsurance contracts, including related liabilities and any sums drawn down under the Commonwealth guarantee.[43]

The scheme is intended to be cost-neutral 'over the longer term'.[44] With respect to contracts involving 'medium to high levels of exposure' to eligible cyclone losses, the Corporation is to 'keep the premiums as low as possible while maintaining incentives to reduce and mitigate the risk of such losses'.[45] For lower levels of exposure, the objective is to keep the premiums 'at levels comparable to what would be charged by other reinsurers'.[46] These high-level, statutory exhortations are consistent with the overall objectives of the scheme, as detailed in the Explanatory Memorandum to the Amending Act, of reducing the consumer cost of property insurance in cyclone-exposed areas to manageable levels without competing on unfair terms with the commercial reinsurance market or disincentivising prudent risk management on the part of policyholders, developers and local authorities.

X. Monitoring

The Australian Competition and Consumer Commission (ACCC) has been instructed to use its price monitoring powers, to measure the impact of the Pool on premiums charged to consumers and ensure that whatever reinsurance cost savings it generates are passed through to them. Nevertheless:

> Responsibility for setting insurance premiums stays with insurers, and they are responsible for commercial decisions on how they set them. Costs may be affected by other factors, including changing calculations of risk, changes to labour costs and changes in building costs.[47]

In addition to Observers,[48] the ARPC is required to appoint and maintain a Reviewing Actuary.[49] The term of appointment is three years and the first person to be appointed is the Australian Government Actuary.[50] The Reviewing Actuary's

[43] Terrorism and Cyclone Insurance Act 2003 (Cth) s 8D (a).
[44] Terrorism and Cyclone Insurance Act 2003 (Cth) s 8D (a).
[45] Terrorism and Cyclone Insurance Act 2003 (Cth) s 8D (b).
[46] Terrorism and Cyclone Insurance Act 2003 (Cth) s 8D (c).
[47] ARPC, 'Premium Rates', *Reinsurance Pools* (30 November 2023) arpc.gov.au/reinsurance-pools/cyclone/premium-pricing/.
[48] Appointed under the Terrorism and Cyclone Insurance Act 2003 (Cth) s 20A (2). They will usually be representatives of APRA and/or the Australian Government Actuary.
[49] Terrorism and Cyclone Insurance Act 2003 (Cth) Division 5A s 33A (1).
[50] Terrorism and Cyclone Insurance Act 2003 (Cth) s 33A (5).

role, as you might expect, is to review the ARPC's most recent Annual Financial Outlook Report[51] and report on how the Cyclone and Flood Damage Reinsurance Pool is travelling. The required subject matter of the Financial Outlook Report, in addition to an overview of the scheme's performance during the previous financial year, includes:

> observations on broader financial risks affecting the scheme's financial outlook; an assessment of the adequacy of:
>
> i) the premiums the Corporation is receiving under cyclone reinsurance contracts; and
>
> ii) the Corporation's reserves that are available to meet claims under those contracts.[52]

The Reviewing Actuary's evaluation of the Financial Outlook Report includes reviewing the premiums which the ARPC proposes to charge for pool reinsurance contracts and its compliance with section 8D in setting them.[53] He/she also must inform the Corporation as soon as reasonably practicable of any 'significant concerns' about the financial sustainability of the scheme or the Corporation's risk management processes.[54]

Whilst the Minister has power under the Act to give directions to the ARPC concerning the way it conducts its business, including the premiums it charges under reinsurance contracts, this explicitly does not extend to telling it what it can charge for cyclone reinsurance contracts.[55] The scheme, therefore, is well provided with actuarial and other technical support and subject to rigorous oversight and is substantially insulated from political interference.

XI. Insurance Implications of the Scheme

Losses arising from the occurrence of any contingent event ultimately can be managed only in either of two ways: by allowing them to lie where they fall or by sharing them, wholly or partly, with others. The great achievement of the modern insurance industry has been to develop a method – actuarial pricing of risk based upon probabilistic analysis of loss frequency and magnitude, otherwise known as underwriting – by which the second option can be efficiently and securely implemented. The concept of premium-based underwriting, in contrast to traditional risk-sharing by the participants in a common enterprise or marine adventure, depends for its effectiveness upon three fundamental aspects of probability – the law of large numbers, regression to the mean and central limit theorem.

[51] Prepared in accordance with the Terrorism and Cyclone Reinsurance Act 2003 (Cth) s 40A. The Minister is to review the Act itself as soon as practicable after 1 July 2025 and at not more than five yearly intervals thereafter, reporting to Parliament on the need for it to continue in operation.

[52] Terrorism and Cyclone Insurance Regulations 2003, Reg 5E (b) and (c).

[53] Terrorism and Cyclone Insurance Act 2003 (Cth) s 33B (1) (a).

[54] Terrorism and Cyclone Insurance Act 2003 (Cth) s 33B (3).

[55] Terrorism and Cyclone Insurance Act 2003 (Cth) s 38 (2) (d).

The first of these principles shows that the greater the number of occurrences of an event, the closer the experienced outcome will approximate the theoretical result predicted by the law of averages. For example, if you toss a fair coin 1,000 times you will get a result much closer to 50/50 heads/tails, than if you toss it just 10 times or even 100 times. The second says that if you measure any random variable from a standard distribution, such as the speed of a gale or the height of a flood, and the result is significantly above or below the mean for the sample period, then the next measurement of the same variable is likely to be closer to it, which is inherent in the very concept of a mean. The third principle, central limit theorem, proves that a sufficiently large set of disparate populations will follow the standard probability distribution, notwithstanding that some or all of them individually may not do so. In other words, the mean of the means will wear a bell curve even if some of the individual means don't.

The insurance industry's reliance on historic, statistical data in its application of these three principles, at a time when means are shifting unpredictably due to rapid changes in the underlying climatic conditions and associated weather patterns over areas with high concentration of property values, has led to serious under-pricing of property insurance against weather risk in such areas. The resultant severe underwriting losses in those classes and locations has led to capacity contraction and consequent pricing adjustments, in turn giving rise to socio-economic concerns in the affected areas and resulting ultimately in the ARPC's Cyclone and Flood Damage Reinsurance Pool. The latter, it is suggested, should not be considered subversion of the traditional underwriting process but a supplementation or expansion of it.

While the Cyclone and Flood Reinsurance Pool claims trigger may be parametric, requiring only the occurrence of a cyclone event and the ARPC's declaration of a claims period in respect of it, the response of the underlying policies remains indemnity-based and the Pool reinsurance contracts operate in the same manner. Insurers remain free to set their own premiums, sums insured and deductibles on whatever terms best enable them to comply with their prudential obligations, and can still compete at the margins. Insurance-based incentives to loss mitigation at the individual policyholder and community levels therefore are still cogent. The objective, bright line trigger for the Pool reinsurance contracts' response enables a clear demarcation between cyclonic winds and their attendant flooding and other, less severe weather damage occurrences such as rainwater ingress, hailstorm, lightning and fire, which may be covered under the same primary policies and either retained or separately reinsured.

The Terrorism and Cyclone Insurance Act does not make it compulsory for property insurers underwriting in northern Australia to cover flood, nor does it prescribe the premium rates they may charge for such protection. All it requires is that to the extent that their pool insurance contracts provide cover for eligible cyclone losses, that portion of the risk must be reinsured out to the Corporation. Insurers can still exclude damage attributable to cyclones and flooding entirely from coverage under their policies,[56] although of course such a contract would scarcely be worth purchasing even at a heavily discounted price.

It seems reasonable to conclude, therefore, that the ARPC's Cyclone and Related Flood Damage Reinsurance Pool represents the lightest touch intervention in the global reinsurance industry's Australian operations which the Commonwealth Government could contrive, consistently with its objectives of ameliorating the cost to private and small business purchasers of building, contents and business interruption insurance and thereby preserving the viability of relevant communities, without compromising wider risk mitigation measures in response to evolving climate perils or positioning itself as the underwriter of last resort. Whether and how these potentially discordant objectives can be reconciled and to what extent they will be achieved, only time will tell.

There is obvious tension between the scheme's primary purpose, that of reducing the cost of domestic and small business property insurance enough to fix the problem of chronic underinsurance in cyclone-affected areas, and the requirements to do so without abrogating either individual responsibility for risk mitigation or local community adjustment to changing risk, in a way which minimises government interference with the private insurance and reinsurance markets and is cost neutral over the 'longer term'.[57] One suspects that the latter phrase has purposely been left undefined, to allow the ARPC's actuaries some discretion in the setting of annual reinsurance rates; however, the Financial Outlook Report must include an assessment of the adequacy of the premiums the Corporation is receiving and its reserves[58] and there are limits to flexibility of regulatory interpretation.

The obvious question to ask is what will happen should achievement of the main objective prove not to be possible within the ARPC's mandatory reinsurance pricing framework? In other words, if removal of the reinsurance profit margin so that over whatever period is considered the longer term, the Pool breaks even, does not bring down the cost of primary cover enough to achieve the desired socio-economic outcome.[59] At that point, either the consequences of uninsurability for the affected areas will just have to be accepted or more drastic intervention contemplated.

[56] Subject to compliance with the derogation requirements of s 35 Regs 19 and 22 of the Insurance Contracts Act 1984 (Cth) and the definitional provisions of Division 1A ss 37B–37D Regs 33–35 of that statute.

[57] Terrorism and Cyclone Insurance Act 2003 (Cth) s 8D(a).

[58] Terrorism Insurance Amendment (Cyclone and Related Flood Damage Reinsurance Pool) Regulations 2022 Reg 5E (c).

[59] According to a statement on the ARPC's website, its pricing formula is designed to be cost neutral to Government 'over the longer term', not to include a profit margin thereby increasing savings available to policyholder and insurers, to lower the reinsurance cost for 'most policies' with medium to high exposure to cyclone risk while maintaining incentives for risk reduction and offering discounts for properties which undertake mitigation of cyclone and related flooding risk: ARPC, "Premium Rates' *Reinsurance Pools* (1 December 2023) arpc.gov.au/reinsurance-pools/cyclone/premium-pricing/.

In setting its reinsurance premiums for pool insurance contracts, Section 8D of the Act requires the ARPC to perform a sort of actuarial tightrope walk while spinning a plate on a stick in each hand. The competing factors which the provision requires it to take into consideration must be balanced against one another and a proper weighting accorded to each. The Corporation is not permitted to ignore or suspend consideration of any of them, the better to advance the others. For example, dispensing with the requirement of cost neutrality over the longer term or that of maintaining incentives to risk management and loss mitigation, in order to maintain the affordability of insurance in areas of medium to high cyclone exposure, is not allowed for by the section or the Regulations.

Once a rate set has been struck which in the Reviewing Actuary's opinion complies with all the requirements of section 8D, there is no provision for it to be revised until the next reporting period and any mid-term adjustments will risk breaching the provision.[60] For the next rate set period, the premium calculation inputs' relative weightings may alter to reflect changed conditions but none of them can be entirely disregarded. Under this legislation in its present form, it does not seem to be an option for a future Commonwealth Government to subsidise premiums further through the back door, so to speak, by directing the ARPC to continue to provide the necessary reinsurance on a net underwriting loss basis. Accordingly, should the cyclone and flooding claims experience of property risks in the affected regions continue to deteriorate, to the point where even the provision of reinsurance at cost does not suffice to maintain their insurability at prices which the communities can afford, other ways of dealing with the problem will have to be found.

The Commonwealth could, of course, amend the Act to enable the Minister to give such directions, at the risk of compromising the ARPC's prudential reserves and increasing the likelihood of draw-down on the guarantees, but that could be a politically fraught step to take. Whilst resort to such measures cannot be ruled out, in view of the significance of functioning northern Australian communities for the country's regional security, it is to be hoped that in such an event direct risk reduction and loss mitigation initiatives would receive funding priority over continued artificial underwriting of risks which are no longer commercially insurable. The insurance industry's long-ignored pleas for proper consideration of weather risks, in the local government property development approval process, might also at last be heard.

[60] Some flexibility is allowed by the undefined phrase 'over the longer term', as to the exact length of which lawyers and even actuaries may reasonably differ. If, however, the frequency and intensity of cyclones in a designated area is persistently increasing and there are no meteorological or other data to suggest abatement of this trend in the foreseeable future, then arguments to the effect that some assumption in the modelling could change or things might be different in a hundred or a thousand years' time, would probably be seen as sophistry.

XII. The Insurers' Dilemma

Underwriting algorithms, enhanced by artificial intelligence, enable risk selection, risk analysis and pricing to be refined with ever increasing precision, but every increase in the predictability of frequency and quantum of loss in a defined area reduces its uncertainty, which is an essential element of its insurability. As the Explanatory Memorandum to the Amending Act makes clear, it is the reduction in cross-subsidisation of risks through insurance as a result of the industry's more sophisticated pricing of it ('address level pricing'), which has contributed at least as much as adverse claims experience to the unaffordability of insurance problem in northern Australia which the Pool is intended to rectify. Compounding this effect is the common requirement for insurance businesses to deliver underwriting profit[61] across regions, as well as by class and portfolio.

If the general insurance industry, in deciding whether to accept and how to price risk, instead of continuing to fulfil its traditional function of facilitating the diversification of risk and cross-subsidisation of losses across the wider community, instead allows itself to become trapped in an underwriter's version of the fund managers' interminable 'quest for alpha',[62] then its range of acceptable risks, available premium pool and relevance to society can all be expected rapidly to decline, in the same order. All risks lie on a spectrum of probability, between vanishingly remote at one end and practically inevitable at the other. The goal of underwriting is to evaluate, with as much precision as the current state of the art allows, whereabouts on the spectrum of frequency and seriousness a particular hazard sits and to price it accordingly.

The more technologically sophisticated this process becomes, the more precisely and accurately risks can be segregated and classified in order of investment desirability, thereby refining pricing but reducing uncertainty and cross-subsidisation. Commercial insurers compete more intensely for risks the closer they lie toward the remote end of the probability scale and less for those on the other side of the mid-point. The latter become less attractive the farther they get from it. None of that should surprise anyone. However, if the process of risk classification and selection becomes too efficient there may be adverse consequences for both insurers and governments.

The more the commercial insurance industry's ability to cherry-pick the more desirable areas of risk within a polity is enhanced, the greater the withdrawal of cross-subsidisation of those less desirable. Higher premiums for the latter then need to be charged to ensure profitability, leading to underinsurance and the need

[61] The term 'underwriting profit' in its simplest form refers to the situation in which, for a given portfolio of risks over a stipulated period, $(A+B) + C < D$, where A = losses paid, B = losses incurred but not reported, C = allocated and operating expenses including cost of sales and D = earned premium.

[62] A term used by stockbrokers and other finance professionals, to describe the small set of investments in every class which consistently outperform the market average.

for further rate increases to support the premium pool. A vicious circle develops which makes insurance still harder to buy and further shrinks the overall proportion of risk in that polity which is managed by means of it. Government then needs to step in and assume responsibility, one way or another, for the redistribution of risks which previously were the preserve of the commercial insurance industry.

If private insurers go too far in narrowing acceptance criteria and excluding cross-subsidisation from the rate-setting process, then rather than promoting improvements in risk management and loss mitigation improvement, they risk progressively pricing themselves out of underwriting the less profitable categories of risk. They then must compete ever harder to insure the attractive ones for which, by their nature and the intensity of the competition, they cannot charge as high a premium. The need to deliver a sufficient rate of return on their capital then forces them to merge or go under, so we finish up with a relatively small group of large insurers trying to sell insurance to an ever more select class of prime risk policyholders, who are the people in the community least likely to need it and smart enough to realise as much. Another vicious circle.

Eventually it dawns on the government that it has been handed the rough end of the pineapple,[63] with a small number of large insurers squabbling over and profiting from the choicest categories of risks and leaving the remainder to be underwritten effectively by the taxpayers. At that point, the talk usually turns toward one or another form of additional tax impost on the remaining insurers which they then pass through to their policyholders, thus restoring a measure of risk cross-subsidisation.

To re-state the obvious, the property insurance problem in cyclone-prone areas of northern Australia is not one of uninsurable risk but of un-affordably insurable risk. That unaffordability is not just a function of the frequency and magnitude of losses in the affected areas. It is due at least as much to the insurance industry's narrowly focussed risk selection and rating algorithms, which in this instance narrow the population of policyholders whose premiums are counted, in determining whether a class of insurance in a designated region delivers an underwriting profit for the insurer, to those payable by the inhabitants of that region. Since there are fewer contributors to the relevant premium pool out of which losses are notionally paid, they all must pay more in order to accumulate a premium pool adequate to cover those losses, pay expenses and deliver a profit margin sufficient to ensure a reasonable ROE for the insurer.

XIII. Conclusion

As the proposition that major climate change this century can be avoided becomes more obviously untenable and is eventually abandoned by governments,

[63] To employ a popular far north Queensland metaphor.

adaptation will become the new socio-political imperative. As well as greater forethought in urban planning and deployment of more robust materials, designs and construction methods, ameliorating the effects of major weather events on local communities though risk sharing with the wider population by all feasible methods will form an essential part of social adaptation and the preservation of viable remote communities.

Ways of attenuating the direct financial risks of climate change for individuals, alternative to insurance underwritten at the local level, need to be evaluated. Parametric trigger-based financial products such as weather swaps, contingent capital and contingent credit bonds, complemented by capital market securitisations of the underlying asset portfolios, have long been used for managing risks at the margins of insurability and now are well understood and regulated. Like insurance itself, the original form of derivative contract, these 'alternative risk transfer' instruments all represent just different methods of funding, transferring and investing in risk to underlying assets, a concept which is as old as human cooperation.

9

Climate Litigation Risk: The Limits of Insurance and Tort Law

LIVASHNEE NAIDOO

I. Introduction

Climate change is a global issue which has widespread effects.[1] Legal and regulatory commitments from governments and corporates, as well as growing awareness of the effects of climate change has necessitated evolving legal and policy commitments to address climate change. From an insurance perspective, initiatives include measures to transition to a low carbon economy, such as, innovative insurance products that involve impact underwriting and investment to shape and incentivise customer behaviours to mitigate the impact of climate change and withdrawing from certain carbon-intensive markets.[2] Whilst these ex-ante measures are important as part of the climate change dialogue, the related ex-post issue of climate litigation is receiving increasing attention both in law and scholarship.[3] Climate litigation is an emerging risk for insurers both as corporate actors and for exposure for climate litigation against their policyholders due to the policies which they underwrite, and therefore presents novel challenges for insurance law rules and doctrine.

Climate change can be conceptualised into three categories: physical risk, transition risk, and liability risk.[4] Whilst there are many categorisations of climate

[1] The Framework Convention on Climate Change (UNFCCC) Article 1, defines climate change as: 'a change of climate which is attributed directly or indirectly to human activity that alters the composition of the global atmosphere and which is in addition to natural climate variability observed over comparable time periods'.

[2] See F Arnold-Dwyer, *Insurance, Climate Change and the Law* (Abingdon, Routledge, 2024) Ch 1.

[3] 'Climate litigation broadly defined includes lawsuits brought before administrative, judicial and other investigatory bodies, in domestic and international courts and organisations, that raise issues of law or fact regarding the science of climate change and climate change mitigation and adaptation efforts', J Setzer and C Higham, 'Global Trends in Climate Change Litigation: 2021 Snapshot' (2001) *Grantham Research Institute on Climate Change and the Environment and Centre for Climate Change Economics and Policy* 8.

[4] M Carney, 'Breaking the Tragedy of the Horizon – Climate Change and Financial Stability' (Speech at Lloyd's of London, September 2015) www.bankofengland.co.uk/speech/2015/breaking-the-tragedy-of-the-horizon-climate-change-and-financial-stability.

litigation risk, the focus of this chapter is where a carbon emitter (the policyholder) is sued based on a cause of action in the (English) law of torts for climate-related damages, and the policyholder's liability insurer may have to respond to such claims (often referred to as the 'carbon majors' cases).[5] Tort law is one of the primary legal grounds which may support a cause of action for climate-related damages and which may expand insurers' liabilities for these novel claims. Climate change impacts different policy lines but will have a particularly prominent effect on liability insurance. Liability policies protect the defendant policyholder as the claimant can only access funds if they establish liability on the part of the defendant.

Climate litigation raise complex and evolving considerations for tort law and liability insurance. There are over 2,000 climate change cases currently being litigated in more than 40 jurisdictions.[6] Whilst climate litigation scholarship has grown exponentially, the insurance perspective is usually included as peripheral to the main discussion largely due to an absence of case law.[7] This chapter remedies that by shifting the analysis so that insurance is central to the enquiry. Section 2 presents an overview of the different classifications of climate change risk and their insurability, and then proceeds to discuss the different types of climate litigation risks which sets the scope of this chapter. Section 3 examines the insurance principles and doctrines that are implicated by climate litigation through the example of commercial general liability (CGL) policies. Section 4 examines the more 'traditional liability setting' in tort law and draws out the important nexus with liability insurance in the context of climate litigation. In doing so, it considers whether insurance and tort law principles may chaff against each other. Section 5 revisits the intersection between tort and insurance in the context of climate litigation. It discusses how law and practice in insurance law should develop, and how to balance the value of liability insurance as a product against the regulation of climate litigation.

II. The Insurability of Climate Risks

A. Insurability in Brief

Insurability is not a dichotomy between insurable and uninsurable risks, but rather insurability exists on a spectrum. Risks that are catastrophic, too unpredictable in occurrence and effect, difficult to quantify and price, or cannot be priced at

[5] The focus is English law, but reference will be made to other jurisdictions as necessary.

[6] Sabin Centre for Climate Change Law (January 2023) climatecasechart.com/about/.

[7] An exception is: J W Stempel, *Insurance and Climate Change Litigation*, in W C G Burns and H M Osofsky (eds) *Adjudicating Climate Change: Sub-National, National and Supra-national Approaches* (Cambridge, Cambridge University Press, 2009).

an affordable level are uninsurable. Climate-related risks, emerging and dynamic, present several challenges to insurability due to the difficulties with financial measurement in calculating premiums and losses, and because climate risks can be correlated risks.[8] Insurability challenges can render insurance cover for climate risk unavailable in certain markets, premiums can be set too high which affects affordability, and/or insurers could withdraw insurance cover from particular perils or geographical areas because losses have become incalculable.[9] Recognising the risk to the insurance sector, the UK's Prudential Regulation Authority (PRA) set out its expectations for UK insurers in its Supervisory Statement 3/19 to the effect that insurers should review their exposure to policyholders' climate liability through scenarios developed by regulators.[10]

Climate change risks can be classified into three categories; physical risks, transition risks, and liability risks – each of which raise different questions for insurability.[11] The former two will be considered briefly as it is not the focus of this chapter. Physical risks associated with climate change include flooding, wildfires, rising sea levels and these risks can result in direct physical loss or damage to property (eg, a policyholder may file a first party insurance claim to cover the costs of repair or replacement), or indirect losses such as supply chain interruptions, due to the increasing severity and frequency of extreme weather events (acute risks) and long-term shifts in climate patterns (chronic risks) caused by climate change.[12] The insurability of physical risks has become more pressing due to projected increases in the frequency and severity of natural disasters and the increase in insurance claims for climate-related losses. Transition risks, on the other hand, refer to financial impacts of transitioning to a low carbon economy, and these risks (eg, regulatory, technological, reputational, market risk) generally lean towards the uninsurability spectrum as 'they lack specificity, calculability and insurable interest'.[13]

Liability risk arises from climate-related litigation and is a claims risk. Climate litigation risks can implicate several policy lines, notably, CGL policies, professional indemnity, and Directors & Officers (D&O). This chapter examines

[8] Climate change presents the possibility of correlated risks where a single event can result in greater exposure leading to several claims arising from the same event (eg, a hurricane that causes property damage to an entire geographical area).

[9] eg, see Arnold-Dwyer (n2) 7, citing the example of California homeowners who can no longer buy any property insurance covering for wildfires or where coverage has become unaffordable.

[10] Prudential Regulation Authority, 'Supervisory Statement SS3/19: Enhancing Banks' and insurers' approaches to managing the financial risks from climate change' (Bank of England, 2019) www.bankofengland.co.uk/-/media/boe/files/prudential-regulation/supervisory-statement/2019/ss319.

[11] Carney (n4). See also: The Geneva Association, 'Anchoring Climate Change Risk Assessment in Core Business Decisions in Insurance' (September 2022) 14 www.genevaassociation.org/publication/climate-change-and-environment/climate-change-risk-3-report.

[12] M Golnaraghi and J Setzer et al, 'Climate Change Litigation: Insights into the Evolving Global Landscape' (2021) www.genevaassociation.org/publication/climate-change-and-environment/climate-change-litigation-insights-evolving-global. Personal injury policies will not be considered in this chapter.

[13] Arnold-Dwyer (n2) Ch 3. *Lucena v Craufurd* [1806] 2 Bos & P NR 269, 321.

exposure to climate litigation risk arising from current portfolios of CGL underwritten policies, and whether such policies may respond to a climate-related claim for monetary damages due to bodily injury and/or property damage that took place during the policy period. Climate liability is not an uninsurable risk; however, insurers often struggle to estimate their exposure to climate litigation risk.[14] Whilst climate litigation scholarship is burgeoning, a framework to understand the costs that can arise from climate litigation remains elusive in the absence of legal precedents and can impact insurability under existing liability portfolios.[15]

B. Climate Litigation Risks and Insurance

Climate litigation cases can be categorised in various ways based on temporal factors, the motivation of the litigation (although these aims may overlap), and the type of litigants or claimants. The first type of climate litigation cases includes those against governments and public bodies for failing to mitigate or adapt to climate change where the outcome is deterrence or regulatory change. This type of litigation has constituted the bulk of claims in the USA and is rooted in regulatory frameworks regulating greenhouse gas emissions (GHG emissions).[16] The primary claimants would be environmental groups, but Kaminskaite-Salters states that insurance companies can also be the potential claimants where they are suing to instigate behavioural changes or face the risk that their financial exposure may be increased.[17]

The second category are actions against corporations and boards by shareholders, stakeholders, and investors for failing to disclose or inaccurate disclosure of climate risks and benefits in public corporate documentation or product information. Greenwashing could also create liability risks where policyholders

[14] Arnold-Dwyer (n2) Ch 3: 'Climate liability risk shows no signs of becoming uninsurable and instead is being embraced by insurers as a risk to be managed as well as presenting business opportunities for new products'. See also S Doering, M Radcliffe, and M Lockman, 'Climate Litigation Risk: Is there Shelter from the Storm?' www.wtwco.com/en-gb/insights/2023/09/climate-litigation-risk-is-there-shelter-from-the-storm#:~:text=Disputes%20arising%20from%20breaches%20of,its%20activities%20on%20climate%20change; Bank of England, 'Results of the 2021 Climate Biennial Exploratory Scenario (CBES)' www.bankofengland.co.uk/stress-testing/2022/results-of-the-2021-climate-biennial-exploratory-scenario.

[15] J Solana, 'Climate Change Litigation as Financial Risk' (2020) 2 *Green Finance* 344, 347, 362, citing C P Harding and W McDaniels J, et al 'Turning up the Heat – Climate Risk Assessment in the Insurance Sector' (2019) *Financial Stability Institute Insights* (No 20) *Bank for International Settlements*.

[16] Relevant regulatory frameworks in the UK include eg the Climate Change Act 2008, and the EU Emissions Trading Scheme, the Environmental Liability Directive.

[17] G Kaminskaite-Salters, 'Climate Change Litigation in the UK: Its Feasibility and Prospects" in M Faure and M Peeters (eds), *Climate Change Liability* (Cheltenham, Edward Elgar Publishing, 2011) 170. This is beyond the scope of this chapter but may raise interesting and novel questions about new insurance products and the limits of insurance and tort doctrine.

greenwash their products or services and may face a variety of claims, including, failure to label products correctly or failure to disclose material risks to investors.[18] These types of claims are based on corporate due diligence standards, a potential breach of fiduciary duties and will trigger D&O insurance policies.[19]

The third category and the focus of this chapter is where a private party seek damages through tort law (nuisance, product liability, trespass, or negligence) against policyholders ('carbon majors'). As carbon majors, these companies are viewed as key contributors to GHG emissions that cause climate-related damage but there have been mixed judicial responses to these claims which have yet to be successful in the UK. The defendant may defend that claim on its own but usually the defendant will look to its liability insurer to defend (or indemnify) the claim. Liability insurance protects the insured against the risk of being held legally liable for any loss and/or damage suffered by other parties as a result of the insured's actions, including any potential pay-out resulting from the claim. Under English law the insurer does not have a general duty to defend a claim but the duty to defend can arise through an express contractual term in the policy. If such a contractual duty exists, the liability insurer will determine if its duty to defend is triggered, that is, does the claim fall within the scope of the policy (the insurance question). If the duty has not been triggered, the insurer will refuse to defend, and the defendant will have to defend itself. If the duty has been triggered, the insurer takes over the litigation and defends the claim on behalf of the insured defendant. In both the latter instances, it becomes a tort law question to determine what duty was owed to the claimant by the defendant and if the duty was breached. Where there is no contractual duty to defend, the extent of the insurers involvement in the defence of the claim or in indemnifying the insured depends on the policy language. It is common for subrogation and assignment clauses to be included in policies often as a substitute for the duty to defend clause.[20]

For purposes of this chapter, the focus is on the insurance and tort question, namely, where a contractual duty to defend exists, and the related tort law question. The tort law question in this context is classified as backward-looking than forward-looking climate litigation as the aim is compensation than deterrence. Adopting this classification connects more closely to the later discussion on the purpose and principles of tort law.

[18] See eg, *Australasian Centre for Corporate Responsibility v Santos Limited* NSD858/202, a case filed in Australia.

[19] Such as under Sections 172 and 174 of the Companies Act 2006.

[20] A subrogation clause gives the insurer the right, after it has paid the insured, to step into the shoes of the insured and claim the losses from the relevant third party (see *Castellain v Preston* [1883] 11 QBD 380). Assignment occurs through agreement whereby the rights of the insured are assigned to the insurer.

III. Climate Litigation and the Limits of Liability Insurance

A. The Duty to Defend or Indemnify

Liability policies comprise two key elements: the duty to defend or to indemnify. The duty to defend is triggered when a covered claim is made against the insured and in that case the insurer is required to defend the insured against liability. The insurer (and its legal counsel) effectively takes over the defence, settlement and negotiation regardless of whether the claim is valid. To trigger the duty to defend, the insured must make a timely tender of the claim to its insurer otherwise late notification of the claim can prejudice the insurer's duty to defend.[21] The insurer also has a duty to indemnify the insured against covered losses and this duty is triggered when liability is established arising from a judgment, arbitral award, or settlement. The insurer may take the view that it is not liable under the policy and may refuse to defend the insured, or the insurer may exercise a reservation of rights where even if the insured is successful, the insurer may refuse to indemnify the insured.[22]

The motivation of climate litigation can impose limitations on the duty to defend or indemnify. Liability insurance is ordinarily triggered by a claim for monetary damages against the policyholder for causing property damage (or bodily harm) to the plaintiff. The consequence is that certain types of climate litigation would fall outside the wrongdoer's CGL policies and will not trigger the duty to defend principle. For instance, forward-looking cases that have the aim of deterrence to deter companies and governments from actions that can contribute to climate change damage or losses, or cases seeking injunctive relief, or regulatory compliance on the basis that companies have failed to adapt or mitigate climate effects, or human rights litigation are likely to not trigger CGL policies as the remedy sought is not monetary damages.

In climate litigation there may be a combination of covered claims and uncovered claims as described above. In that instance, the liability insurer's duty to defend will remain alive although recoupment of fees will remain in issue.[23] The duty to defend is considered to be broader than the duty to indemnify as the insurer is required to provide a defence (provided the claim falls within the policy coverage and there are no applicable exclusions) even if the claim turns out to be groundless or the insured is found to have no legal liability. The duty to indemnify is contingent on actual liability but the duty to defend is more

[21] J Birds, B Lynch, and S Paul, *MacGillivray on Insurance Law* (15th edn, London, Sweet & Maxwell, 2023) 28–040.

[22] R Merkin and J Steele, *Insurance and the Law of Obligations* (Oxford, Oxford University Press, 2013) 393. See eg, *AES Corp v. Steadfast Ins Co*, 725 S E 2d 532 (Va 2012).

[23] Stemple (n7) 246.

immediate and is a response to a claim not liability. It could be said that the duty to defend is not broader but merely triggered more often.

The duty to defend is triggered by allegations in the claim (and the terms of the insurance policy)[24] rather than a final determination of liability and may be impacted by how plaintiffs plead their tort claims. The doctrine of the duty to defend (and to a lesser extent the duty to indemnify) will undergo scrutiny if private litigation for climate-related damages becomes more prevalent. Establishing tort liability for climate-related losses remains novel and uncertain, liability insurers' duty to indemnify may not be triggered in these early stages; but with the increase in climate litigation, the duty to defend will become more prominent. The starting basis to trigger the duty to defend is a covered claim and the first battle lines will be drawn in relation to coverage issues under CGL policies.

B. Coverage

When faced with a claim for climate-related liability, policyholders will look to their liability insurers for defence and indemnity. To trigger a liability insurer's duty to defend, the claim must fall within the policy and not be subject to any contractual exclusions. A CGL policy is triggered when a covered event takes place during the policy period, and this depends on whether it is occurrence-based or a claims-made liability policy. The key difference between these policies relate to the trigger for coverage and the fact that the former looks to the past and the latter looks to the future. Occurrence-based policies are triggered by a claim of bodily injury or property damage during the policy period due to an 'occurrence'. The trigger is the date of injury to the third party and not the date of the claim or the date of when the wrongdoing or negligence occurred. In climate litigation contexts, the property damage will have to have occurred during the policy period to trigger the CGL policy for that year.

Occurrence-based policies are the most common and are more suitable for long tail risks where the manifestation of injury may occur after the wrongdoing. Claims-made policies are when a claim is made against the insured during the policy period regardless of when the incident causing the claim occurred. These types of policies tend to have a retroactive date which is a date from when the insured is covered for claims, are more affordable – but can result in coverage gaps when switching claims-made policies.[25] Difficulties may arise in the temporal scope where there is excess liability coverage such as the Bermuda Form, which provides cover that sits on top of the primary liability cover and responds where the primary policy limits are exhausted.[26] For example, Article III.V(1)(a) of the

[24] Such as, that the duty to defend will only be triggered if there is a reasonable chance of succeeding which can also result in interpretative disputes between insured and insurer.

[25] Merkin and Steele (n22) 69.

[26] The Bermuda Form is used for high value risks environmental liability, product liability etc. *AstraZeneca Insurance Company Ltd v XL Insurance (Bermuda) Ltd & ACE Bermuda Insurance Ltd*

Bermuda Form provides for the event itself to take place within the policy period which differs from the typical CGL position where the damage must occur in the policy period.

In what circumstances would a particular climate-change-based event come within the definition of an 'occurrence' in a liability policy. 'Occurrence' is generally defined in the policy along the lines of an 'accident, including continuous or repeated exposure to conditions' which causes 'bodily injury' or 'property damage'. Additionally, it may include a clause that the injury or damage is neither expected nor intended by the insured. Insurers may argue that the climate change event was not 'accidental' or that the injury or damage was 'expected' or 'intended' (fortuity-based defences) and therefore falls outside the scope of the policy coverage.

Liability policies cover only the risk of fortuitous loss as insurance is about uncertainty, and for losses that are not caused wilfully which is closely linked to principles of public policy applicable to insurance contracts. The concept of fortuity – with its roots in marine insurance is necessary for a risk to be insurable.[27] In insurance contract law, as explained by Bennett, 'fortuity is a variable concept that addresses both the likelihood of loss and the cause of the loss'.[28] As Lord Herschell said of perils of the sea in *The Xantho*, '[t]he purpose of the policy is to secure an indemnity against accidents which may happen, not against events which must happen'.[29] Therefore fortuity relates to something unexpected but is fortuity a matter of contractual interpretation or is it an insurance rule about risk?[30] Stempel says, '[a]lthough insurance is available only for fortuitous, accident-like losses and not for losses wilfully brought about by the policyholder, it is unlikely that insurers can defeat policyholder requests for climate change coverage on this basis'.[31]

Fortuity is linked to the express wording of the policy provisions as liability policies frequently include provisions such as those in the CGL policy which excludes coverage for 'expected' or 'intended' harm. Thereby implying that unless

[2013] EWCA Civ 1660 where the underlying policy was a Bermuda Form contract, which is usually governed by New York law with London arbitration, but here there was an express choice of English law and English Courts.

[27] Fortuity is defined in rule 7 of Schedule 1 of the Marine Insurance Act of 1906 which states: '[t]he term "perils of the seas" refers only to fortuitous accidents or casualties of the seas. It does not include the ordinary action of winds and waves'.

[28] H Bennett, 'Fortuity in the Law of Marine Insurance' (2007) *Lloyd's Maritime and Commercial Law Quarterly* 315. For general examination of 'fortuity' see Notes 'The Luck of the Law: Allusions to Fortuity in Legal Discourse' (1989) 102 Harvard Law Review 1862; S Cozen and R Bennett, 'Fortuity: The Unnamed Exclusion' (1985) 20 *The Forum* (American Bar Association) 222.

[29] *Wilson Sons & Co v Owners of Cargo per the Xantho* (*The Xantho*) [1887] 12 App Cas 503, 509. See also *NE Neter & Co Ltd v Licences & General Insurance Co Ltd* [1944] 77 LIL Rep 202 and *The Catharine Chalmers* [1875] 32 LT (NS) 847.

[30] See, *Beresford v Royal Insurance Co* [1938] AC 586 and *British and Foreign Marine Insurance Co Ltd v. Gaunt* [1921] 2 for differing judicial views on 'fortuity'. See also, *Ikergi Compania Naviera SA v. Palmer, The Wondrous* [1991] 1 Lloyd's Rep 400.

[31] Stemple (n7) 241.

there is coverage for a 'known loss' where, for example, a policyholder intended or expected that the release of emissions would have the effect, climate change should fall outside the scope of coverage for CGL. The proposition that only fortuitous loss may be insured does not imply that insurance is only for unpredictable losses; the corollary of this argument being that expected or intentional losses are predictable and falls outside coverage (or is not insurable).[32] The fact that the insured engaged in intentional activities that released emissions which contributed to climate change damage does not necessarily follow that the resultant damage was foreseen.[33] Intentional activity can still result in accidental damage which would trigger coverage; an insured may protect against a risk that he brings about himself provided, as Abraham states, that the assured does not have the intention at the time of contracting as that would not constitute fortuity.[34]

Climate change although, arguably, foreseeable with the growing scientific evidence would not constitute a 'known-loss' when insurance is purchased, and even if it did there is still uncertainty as to whether liability for climate change will be imposed and the extent thereof.[35] In relation to insurability, it should therefore still constitute a fortuitous loss. Nevertheless, insurance policies typically preclude liability for 'expected' or 'intended' harm and the starting point should be the policy terms which either captures or does not capture fortuity, rather than a focus on whether climate change is a non-fortuitous loss as that implies a separate legal rule.[36] If disclosure obligations are met[37] which address information asymmetries about the loss there should be little reason for effect not to be given to the contractual terms as agreed by the parties and for insurers to rely on fortuity defences. Non-fortuity defences raised by insurers to defeat insurance coverage for climate change remain unconvincing and should be assessed as part of the construction of the insurance contract.

In a more recent case of *Steadfast Insurance Co v AES Corp*, an insurance company sought a declaratory judgment that it was not required to defend or indemnify its policyholder, an energy company, in underlying litigation seeking climate change-related damages.[38] A claim had been brought against the policyholder by a native Alaskan village (Kivalina) who claimed on the basis of nuisance that the policyholder's activities (amongst others) had contributed to climate change which led to the destruction of the village. The Virginia Supreme Court reaffirmed its previous holding that the insurance company had no duty to defend

[32] See K S Abraham, 'Peril and Fortuity in Property and Liability Insurance' (2001) 36 *Tort & Insurance Law Journal* 777, 779 as to why predictability matters in insurance. See K Abraham, *Distributing Risk: Insurance, Legal Theory, and Public Policy* (New Haven, Yale University Press, 1986).

[33] This distinction was drawn in *Steadfast* (n22).

[34] K S Abraham, 'Peril and Fortuity' (n32) 792.

[35] Drawing on ibid, 794.

[36] K S Abraham, 'Peril and Fortuity' (n32) 781–782, 778.

[37] Under the Insurance Act 2015 and the Consumer (Insurance and Disclosure Representations) Act 2012.

[38] See *Steadfast* (n22).

or indemnify the insured as there was no coverage for an 'occurrence' for the purposes of the CGL policy in question. The court held there was no coverage as the resulting harm is alleged to have been the 'natural or probable consequence' of the insured's intentional act.[39]

Climate litigation will raise coverage disputes regarding the triggers for CGL policies and on how fortuity-based defences will be interpreted by courts. It will be interesting to see how the fault of the policyholder, that is, if they knew about the effects of their activities which could cause damage would negate 'accidental occurrence' and imply that the damage was expected or intended, thereby falling outside policy coverage. There is robust evidence about the connection between GHG emissions and climate change which raises the question whether climate change can ever be considered 'accidental'.[40] For the reasons mentioned previously, it is unlikely that such a broad (objective) interpretation that any intentional activity that could result in climate change damage would be excluded from coverage. Rather, a more restrictive, subjective approach seems sensible by considering whether the defendant policyholder knew that the damage would occur from its activity.

A further interpretative difficulty will arise with what constitutes 'property damage' arising from an occurrence. 'Property damage' is generally defined as 'physical injury to tangible property, including all resulting loss of use of that property' or as 'loss of use of tangible property that is not physically injured'.[41] Examples include damage to property due to flooding from a rise in sea levels. It is unlikely that *potential* damage, or preventative or mitigative measures to avoid loss will be caught, for example, relocating buildings or building a dam to prevent flooding.

The US case of *Everest Premier Insurance Co v Gulf Oil LP* highlights the interpretative difficulties on 'property damage.[42] The liability insurers' lawsuit sought declarations that the policies did not obligate the insurers to defend or indemnify Gulf Oil LP (the insured) in a lawsuit alleging failure to prepare a bulk petroleum terminal in New Haven, Connecticut for climate change impacts. The basis was that the allegations in the underlying claim against Gulf Oil did not involve any bodily injury or existing property damage that was caused by an occurrence during the policy period. The underlying suit instead alleged 'a risk of *potential* property damage from ongoing and future weather events related to global warming and climate-change'. The insurer also additionally argued that even if there had been property damage, the pollution exclusion amongst others in the policy excluded coverage. Although the insurer has since voluntarily withdrawn its case, this case highlights the interpretative difficulties on 'property damage'. It also leads

[39] These aspects will be discussed further in section 4.

[40] P Minnerop and F Otto, 'Climate Change and Causation: Joining Law and Climate Science on the Basis of Formal Logic' (2020) 27 *Buffalo Environmental Law Journal* 49.

[41] Not all CGL policies cover loss of use of property not physically injured.

[42] No 2284-CV-01291 (Mass Super Ct Oct 18, 2022).

to the next question about policy exclusions for climate-related claims, notably whether the standard pollution exclusion in CGL policies will capture climate change.

C. Pollution Exclusions

In a recent insurance coverage case in the US, *Aloha Petroleum Ltd v National Union Fire Insurance Co of Pittsburgh*, a fossil fuel company sued its liability insurer for breaching its obligations to defend and indemnify the company in underlying climate change cases brought by Honolulu and Maui.[43] The insurer argued that the policy in question contained a pollution exclusion which would exclude cover for Aloha Petroleum's alleged conduct. More specifically, for an 'occurrence' insurance policy, would GHG emissions constitute 'pollutants' under the pollution exclusion? The fossil fuel company argued for a distinction between greenhouse gases and 'traditional environmental pollution' so that bodily injury or property damage arising out of the insured's products would constitute 'products hazard' for which cover would be available.[44]

While GHGs are considered 'pollutants' under a number of legal frameworks, *Aloha Petroleum Ltd* highlights the interpretive difficulties and uncertainties whether climate change effects are a 'pollutant'.[45] Many CGL policies now contain a pollution exclusion clause, and although the clauses differ, they are often broadly worded. In the UK, policies may exclude pollution unless caused by a specific, sudden, accidental event. The Bermuda Form Pollution Exclusion, Article IV.K, provides for what is prima facie an absolute pollution exclusion, albeit with three 'escape' clauses which 'write back' cover in certain circumstances. Pollution exclusions typically provide that there is no cover for 'bodily injury' or 'property damage' that 'would not have occurred but for the actual or alleged, discharge, dispersal, seepage, migration, release, or escape of pollutants'.[46] The precise definition of 'pollutant' varies but is most commonly defined in a CGL policy as '[a]ny solid, liquid, gaseous or thermal irritant or contaminant, including smoke, vapor, soot, fumes, acids, alkalis, chemicals and waste …'.[47]

[43] Civ No 22–372.

[44] N l Brook, W Lawrence and L Williams, 'Climate Change: Liability Risk' in A Tarr, J Tarr et al (eds), *The Global Insurance Market and Change: Emerging Technologies, Risks and Legal Challenges* (Abingdon, Routledge, 2024) 465.

[45] See also USA case examples where GHG emissions seem to constitute 'pollutant': *Am Elec Power Co v Connecticut*, 564 US 410 (2011); *Essex Ins Co v. Tri-Town Corp*, 863 F Supp 38 (D Mass 1994); *Donaldson v Urban Land Interests, Inc*, 564 N W 2d 728 (Wis 1997); *Motorists Mut Ins Co v RSJ, Inc*, 926 S W 2d 679 (Ky Ct App 1996).

[46] D Scorey, D Walsh and H Morton, 'Climate Change and Insurance Law' files.essexcourt.com/wp-content/uploads/2022/07/01115614/Climate-Change-and-Insurance-Law.pdf.

[47] Lloyds' 'General Liability Insurance Policy Wording' prokopius.com/wp-content/uploads/2019/11/lma3150a-wording.pdf.

Given the variation in the wording of pollution exclusions, rather than engage in a discussion about general interpretative principles in insurance law, it is more beneficial to extract the main considerations about the applicability of (pollution) exclusions to climate litigation. If the exclusions are applicable and causation has been established (discussed below), it will operate to exclude coverage – even potential coverage – under the CGL policy which may result in the duty to defend not being triggered. In *Crowden v QBE Insurance (Europe) Limited*, Peter MacDonald Eggers QC sitting as a Deputy High Court Judge held that 'the Court must adopt an approach to the interpretation of insurance exclusions which is sensitive to their purpose and place in the insurance contract'.[48] Exclusion clauses in insurance contract law serve a different purpose from exemption clauses in general contract law, in that the former defines the risk that the insurer is willing to assume, whereas the latter excludes or limits a party's legal liability.[49] A narrow approach to the interpretation of exclusion clauses has been rejected except where there is genuine ambiguity. Further difficulties in interpreting the scope of the 'pollution exclusion' may relate to whether the pollutant (emissions) was knowingly, intentionally, or accidentally emitted and policies may respond differently. This may be compounded by differences in jurisdictional approaches to policy interpretation and where GHG emissions are deemed to be a 'pollutant' under specific policies. Courts are likely to be divided as to whether GHG emissions can be classed as a traditional pollutant or something quite apart.

Given the inherent uncertainty, one can expect that new pollution clauses will need to be drafted depending on the type of policy and whether those exclusions can operate to include GHG emissions. It could be argued that climate change is a known occurrence given the scientific information that is now available, and therefore GHG emissions could easily be caught by typical exclusions which exclude occurrences known to the insured. The Lloyd's Market Association has published LMA5570 a model climate change exclusion for use in liability policies. The clause includes reference to a definition of climate change, the source of which is the UN Framework Convention on Climate Change (1992, Article 1 (2).[50]

> **Climate Change Exclusion**
>
> Notwithstanding any other provision in this Policy or any endorsement hereto, this Policy excludes any loss, liability, cost or expense arising out of any allegation or claim that the (Re)Insured caused or contributed to Climate Change or its consequences. For the purposes of this clause Climate Change means a change of climate which is attributed directly or indirectly to human activity.[51]

[48] [2017] EWHC 2597 (Comm).

[49] *Crowden v QBE Insurance (Europe) Limited* [2017] EWHC 2597 (Comm). See also, *Impact Funding Solutions Ltd v AIG Europe Insurance Ltd* [2016] UKSC 57.

[50] Lloyd's Market Association, 'LMA Model Climate Change Exclusion' www.lmalloyds.com/LMA/News/LMA_bulletins/LMA_Bulletins/LMA21-041-DP.aspx. It was produced with input from the Joint Committees and the Non-Marine market.

[51] ibid.

More innovative exclusions clauses may be linked to an insured's failure to meet ex-ante measures of emissions targets or to use best endeavours to do so, in that case the policy will provide coverage unless insured have failed to reach those targets.[52]

D. Aggregation

Climate change can give rise to correlated losses and the number of occurrences could have severe monetary implications on available policy limits and could exhaust policy coverage. Policies commonly contain an aggregation clause which determines how the policy responds to more than one event, loss, or claim, depending on the type of insurance cover and whether those should be treated as a single event, loss, or claim. If the policy does not include an aggregation clause, it will not ordinarily be possible to imply any such clause. If there is more than one claim, the insured may be able to aggregate the claims as one claim and bear a single deductible. On the other hand, insurers may be able to aggregate the claims against the insured so that the limit of indemnity applies to the total amount of all claims than to each separate claim.[53]

Aggregation is fact specific and context specific as varying terminology can be used in policies to determine whether losses can be aggregated, such as occurrence, event, cause, accident, and claim.[54] Consider, for example, if a CGL policy refers to 'any one occurrence' as a limitation of the losses that can be claimed under that policy. In relation to climate change, a tort-based claim where the insured's conduct has led to multiple losses could lead to questions whether an emission would constitute one occurrence or would separate emissions constitute one occurrence or separate occurrences? It is difficult to provide any general viewpoints as English courts have said that aggregation is matter of context and policy language.[55]

Aggregation clauses are another type of clause that will need to be revisited in the context of climate litigation. Aggregation of claims may be easier in some contexts than others. In *AIG Europe Ltd v Woodman*[56] the case concerned the interpretation of an aggregation clause in a professional indemnity policy which

[52] The Chancery Lane Project, 'Condition to Liability Cover for Climate-Related Claims (Commercial Insureds)' chancerylaneproject.org/climate-clauses/exclusions-from-insurance-coverage-for-climate-harms/.

[53] Merkin and Steele (n22) 71.

[54] ibid 72.

[55] In *Lloyds TSB v Lloyds Bank Group Insurance Co Ltd* [2003] UKHL 48, the House of Lords pointed out that the scope of aggregation depended on the nature of the act or event treated as a unifying factor, so that the choice of language was critical. The court also discussed the difference between tort law and insurance law in ascertaining the proximate cause The approach to interpreting aggregation clauses was summarised by the Court of Appeal *Inspire Healthcare Ltd v Royal & Sun Alliance Insurance Ltd* [2022] EWCA Civ 17. See also *AIG Europe v Woodman* [2017] UKSC 18.

[56] [2017] UKSC 18.

provided for aggregation of all claims arising from 'similar acts or omissions in a series of related matters'. The Supreme Court held that 'related' required a 'real connection', but this provides little guidance to policyholders where the situation is not factually similar to the *AIG Europe Ltd* decision.

There are uncertainties about how aggregation clauses will be interpreted in relation to climate related 'occurrences' and losses. As addressed in the following paragraphs, establishing the relevant linkages between events or claims will involve causational elements. There are various approaches that could be adopted in relation to climate change: are courts likely to find a single proximate cause (eg, a corporate decision taken by the insured to burn fossil fuels), will they focus on the end point (eg, the number of discrete, harmful effects from the emissions),[57] or could there be the possibility of a middle-ground where the cause or effects can be broken down even further.

E. Causation

Causative questions in insurance have developed independently of tort law. In insurance the insurer is liable for losses proximately caused by an insured peril which is the dominant or effective cause.[58] The onus is on the insured to show that the (climate-related) claim falls within the insured coverage, and the burden then shifts to the insurer to prove that the loss falls within a policy exclusion, which if successful will bar coverage. Whilst tort law recognises apportionment through the principle of contribution where there are two or more tortfeasors, causation in insurance law 'responds in an all-or-nothing fashion to the possibility of two (or more) concurrent causes of a loss'.[59] In practice, the rules of proximate cause in insurance are often modified or qualified through an express contractual term,[60] such as 'directly or indirectly' caused by[61] or where the cause is external.[62]

With climate litigation, challenges will centre on the standard of causation as set out in the policy under its insuring clause as well as any relevant exclusions. Insurers could rely on principles of construction to avoid defending claims or paying out successful climate change suits. As shown in the recent case of *Brian Leighton (Garages) Ltd v Allianz* – although not a climate change case – the issue was the applicability of a pollution exclusion based on the standard of causation

[57] *Beazley Underwriting Ltd v The Travelers Companies Incorporated* [2011] EWHC 1520.

[58] Section 55 of the Marine Insurance Act 1906. See also, *Leyland Shipping Co v Norwich Union Fire Insurance* [1918] AC 350.

[59] *Wayne Tank and Pump Co Ltd v Employers Liability Assurance Corporation Ltd* [1974] QB 57; [1973] 3 WLR 483; *Global Maritime Systems Inc v Syarkat Takaful Malaysia Berhad, The Cendor Mopu* [2011] UKSC 5; [2011] 1 Lloyd's Rep 560.

[60] *Financial Conduct Authority v Arch Insurance (UK) Ltd* [2021] AC 649; *Brian Leighton (Garages) Ltd v Allianz Insurance Plc* [2023] EWCA Civ 8.

[61] See eg, *Coxe v Employers' Liability Insurance* [1916] 2 KB 629; *Brian Leighton* ibid.

[62] *The 'Miss Jay Jay'* [1987] 1 Lloyd's Rep 32.

in the policy wording ('caused by').[63] Pollution was part of the chain of causation and the insurer contended that a 'looser standard' of causation applied whereas the insured argued that the exclusion clause would only apply where the pollution or contamination was the proximate cause of the loss. By a 2:1 majority the Court of Appeal held that 'caused by' referred to the proximate cause of the loss, and consequently the exclusion was not applicable. In reaching that decision, the Court relied on the Supreme Court decision of *FCA v Arch* and in doing so was not a 'difference of principle, but rather a difference of outcome arising from the application of the iterative approach to construction to the policy in question construed as a whole'.[64]

Causation questions in the context of climate litigation may not be clear on what the defendant policyholder is being sued for; is it releasing emissions or is it a corporate decision to engage in commercial activities that released GHG emissions and resulted in the climate-related damage. Are certain emissions more likely to constitute a 'pollutant' under an exclusion clause or if sufficient causation can be shown, would that emission constitute a 'pollutant' for the exclusion to bite? Causation brings with it more questions than answers, but questions of this nature may be unnecessary if regulatory thresholds for emissions standards have been exceeded.

F. Damages

Liability policies include cover for damages that the policyholder is liable to pay but does not extend to cover other relief, such as injunctive or declaratory relief. The duty to defend and to indemnify are separate obligations of the insurer with distinct financial limits for liability. The costs of damages would not usually include the costs of defending the claim as the provision as to costs normally applies only where the insurer is liable to indemnify the insured.[65] There will invariably be limits on the costs such as:

> by being included together with damages in the sum insured, or by being limited to the same proportion which the indemnity provided bears to the insured's loss where the latter exceeds the former because it is greater than the sum insured by the policy.[66]

Defence costs are likely to be substantial especially given that the duty to defend can be triggered for novel claims that are 'founded (at least) on arguable non-trivial harm'.[67] An insured must therefore determine if its CGL policy will pay

[63] [2023] EWCA Civ 8.

[64] *MacGillivary* (n21) (15th ed, London, Sweet and Maxwell, 2023) 19-004.

[65] *Cross v British Oak Insurance Co* [1938] 2 KB 167 at 174.

[66] J Birds & K Richards, *Birds' Modern Insurance Law* (12th edn, London, Sweet & Maxwell, 2022) 20–17.

[67] *Smith v Fonterra* [2024] NZSC 5 at [83]: 'the cornerstone of the reversal is adherence to the long-established principle that where a claim is novel but is founded (at least) on arguable non-trivial harm, the court should lean to allowing the claim to proceed to trial, rather than pre-emptively eliminate it'.

defence costs in addition to the policy's per occurrence or aggregate limits of liability, in which case defence costs will not erode the policy's limits, alternatively, defence costs will be paid as part of the policy limits which will erode the policy's limits. These changes will expose policyholders to the risk of having to meet a larger proportion of any potential pay-outs with their own resources.[68]

IV. The Limits of Tort Law and its Relationship to Liability Insurance

Allied to the insurance question is the challenge which climate litigation presents for tort law and policy. At the time of writing, there is no tort-based litigation alleging climate-related damage in the UK.[69] There are various routes to a cause of action in tort: negligence, product liability, the Environmental Liability Directive, public nuisance.[70] Within those causes of action the primary hurdles are in relation to the duty of care, causation, damages, and preliminary jurisdictional challenges.

Negligence could support a climate-related claim as it is conceivable that English courts may be willing to find that a carbon emitter owes a duty of care to others, thereby providing scope for negligence to be developed to respond to climate change damage. As the 'gatekeeper to tort liability',[71] the duty of care is the legal obligation that a party owes to another to exercise reasonable care to avoid causing harm or injury. Uncertainties about climate change render it challenging to establish proximity between the carbon emitter and the claimant, and consequently to establish a duty of care and breach of that duty (which would necessitate an enquiry about the standard of care).

Establishing a (potential) duty of care and breach of that duty is a pre-requisite to trigger the duty to defend for insurance purposes. This will be done at the stage of the allegation by the claimant and the wrongdoer will look to its liability insurer to respond to that allegation. The phrasing of the allegation by the claimant influences whether there is enough of a potential breach of duty of care for the insurer to defend. Plaintiff's may plead claims so that it falls within the scope of liability policies, or they may plead it in a manner that leaves the wrongdoer without the protection of its liability insurer. The former renders it easier to trigger the duty to defend of insurers and is closely related to the aim of receiving compensation (assuming that the claim is successful), and that aim is more likely to be met if there is insurance available. On the other hand, the plaintiff

[68] Solana (n18) 352.

[69] See Kaminskaite-Salters (n17).

[70] Negligence and public nuisance are considered here as they are the most viable causes of action for climate-related damages.

[71] Kaminskaite-Salters (n17).

may have the added aim of deterrence or punishment and may seek to bypass the liability insurer to ensure responsibility falls on the wrongdoer by triggering the exclusions under the insurance policy. This may be a risky tactic as the plaintiff will have to rely on assumptions that the wrongdoer is in fact able to financially meet any claims but at the same time it can render the wrongdoer more open to a settlement.

Public nuisance is a second (narrower) potential cause of action that could support climate change suits and cases have been brought on this basis in other jurisdictions. In English law, public nuisance requires an actionable wrong (act or omission) that has a material effect on the safety or health of significant group of people to constitute a class.[72] It offers a potential remit for climate litigation as it does not require a proprietary interest in land or a duty of care, rather it focuses on a range of potential claimants as it arises in the context of an effect on a large part of the population. The types of damages that are recoverable are particular damage, that is, damage that is separate from that experienced by the public at large.[73] Public nuisance remains an unpredictable area for judicial development in the context of novel climate litigation.

The recent New Zealand case of *Smith v Fonterra* highlights the emergence of a climate-related claim suit within existing legal doctrines and on novel legal bases.[74] The facts are that Smith brought tort claims against New Zealand's seven corporate defendants on the basis that they contributed to GHG emissions. He argued their activities amounted to torts of public nuisance, negligence, and a novel climate duty 'to cease materially contributing to: damage to the climate system; dangerous anthropogenic interference with the climate system; and the adverse effects of climate change'. As a Māori leader with an interest in customary land, Smith argued that the defendants' actions would harm him through impacts related to rising sea levels, loss of sites of cultural and spiritual significance, damage to fisheries, and adverse health impacts. The remedy that Smith sought was for the court to issue declarations against the defendants to require them to reduce emissions – but he did not seek damages.

The New Zealand Supreme Court reversed the decisions of the lower courts by refusing to strike out any of the causes of action. The court was also very clear that refusing to strike out the application was not indicative of the eventual likelihood of success. Distinguishing the position under English law, the Supreme Court said that public nuisance under New Zealand law does not require the act or omission complained of to be independently unlawful and that there was no need for Mr Smith to have suffered 'special damages' – damages which are distinguishable from general harms suffered – but that in any event Mr Smith and those he represents had 'both a legal interest and distinct tikanga interests',

[72] J Bates et al, *Liability for Environmental Harm* (Amsterdam, Reed Elsevier, 2004) para 2.72. See also: *Attorney General v PYA Quarries Ltd* [1957] 2 QB 169 at 184.

[73] ibid 2.83 to 2.87.

[74] *Smith v Fonterra* (n67).

therefore meeting the requirements of the special damages rule for standing. In considering causation, the Supreme Court said that this is challenging as no single emitter is the cause of any person's harm due to it being a global problem. Whilst, on the face of it, this decision appears to pave the way for further developments in tortious claims relating to climate change, it was a procedural decision which followed existing procedural rules applicable in New Zealand. The impact of this case on English law is uncertain due to the heavy reliance on indigenous principles and law in New Zealand.

Turning to the permeating factor of causation which is a vital element of any case premised on the law of torts as it attributes liability by establishing a causal connection between the breach of the duty of care by the emitter and the damage suffered by the claimant.[75] Causation – which is an important part of responsibility in tort law – is one of the key challenges to climate litigation cases.[76] GHG emissions may be the result of several emitters and climate change damage is incremental and cumulative over time which raises temperatures and the potential for injury or harm. Tobacco and asbestos precedents might be more instructive for future tort-based climate litigation.

In the English tort case of *Fairchild v Glenhaven* the House of Lords departed from the 'but for' test for causation – which asks whether the harm would have occurred but for the defendant's alleged negligence – to a test that allowed for causation where the defendant's conduct made a material contribution to the damage. The facts were the plaintiff contracted mesothelioma due to exposure to asbestos whilst working for different employers. In *Fairchild* the difficulty for the House of Lords was in establishing causation (ie, which employer caused the harm through the lack of a scientific link to determine causation) and climate litigation faces similar causation challenges. This decision was not immune from criticism, and it has been limited to cases of clinical negligence or the negligence of an employer. Parallels can be drawn with climate litigation as asbestos litigation was also initially viewed with scepticism yet there is growing reliance on the value of attribution science to provide a clearer basis for causation between emissions and resultant damage. It remains to be seen whether judicial attitudes will respond to climate change in much the same way as it did to asbestos and tobacco litigation.

Damages will be the appropriate remedy in situations where climate change-related harm has already occurred (backward-looking litigation). Consequential loss stemming from the original damage will also be claimed for, as will the cost of mitigation of the potential harm.[77] Deterrence – that is, the objective of preventing

[75] J Lowry and R Edmunds (eds), *Environmental Protection and the Common* Law (Oxford, Hart Publishing, 2000) 77.

[76] M Faure and A Nollkaemper, *International Liability as an Instrument to Prevent and Compensate for Climate Change*, SELJ Volume 26A and SJIL Volume 43A, Number 1, June 2007, 157.

[77] Kaminskaite-Salters (n17). Pure economic loss (ie, economic loss that is not linked to damage to land or goods) will not normally be recoverable under English law and is therefore unlikely to be claimed.

a person from engaging in a harmful activity, or even triggering a behavioural change in him – represents another fundamental goal served by the law of torts. Much climate litigation has deterrence as its aim to deter the wrongdoer from continuing to emit GHG emissions and this may not be achieved where the damages awarded are compensatory rather than punitive, as the damages awarded will have limited financial repercussions for the defendants. English law does not allow parties to insure against awards of punitive damages, although this is not without controversy.[78] A wrongdoer who makes an insurance claim in respect of liability to pay punitive damages would likely have to pay higher premiums and may encounter difficulties in obtaining renewal insurance.[79] Damages are likely to be of secondary importance to injunctions which has implications for insurance coverage. It is generally thought that insurers attach more weight to contesting damages than breach of duty. However, given the challenges in establishing a duty of care in tort law, it is likely that insurers will hold the line at the duty to defend by relying on coverage disputes.

V. Charting the Regulatory, Judicial, and Market Responses to Climate Litigation Risk

Climate litigation is a 'polycentric issue'[80] which raises important regulatory and normative considerations. It is underpinned by varying motivations and is being used a strategic tool in some cases to influence behaviour and regulatory responses to climate change. Pursuing such litigation and the outcome of such litigation has implications for tort law, insurance doctrines, behaviour, and the insurance product itself. Climate litigation is gaining momentum but (tort-based) climate litigation faces hurdles, both within existing legal doctrines and in terms of who should be driving the climate change response. The magnitude of climate change confronts the insurance market with two related questions: first, how does (liability) insurance respond to climate-related claims, and the secondly, how should insurance respond to climate litigation.

Tort and insurance are seen as interrelated due to their role in compensating victims and distributing losses, yet the tort-insurance relationship has divided scholars on both sides of the Atlantic.[81] The main arguments about why insurance

[78] In the same 1997 report, for example, the Law Commission recommended that punitive damages be insurable clpure.kcl.ac.uk/ws/portalfiles/portal/197215007/Rowan_S_ECOMPL_entry_Punitive_Damages.pdf p3. This view was shared by Simon Brown LJ in *Lancashire County Council v Municipal Mutual Insurance Ltd* [1996] 493, who argued that punitive damages were still 'likely to have punitive effect' despite insurance.

[79] ibid.

[80] *Smith v Fonterra* (n67) at [26].

[81] P Cane, *The Anatomy of Tort Law* (Oxford, Hart, 1997), 11–15. See eg, *McFarlane v Tayside Health Board* [2000] 2 AC 59 at 83 described the duty of care as 'a mosaic in which the principles of corrective and distributive justice are interwoven'. Lord Hoffmann said that corrective justice '... has been

is (or should be) extrinsic to tort law, centres on the loss-spreading logic of insurance law which chaffs against the notion of responsibility, thereby undermining the doctrinal integrity of tort law. Lord Steyn explained this in a lecture:

> The primary aim of tort law is the pursuit of corrective justice. It requires somebody who has harmed another without justification to indemnify the other. There is, however, another perspective, namely considerations of distributive justice. It concentrates on the place of the plaintiff and the defendant in society …. Not surprisingly, our courts have not shut their eyes to such considerations: the insurance position of the parties has sometimes been treated as relevant.[82]

As to whether insurance has had an expansionary effect on tort *liability*, there are arguments on both sides of the fence, but it is generally accepted that insurance does not have a direct impact on tort liability.[83] The more difficult question – on which there are several well-known dissenting voices[84] – is whether insurance has had an indirect influence on tort law as this raises policy issues, such as whether judicial decisions are based on a party's means and insurability. The indirect influence of insurance may be at work if the presence or absence of insurance influences tort victims in whether to pursue claims where the tortfeasor does not have the financial backing of insurance to satisfy damages awarded, or policy limits (assuming that the information is available) can influence the award sought by the victim. Courts may be slow to extend liability for climate-related claims without insurance in place or may award damages in line with policy limits. Economists have adopted a broader view of the link between tort and insurance as extending beyond the product of insurers but is part of an economic relation wherever risk is involved.[85] This debate cannot be resolved in this chapter, but climate litigation will influence the tort-insurance relationship as the driving force at present is on the outcomes of climate litigation than on the principles of tort law. Climate litigation (including how cases are pleaded) will influence contracting behaviour and the drafting and construction of insurance policies.

abandoned in favour of a cautious pragmatism'. See also *Frost v Chief Constable of South Yorkshire Police* [1999] 2 AC 455.

[82] Lord Steyn, 'Perspectives of Corrective and Distributive Justice in Tort Law' [2002] 23 *Irish Jurist*. See E J Weinrib, 'Corrective Justice' (1992) 77 *Iowa Law Review* 403.

[83] *Davie v New Merton Board Mills* [1959] AC 604 at 627; *Lister v Romford Ice Storage Co Ltd* [1957] AC 555 at 576; *Hunt v Severs* [1994] 2 AC 350 at 393; *Morgans v Launchbury* [1973] AC 127 at 137. See also Lord Denning in *Nettleship v Weston* [1971] 2 QB 691 at 699; *Morris v Ford Motor Co Ltd* [1973] QB 792 at 798. See further P Cane, 'Insurance and Tort Law' in *Tort Law and Economic Interests* (OUP, 1991); J Stapleton, 'Tort, Insurance and Ideology' (1995) 58 *Modern Law Review* 820; J Morgan, 'Tort, Insurance and Incoherence' (2004) 67 *Modern Law Review* 384; Merkin and Steele (n 25); R Merkin, 'Tort, Insurance and Ideology: Further Thoughts' 2012 (75) 3 *Modern Law Review* 301.

[84] ibid. See also: K Abraham, *The Liability Century* (Cambridge MA, Harvard University Press, 2008); T Baker, 'Liability Insurance as Tort Regulation: Six Ways that Liability Insurance Shapes Tort Law in Action' (2005) *All Faculty Scholarship* 2337; T Baker, 'On the Genealogy of Moral Hazard' (1996) 75 *Texas Law Review* 237.

[85] Baker, 'On The Genealogy of Moral Hazard' (n84) 272. See also J Stiglitz, 'Risk, Incentives and Insurance: The Pure Theory of Moral Hazard' (1983) 8 *Geneva Papers on Risk and Insurance* 4.

Backward-looking litigation is best regulated through the insurance market, legislature, and courts – in that order. The most prominent barrier at present is whether climate-related claims will trigger existing liability policies, and consequently coverage disputes will be at the forefront. Due to the uncertainty as to whether climate litigation will fall within existing coverage or will be caught by existing exclusions, the insurance market will be the driver to ensure that existing wording is clarified to minimise coverage disputes. The insurance market should take the lead to clarify existing policy wording and to draft new types of policies or clauses to address climate change. Regulatory authorities such as PRA have expressed concerns about the unpredictable costs associated with climate litigation, and clear wording and exclusions will go some way in enhancing clarity of coverage. Insurability can impact the assessment of climate-related risks, and this may impact the boundaries of liability for insurers. Insurance for climate risks may follow tort liability in this area in much the same way as has been done historically in relation to workers compensation and road accidents.[86]

For courts faced with climate-related claims, judicial attitudes will determine how far tort doctrines can be stretched and how insurance contracts should be interpreted. Courts may adopt more creative approaches to interpretation persuaded by regulatory trends, or there may be judicial reluctance to engage with novel climate litigation. Causation in English tort law is one of the biggest hurdles for climate litigation and it raises the question whether tort law is 'too restrictive' to address complex causal relationships such as climate change. As demonstrated in *Fairchild*, the courts extended tort doctrine to allow for broader causal relationships and multiple tortfeasors. Could the availability of insurance or the urge to compensate the victims have indirectly influenced this view of causation, or does this extension reflect policy reasons to effect behavioural changes in cases of mesothelioma or the difficulties faced by the victim of mesothelioma and how justice can be provided for them?[87] The doctrinal integrity of tort law and insurance should be maintained to avoid opening the floodgates to climate litigation in the UK. A *Fairchild*-esque approach should be resisted in relation to climate litigation (if the lower standard of 'material increase in risk' can indeed be met in climate emissions cases with multiple tortfeasors). In *Smith v Fonterra* the court said:

> The magnitude of the crisis which is climate change simply cannot be appropriately or adequately addressed by common law tort claims pursued through the courts. It is quintessentially a matter that calls for a sophisticated regulatory response at a national level supported by international coordination.[88]

[86] Although these two areas present a skewed perspective as they represent the two major areas of compulsory insurance. K Abraham, *The Liability Century: Insurance and Tort Law from the Progressive Era to 9/11* (Cambridge MA, Harvard University Press, 2008).

[87] *Bonnington Castings Ltd v Wardlaw*; *McGhee v National Coal Board*; *Fairchild v Glenhaven Funeral Services Ltd and others* has confirmed the Courts' willingness to depart from the restrictive 'but for' test in special circumstances. The details of *Fairchild* and these arguments cannot be discussed in detail here.

[88] *Smith v Fonterra* (n67) at [11].

It is likely that English courts will share the above sentiments when faced with novel climate litigation and will be reluctant to develop the common law of torts or depart from insurance coverage and principles. There is, nevertheless, scope for such judicial nudging to highlight a need for legal change or a role for the legislature as seen through the tobacco and asbestos litigation to provide systemic redress to victims. Climate litigation, particularly forward-looking litigation, is being used in this manner to influence legislative change. The UK has a fairly developed regulatory system but the difficulties in bringing a tort-based climate claim may indicate that climate litigation may not be as forthcoming in the UK.

There is an important role for the insurance market in relation to forward-looking litigation that aims to deter behaviour or conduct that can contribute to climate-related damage. With the increasing regulatory focus and industry focus on mitigation or adaptation measures to combat GHG emissions,[89] there is a need for insurance products that are geared at ex-ante measures to help policyholders meet their emissions targets. These types of insurance products could combat arguments that the insurance sector should be doing more and that traditional liability policies do not address the climate crisis but only protect policyholders against financial consequences. Insurance products focusing on ex ante measures to incentivise or aid mitigation and adaptation efforts of policyholders, may arguably be able to accomplish more as both a loss-spreading device and to build resilience to climate change effects.[90] This would align with the law and economics view where insurance is not perceived as confined to the products of insurers, but as provided 'any time that one party's actions have consequences for the risk of loss borne by another'.[91]

It is difficult to dispute that tort law is linked to claims handling and settlement where liability insurers involvement can be significant to the nature of tort liability. Due to uncertainties with existing policy coverage and the difficulties in satisfying the thresholds in tort law, insurers are likely to deny that they have a duty to defend rather than settle claims. There is, however, also an argument to be made about insurers influencing precedents by settling matters that would set an unfavourable precedent for the insurance market. A more positive perspective is that insurer participation in climate litigation can create a value-added liability product for insureds. Insurers bring a weight of capital and expertise in the defence of a claim, and insurer involvement can shape attitudes to how climate-related claims are litigated – and looking ahead, how climate change can be managed by their policyholders.

[89] See eg, L Naidoo, 'The Poseidon Principles for Marine Insurance: Legal and Regulatory Issues for Sustainable Marine Insurance' in O Gurses, *Research Handbook of Marine Insurance Law* (Cheltenham, Edward Elgar Press, 2024).

[90] See Arnold-Dwyer (n2).

[91] Baker, 'On the Genealogy of Moral Hazard' (n84) 272.

The potential expansion of tort law to novel duties of care like in *Smith v Fonterra*, may be fuelled by the availability of funds to satisfy claims. If insurance is not available or the insured deliberately pleads in a manner that excludes insurance coverage, or the insurer adopts a strict approach to resisting the duty to defend, the effect of insurance can 'create an incentive to argue for new duties, drawing in new parties to the tort frame'.[92] Climate change is an economic and financial risk and insurance is an important way to spread the risk of loss. Creative ways of pleading based on differing motivations for climate litigation to circumvent insurance pose a financial risk and should not be encouraged. The effect of insurance on climate litigation is not simply procedural but may well impact the substance of how climate litigation claims are framed, defended, and the ultimate outcome.[93]

Returning to the tort-insurance interface, if tort law is to incentivise potential wrongdoers to implement measures to minimise climate-related damages, liability insurance can either promote or hinder that goal depending on insurability criteria (eg, premiums and affordability of coverage) and regulation. If the premise is indeed that tort law is about corrective justice, the original controversy will stand, namely that liability insurance will negate responsibility on the insured wrongdoer by shifting that to its insurer. It is conceivable that if the purchase of insurance is in anticipation of the imposition of risk one's activities will impose on others (eg, to cover potential climate damage caused to third parties due to the release of GHG emissions), the purchase of liability insurance is arguably a form of corrective justice.

VI. Conclusion

Climate litigation is playing an important role in shaping behaviours, and the legal and regulatory responses to climate change. The close connection between tort liability and insurance makes insurance a fundamental part of the climate litigation dialogue. This chapter has examined how existing insurance and tort doctrines can cope with climate litigation. Whilst the tort law implications have been well documented, the implications for insurance law and practice are less well developed. This chapter is a starting point for further research on how insurance doctrines may evolve in light of climate litigation. It has demonstrated that insurance and tort law may chaff against each other not only in relation to the policies and perceptions stemming from the traditional tort-insurance interface, but in terms of the practice of litigation as well. Whether climate litigation presents new considerations for the tort-insurance interface

[92] Merkin and Steele (n22) 62.
[93] ibid, 383.

is difficult to predict given the dynamic and evolving nature of climate change and climate litigation. The policy setting for climate litigation is also not clear due to multiple motivations and aims. Liability insurance will need to be revisited in the context of climate litigation – but the insurance *product* (broadly construed) will need to be reconsidered in the context of climate change. The insurance market and legislature, rather than the judiciary, are likely to play a primary regulatory role in climate litigation.

PART III

Insuring Various Emerging Risks: Technology Related Risks

10

Tort and Autonomous Vehicle Accidents: The Automated and Electric Vehicles Act 2018 and the Insurance Solution

PHILLIP MORGAN*

I. Introduction

Even if autonomous vehicles (AVs) prove to be safer than human drivers, accidents will still occur. The law will need to be able to compensate the victims of such accidents. The current motor accident compensation system within England and Wales is based on the tort of negligence, combined with compulsory motor insurance. Given the compulsory insurance context driver 'fault' is assessed at a standard which can tend towards strict liability. This accident compensation system is threatened by AVs.

With AV accidents, since AVs are machines not persons, where an AV causes an accident there is no negligent driver, and thus no 'driver' to sue. AVs also generate further difficulties for an accident compensation system based on negligence. Due to inherent features of AVs they challenge a number of key tort concepts such as causation, and remoteness of damage. Alternative actions based on product liability, and/or direct duties against designers, maintainers, data-suppliers and the like are not a substitute for the absence of a negligence action against a driver. These actions contain a number of additional legal hurdles when compared to negligence, are also challenged by AVs, are forensically more difficult, and require complex expert evidence. They are also simply not viable as alternatives in low value claims which characterise many motor vehicle accidents.

The difficulties AVs cause for tort has been recognised by the UK Parliament. In a bid to get AVs on the road, Parliament has enacted the Automated and

* This work is supported by the UK Research and Innovation (UKRI) Trustworthy Autonomous Systems programme [EPSRC ref: EP/W011239/1].

Electric Vehicles Act 2018 (AEV Act). It is a pre-emptive, hurried, and sticking-plaster solution. This Act provides victims of AV accidents with a direct, strict liability claim, against the AV's insurers. In doing so it inadvertently violates technology impartiality ('tech-impartiality', the idea that tort law should not favour any particular technology over another where the risks of harm are equal). However, the AEV Act is more subtle than its drafters and enactors may have thought. Whilst unarticulated in its enactment history the Act co-opts the insurer as an indirect regulator of AVs. This is not simply through differential insurance pricing based on product risks, but also through the role of subrogated litigation.

As with any vehicle, insurers will have the ability to monitor accidents, and price insurance accordingly. However, the real value of the AEV Act's model is the insurers' subrogated claims. Here insurers have the opportunity to use their litigation expertise, resources, ability to combine claims, and their ability to engage in strategic litigation, which will justify the services of the expensive experts and the litigation resources necessary to pursue claims against AV manufacturers and Big Tech. Nevertheless, the AEV Act does not solve the core problems raised by the tort/AV interface, and simply displaces these problems and places them onto insurers.

II. AVs and Accidents

AVs have the potential to reduce motor vehicle accidents. However, even if they prove safer they will also cause accidents, including in some situations where a human driver would not since the nature of their errors may differ from those made by human drivers. There have been a number of well-publicised AV accidents. Perhaps the most famous is the Tempe incident,[1] where an Uber automated test vehicle which was operated by an automated driving system (ADS) struck, and fatally injured a pedestrian pushing her bicycle. This resulted from the ADS repeatedly misclassifying the pedestrian and not predicting her actual path of movement. Immediately before the collision the system determined that a collision was imminent, but the ADS's response specifications were exceeded, and the human safety driver in the vehicle failed to intervene in time.[2]

In addition to these well-publicised accidents, data published by the United States National Highway Traffic Safety Administration (NHTSA) also indicates

[1] eg, S Levin and J Ce Wong, 'Self-Driving Uber Kills Arizona Woman in First Fatal Crash Involving Pedestrian' (19 March 2018) *The Guardian*. www.theguardian.com/technology/2018/mar/19/uber-self-driving-car-kills-woman-arizona-tempe; D Shepardson, 'In Review of Fatal Arizona Crash, U.S. Agency Says Uber Software Had Flaws' (5 November 2019) *Reuters*. www.reuters.com/article/us-uber-crash-idUSKBN1XF2HA.

[2] National Transportation Safety Board, *Collision Between Vehicle Controlled by Developmental Automated Driving System and Pedestrian, Tempe, Arizona, March 18, 2018* (Highway Accident Report NTSB/HAR-19/03, 2019) 15–17.

that AV accidents are with us, and that the law will need to be able to deal with them.[3] From July 2021–December 2023 the NHTSA received reports for 508 crashes involving ADS equipped vehicles, four of which involved serious injuries, and 20 involved minor injuries.[4] Normal accident theory further suggests that some AV accidents are inevitable.[5] Potential industrial users of such technologies appear to be highly aware of the potential for AV accidents as well.[6] Thus as AVs replace human drivers the law needs an adequate way to respond to these accidents and to compensate those wrongfully injured.

III. Current Motor Accident Compensation System

Previous major advances in transportation have led to significant developments in tort law. It is difficult to underestimate the impact of the development of the railways, and the motor vehicle on tort,[7] and on the tort/insurance ecosystem.

The current motor accident compensation system in England and Wales is a fault-based system which uses the tort of negligence with road users owing a duty of care to one another. This system examines individual driver fault. Importantly it operates alongside compulsory motor insurance,[8] with significant limitations on insurance exclusions[9] and on the ability of insurers to assert defences ordinarily available in insurance law.[10] A motor accident victim may also pursue the

[3] NHTSA Standing General Order 2021-01 requires manufacturers and operators to report crashes occurring on public roads in the US involving Automated Driving Systems.

[4] NHTSA, 'Standing General Order on Crash Reporting' (January 2024) *NHTSA*. www.nhtsa.gov/laws-regulations/standing-general-order-crash-reporting#:~:text=ADS%3A%20Entities%20named%20in%20the,in%20property%20damage%20or%20injury. However, the number of reports is not the same as the total number of crashes, and crashes involving ADS equipped vehicles are recorded irrespective of whether the system was engaged, but they are still illustrative of the fact that AVs are likely to be involved in accidents.

[5] C Perrow, *Normal Accidents. Living with High-Risk Technologies* (2nd edn, Princeton, Princeton University Press, 1999) 141; R Williams and R Yampolskiy, 'Understanding and Avoiding AI Failures: A Practical Guide' (2021) 6 *Philosophies* 53.

[6] European Commission, Directorate-General for Communications Networks, Content and Technology, 'European Enterprise Survey on the Use of Technologies Based on Artificial Intelligence: Final Report' (2020) *Publications Office*. data.europa.eu/doi/10.2759/759368.

[7] J Morgan, 'Technological Change and the Development of Liability for Fault in England and Wales' in M Martín-Casals (ed), *The Development of Liability in Relation to Technological Change* (Cambridge, Cambridge University Press, 2010) 40–41, 48; D Gifford, 'Technological Triggers to Tort Revolutions: Steam Locomotives, Autonomous Vehicles, and Accident Compensation' (2018) 11 *Journal of Tort Law* 71; K Oliphant, 'Tort Law, Risk, and Technological Innovation in England' (2014) 59 *McGill Law Journal* 819.

[8] This obligation is now to be found in Road Traffic Act 1988 (RTA), s 143.

[9] eg, RTA, s148; Directive 2009/103/EC of the European Parliament and of the Council of 16 September 2009 relating to insurance against civil liability in respect of the use of motor vehicles, and the enforcement of the obligation to insure against such liability, Arts 3, 13.

[10] R Merkin and S Dziobon, 'Tort Law and Compulsory Insurance' in TT Arvind and Jenny Steele (eds), *Tort Law and the Legislature* (Oxford, Hart, 2012) 308.

tortfeasor's insurer directly.[11] There is also a tapestry of provisions which establish insurer liability in circumstances other than simple coverage of a negligent driver within the terms of the policy. For instance, the insurer may also retain liability in circumstances where it is entitled to avoid the insurance policy, and does not indemnify the tortfeasor who is unable to satisfy judgment,[12] or where it has avoided the policy.[13] A victim may also pursue an insurer of an at fault vehicle even if the individual driver was uninsured, for instance where an unauthorised driver is driving the vehicle.[14] These provisions partially reshape the terrain of the motor vehicle accident compensation system towards insurance of the vehicle, rather than merely insurance of the driver(s) covered by the policy. Nevertheless, there still needs to be a negligent driver for liability to be present. There is also a privately operated fund of last result, the Motor Insurance Bureau (MIB), which compensates the victims of uninsured or untraced driver torts, and which is funded by the motor insurance industry.

A number of other jurisdictions now use strict liability for motor vehicle accidents.[15] Initially the development of a leisured motoring class in England, its concerns about individual liability, and the development of a motorist lobby, meant that English law when initially faced with motor vehicle accidents adopted a fault-based approach to motor accident liability, in contrast to its approach to liability for industrial traction engines and steam rollers, which used strict liability.[16] Once motoring had become more democratised, and motor insurance had become compulsory,[17] the law evolved, and the fault-based requirement of the tort of negligence in a motor vehicle accident context shifted towards a more strict liability system,[18] the standard of care applicable to drivers evolving to that of an experienced, skilled, and careful driver, even if the driver in question could not meet that standard, for instance due to them being a learner driver, or due to the driver's infirmity.

[11] Under the European Communities (Rights against Insurers) Regulations 2002.

[12] RTA, s 151(5).

[13] As an Article 75 insurer.

[14] RTA, s 151.

[15] J Bell and D Ibbetson, *European Legal Development, The Case of Tort* (Cambridge, Cambridge University Press, 2012) 34.

[16] *Mansel v Webb* [1918–19] All ER Rep 794, 796 (Swinfen Eady MR); J R Spencer, 'Motor-Cars and the Rule in *Rylands v. Fletcher*: A Chapter of Accidents in the History of Law and Motoring' (1983) 42 *Cambridge Law Journal* 65, 69.

[17] Via the Road Traffic Act 1930.

[18] *Nettleship v Weston* [1971] 2 QB 691 (CA) 699–701 (Lord Denning MR); *Henderson v Henry E Jenkins & Sons* [1970] AC 282 (HL); *Daly v Liverpool Corporation* [1939] 2 All ER 142 (AS) 144; *Government Insurance Office of New South Wales v Ergul* [1993] NSWCA 108 [35]–[40] (Clarke JA): 'since the advent of compulsory insurance, and consequential notions of risk sharing, the courts have, in substance, elevated the "reasonably prudent driver" to the role of the perfectionist'. *Lunt v Khelifa* [2002] EWCA Civ 801 [20] (Latham LJ): 'this court has consistently imposed on the drivers of cars a high burden to reflect the fact that a car is potentially a dangerous weapon'. See generally J Goudkamp, 'The Spurious Relationship Between Moral Blameworthiness and Liability for Negligence' (2004) 28 *Melbourne University Law Review* 343.

However, motor vehicle accident litigation is still nominally fault based, and fault needs to be pleaded. An at fault driver is still labelled as negligent, and there are also financial consequences for them, including the payment of any insurance excess, increased motor insurance premiums in future years, and loss of no-claims bonuses. A professional driver may also face career consequences with a finding of negligence against them. With uninsured drivers the MIB may also pursue uninsured drivers for contribution. Thus a collision in the absence of evidence of fault does not justify the imposition of liability.[19]

Most motor vehicle accident cases are settled prior to trial. This is since fault is relatively easy to establish in many circumstances, particularly through the use of rough and ready rules by insurers, or fault may simply be irrelevant when an accident is dealt with through a knock for knock agreement. However, when such cases are tried, (most frequently in the County Court since most motor accident litigation concerns low value claims), advocates will spend time cross examining witnesses in order to elicit evidence which illuminates the question of fault and also contributory negligence. Expert evidence is typically not used in such litigation since fault in such cases is treated as one of common sense, which can be resolved without the need for expert opinion.[20] This helps to keep costs down in this high volume litigation field.

A. Insurance and Tort

Insurance is integral to tort litigation. Notwithstanding arguments that questions of liability in tort law, such as the applicable standard of care, should not be shaped by the presence of insurance,[21] arguments invoked by courts in a number of contexts, including loss spreading,[22] and also claims which stretch the ambit of duties of care to reach insured parties,[23] appear to contradict this contention. Insurers have also themselves directly shaped tort, for instance by seeking new parties with whom to share liability burdens,[24] and as repeat players by strategically deciding whether to settle or bring claims, appeal, or lobby Parliament. The presence of insurance also influences the development of tort through the fact

[19] *Knight v Fellick* [1977] RTR 316 (CA); *Ng Chun Pui v Lee Chuen Tat* [1988] RTR 298 (PC). Note Mark Armitage et al (eds), *Charlesworth & Percy on Negligence* (15th edn, London, Sweet & Maxwell, 2023) [11–203]: a motorist will rarely be held liable for a split-second decision which requires them to take one of a number of courses of action, each of which having potential disadvantages.

[20] A Tettenborn et al (eds), *Clerk and Lindsell on Torts* (24th edn, London, Sweet & Maxwell, 2023) [7-214]; *Liddell v Middleton* [1996] PIQR P36.

[21] J Stapleton, 'Tort, Insurance and Ideology' (1995) 58 *Modern Law Review* 820; cf R Merkin and J Steele, *Insurance and the Law of Obligations* (Oxford, Oxford University Press, 2013) Ch 5; R Merkin, 'Tort, Insurance and Ideology: Further Thoughts' (2012) 75 *Modern Law Review* 301.

[22] Loss spreading arguments are found in a range of tort contexts, most prominently within vicarious liability hybridised with enterprise liability.

[23] *Moore Stephens v Stone and Rolls* [2009] UKHL 39, [2009] 1 AC 1391.

[24] See *Home Office v Dorset Yacht* [1970] AC 923 (insurance stated to be irrelevant).

that tort litigation which pursues an uninsured defendant, who is not a solvent self-insured defendant, is either not brought, or may be viewed with suspicion by many lawyers.[25]

It is undoubtedly the case that insurance has had a significant impact on the law of tort,[26] particularly with motor vehicle accidents, which have been shaped by the presence of compulsory insurance and a fund of last resort.[27] It was also the potential for the individual liability of members of the leisured motoring classes in the early twentieth century that ensured the adoption of fault-based liability for motor vehicle accidents in the first place, instead of using the strict liability approach then applied to industrial steam road vehicles. With accidents involving the latter loss could be spread through the enterprise, and was less likely to be concentrated on one individual tortfeasor. The introduction of compulsory insurance for motor vehicles then led to shifts within the applicable standard of care, such that it is now the case that many drivers doing their best simply cannot meet this standard. Indeed maintaining an approach to the standard of care in a motor vehicle context which is more typically found in other negligence contexts which are less pro-claimant, would likely have led to legislative reform of the motor vehicle accident compensation system.

Merkin and Dziobon argue that the existence of compulsory insurance demonstrates a legislative intent for the compensation of victims of accidents and that courts *should* take this into account.[28] It is hard not to agree. All of the players in the litigation are aware that the individual motorist is not paying for the damage themselves, and that the cost of the accident is primarily spread amongst fellow motorists via their compulsory premiums, or via the MIB. Whereas for the victim to shoulder the costs of the accident is to concentrate the costs on a single person, with potentially life changing financial consequences for them, particularly in the case of some personal injury claims which result in disabilities significantly impacting on an individual's ability to work, or requiring long term personal care. The lawyers on both sides are also likely to be instructed by the respective insurers, save in the case of pedestrian or cyclist victims. A failure to recognise the significant role of compulsory insurance in shaping the unique motor vehicle accident tort architecture is potentially dangerous, and runs the risk of perverting the law of negligence in other contexts. Such a failure may run the risk that any stretching of negligence doctrines in a motor vehicle context will not be viewed with suitable caution in other contexts, where compulsory insurance is not present, and when some defendants are not insured, or able to spread the loss

[25] T Baker, 'Blood Money, New Money, and the Moral Economy of Tort Law in Action' (2001) 35 *Law & Society Review* 275.

[26] R Lewis, 'Insurance and the Tort System' (2005) 25 *Legal Studies* 85; T Baker, "Liability Insurance as Tort Regulation: Six Ways that Liability Insurance Shapes Tort Law in Action" (2005) 12 *Connecticut Insurance Law Journal* 1.

[27] Note P S Atiyah, *The Damages Lottery* (Oxford, Hart, 1997).

[28] Merkin and Dziobon (n10) 315.

in other ways, and/or where any finding of fault may have significant financial or professional, even career ending, consequences for a defendant.

IV. The AV Challenge

When discussing AV technologies, it is typical to cite the Society of Automotive Engineers ('SAE') J3016 levels of driving automation. These range from Level 0 to Level 5. Levels 0–2 concern driver support features, and the human driver remains in control of the vehicle. With Levels 3–5, the vehicle drives itself, but with Level 3 systems a human driver may need to take control when requested to do so, whereas with Level 4 and Level 5 technologies they do not, and such vehicles might not in fact be fitted with steering wheels or pedals. Level 4 systems might include driverless taxis, which operate in limited conditions, whereas Level 5 systems can drive anywhere in all conditions.

Levels 0–2 cause limited difficulties for tort, although a minor difficulty emerges with Level 3. With Levels 0–2 the human remains driving the vehicle, and with a Level 3 system a human driver is available to step in when need be. With tort it is possible to target a safety driver, or remote operator for negligent supervision, or failure to intervene, or for improperly responding, and also their employer (where they are carrying out such a role when employed) via vicarious liability for this negligence. However, for fully autonomous systems such a route is not available.

Nevertheless, with a claim for negligent supervision by the safety driver human factors research would suggest that this claim is not entirely coextensive with a claim that might be brought against a negligent driver themselves. This is since there may be situations where it is not humanly possible for a safety driver (who is in an observational role and not actively driving), to obtain the same level of situational awareness and react with the same speed as a driver actively driving the vehicle.[29] This may be particularly problematic where the handover time provided by the AV is insufficient for the safety driver to be able to obtain sufficient situational awareness, and/or react in time in order to make a difference. To hold a safety driver to be at fault, might be unjust where it is a situation where no reasonable human safety driver would be able to properly obtain sufficient situational awareness, intervene, and prevent the accident in time, even where a driver actively driving the vehicle at the time could have. It is significantly more objectionable to hold a safety driver to be at fault for not meeting a standard of

[29] A McKerral, K Pammer, and C Gauld, 'Supervising the Self-Driving Car: Situation Awareness and Fatigue During Highly Automated Driving' (2023) 187 *Accident Analysis & Prevention* 107068; J De Winter, R Happee, M Martens, and N Stanton, 'Effects of Adaptive Cruise Control and Highly Automated Driving on Workload and Situation Awareness: A Review of the Empirical Evidence' (2014) 27 *Transportation Research Part F: Traffic Psychology and Behavior* 196.

care that no human can reach, than the situation where an inexperienced driver is held to be at fault in not meeting the standard of a competent driver.

With AVs where a human is in or on the loop, such as with AV technologies up to and including Level 3, it will still be possible to bring actions against the operator/supervisor/safety driver for negligence in their operation or supervision of the system, and also against their employer via vicarious liability. However, with fully autonomous AVs (Level 4–5 technologies) this liability route is not available. Such an AV which drives in a manner which would be negligent if it were driven by a human driver, and which as a result causes an accident, does not trigger the tort of negligence in the same way as a human driver does, and here there is no safety driver on whom to pin a negligence claim. AVs are not legal persons,[30] instead AVs are personal property. Only persons, legal or natural, can commit torts.[31] Property, such as an AV, cannot commit a tort. Instead we hold those associated with it to account.[32] This creates a potential liability gap for AVs.[33]

V. Alternative Claims

Where an injured victim cannot sue an at fault driver (or safety driver) since there is no human driver, what should the victim do?[34] Where a fully autonomous AV causes an accident in a manner that would be considered negligence if a human were driving the vehicle, there are a range of potentially available alternative claims, although as we will see below they do not address the gap, and this in part led to the enactment of the AEV Act. It is also necessary to examine such claims in detail since they are also the subrogated claims available to insurers as a result of the AEV Act.

A. Negligence

In the absence of a driver the first possibility is to find another person (legal or natural) who is at fault and whose fault caused the accident, and to bring a

[30] See generally K Low, WW Yee and W Ying-Chieh, 'Property/Personhood and AI: The Future of Machines' in E Lim and P Morgan (eds), *The Cambridge Handbook of Private Law and Artificial Intelligence* (Cambridge, Cambridge University Press, 2024) 307; S Chesterman, 'Artificial Intelligence and the Limits of Legal Personality' (2020) 69 *International and Comparative Law Quarterly* 819.

[31] G Wagner, 'Robot, Inc.: Personhood for Autonomous Systems?' (2019) 88 *Fordham Law Review* 591.

[32] Note R van den H van Genderen, 'Legal Personhood in the Age of Artificially Intelligence Robots' in W Barfield and U Pagallo (eds), *Research Handbook on the Law of Artificial Intelligence* (Cheltenham, Edward Elgar Publishing, 2018) 245–46.

[33] Such a gap has led some AV manufacturers to publicly declare that they will accept liability if their car causes an accident 'Who Is Responsible for a Driverless Car Accident?' (8 October 2015) *BBC*. www.bbc.co.uk/news/technology-34475031.

[34] For a fuller account see P Morgan, 'Tort Law and AI – Vicarious Liability' in Lim and Morgan (n30) 135–171, on which this section is based.

negligence claim against them.[35] Such claims may potentially be brought against manufacturers, programmers, designers, users of the AVs, and so on, provided that they owe a duty of care to the claimant, and that breach of this duty led to the accident. For instance it is likely that those who use AVs commercially will owe a duty of care to appropriately monitor them, and to maintain them,[36] a failure to properly do so, which leads to an accident is likely to found a claim in negligence. Manufacturers also owe duties of care to the world at large for negligence in the production of their goods, and analogous duties have also been placed on designers, repairers, maintainers, and distributors of products.[37] It is likely that programmers, developers, and those responsible for training data will hold similar duties. There may also be a duty of care on producers of AVs to monitor them after they have put them into circulation.[38] In assessing whether there is a breach of duty, courts will consider whether the defendant met the required standard of care, which in this context is that of the ordinary competent practitioner in the relevant calling.[39]

However, there are considerable problems with such a claim, when compared with a claim brought against a human driver for negligence. The first is in identifying the relevant tortfeasor. Many parties may be involved in the creation, commercialisation, and operation of an AV.[40] AVs will consist of multiple component parts – there may be different entities responsible for the motor vehicle, the technology which controls this platform, the learning systems, the data on which that system was trained,[41] and for updates to the system.[42] Interconnectivity and information sharing with systems outside of the control of the parties,[43] for example the highway infrastructure systems and other AVs designed, produced, and operated by others will also occur, and will complicate the claim. The complexity of AVs, and their inputs means that it may be extremely difficult to identify the relevant tortfeasor.

Further, adaptability, interactivity, and autonomy will make it particularly difficult for users to prove that manufacturers, developers, and designers did not meet the required standard of care.[44] The evidence necessary to do so may be difficult to obtain, and extremely difficult to comprehend, and may necessitate specialised expert evidence. This means that the cost of bringing such actions

[35] Note J Morgan, 'Torts and Technology' in R Brownsword, E Scotford, and K Yeung (eds), *The Oxford Handbook of Law, Regulation and Technology* (Oxford, Oxford University Press, 2017) 522.

[36] Expert Group on Liability and New Technologies, *New Technologies Formation, Liability for Artificial Intelligence and Other Emerging Digital Technologies* (European Union 2019) 44.

[37] *Donoghue v Stevenson* [1932] AC 562 (HL); Tettenborn (n 20) [10-08]–[10-16].

[38] Expert Group (n36) 44.

[39] Armitage (n19) [10-01]–[10-04].

[40] Miriam Buiten, 'Towards Intelligent Regulation of Artificial Intelligence' (2019) 10 *European Journal of Risk Regulation* 41.

[41] C Reed, "How should we regulate artificial intelligence?" (2018) 376 *Philosophical Transactions of the Royal Society A* 20170360.

[42] Expert Group (n36) 21.

[43] U Pagallo, *The Laws of Robots, Crimes, Contracts, and Torts* (New York, Springer, 2013) x.

[44] ibid, 117.

may be high, and may only be viable in larger value actions,[45] and not in low value motor accident claims. In addition the behaviour of some systems may vary significantly, even after a short period of time, from their interactions with others such that fault is unlikely to be found on the part of those who design, manufacture, or supply AVs.[46]

Even if it is possible to establish duty, and breach, the issue of causation arises. Negligence requires causation of the harm. The models of causation used by negligence require a tracing back process, whereby the harm is traced back to a breach of duty committed by a person. The number of potential parties involved in an AV further complicates this process.[47] The complexity of AVs complicates proof, and may make proving causation of damage extremely difficult.[48] Establishing causation involving AVs may require significant forensics, simulations, and examination of logs. This may lead to protracted and costly litigation, in turn delaying or denying victims compensation. Again these costs may not be viable in smaller value claims representing the majority of motor accident claims.

Further, causation is extremely problematic in a machine learning context. Traditional common law tests of causation may fail.[49] It is also possible that defendants may seek to rely on the doctrine of *novus actus interveniens* where post-delivery, an AV is exposed to unusual circumstances, resulting in the system learning inappropriate responses, or where the system has been hacked.[50] The evidential doctrine of *res ipsa loquitur*, may assist claimants,[51] but for this doctrine to apply, the thing that inflicted the harm needs to be under the sole management and control of the defendant.[52] It is thus not a complete solution in the AV context,[53] since it will often be the case that the system is not under the sole management and control of the defendant.[54]

[45] F P Hubbard, 'Allocating the Risk of Physical Injury from "Sophisticated Robots": Efficiency, Fairness, and Innovation' in R Calo, A M Froomkin, and I Kerr (eds), *Robot Law* (Cheltenham, Edward Elgar Publishing, 2016) 43.

[46] Pagallo (n43) 124–126. However, note that there may be some cases where AVs make the determination of fault easier, for instance where the AV's system produces accurate logs and recorded footage, and a third party is responsible for the accident.

[47] J Lehmann, J Breuker, and B Brouwer, 'Causation in AI and Law' (2004) *Artificial Intelligence and Law* 279, 280–86.

[48] C Holder, V Khurana, F Harrison, and L Jacobs, 'Robotics and Law: Key Legal and Regulatory Implications of the Robotics Age (Part I of II)' (2016) 32 *Computer Law and Security Review* 383, 386.

[49] Y Bathaee, 'The Artificial Intelligence Black Box and the Failure of Intent and Causation' (2018) 31 *Harvard Journal of Law and Technology* 889; C Karnow, 'Liability for Distributed Artificial Intelligences' (1996) 11 *Berkeley Technology Law Journal* 147.

[50] M Hervey and M Lavy, *The Law of Artificial Intelligence* (London, Sweet & Maxwell, 2021) [5-023].

[51] D Vladeck, 'Machines without Principals: Liability Rules and Artificial Intelligence' (2014) 89 *Washington Law Review* 117, 142–4.

[52] Tettenborn (n20) [7-208].

[53] Note Singapore Academy of Law, *Report on the Attribution of Civil Liability for Accidents Involving Autonomous Cars* (SAL LRC, 2020) [5.12]–[5.13]; cf B Casey, 'Robot Ipsa Loquitur' (2019) 108 *Georgetown Law Journal* 225, 269–273.

[54] J Buyers, *Artificial Intelligence, The Practical Legal Issues* (Somerset, Law Brief Publishing, 2018) 30.

A claim in negligence also presupposes foreseeability of harm. A defendant is only liable for damage of a kind which would have been reasonably foreseeable at the time of the breach of duty.[55] This requirement may be problematic in an AV context,[56] particularly since it is assessed at the time of the breach of duty, and not when the harm was suffered. The systems may be so complex that they may perform actions which are unforeseeable, and which result in unforeseeable harm,[57] particularly where they draw on constantly shifting vast real world data, or the internet,[58] interact with other systems,[59] or where the systems continue to learn from interacting with their surrounding environment once they have left the hands of the designer/producer/supplier.[60]

It is thus clear that a claim in negligence against a person associated with an AV, which drives in a manner which would be considered negligent if it were driven by a human, is not a substitute for a claim in negligence against a human driver. Firstly, no one person may be negligent for this occurrence, and even if they were there are considerable hurdles in the way of the claim, and additional costs when compared to typical motor accident claims.

B. Consumer Protection Act 1987

A second alternative is to use a claim under the Consumer Protection Act 1987 (CPA). However, there are significant problems with such a product liability claim in an AV context.[61] The CPA defines products as 'any goods or electricity', thus whilst the provision includes AVs, or updates to the AV's software which are provided via a tangible medium, there are real problems in applying this to software, or to defective updates provided to the AV over the air.[62] The CPA regime makes producers, suppliers, or importers liable for damage resulting from

[55] *Overseas Tankship (UK) Ltd v Morts Dock & Engineering Co Ltd (the Wagon Mound No 1)* [1961] AC 388 (PC); *Overseas Tankship (UK) Ltd v The Miller Steamship Co Pty (the Wagon Mound No 2)* [1967] 1 AC 617 (PC).

[56] M Geistfeld, 'A Roadmap for Autonomous Vehicles: State Tort Liability, Automobile Insurance, and Federal Safety Regulation' (2017) 105 *California Law Review* 1611, 1621.

[57] W Barfield, 'Towards a Law of Artificial Intelligence' in Barfield and Pagallo (n32) 4.

[58] J Miller and I Kerr, "Delegation, Relinquishment, and Responsibility: The Prospect of Expert Robots' in Calo, Froomkin, and Kerr (n45) 107; C Karnow, 'The Application of Traditional Tort Theory to Embodied Machine Intelligence' in Calo, Froomkin, and Kerr (n45) 60.

[59] Expert Group (n36) 54.

[60] Pagallo (n43) 47, 138.

[61] For a detailed discussion, see V Ulfbeck, 'Product Liability Law and AI: Revival or Death of Product Liability Law' in Lim and Morgan (n30), and J De Bruyne and O Dheu, 'Liability for Damage Caused by Artificial Intelligence – Some Food for Thought and Current Proposals' in P Morgan (ed), *Tort Liability and Autonomous Systems Accidents* (Cheltenham, Edward Elgar Publishing, 2023).

[62] K Oliphant and V Wilcox, 'Product Liability in England and Wales' in P Machnikowski (ed), *European Product Liability: An Analysis of the State of the Art in the Era of New Technologies* (Cambridge, Intersentia, 2016) 204; R Bagshaw, 'Product Liability: Autonomous Ships' in B Soyer and A Tettenborn (eds), *Artificial Intelligence and Autonomous Shipping* (Oxford, Hart, 2021) 119.

defective products.[63] Defective being defined as where the 'safety of the product is not such as persons generally are entitled to expect',[64] and in determining this, the manner and purposes for which the product has been marketed, and what might be reasonably be expected to be done with or in relation to it are considered.[65] With self-learning systems, it is unclear if unpredictable deviations will be treated as defects.[66]

The claimant will need to identify and prove the defect. With AVs which may be sophisticated, opaque, and interconnected systems this may be an extremely difficult and costly exercise requiring significant expertise.[67] The defect needs to be present at the relevant time, that is the time when the product was supplied, otherwise the defendant has a defence to the claim.[68] This means that the regime has trouble accommodating claims arising from updates to systems, third party activities, interconnected systems, data sharing, and post-supply self-learning.[69] This causes significant problems in an AV context. Likewise the defect must cause the damage. Similar problems with proving causation are present as with a claim in negligence, although foreseeability of damage is not required.

Further weakening the claimant's position is the state of the art defence. This defence means that the defendant is protected from liability if they can show that 'the state of scientific and technical knowledge at the relevant time was not such that a producer of products of the same description as the product in question might be expected to have discovered the defect if it had existed in his products while they were under his control'.[70] Whilst a fairly narrow interpretation is given to this defence[71] since many defects, particularly with machine learning might not be discoverable under the existing state of scientific and technical knowledge until after an accident,[72] this defence may render the CPA claim of limited value in an AV context.[73] Finally the need for costly expert evidence to establish defectiveness, causation, and to counter any state of the art defence,[74] means that this claim

[63] CPA, s 2.
[64] CPA, s 3(1).
[65] CPA, s 3(2).
[66] Expert Group (n36) 28.
[67] ibid.
[68] Under CPA, s 4.
[69] Note P Cerka, J Grigiene, and G Sirbikyt, 'Liability for Damages Caused by Artificial Intelligence' (2015) 31 *Computer Law and Security Review* 376, 386.
[70] CPA, s 4(1)(e).
[71] J Morgan, "Torts and Technology" (n 35) 534.
[72] Note Expert Group (n 36) 28–9.
[73] Although the EU is considering reforms to the Product Liability Directive ('PLD') (Council Directive 85/374/EEC of 25 July 1985 on the approximation of the laws, regulations and administrative provisions of the Member States concerning liability for defective products) (see European Commission, Proposal for a Directive of the European Parliament and of the Council on liability for defective products (COM(2022) 495 final; and European Parliament, "New Product Liability Directive" (EP, 20th February 2024) <www.europarl.europa.eu/legislative-train/theme-a-europe-fit-for-the-digital-age/file-new-product-liability-directive>), these do not address the liability gap, and the reforms will not apply to the UK's CPA regime.
[74] Department for Transport, *The Pathway to Driverless Cars: A Detailed Review of Regulations for Automated Vehicle Technologies* (DfT 2015).

against the supplier/producer/importer is a poor substitute for a claim that could be brought against a negligent driver.

C. Liability Gap

Since both of these alternative claims do not offset the loss of the claim in negligence against a human driver, the position of the claimant injured by an AV is significantly weaker, both in legal and practical terms, than that of a victim injured by a human driver. This results in a liability gap. There will undoubtedly be situations where an AV drives in a manner which would be negligent if driven by a human driver, but where no one individual designer, programmer or the like is at fault, and the AV is not itself 'defective'. Further, the alternative claims are not suitable to low value motor accident claims. It is also important to note that these claims are *also* available in the context of ordinary motor vehicle accidents (for instance for negligence in designing the vehicle, or defective braking systems etc), but they are inevitably not brought, since they are considerably more complicated to bring than a claim which alleges driver fault. Proving fault on the part of someone other than a driver, such as a designer, is a complicated, and expensive process. Even strict liability product liability claims are also significantly less attractive than claims against a negligent driver. Further, these alternative claims are not subject to the compulsory motor insurance regime.

VI. The AEV Act

Recognising some of these significant problems with the alternative actions Parliament introduced a bespoke regime for AV accidents, which is to be found in the AEV Act. The Act, which came into force in 2021, is part of a Government strategy to put the UK at the forefront of AV deployment,[75] and partly motivated by a desire to help ensure that the public is receptive to AVs.[76] The Act is pre-emptive in that it was enacted prior to approved AVs operating on UK roads. This was done in order to permit parties to know the relevant civil liability regimes for AV accidents in advance of their deployment.

The provisions dealing with AVs are found in Part I of the statute. Part II is concerned with electric charging, and does not concern us here. Part I is short, and does not seek to be a comprehensive regime, instead it seeks merely to set out a liability regime which is sufficient in order to enable the deployment of AVs, whilst

[75] HM Queen Elizabeth II, 'The Queen's Speech 2016' (18 May 2016) *HM Government*. www.gov.uk/government/speeches/queens-speech-2016.

[76] K Oliphant, 'Liability for Road Accidents Caused by Driverless Cars' (2019) *Singapore Comparative Law Review* 190.

providing for accident victims. It does not seek to deal with regulatory standards or approval processes, which AVs need to meet in order to be able to be deployed on the road. It also does not deal with the data storage or sharing requirements[77] which may in fact be necessary for the proper functioning of an AV insurance market.

A. Definition?

The AEV Act does not set out a technical definition of an AV.[78] Instead, prior to the relevant provisions of the Automated Vehicles Act 2024 (AVA) coming into force, AVs are defined in accordance with whether or not they are included on a list kept by the Secretary of State.[79]

Section 1(1) states:

> (1) The Secretary of State must prepare, and keep up to date, a list of all motor vehicles that—
>
> (a) are in the Secretary of State's opinion designed or adapted to be capable, in at least some circumstances or situations, of safely driving themselves, and
>
> (b) may lawfully be used when driving themselves, in at least some circumstances or situations, on roads or other public places in Great Britain.

Considerable discretion is given to the Secretary of State,[80] and the Act does not provide any guidance as to how to exercise it. The word 'capable' means that the vehicle does not need to use this capability all of the time, for instance where it can only be used in particular conditions such as motorway driving, or where the capability can be turned off and on. The phrase 'safely driving' is not defined, but this is likely to include a consideration of test results, accident records, and soft law standards. Since the cause of action which the AEV Act creates only applies to vehicles on the list,[81] there is a significant risk that liability under the Act may either be too broad, or too narrow, depending on how the list is compiled. A list which is too narrow will mean that accident victims may be forced to bring complicated and difficult product liability claims.

In place of this approach Parliament considered using the SAE levels, but this proposal was rejected on the basis that they were considered too imprecise, and insufficiently robust for legislative use.[82] Although their use in US regulation might imply that they may be adequate for such purposes.[83] However, since they

[77] J Goudkamp, 'Automated Vehicle Liability and AI' in Lim and Morgan (n30) 175.

[78] J Marson and K Ferris, 'The Lexicon of Self-Driving Vehicles and the Fuliginous Obscurity of "Autonomous Vehicles"' (2021) 44 *Statute Law Review* 1, 6.

[79] AEV Act, s 1(4).

[80] J Marson, K Ferris, and J Dickinson, 'The Automated and Electric Vehicles Act 2018 Part 1 and Beyond: A Critical Review' (2020) 41 *Statute Law Review* 395, 401.

[81] Even if the vehicle should not have been added to the list it is an AV if it is on the list, see Goudkamp, 'Automated Vehicle Liability' (n77), 178.

[82] Marson, Ferris, and Dickinson (n80), 401.

[83] Marson and Ferris (n78) 11.

are American rather than international standards, are not the only categories used to define AV technologies, and are not used by the United Nations Economic Commission for Europe (which sets regulations for vehicle standards), this may also have played a role in not tying the cause of action provided by the AEV Act to the SAE levels.[84] It also may help prevent litigation regarding categorising AV technologies, which as experience shows are sometimes misclassified in different contexts, including over-classified for marketing purposes. The absence of statutory definitions or guidance may therefore be a deliberate attempt to future proof the Act in that it allows the legislation to adapt to the prevailing technology, and any emerging future consensus on international definitions for AVs.

Notwithstanding the Secretary of State's discretion, for the practical operation of the liability mechanism in the Act currently (prior to the provisions of the AVA coming into force), an AV appears to be limited to Level 4 and 5 technologies,[85] since the statutory cause of action is limited to a vehicle 'driving itself'. This is defined in Section 8(1)(a), which states that 'a vehicle is "driving itself" if it is operating in a mode in which it is not being controlled, and does not need to be monitored, by an individual'. Driver assist systems are therefore not included. This may be problematic since if the accident is caused by a defect in a Level 3 system, and the driver is not at fault in monitoring it (and as we have seen above human capabilities monitoring may be different from human capabilities driving), the victim will be left to pursue a difficult, and expensive product liability claim against the manufacturer.[86] It is therefore arguable that the Act is under-inclusive. The AVA reforms, when in force, potentially partially sidestep this problem by substituting a new definition into Section 8(1)(a) which will then define 'driving itself' to be when the authorised automated vehicle 'is travelling while an authorised automation feature of the vehicle is engaged'.

As part of a broader review of the AV legal framework the Law Commission has proposed a new AV authorisation process. This will render the AEV Act listing system unnecessarily duplicative, and potentially contradictory, and the Law Commission therefore recommended an amendment to Section 1 so as to integrate it into a new AV authorisation process.[87] This proposal was accepted by the Government,[88] and is found within the Automated Vehicles Act 2024,[89] which (when in force) removes Section 1, and inserts the word 'authorised' in front of

[84] A Glassbrook, 'An A to Z of Automated and Electric Vehicle Law' (2021) *Journal of Personal Injury Law* 140; Hansard, HL, vol 791, 'Automated and Electric Vehicles Bill Committee', 9 May 2018, col 174–5 (Baroness Sugg).

[85] This is also the position of the Government, see Sugg (n84); see also Oliphant, 'Liability for Road Accidents' (n76). cf M Chatzipanagiotis, 'Insurance Aspects of Automated Vehicles' in S Jovanovic and P Marano (eds), *Insurance and Legal-Economic Environment – Wider and Narrower Framework* (AIDA, 2022) 159, 162, who considers that some Level 3 technologies will be covered. This is, however, unlikely as these technologies need to be monitored.

[86] Goudkamp, 'Automated Vehicle Liability' (n77), 180.

[87] Law Commission, *Automated Vehicles* (Law Com No 404, 2022), [13.12].

[88] HM Government, *Connected & Automated Mobility 2025: Realising the benefits of self-driving vehicles in the UK*, CP 719 (HMSO 2022) 126.

[89] AVA, s 5(2).

the words 'automated vehicle' in other sections of the AEV Act, thus referring to the new authorisation procedure. Whilst the authorisation procedure will still be carried out by the Secretary of State,[90] and will use as yet to be drafted secondary legislation, the Secretary of State's discretion is less arbitrary. There is a requirement for the Secretary of State to identify how the AV meets the self-driving test,[91] and also to prepare a statement of safe principles which they propose to apply in assessing whether the vehicle is capable of travelling autonomously and safely. In drafting these principles the Secretary of State is required to consult with representative organisations, and to frame them with a view to securing that AVs will be as safe, or safer than careful and competent human drivers, and that road safety will be improved by the use of such vehicles.[92] The Law Commission did not propose any other alterations to the AEV Act, and the AVA makes no other amendments to the statute.

B. The Liability Regime

The core of the AEV Act is Section 2 which introduces an insurer pays system. Its purpose is to plug the gap in insurance cover which arises due to the removal of the human driver,[93] and to ensure that accident victim claims remain within the motor insurance framework and that victims do not have to pursue product liability claims against AV manufacturers.[94] Section 2 provides that where an AV is driving itself, and causes an accident the insurer is strictly liable for any damage suffered by the insured person, or by any other person as a result of the accident.[95] Damage under this section includes death, personal injury, and property damage. However, it does not include liability for property damage to the AV itself, or goods which are carried for hire and reward in the AV or in a trailer drawn by it.[96] Liability for property damage under this section is capped at £1.2 million.[97]

Where the AV is not insured the owner is instead strictly liable for the damage.[98] However, there is a lacuna in this AV liability regime when compared to the regime applying to conventional motor vehicles since there are currently no agreements in place with the MIB to cover uninsured owners of AVs, who may be men of straw. Further work is needed to get an agreement in place with the MIB, and it is understood that negotiations are ongoing.

[90] AVA, s 3.
[91] AVA, s 4.
[92] AVA, s 2.
[93] Goudkamp, 'Automated Vehicle Liability' (n77), 177.
[94] House of Commons Library, *Briefing Paper, Number CBP 8118, Automated and Electric Vehicles Act 2018* (HC Library, 2018) 3.
[95] AEV Act, s 2(1).
[96] AEV Act, s 2(3).
[97] AEV Act, s 2(4), being the amount specified in RTA, s 145(4)(b).
[98] AEV Act, s 2(2).

For strict liability to be present under Section 2(1) the AV must be 'driving itself'. This as we have seen above is defined in Section 8(1)(a). However, there is a lack of clarity in its application. The use of this phrase means that this statutory liability will not apply to all AV accidents. For instance it is unlikely that it will cover an accident caused by an AV being parked in a dangerous position, even if it parked itself, since it is not at this time being 'operated'.[99] This position appears not to be changed by the revisions to be made by the AVA to Section 8(1)(a) since in this example it also could not be said that the automation feature is 'engaged'. It is also possible that an AV will not be considered 'driving itself' if it is stationary in traffic, with its engine turned off, and where it is hit by a third party motor vehicle from behind, which shunts it into the vehicle in front.

The requirement for the AV to be 'driving itself' means that vehicles will move in and out of this strict liability system depending on whether they are driving themselves, or whether the human driver has intervened, and/or the autonomous driving system has been turned off. With the latter two situations ordinary fault-based liability against the human driver will be in operation. The fact that AVs require a single policy of insurance covering both the vehicle and the driver will help to reduce the potential for disputes as to whether the vehicle is driving itself, since the same insurer will cover both the driver and the AV.[100] This in turn stops two different insurers from disputing which insurer covers the accident, which might occur if separate insurers covered the AV and the driver. Nevertheless, there will be incentives to argue that the vehicle was not driving itself at the time of the accident, since notwithstanding the fairly strict approach taken to fault in a motor accident negligence context, if the vehicle is not driving itself it will slightly strengthen the hand of the insurer in defending against the claim. This may be particularly tricky during handover situations. Secondly, where it is the driver of the vehicle themselves who is injured whether or not the vehicle is driving itself will determine if the insurer is liable to the driver. If the driver is in fact driving themselves, the insurer will not be so liable,[101] and the loss will lie with the injured driver if no other party is at fault, and no product liability claim is available. It may thus be necessary for such litigation to involve consideration of data produced by the AV, particularly in handover cases. In some circumstances the Act will not have sidestepped the need for courts to forensically examine data in order to compensate accident victims.

Section 2 uses the word 'caused', which also includes accidents which are 'partly caused' by the AV.[102] This is likely to be construed as importing a but for test, and is narrower than 'caused by, or arising out of, the use of', which is found within Section 145(3)(a) of the Road Traffic Act 1988. Given the use of the word 'accident' in Section 2 it is not clear if the strict liability claim would cover

[99] Goudkamp, 'Automated Vehicle Liability' (n77), 178.
[100] RTA, s 145(3A).
[101] Note Goudkamp, 'Automated Vehicle Liability' (n77), 179.
[102] AEV Act, s 8(3)(a).

deliberate harm, for instance the situation where the collision results from the AV being hacked by a malicious third party and turned into a weapon,[103] or where an AV deliberately hits another vehicle or pedestrian so as to minimise harm to others or the AV's occupants (as with a classic trolley problem situation). If a similar approach is taken to interpreting this word as with conventional vehicles it is possible that the cause of action may also cover deliberate harms.[104]

Notwithstanding the regime's strict liability approach, Section 3 introduces a contributory negligence defence. Where the accident or the damage which results from it was to any extent caused by the injured party the liability is reduced by whatever reduction would apply to the claim under the Law Reform (Contributory Negligence) Act 1945, if the claim was brought via a route other than the AEV Act claim.[105] This complicated provision, which Goudkamp describes as 'nothing short of an embarrassment in account of [its] complexity',[106] appears to require the court to imagine that the AV is a conventional motor vehicle and apply the contributory negligence approach which would apply in such an accident, or that it is a defective product which has caused the accident, and apply the relevant contributory negligence approach to that claim. This requires consideration of the respective faults of the AV and the victim, and runs the risk of importing human standards to AVs via the back door, in spite of the strict liability claim. Section 3(2) imports 100% contributory negligence, which excludes insurer liability to a person in charge of an AV (but not third parties), where the accident was wholly due to their negligence in allowing the vehicle to drive itself when it was not appropriate to do so. Despite some criticism of Section 3 the Law Commission has declined to propose changes to the section, considering that it is best reviewed in the light of AEV Act litigation, and since most insurers consider it sufficiently 'fit for purpose'.[107]

Section 4 deals with unauthorised software alterations or failures to update software. It permits an insurance policy to exclude or limit the insurer's liability under Section 2(1) for damage which is suffered by an 'insured person' where the accident occurs as a 'direct result' of software alterations made by the insured person, or with their knowledge, which are prohibited by the policy, or as a result of a failure to install safety-critical software updates, which the insured person knows (or ought reasonably to know) are safety-critical. Safety-critical is given a narrow definition, such updates being safety-critical only where it would be unsafe to use the AV without the updates.[108] This appears not to include mere safety

[103] cf Oliphant, 'Liability for Road Accidents' (n76).

[104] M Channon, 'Automated and Electric Vehicles Act 2018: An Evaluation in Light of Proactive Law and Regulatory Disconnect' (2019) 10 *European Journal of Law and Technology* 26.

[105] AEV Act, s 3(1).

[106] Goudkamp, 'Automated Vehicle Liability' (n77) 184. He suggests that a simpler approach would be to consider only to what extent the claimant has departed from the standard of a reasonable person in their position.

[107] Law Commission, *Automated Vehicles: Consultation Paper 3 – A regulatory framework for automated vehicles* (Law Com CP No 252, 2020) [16.3], [16.20].

[108] AEV Act, s 4(6)(b).

improvements to a generally safe vehicle. Where the insured person is not the holder of the policy the exclusion in relation to software alterations only applies where the victim knows that the alterations are prohibited under the policy. Section 4(3) also permits the policy to include provisions which allow the insurer to recover sums which it has paid to victims under Section 2(1) from an insured person who makes such alterations, or fails to install safety-critical software.

This section is likely to lead to insurers including clauses prohibiting software alterations, or penalising a failure to update software in their AV insurance policies, thus placing market pressure on AV owners not to modify their vehicles, and to ensure updates are installed, although specialised 'tinkerer's insurance' may emerge with higher premiums.[109] It is submitted that the failure to install safety-critical software provision is too harsh, and a contributory negligence approach would be more appropriate, which is tailored to the fault of the insured person. There is a significant difference between a failure to install which is caused by a genuine oversight such as by storing the AV inside a garage at a house where there is limited signal, perhaps in a rural and hilly location, with limited mobile coverage/radio coverage, thus preventing regular over the air updates, and a situation where an individual deliberately blocks signals to the AV by removing parts of the AV, or covering parts of the AV in signal absorbent materials. Further, it is unclear what level of knowledge is expected of an AV owner in this context. Some owners will be sophisticated early adopters of the technologies, but AVs also offer opportunities for those with significant disabilities to gain mobility. There is thus also a risk that 'ought reasonably' will be construed in a way which is harsh to unsophisticated parties, and also to those with mental or developmental disabilities, groups for whom AVs offer significant opportunities for increased independence, and for whom some classes of AV will be specifically designed for.

C. Superior Position

Through the AEV Act regime victims of AV accidents are placed in a superior position over victims of conventional motor vehicle accidents. Firstly, the strict liability claim against insurers means that AV accident victims, unlike the victims of human driven motor vehicle accidents, do not have to prove fault. Thus AV accident victims will be able to recover even where the AV is not defective, and where it drives with all due care and skill, such that if it were driven by a human driver there would be no negligence. Secondly, Section 2(1) provides for strict liability for 'damage', including 'personal injury', but the latter is not further defined in the Act, and it would appear to include pure psychiatric harm. Recovery for psychiatric harm for secondary victims under the AEV Act appears not to have

[109] M Marynowski, 'Car Insurance in the Age of Self-Driving – Analysis of the Automated and Electric Vehicles Act 2018' (2019) 4 *Insurance Review* 25.

the ordinary restrictions found in a negligence claim.[110] Thus a secondary victim, a passive witness of the AV accident, may be able to claim for pure psychiatric harm even where they do not have a close tie of love and affection with an individual involved in the physical accident. Parliament did not seem to recognise that it had placed AV accident victims (both primary and secondary) in a superior position to the victims of ordinary motor vehicle accidents.[111] However, such an approach, could be favoured by policy makers as a result of a need to obtain public acceptance of AVs, particularly in the light of the problems encountered in San Francisco, where members of the public have deliberately disrupted the operation of AV taxis.[112]

However, there is one aspect where the Section 2(1) claim is less favourable than a claim in negligence, and that is in regard to limitation. With property damage the AEV Act contains a limitation period for property damage of three years,[113] which matches the limitation period for a tort personal injuries claim, rather than the usual six-year limitation period in tort for property damage.[114]

In constructing a different liability system for AVs to ordinary motor vehicles Parliament has infringed 'tech-impartiality'.[115] This doctrine has two aspects deterrence and victim rights. The doctrine recognises that tort can shape behaviour including by deterring harms. Here it is the first aspect of tech-impartiality, deterrence, which is problematic in this context. The first aspect is that tort law should neither encourage nor discourage the use of new technologies, where the risk of legally recognised harms that such technologies pose to third parties are the same when compared to older technologies and methods of work. Tort should only play a role in encouraging or discouraging the use of new technologies where the systems are more, or less safe, than the alternatives. This aspect prevents a perversion of tort's deterrence role. By adopting strict liability for AVs, and fault-based liability for conventional motor vehicles, deterrence is not being equally applied, and tort law exerts a greater deterrent effect on the deployment of AVs, than with conventional vehicles, even where the risk of harm is the same. There was no consideration of whether there should be a 'reasonable robot' standard for AVs,[116] or a standard of care which matches that of a human driver. This will discourage the adoption of AVs even where they are equally as safe as human drivers. Further, equalising the liability exposure will prevent any advantage from being gained from asserting that the vehicle was not driving itself at the time.

[110] For a discussion of the ordinary restrictions see Tettenborn (n 20) [7-76]–[7-78].
[111] Note Goudkamp, 'Automated Vehicle Liability' (n77) 182–183, 188.
[112] See eg, R Luscombe, 'Driverless Taxi Vandalized and Set on Fire in San Francisco's Chinatown' (12 February 2024) *The Guardian*. www.theguardian.com/us-news/2024/feb/12/waymo-car-fire-san-francisco.
[113] Limitation Act 1980, s 11B(3)–(4).
[114] Limitation Act 1980, ss 2, 11(4).
[115] Introduced in P Morgan 'Tort Law and AI' (n34).
[116] See R Abbott, *The Reasonable Robot* (Cambridge, Cambridge University Press, 2020) 9, 69.

However, rather than lowering the standard expected of AVs from strict liability to the standard expected of human drivers, it is perhaps time to consider whether it is time to apply a regime of strict liability to both human drivers and AVs.[117] As AVs become widespread, and freely mix with conventional vehicles which are likely to remain on our roads for a long time, operating two distinct models of liability, one less favourable to accident victims, is likely to come under increasing public scrutiny. It will also help to prevent confusion. Should a fault-based claim or an AEV Act claim apply in the case of an untraced driver/vehicle where it is not clear if the vehicle was an AV or not, or if it was an AV whether it was driving itself at the time? This might also reduce the perverting effect of motor vehicle accidents on the law of negligence generally. It will also help alleviate the situation where human drivers are labelled as being negligent, when their conduct is not in fact blameworthy.

D. Insurer Claims

The statutory cause of action provided by the AEV Act does not affect any other person's liability,[118] but since the Act provides the victim with a strict liability claim against the insurer there is little incentive on a victim to pursue other parties.[119] However, Section 5 provides the insurer on whom the Section 2 liability is placed, with the right to a subrogated claim against any person liable to the injured person in respect of the accident. Such claims would include for example claims brought against at fault drivers of conventional vehicles involved in accidents, or product liability claims against manufacturers of AVs, or contractual claims where the damage was sustained by the person who purchased the AV. The justification for this approach, of placing strict liability on the insurer, but the right for the insurer to pursue other parties, is to ensure speedy and smooth compensation for victims.[120] Differential pricing of insurance for different classes of AVs with different safety records may exert some additional deterrent effect on manufacturers, in that less safe vehicles may be more expensive to insure, and thus perhaps harder to sell once the market is aware of this greater insurance expense.

This approach could also help to maintain both tort deterrence and the forensic role of tort in accident investigation in that insurers, unlike many third-party victims of AV accidents, are likely to have greater expertise in technology and litigation, the resources to investigate, and to bring claims against manufacturers, designers, and so on. The AEV Act channels the liability to ensure that in

[117] See also Oliphant, 'Liability for Road Accidents' (n76).
[118] AEV Act, s 2(7).
[119] Goudkamp, 'Automated Vehicle Liability' (n77) 182.
[120] Law Commission, *Automated Vehicles A Joint Preliminary Consultation Paper* (Law Com CP No 240, 2018) [6–26].

any subrogated product liability litigation, there are sophisticated parties on both sides. An insurer is more likely to have the resources to take on Big Tech. They are also likely to be able to monitor common problems arising from different models of AVs. Insurers have the litigation expertise that injured victims do not, and they may be able to embark on test cases as appropriate, based on their monitoring of AV accidents, even where in the instance of a particular case it would not be financially viable to bring a claim, but where it might make a difference to their overall profitability. However, there are a number of obstacles to maintaining this tort deterrence through subrogated actions.

Firstly, some insurers may enter into commercial relationships with AV manufacturers and will not wish to disrupt this relationship through litigation.[121] This is a more limited problem since many will not. The second problem is one of data access. The AEV Act does not require data capture or storage. The ability of an insurer to pursue other parties (or even to assert contributory negligence) may be limited unless an AV collects and stores data related to the crash.[122] This data will help establish key facts about the accident. Manufacturers may be reluctant to share sensitive data with others, particularly where they have set up their own insurers and wish them to have a competitive advantage, or where they fear that an insurer may use this data against them.[123] This problem may however be overstated in that AVs will require insurance, and insurers will not be compelled to provide it for AVs produced by any particular AV manufacturer. Lack of manufacturer co-operation to these subrogated claims may not be in their commercial interest, since an insurer may simply cease to offer insurance for particular makes/models of AV.[124] The data problem has been considered by the Law Commission which has proposed data storage recommendations, including records of activation and deactivation of self-driving and when a collision is detected.[125] The Government has agreed to consult on a new data sharing regime, which will be subject to secondary legislation, and is considering a new code of practice on data sharing.[126] This problem may thus be addressed by the time of AV deployment. Additionally in the absence of manufacturer co-operation insurers might require the use of black box technologies (telematics) in AVs in order to collect the data necessary for litigation.

Thirdly, and more significantly the AEV Act does not provide any new routes for the insurer to recover, or address the defects in the existing causes of action. This means that the insurer faces many of the same problems that an individual victim would face in the absence of the AEV Act, where an AEV causes the harm, since the causes of action which they can deploy (as set out above) are significantly flawed in an AV context. Without reform to the CPA product liability regime, for

[121] Channon (n104).
[122] Law Commission 2022 (n87) [13.41].
[123] Chatzipanagiotis (n85).
[124] Singapore Academy of Law (n53) [3.12].
[125] Law Commission 2022 (n87) [13.50]–[13.52].
[126] HM Government (n88) 126.

instance coverage of over the air updates, re-examination of the state of the art defence and proof of defectiveness in an AV context (amongst others), it is likely that where an AV itself causes an accident the loss will lie with the insurer. Although insurers may be less disadvantaged than an accident victim in any product liability litigation against a manufacturer given their litigation resources, expertise, greater ability to access and analyse data, and to choose favourable test cases, they still face significant, if not insurmountable legal hurdles.

VII. Conclusion

The AEV Act is a sticking plaster to get AVs on the road, and to ensure compensation for AV accident victims, but it does not resolve the underlying problems regarding the interface between AVs and the law of tort.[127] It also does not deal with the problem regarding Level 3 system accidents. Parliament has temporarily avoided the issue of how the broader law of tort should evolve in an AV context. The same problems (and legal gaps) remain, but the Act shifts these problems onto the insurer, and away from the accident victim. This does have the advantage that insurers are more likely than accident victims to have the litigation expertise, resources, and ability to engage in strategic litigation, which will be needed to pursue claims against AV manufacturers and Big Tech. Insurers may also indirectly regulate AV safety through increased premiums, but despite the subrogated actions that insurers can bring tort deterrence and the forensic role of tort in this context is undermined given that the causes of action which they will have to rely on are poorly adapted to AV technologies. Parliament will need to revisit tort, particularly product liability claims, in an AV context, since the existing mechanisms are unable to deal with AI systems such as AVs. The European Union has been pro-active in considering the problems that AI causes for the Product Liability Directive, which the CPA implements.[128] It is time for the UK to do likewise.

The AEV Act also places the victims of AV accidents in a stronger position than the victims of conventional motor vehicle accidents. It is unlikely that this was deliberately intended, particularly the preferencing of secondary victims of AV accidents. In doing so the AEV Act infringes tech-impartiality, by exerting greater tort deterrence on AVs compared to conventional motor vehicles even where the risk of harm is the same. It is time for Parliament to openly acknowledge this preferencing of AV accident victims and to consider whether a strict liability system is also the appropriate method of compensation for conventional motor vehicle accidents too.

[127] Note Law Commission 2020 (n107) [16.12].

[128] P Morgan, 'Tort Liability and Autonomous System Accidents – Challenges and Future Developments' in Morgan (n61) 1–26. The UK Government states that it will be engaging more widely with Government to understand the next steps (HM Government (n88) 126).

11

The Changing Landscape of Professional Liabilities

GARY MEGGITT

I. Introduction

Once upon a time, it was relatively easy to identify who was 'a professional'. As the authors of *Jackson & Powell on Professional Liability* put it, 'the occupations which are regarded as professions have four characteristics'. These are the 'mental' rather than 'manual' nature of their work; the 'moral' or 'societal' aspects of their role; the existence of collective organisations to which they belong and which oversee their activities; and the elevated social status which they enjoy.[1]

Those characteristics are passing into history. Professionals' work may still be mental rather than manual, but the quality of their work is no longer 'judged' by their professional peers but by the managers of the corporate entities in which they are now often employed. Moreover, emerging technology, including artificial intelligence (AI), presents an even greater challenge. Can a 'bot' be a barrister? If not, why not? If an architect uses AI to design a building and that design is defective, who is to blame? The architect or the AI or the AI's developer? If the design is superlative, who takes the credit?

The demise of traditional partnerships and the 'commercialization' of their practices has exacerbated the tensions between professionals' disparate ethical duties to their colleagues, clients and the wider community. The supervisory role of collective organisations such as national law societies has been diluted by the growth of statutory regulatory bodies and, in the view of some, sidestepped by multinational professional service firms. Finally, professionals' supposed social status has been all but eradicated by the public's disinclination to defer to their 'betters'. This is reflected, most importantly for professional indemnity (PI) insurers, in the growth of claims against professionals for both their own alleged misconduct and in 'facilitating' the misconduct of others.

[1] M Cannon, H Evans, R Stewart, QC, K L Marshall, Sir Rupert Jackson and J Powell (eds) *Jackson & Powell on Professional Liability* (9th Edition, London, Sweet & Maxwell, 2022) para 1–003. Hereinafter referred to as *Jackson & Powell*.

This chapter addresses the changing nature of the work, obligations and regulation of professionals by reference to the 'four characteristics' in *Jackson & Powell*.[2] It considers the possible risks that may be brought about by these changes. It discusses the need for policyholders and insurers to familiarise themselves with these risks and to address them when it comes to their practices (in the case of the former) and underwriting, claims management possible development of alternative forms of cover (in the latter's case). Although this chapter focuses on legal professionals (so as to keep it to a manageable length) it touches upon the experiences of other professions where appropriate. Finally, although it concentrates on developments in the UK, it does not neglect those in other significant jurisdictions.

II. A Professional and a Professional's 'Skills'

Whilst this chapter began by identifying the characteristics of a 'professional', it is conceded that there is no comprehensive definition of such individuals in UK statute or case law. That said, in *Commissioners of Inland Revenue v Maxse*[3] Scrutton LJ observed:

> [A] 'profession' in the present use of language involves the idea of an occupation requiring either purely intellectual skill, or manual skill controlled, as in painting or sculpture, or surgery, by the intellectual skill of the operator, as distinguished from an occupation which is substantially the production or sale or arrangements for sale of commodities.

This judicial remark serves the valuable purpose of identifying the prominence and significance of 'skill' – especially 'intellectual skill' – to a professional's work. If someone undertakes a task that requires such 'skill', he is expected to exercise the same level of 'skill' as an ordinarily competent practitioner. As Tindal CJ put it in *Lanphier v Phipos*:[4]

> Every person who enters into a learned profession undertakes to bring to the exercise of it a reasonable degree of care and skill. He does not undertake, if he is an attorney, that at all events you shall gain your case, nor does a surgeon undertake that he will perform a cure; nor does he undertake to use the highest possible degree of skill. There may be persons who have higher education and greater advantages than he has, but he undertakes to bring a fair, reasonable and competent degree of skill.[5]

[2] That is not to say that this is the only formulation of such professional characteristics. In H Gardner and L S Shulman 'The Professions in America Today: Crucial but Fragile', 134 *Daedalus* 13–18, six 'commonplaces' are identified as being 'characteristic of all professions, properly construed' including 'a commitment to serve in the interests of clients in particular and the welfare of society in general' and 'the development of a professional community responsible for the oversight and monitoring of quality in both practice and professional education'.

[3] [1919] 1 KB 647, 657.

[4] [1838] 8 C & P 475, 479.

[5] Most of the judgments cited in this chapter, especially the older ones, use the terms 'he' or 'his' or 'man' when referring to professionals. This chapter will adopt that terminology for sake of

This expectation is embodied in the 'Bolam Test':

> The test is the standard of the ordinary skilled man exercising and professing to have that special skill [...] A man need not possess the highest expert skill; it is well established law that it is sufficient if he exercises the ordinary skill of an ordinary competent man exercising that particular art.[6]

Consequently, as noted by Bingham LJ in *Eckersley v Binnie*,[7] a professional should 'command the corpus of knowledge' of his field of expertise; be aware of any 'gaps' in his knowledge and ensure that he keeps up-to-date with new developments; and be conscious of the risks arising from his work.[8] The standard applies irrespective of the length of time that someone has been a member of the profession in question.[9]

The courts assess the standard of care and skill expected from a professional by reference to his colleagues' 'corpus of knowledge', which generally requires the input of expert witnesses.[10] Such expert opinion often includes references to a profession's relevant codes of conduct.[11] Any failure to follow a profession's usual practices is not, however, automatically indicative of negligence and, moreover, the courts have occasionally found such practices themselves to be at fault.[12] The crucial point is, as identified by Lord Browne-Wilkinson in *Bolitho v City and Hackney HA*,[13] whether or not the usual practice has a 'logical basis'.[14]

Determining whether someone had complied with his profession's expected standards of care and skill was relatively straightforward in the days when the professions 'kept to themselves'. In many jurisdictions, including the UK, the position has since changed and traditional partnerships have been displaced by alternative business structures (ABS), including multidisciplinary practices (MDPs) staffed by a variety of professionals. These developments are addressed in detail in the next section, but it is important to appreciate, for now, that they are linked to and driven (in part) by what Susskind described as the 'commoditization'

consistency and brevity only, it being recognised that – in many professions, including the law – 'he' is often 'she'.

[6] McNair J in *Bolam v Friern Hospital Management Committee* [1957] 1 WLR 582, 586.

[7] [1988] 18 Con LR 1, 79.

[8] Many professions require their members to undertake regular training after qualification as a condition of ongoing certification. See eg, the Solicitors Regulation Authority (SRA) continuing competence requirements available at www.sra.org.uk/solicitors/resources/continuing-competence/cpd/continuing-competence/.

[9] Whilst inexperience is no defence to a professional negligence claim, the standard of care required may vary according to the nature of the client and his experience and/or needs, see *Carradine Properties Ltd v DJ Freeman and Co* [1999] Lloyds Law Rep P N 483.

[10] As provided for by the Civil Procedure Rules (CPR), in particular CPR Part 35 and its accompanying practice Direction 35, both available at www.justice.gov.uk/courts/procedure-rules/civil/rules/part35.

[11] As in *Barber v Somerset CC* [2004] 1 WLR 1089.

[12] *Edward Wong Finance Co Ltd v Johnson, Stokes and Master* [1984] AC 296. See also *Patel v Daybells* [2001] EWCA Civ 1229.

[13] [1998] A.C. 232. See also R Heywood, 'The logic of Bolitho' (2006) 4 *Professional Negligence* 225.

[14] See also *McCulloch v Forth Valley Health Board* [2023] UKSC 26; [2023] 3 WLR 321 on the continuing applicability of the *Bolam* Test.

of legal services,[15] which is itself related to increased use of emerging technology by various professionals.

Such emerging technology, as far as legal practice is concerned, is generally referred to as 'LawTech' or 'LegalTech' and embraces processes such as electronic document management; computerised time-management and billing systems (or 'e-Billing'); electronic discovery or disclosure of documents in litigation (or 'e-Discovery'); legal research software; and due diligence tools.[16] Equivalent technology has been developed for other professions and industries, such as 'FinTech' for those in the banking and financial services sector and 'InsurTech' for insurers.[17] The emerging technologies themselves range from blockchain and other distributed ledgers, chatbots, the Internet of Things (IoT) and AI. Some of these processes and tools, such as search engines, are relatively simple whereas others are much more sophisticated and can carry out complicated tasks with very little human intervention with, arguably, the most impressive being autonomous ships.[18]

It is perhaps indicative of the dangers of thinking about such matters in human terms that when we contemplate LawTech, the image of a robot sporting a barrister's wig often springs to mind. Interestingly, Devanović referred to Isaac Asimov's character of Stephen Byerley – a district attorney who may or may not have been a robot – in her valuable discussion of the development of 'true' AI lawyers.[19] It is important, however, to appreciate that AI lawyers need not look like humans; not all emerging technology is AI; and not all AI is 'autonomous' in the manner suggested by Asimov's writings. So what is meant by 'AI'? The term was coined by McCarthy, for a conference at Dartmouth College in 1956, as 'the science and engineering of making intelligent machines'.[20] In the six decades since then, the

[15] See, inter alia, R.Susskind, *The Future of Law: Facing the Challenges of Information Technology* (Oxford, Oxford University Press, 1996); *Transforming the Law: Essays on Technology, Justice and the Legal Marketplace* (Oxford, Oxford University Press, 2000). *The End of Lawyers? Rethinking The Nature of Legal Services* (Oxford, Oxford University Press, 2008); *Tomorrow's Lawyers: An Introduction to Your Future* (Oxford, Oxford University Press, 2013); and, with D Susskind, *The Future of the Professions: How Technology Will Transform the Work of Human Experts* (Oxford, Oxford University Press, 2015).

[16] See S Chishti, S Adams Bhatti, A Datoo and D Indjic (ed), *The Legaltech Book: The Legal Technology Handbook for Investors, Entrepreneurs and FinTech Visionaries* (Hoboken, John Wiley & Sons, 2020).

[17] See R Buckley, D Arner and D Zetzsche, *FinTech: Finance, Technology and Regulation* (Cambridge, Cambridge University Press, 2023).

[18] See S Doll, 'Autonomous Cargo Ship Completes 500 Mile Voyage, Avoiding Hundreds of Collisions' (May 13 2022) electrek.co/2022/05/13/autonomous-cargo-ship-completes-500-mile-voyage-avoiding-hundreds-of-collisions/. If you wish: For a comprehensive analysis on how such ships can be integrated into the current legal system, see B Soyer and A Tettenborn (eds), *Artificial Intelligence and Autonomous Shipping- Developing the International Legal Framework* (Oxford, Hart Publishing, 2021).

[19] 'True' as in autonomous, decision-making agents that can provide legal advice and represent clients at court. See D Dervanovic 'I, Inhuman Lawyer: Developing Artificial Intelligence in the Legal Profession' in M. Corrales et al (eds), *Robotics, AI and the Future of Law, Perspectives in Law, Business and Innovation* (New York, Springer, 2018).

[20] He subsequently published 'Ascribing Mental Qualities to Machines' in M Ringle (ed), *Philosophical Perspectives in Artificial Intelligence.* (London, Humanities Press, 1979) and *The Little Thoughts of Thinking Machines* (1983) available at www.semanticscholar.org/paper/The-Little-Thoughts-of-Thinking-Machines-McCarthy/25a384720fb178e6a848f6814278034181489 8aa. See also J Roberts,

meaning of the term and its relationship with the rival term 'machine intelligence' has been debated at length.[21]

In its 2023 White Paper 'A Pro-innovation Approach to AI Regulation', the then Conservative UK government acknowledged that there 'is no general definition of AI that enjoys widespread consensus' and offered its own explanation 'by reference to the 2 characteristics that generate the need for a bespoke regulatory response', these being its 'adaptivity' and 'autonomy'.[22] Unfortunately, the White Paper did not address the important distinction between 'Narrow AI', where the 'agent' carries out a specific task (eg, speech or facial recognition) and 'Artificial General Intelligence' (AGI) in which the 'agent' is able to carry out a wide variety of tasks including those which it has not carried out before, much like a human being.[23] This distinction is important in the context of the application of AI to the work of lawyers or other professionals. Nor did it address such issues as data access and sustainability and, most importantly, the question of liability.[24]

On this last point, although the White Paper acknowledged that 'The clear allocation of accountability and legal responsibility is important for effective AI governance' it continued 'It is too soon to make decisions about liability as it is a complex, rapidly evolving issue which must be handled properly to ensure the success of our wider AI ecosystem'. Its response to the consultation on its White Paper in February 2024 continued in that vein.[25] Although the new Labour UK government has announced that it will legislate on these issues, no details have been revealed as at the date of writing.

By contrast, the European Union has published a draft AI Liability Directive,[26] which is intended to complement the AI Act (which was formally adopted by

'Thinking Machines: The Search for Artificial Intelligence' (2016) 2 *Distillations* 14–23, available at https://www.sciencehistory.org/distillations/magazine/thinking-machines-the-search-for-artificial-intelligence and J Kaplan, *Artificial Intelligence, What Everyone Needs to Know* (Oxford, Oxford University Press, 2016).

[21] The term 'machine intelligence' was employed by Donald Michie, whose long and distinguished career in computer sciences began when he worked at Bletchley Park with Alan Turing and others on decrypting German military communications during World War II. For his part, Turing published 'Computing Machinery and Intelligence' (1950) 49 *Mind* 433.

[22] UK Department for Science, Innovation and Technology, 'A Pro-Innovation Approach to AI Regulation' (CP815, March 2023) www.gov.uk/government/publications/ai-regulation-a-pro-innovation-approach.

[23] An 'agent' is defined by SJ Russell and P Norvig in *Artificial Intelligence: A Modern Approach 4th Edition* (Prentice Hall, 2020) as 'Anything that can be viewed as perceiving its environment through sensors and acting upon that environment through actuators'.

[24] Other important concepts relevant to AI include 'Machine learning', by which algorithms 'learn' from examples and improve their performance with more data over time. Machine learning involves decision trees and Bayesian networks. 'Deep machine learning' involves complex statistical models and algorithms in 'neural networks.' See www.ibm.com/cloud/blog/ai-vs-machine-learning-vs-deep-learning-vs-neural-networks.

[25] assets.publishing.service.gov.uk/media/65c1e399c43191000d1a45f4/a-pro-innovation-approach-to-ai-regulation-amended-governement-response-web-ready.pdf.

[26] commission.europa.eu/system/files/2022-09/1_1_197605_prop_dir_ai_en.pdf.

the European Parliament in March 2024) and the revised Directive on Liability for Defective Products (which was also adopted in March 2024).[27] The AI Act, which regulates AI systems by reference to 'risk' but does not address individual claims for compensation, provides its own definition of AI:

> 'artificial intelligence system' (AI system) means a system that is designed to operate with elements of autonomy and that, based on machine and/or human-provided data and inputs, infers how to achieve a given set of objectives using machine learning and/or logic- and knowledge based approaches, and produces system-generated outputs such as content (generative AI systems), predictions, recommendations or decisions, influencing the environments with which the AI system interacts[28]

This definition is adopted in the draft AI Liability Directive, which will apply it to 'non-contractual fault-based civil law claims for damages'. The draft Directive lowers the evidential burden for claimants; empowers the courts to compel the disclosure of evidence related to AI systems; permits representative and class actions; and introduces a 'rebuttable presumption of a causal link in the case of fault'. Crucially, the Directive does not 'harmonise general aspects of civil liability which are regulated in different ways by national civil liability rules', it simply shifts the evidential burden in favour of claimants and against the 'users' and 'providers' of AI systems i.e. the defendants. In that respect, the question of 'fault' remains unanswered.[29]

Other jurisdictions, such as China and the US, are also addressing the question of AI liability. In August 2023, the Cyberspace Administration of China's 'Interim Measures for the Management of Generative Artificial Intelligence Services', which are intended to regulate the provision of generative AI services, came into force. Comprehensive 'final' legislation is still under consideration.[30] US President Biden issued an executive order on the 'Safe, Secure, and Trustworthy Development and Use of AI' in October 2023 and, in September 2024, the US, UK and EU signed the first legally binding treaty aimed at regulating the use AI.[31] Whether or not states opt for a 'light touch' or a more prescriptive approach is something which the users of AI and their insurers will need to address. Moreover, insofar as lawyers are concerned, there is not just the question of apportioning liability but the wider issue of professional ethics. Devanović proposes the concept of 'Fairness by Design', 'inspired by data

[27] www.europarl.europa.eu/doceo/document/TA-9-2024-0132_EN.html. The revised Directive includes 'software' within the definition of 'product' and widens its predecessor's concept of 'damage", among other changes to the relevant law and procedures.

[28] Article 3(1) of the Act. See data.consilium.europa.eu/doc/document/ST-14954-2022-INIT/en/pdf.

[29] The details of the relationship between this triumvirate of EU measures are beyond the scope of this article. See, however, P Hacker, 'The European AI Liability Directives – Critique of a Half-Hearted Approach and Lessons for the Future' (November 25, 2022). ssrn.com/abstract=4279796.

[30] See the CSET translation of the draft AI law available at https://cset.georgetown.edu/publication/china-ai-law-draft/. See also A H Zhang, *High Wire: How China Regulates Big Tech and Governs Its Economy* (Oxford, Oxford University Press, 2024).

[31] US President Biden issued an executive order on the 'Safe, Secure, and Trustworthy Development and Use of AI' in October 2023 and, in September 2024, the US, UK and EU signed the first legally binding treaty aimed at regulating the use AI.

protection law and its Privacy by Design principles', to ensure that LawTech systems are free from bias. Ng discusses AI in the legal profession but her co-authors address AI liability and an ethical framework for AI more broadly.[32] As Davis identifies:

> Artificial intelligence (AI) has profound ethical implications. It poses grave threats – maybe even existential ones – to humanity. But we have yet to develop a theoretical framework for determining what it can and cannot do or, relatedly, for what it should and should not do. That gap is understandable. Applying ethics and law to AI is not easy. Doing so raises deep philosophical problems. The result is a formidable strategic challenge.[33]

Although Davis is discussing the strategic challenge of developing an ethical framework for AI generally, the challenge is no less formidable when it comes to ensuring that LawTech is ethical. Barristers and solicitors have an array of ethical duties, including but not limited to the duty to be competent; the related obligations of confidentiality and legal professional privilege; the duty to maintain professional disinterest or 'independence' (which is especially important for barristers); and the responsibility to assist in the administration of justice.[34] There are equally important ethical duties for doctors, financial advisers and other professionals.[35]

Ensuring that these duties are complied with by a human lawyer using Lawtech or by a 'barrister bot' and that there are effective ways of apportioning liability when they are not is a substantial technical and legal challenge. The task will be made much harder by the opacity of AI decision-making – the proverbial 'black box'.[36] The EU AI Liability Directive is an attempt to sidestep the 'black box' problem but, unless one uses a 'transparent' AI system or one of the tools that can explain its conduct (and determine why it was 'wrong') the opacity issue remains.[37] Moreover, there is the simple fact that AI systems do not 'think' or 'judge' as humans do. For example, Fleming has identified that 'while the algorithms […] can seem stunningly intelligent, they currently differ from humans in that one crucial respect – they don't know what they don't know, an ability

[32] C Ng 'AI in the Legal Profession' in L A DiMatteo et al (eds) *The Cambridge Handbook of Artificial Intelligence: Global Perspectives on Law and Ethics* (Cambridge, Cambridge University Press, 2022).

[33] J D Davis 'AI, Ethics, and Law: A Way Forward' in L A DiMatteo, C Poncibo and M Cannarsa (eds), *The Cambridge Handbook of Artificial Intelligence* (Cambridge, Cambridge University Press, 2022).

[34] See M Legg and F Bell, *Artificial Intelligence and the Legal Profession* (Oxford, Hart Publishing, 2020), in particular Chapter 11 'Legal Ethics, Liability and Regulation in an AI World'. For a comprehensive discussion of the law in relation to solicitors, see W Flenley and T Leech, *The Law of Solicitors' Liabilities* (4th Edition, London, Bloomsbury Professional, 2020).

[35] As are discussed in *Jackson & Powell* and elsewhere.

[36] In computing, the term 'black box' refers to those systems whose internal operations cannot be easily monitored or analysed (if at all). One may know what information or instructions they received and the output they produced but not how they got from the one to the other.

[37] See M Bischoff, 'New Tool Reveals How AI Makes Decisions' (15 June 2023) *Scientific American*. www.scientificamerican.com/article/new-tool-reveals-how-ai-makes-decisions/.

psychologists refer to as metacognition'.[38] In a recent speech, Sit Geoffrey Vos opined that AI's lack of any conscience was a great weakness insofar as its application to legal work was concerned given that 'the concept of justice itself depend[s] upon empathy, conscience, even guilt'.[39] Thus, a barrister bot could well fail the test in *Eckersley v Binnie* but a barrister expert witness would not be able to give evidence on how or why it had. An AI expert witness would be needed … but that expert wouldn't necessarily know about lawyers' professional obligations.

These difficulties will be replicated, with different outcomes, in each jurisdiction and for each profession in which such technology is used. Legislation may be needed to address the nuances in liability when humans and autonomous 'bots' both contribute to the services provided to (and loss suffered by) a client or third party. One temptation would be to cut through the proverbial 'Gordian Knot' and apply a strict liability rule or presumption of negligence when a professional's use of emerging technology (or failure to use it) may have resulted in loss or damage to a client or third party. There may be a similar desire for such simplicity when one is dealing with the work of MDPs. This would be an error. As Tindal CJ put it almost 200 years ago, professionals are not expected to guarantee a favourable outcome for their clients. Nor should they be. They are fallible human beings and AI, for all its promise, is but a creation of humans. The standard of care should remain that of a reasonably competent professional and the attribution of responsibility should, in the first instance, be to the supplier of the professional service, ie the law firm.[40] Ultimately, a compromise between or amalgam of professional liability and product liability seems the likeliest outcome.[41]

III. The 'Societal' Role

It will come as no surprise that the 'socio-economic' role of the professions has been the subject of much academic (and non-academic) discussion. It would be impossible to adequately review that discussion here but there are two aspects which are important to this chapter. The first, which shall be considered in this section, is the 'commercialization' of the professions. The second, which shall be examined in the next section, is what has been described as the 'regulative bargain' between the professions and states (or governments).[42]

[38] S Fleming, 'Opinion: What separates humans from AI? It's doubt' (16 April 2021) *UCL News*. www.ucl.ac.uk/news/2021/apr/opinion-what-separates-humans-ai-its-doubt#:~:text=But%20while%20the%20algorithms%20behind,psychologists%20refer%20to%20as%20metacognition.

[39] Sir Geoffrey Vos, Speech to Professional Negligence Bar Association 22 May 2024, available at https://www.judiciary.uk/speech-by-the-master-of-the-rolls-to-the-professional-negligence-bar-association/.

[40] Much in the way that a firm would be vicariously liable for the faults of its individual staff.

[41] See Allianz Commercial 'Professional indemnity insurance claims insights 2023' p 12. commercial.allianz.com/content/dam/onemarketing/commercial/commercial/reports/commercial-professional-indemnity-insurance-claims-2023.pdf.

[42] D Cooper, 'Regulating the UK Accountancy Profession: Episodes in the Relation between the Profession and the State' (Economic and Social Research Council Conference on Corporatism at the

In September 2023, the International Bar Association (IBA) launched its 'Impact Project', which is intended to be a 'comprehensive [...] assessment of the socioeconomic impact of the legal profession'.[43] In doing so, Almudena Arpón de Mendívil Aldama, the IBA President, declared:

> Lawyers are an undeniable pillar of society. Through our day-to-day work, we contribute to strengthening and maintaining the Rule of Law, which is fundamental to socioeconomic development.

Similarly, the Bar Council of England & Wales asserts:

> A strong and independent Bar exists to serve the public. As specialist, independent advocates, barristers enable people to uphold their legal rights, often acting on behalf of the most vulnerable members of society.[44]

These statements, although they contain some truth, echo what is now often seen as the archaic view that to join a profession – especially the legal profession – was to 'answer' a 'calling' rather than merely than do a 'job'. There was an emphasis on 'service' over the pursuit 'profit'. This outlook is evident in Carr-Saunders and Wilson's observation (almost 90 years ago) that the professions:

> inherit, preserve and pass on a tradition ... [T]hey engender modes of life, habits of thought and standards of judgement which render them centres of resistance to crude forces which threaten steady and peaceful evolution ... The family, the church and the universities, certain associations of intellectuals, and above all the great professions, stand like rocks against which the waves raised by these forces beat in vain.[45]

It would, of course, be foolish to be too misty-eyed about a long-lost age of morally upstanding professional gentlemen who would never stoop so low as to engage in what was pejoratively described as 'trade'.[46] Flood, among others, has pointed out that, although numerous professionals saw (and continue to see) themselves as superior to mere 'businessmen', many were engaged in lucrative commercial work.[47] It was this work that laid the foundations of many of today's 'Magic Circle' City law firms and the 'Big Four' accountants. Nevertheless, it is true to say that the typical law firm in England was, until the 1970s, a relatively small enterprise and

Policy Studies Institute, London, January 1988) is said to be the first appearance of the term 'regulative bargain' albeit the concept predates this address. See also K M Macdonald, *The Sociology of the Professions* (Thousand Oaks, Sage Publications, 1995).

[43] See the Impact Project page on the IBA website: www.ibanet.org/Impact-Project.

[44] www.barcouncil.org.uk/about/about-the-bar.html. The Law Society, among many others, makes similar declarations, see www.lawsociety.org.uk/about-us/.

[45] A M Carr-Saunders and P A Wilson, *The Professions* (Oxford, Clarendon Press, 1933) 497. See also C T Bogus, 'The Death of an Honorable Profession' (1996) 71 *Indiana Law Journal* 911, 937–38 for a similar sentiment.

[46] As demonstrated in the exchange between Louis D'Ascoyne Mazzini and his mother in the classic Ealing comedy 'Kind Hearts and Coronets' in which the latter despairs of her son, the impoverished and outcast scion of a noble family, having to seek employment with the agonised cry 'A D'Ascoyne in trade!'.

[47] J A Flood, 'From Ethics to Regulation: The Re-Organization and Re-Professionalization of Large Law Firms in the 21st Century' (September 20, 2011). ssrn.com/abstract=1592324.

as such was subject to the authority of the Law Society and courts when it came to matters of 'correct behaviour'.

The change, as far as England is concerned, began with the passage of the Companies Act 1967, s 120 of which lifted the twenty-member 'cap' upon professional partnerships. Hitherto, firms that exceeded this limit were required to register as a company rather than operate a partnership.[48] The consequences of this change can be seen in the growth of one of the oldest City firms. In 1950, Slaughter & May was the largest solicitors' firm in the city with 14 partners.[49] By 1975, it had 36 partners, and, by the mid-1980s, there were 63 partners. The rise in the number of partners and assistant solicitors in Slaughter & May, its peers in the City and many other firms has continued ever since.

At the same time, there were changes in the way in which solicitors operated. In 1970, the UK's Monopolies and Mergers Commission (MMC) criticised the allegedly restrictive practices of various professions, which was followed by a similar report on the legal profession in 1976.[50] Further, although the 1979 Royal Commission on Legal Services (known as the *Benson Commission*)[51] did not itself produce any major reforms it is regarded as having laid the basis for the Courts and Legal Services Act 1990, which ended barristers' monopoly on advocacy in the higher courts.[52] In addition, the Law Society lifted its ban on advertising by solicitors in 1984 and the Administration of Justice Act 1985 terminated solicitors' traditional monopoly over conveyancing.[53]

The introduction of limited liability partnerships (LLPs) in the UK in the early 2000s was the next significant change.[54] The 'attacks' on the restrictive practices of the legal profession also continued in the form of the (then) Office of Fair Trading (OFT) report *Competition in the Professions* in 2001[55] and (most significantly) the so-called *Clementi Review* of 2004.[56] This recommended the creation of alternative business structures (ABS) that would permit both lawyers *and* non-lawyers to manage and own legal practises. The UK government responded with

[48] The full text of the 1967 Act is available at www.legislation.gov.uk/ukpga/1967/81/enacted.

[49] See M Galanter and S Roberts, 'From Kinship to Magic Circle: The London Commercial Law Firm in the Twentieth Century' (2008) 15 *International Journal of the Legal Profession* 143–178.

[50] Monopolies and Mergers Commission (1970), *A Report on the General Effect on the Public Interest of Certain Restrictive Practices so far as they prevail in relation to the Supply of Professional Services*, Cmnd 4463, HMSO and Monopolies and Mergers Commission (1976), *Services of Solicitors in England and Wales in Relation to Advertising*, HC 457, London, HMSO.

[51] *The Royal Commission on Legal Services: Final Report* (Cmnd. 7648) H.M. Stationery Office, 1979. See also R Luckham 'The Final Report of the Royal Commission on Legal Services: A Sociologist's View' (1980) 43 Michigan Law Review 543–548.

[52] The text of the 1990 Act is available at www.legislation.gov.uk/ukpga/1990/41.

[53] The text of the 1985 Act is available at www.legislation.gov.uk/ukpga/1985/61/contents.

[54] The text of the Limited Liability Partnerships Act 2000 is available at www.legislation.gov.uk/ukpga/2000/12/contents.

[55] The report is available on the OFT's archived website at webarchive.nationalarchives.gov.uk/ukgwa/20140402160349/http://www.oft.gov.uk/OFTwork/publications/publication-categories/reports/professional_bodies/.

[56] The text of the Review is available at www.avocatsparis.org/Presence_Internationale/droit_homme/PDF/Rapport_Clementi.pdf.

a series of White Papers, leading ultimately to the Legal Services Act 2007.[57] This legislation not only permitted the creation of ABSs but also led to significant changes in the regulation of the legal professions (addressed further in the next section).

So what does the legal services 'industry' of the UK (or, rather, England and Wales) look like in 2024? At the time of writing, there were 198,456 solicitors on the Roll, of whom 163,189 held a current practicing certificate.[58] There were 9,465 'recognised' legal practices, comprising 1,635 sole practitioners (17% of the total); 1,133 partnerships (12%); 5,185 incorporated companies (55%); and 1,478 LLPs (16%).[59] Thus, the majority of legal practices are now incorporated (or limited) companies rather than traditional partnerships or LLPs.[60] According to some commentators, the rise of 'corporate' legal practices in the UK is attributable to the tax advantages of operating as a limited company.[61] Incorporation also provides solicitors with the opportunity to operate as an ABS and, for those who have truly embraced 'trade', to seek a stock exchange listing.[62]

Such has been the rate of change in the profession that the largest UK-based law firm by number of lawyers is Dentons, with 11,000 legal staff based in over 160 offices in 80 countries.[63] Some commentators have argued that such large practices have grown beyond the supervisory reach of professional bodies such as the Law Society. In the words of Rogers, Smith and Chellew:

> They have become their own locations of professional regulation in which junior employees are most powerfully managed [...] by the partner, elite and demands of largely corporate clients, rather than traditional wider professional hierarchy or the community[64]

If so, this places a great deal more responsibility on these firms to set appropriate working practices. Although it is not suggested here that such practices may be deficient compared to those set down by the 'profession' in the past (indeed, the contrary may well be true), the very fact that they are set down by a multitude of individuals in a multitude of firms means that they are not uniform.

[57] The text of the 2007 Act is available at www.legislation.gov.uk/ukpga/2007/29/contents.

[58] There were also 17,782 practicing barristers in chambers and elsewhere.

[59] The SRA statistics are available at www.sra.org.uk/sra/research-publications/regulated-community-statistics/. There are also 34 'other' legal service providers. These statistics are updated every month.

[60] Interestingly, Slaughter and May remains a traditional partnership.

[61] J Ames 'Most Law Firms Are Now Limited Companies but Corporation Tax Change Could Reverse Trend' (27 June 2022) *The Times*.

[62] It is of note that many large, long-established City firms, including Clifford Chance and Allen & Overy, are LLPs whereas some of the large 'regional' firms, such as DWF (once known as Davies Wallace Foysters), have incorporated and subsequently sought a stock exchange listing to enable their expansion into a multinational practice. CMS Cameron McKenna Nabarro Olswang, on the other hand, operates as part of CMS Legal Services EEIG, a European economic interest grouping.

[63] It is also the sixth largest in terms of fee income, estimated to be US $2.9 billion in 2021.

[64] See J Rogers, D Kingsford Smith and J Chellew, 'The Large Professional Service Firm: A New Force in the Regulative Bargain' (2017) 40 *UNSW Law Journal* 218.

Similar problems are faced by in-house lawyers.[65] This, in itself, may present as many problems to the courts and insurers in assessing risk and liability as those presented by the opacity of the AI 'black box'.

This problem is exacerbated when one comes to consider an ABS or MDP. Who is in a position to assess the professional standards of a disparate group of professionals – lawyers, bankers and accountants – engaged on a 'project' for a client? Even the nominal 'head' of the firm or the project team may find it difficult to do so. Even if the team is restricted to 'lawyers', one is now confronted with Susskind's seven models of '[p]roduction and distribution of [legal] expertise', which he posited in *The Future of the Professions*, or his five models of legal work from *The End of Lawyers*. In his critique of Susskind's work, Greenleaf subsequently reduced these models to four categories – traditional experts; para-professionals; networked experts; and knowledge engineers.[66] The 'traditional expert' may have little grasp of what is entailed in 'knowledge engineering' and yet he may well have overall responsibility for this activity. As noted above, the temptation for regulators and the courts will be to impose some form of strict liability or presumption of negligence, which should be resisted.

Although Susskind and Greenleaf differ on who will control and benefit from such developments (the former is an optimist and the latter is not), they appear to agree that 'On both the optimistic and dystopian scenarios, the future will see a gradual decline in traditional professional work (and its job satisfactions), or control by professional bodies'. A decline in job satisfaction, exacerbated by the Covid-19 pandemic, and its consequences are already being seen. Further, an increase in 'working from home' (WFH) or hybrid working (a combination of WFH and time in the office) and resistance to returning to returning to the office has potentially adverse consequences in terms of staff competence and supervision.[67] The law firm Kennedys observed:

> Post-pandemic working has created the perfect storm for pure process error claims. Junior lawyers (particularly at smaller firms) are exposed to increasing workloads and pressure to meet financial targets, whilst receiving less supervision due to hybrid working patterns.[68]

Others have reported or expressed similar concerns, along with warnings over the mental health of 'isolated' staff and the vulnerability of their 'home/work' computers to cybercriminals.[69]

[65] See R Moorhead and S Vaughan, *Legal Risk: Definition, Management and Ethics* (March 31, 2015). ssrn.com/abstract=2594228 or http://dx.doi.org/10.2139/ssrn.2594228.

[66] G Greenleaf, 'Review Essay – Technology and the Professions: Utopian and Dystopian Futures' (2017) 40 *UNSW Law Journal* 302–321.

[67] See J Ames 'Law Firm Names and Shames Employees Who Always Work from Home' (12 January 2024) *The Times*.

[68] Kennedys LLP, *Professional Liability Report 2023: trends and future risks* (July 2023). kennedyslaw.com/en/thought-leadership/reports/2023/professional-liability-report-2023-trends-and-future-risks/.

[69] See Allianz Commercial, *Professional Indemnity Insurance Claims Insights 2023*, p 11, where it is stated 'For design professionals […] The sharing of knowledge relating to design, risks, solutions and new methods of working is vital. If agile working tends to reduce that interaction, we may see more professional indemnity claims'. See also *PWC Strategy & UK Legal Services Market Report 2022*

Allied to the risks of WFH or hybrid working is the challenge of the so-called 'Great Resignation' or 'Great Retirement'. It seems that the Covid-19 pandemic; the 'commoditization' of professionals' roles; decline in a sense of 'collegiality'; and focus on turnover and profit has resulted in more part-time working and early retirements. As DWF observed of insurers themselves 'Following the so-called "Great Resignation" many employers have struggled with labour supply and ensuring the right people are in the right place with the right skill set'.[70]

The departure of experienced professionals and the need for junior staff to take up their responsibilities, without supervision by their departed mentors, is a recipe for increased claims in both the short-term and until the 'skills deficit' is repaired, whenever and however that may be.[71] It is incumbent on both professionals and their insurers to anticipate and, if possible, avoid such claims by taking appropriate action. Given that the 'Great Resignation' appears to be driven by a shift in attitudes about 'work-life balance' and 'wellbeing', such action should focus on the interests, motivation and abilities of staff. Among the measures to be taken are the recruiting of competent individuals (especially from less flexible competitors); providing a collaborative and inclusive working environment in which staff feel valued; enhanced and appropriate training; disposing of unnecessary internal bureaucracy; succession planning; and the intelligent use of emerging technology. Ultimately, competent and happy professionals are less likely to make the mistakes that lead to expensive negligence claims.

IV. Private versus Public Regulation

The 'regulative bargain' referred to in the preceding section may be described as the state's award of self-regulation, monopolies (or partial monopolies) over their areas of practice and other rights to the professions in return for a commitment to serve the proverbial public good. Insofar as legal professionals are concerned, this amounts to preserving of the rule of law, assisting in the administration of justice and upholding individuals' legal rights.[72] As seen above, the Bar Council and the

(July 2022) www.pwc.co.uk/industries/legal-professional-business-support-services/strategy-and-uk-legal-services-market-report-2022.html in which it is noted that there had been a 'sharp increase' in 'stress-associated illnesses in the workplace' since 2019 to the extent that, by 2021, half of all workplace illnesses were mental health related. See also Clyde & Co LLP *London Market Professional Indemnity July 2022 Report* www.clydeco.com/en/reports/2022/07/london-market-professional-indemnity-report-ju-1.

[70] DWF LLP, *InsureInsight: Insurance Sector Trends 2023* (January 2023). dwfgroup.com/en/news-and-insights/reports-and-publications/insureinsight-2023-insurance-sector-trends.

[71] In December 2023, the Australian government sought to address this deficit by announcing the creation of a new class of financial advisers called 'qualified advisers'. These 'qualified advisers' will focus on providing advice on simple matters to ordinary consumers. See ministers.treasury.gov.au/ministers/stephen-jones-2022/media-releases/government-unveils-comprehensive-financial-advice.

[72] Some, rightly, question what this 'public service' actually is and point to the absence of detail on the same. See J Goldsmith, 'Put Lawyers at the Heart of the Rule of Law' (27 October 2023) *Law Society Gazette* www.lawgazette.co.uk/commentary-and-opinion/put-lawyers-at-the-heart-of-the-rule-of-law/5117715.article.

IBA (among others) believe in and support such 'public service'. In return, English solicitors and barristers enjoyed (and continue to enjoy, in part) monopolies over such practices as conveyancing and trial advocacy.

This 'regulative bargain' in the UK came under attack from the late 1960s onwards. The Banking Act 1979 ended the informal regime of financial regulation by 'the club' of City professionals and the Bank of England, with the latter's role put on a statutory footing.[73] This was followed by the Financial Services Act 1986 and the Banking Act 1987.[74] The Estate Agents Act 1979 introduced statutory duties covering competence, disclosure and the safekeeping of clients' funds, with their enforcement by the Director General of Fair Trading. The work of accountants, especially the conduct of audits, has long been subject to statutory controls[75] but the creation of the Financial Reporting Council (FRC) in 1990 was another step away from self-regulation.[76] Whilst the Solicitors Act 1974 maintained – for a time – the self-regulation of solicitors, the profession was forced to assuage adverse public opinion by setting up the independent Office for the Supervision of Solicitors in 1983.

In the late 1990s the balance between partial state and partial self-regulation began to shift decisively towards the former. The Financial Services and Markets Act 2000 (FSMA 2000) created a single statutory regulator, the Financial Services Authority (FSA), for all financial services business.[77] The FSA was subsequently replaced as sole regulator by the 'twin peaks' of the Financial Conduct Authority (FCA) and Prudential Regulation Authority (PRA). Further reforms have since taken place, the latest being under FSMA 2023,[78] but the principle and reality of state regulation of financial services remains uncontested.

For legal professionals, not only did the *Clementi Review* change the way in which solicitors' practices were organised, it also had a profound effect on regulation. Hitherto, the Law Society had been solely responsible for the supervision of solicitors, albeit this supervision was enshrined in series of Solicitors Acts, including the 1974 Act (which remains in force). Similarly, the Bar Council was the representative and regulatory body for the barristers' profession.[79] The 2007 Act replaced this essentially bipartite self-regulation of legal services by the Law Society and Bar Council by a convoluted multi-party regulatory structure, with the Legal Services Board (LSB) at its apex.[80] The LSB is what is known as an 'oversight

[73] The text of the 1979 Act is available at www.legislation.gov.uk/ukpga/1979/37/contents.

[74] The text of the 1986 Act is available at www.legislation.gov.uk/ukpga/1986/60/contents and the 1987 Act at www.legislation.gov.uk/ukpga/1987/22/contents. Both since repealed.

[75] Insofar as the form and content of company accounts are determined by the Companies Acts.

[76] The FRC website is available at www.frc.org.uk/.

[77] The text of the 2000 Act is available at www.legislation.gov.uk/ukpga/2000/8/contents. Prior to this legislation, the the UK had nine separate financial regulators (including self-regulatory bodies) covering distinct business activities.

[78] The text of the 2023 Act is available at www.legislation.gov.uk/ukpga/2023/29/contents/enacted.

[79] The 1990 Act formally designated the Bar Council as the professional body for the barristers' profession and restated its regulatory authority in this regard.

[80] The LSB website is available at legalservicesboard.org.uk/about-us.

regulator' and 'oversees' the ten 'approved regulators' under the 2007 Act and the Office for Legal Complaints (which is responsible for the administration of the Legal Ombudsman scheme).

The ten approved regulators are responsible for the day-to-day supervision of those businesses and individuals who are authorised to carry out 'reserved legal activities'.[81] The approved regulator for solicitors is the Solicitors Regulation Authority (SRA).[82] The Law Society itself continues to operate as the representative body for solicitors in England & Wales but it has lost its regulatory role. Similarly, the Bar Council has lost its regulatory powers over the barristers' profession, in its case to the Bar Standards Board (BSB).[83] Of the other eight regulators, Legal Executives, for example, are – for now – regulated by Chartered Institute of Legal Executives (CILEx) Regulator and Patent Attorneys by the Intellectual Property Regulation Board.[84]

The shift from private self-regulation to statutory-based public regulation of the professions in the UK and in other jurisdictions was driven, in part, by the alleged deficiencies of the former. These allegations were not altogether inaccurate or unjustified and, consequently, the shift was not surprising. Indeed, it was suggested by Smith, Paynter and Donley that some that public regulation 'may in fact prevent a profession from being impacted by an [adverse] issue or an event that would, otherwise have had a broad ranging impact' and therefore should be welcomed by insurers.[85] The difficulty comes when such regulation becomes too oppressive. Nor should the potential imposition of regulations and sanctions for 'political reasons' be neglected.[86]

For example, accountants and auditors are facing the possibility of greater scrutiny (and sanctions for misconduct) with the imminent replacement of the FRC by the Audit, Reporting and Governance Authority (AGRA) in 2024. The creation of AGRA was first mooted in 2019, following a review of the (then) regulatory regime for the FRC by Sir John Kingman, in light of sundry irregularities at Carillion, Patisserie Valerie and BHS. AGRA will have greater powers than the FRC to investigate breaches of corporate reporting and audit-related responsibilities.

[81] Section 12 of the 2007 Act defines 'reserved legal activity' as the exercise of a right of audience; the conduct of litigation; reserved instrument activities; probate activities; notarial activities; and the administration of oaths. By section 14 it is an offence to carry on a reserved legal activity if one is not entitled to do so.

[82] The SRA website is available at www.sra.org.uk/. The SRA may also take over regulation of legal executives from CILEx, see www.lawsociety.org.uk/contact-or-visit-us/press-office/press-releases/sra-regulation-of-cilex-could-risk-consumer-confusion.

[83] The BSB website is available at www.barstandardsboard.org.uk/.

[84] The future of CILex Regulator is uncertain, as there are ongoing discussions about the possibility of the SRA taking over the regulation of Legal Executives. See the SRA statement on CILEX (1 July 2024) available at https://www.sra.org.uk/sra/news/sra-statement-cilex/.

[85] See D Smith, K Paynter and S Donley 'Professional Indemnity Insurance' in A Tarr et al (ed) *The Global Insurance Market and Change Emerging Technologies, Risks and Legal Challenges* (Abingdon, Routledge, 2023).

[86] The recent 'debanking' scandal in the UK is an example of ostensibly politically neutral institutions, in this case banks rather than regulators, behaving in a 'partisan' manner.

As a consequence, it is possible that accountants and auditors may face more claims from disgruntled shareholders, participants in M&As and liquidators.

Similarly, construction professionals in the UK face increased regulatory controls. Following the horrific fire at Grenfell in 2017, the liability periods for claims under the Defective Premises Act 1972 was increased by the Building Safety Act 2022 from six years to 30 years for works completed prior to June 2022 and from and from six to 15 years prospectively.[87] Moreover, a new Building Safety Regulator will oversee the safety and standards of all buildings; act as the building control authority for 'higher-risk' buildings; and register higher-risk buildings and assess their safety during their occupation.[88] Similar measures have been considered and/or introduced in the EU, Australia and other jurisdictions.[89] These measures, and associated ones, may well lead to increased numbers of claims against the manufacturers and suppliers of construction materials; building contractors; sub-contractors and professionals such as architects, quantity surveyors and engineers.

Legal professionals will be affected by these changes too. Those advising on commercial and domestic conveyancing may be exposed to claims relating to infringements of the 2022 Act by their clients and those involved in M&As – and corporate work generally – may find themselves on the wrong end of complaints and claims by directors, shareholders and liquidators. They have also found themselves subject to increased scrutiny from their own regulators, especially in respect of their activities outside of the office or chambers. A number of UK solicitors and barristers have been suspended or struck off for 'offensive' tweets (NB which were unrelated to their work) over the past few years.[90]

Finally, it would be remiss to omit the FCA's Consumer Duty, which came into force in July 2023.[91] This duty applies to the 'regulated activities and ancillary activities of all firms authorised under [FSMA]' and associated legislation 'in respect of products and services for prospective and actual retail customers'. The duty is aimed at ensuring that such firms 'pro-actively act to deliver good outcomes for customers generally and put 'customers' interests at the heart of their activities'. To this end, financial services providers must– among other things – act in good faith; avoid causing any harm to their customers; and enable them to 'achieve their financial objectives'. The FCA's finalised guidance 'FG22/5 Final non-Handbook

[87] The text of the 2022 Act is available at www.legislation.gov.uk/ukpga/2022/30/contents.

[88] See the HSE details on the BSR available at www.hse.gov.uk/building-safety/regulator.htm.

[89] See the UK House of Commons European Scrutiny Committee report (28 June 2022) on the EU's new Construction Products Regulation, available at publications.parliament.uk/pa/cm5803/cmselect/cmeuleg/119-iv/report.html. See also Urban Lawyers, 'Limitation Period for Combustible Cladding Claims Extended to 15 Years' (March 27, 2022), which discusses sundry Australia legislative proposals on building safety reform, available at www.urbanlawyers.com.au/blog/2022/3/27/limitation-period-for-combustible-cladding-claims-extended-to-15-years.

[90] See www.lawgazette.co.uk/news/tweeting-solicitors-behaviour-went-well-beyond-bounds-of-acceptable-conduct/5117277.article.

[91] See the details of the Code on the FCA website, available at www.fca.org.uk/firms/consumer-duty.

Guidance for firms on the Consumer Duty elaborates on these requirements over 121 pages of detailed text.

It is incumbent upon professionals and their insurers to be familiar with the reams of – regularly updated and amended – rules, guides and codes that are churned out by regulators. 'Old-fashioned' methods such as regular staff newsletters, email alerts and continuous education programs can continue to contribute to this process. The frequency and volume of regulatory change necessitates going further, however, and integrating regulatory requirements into a firm's very culture is becoming increasing de rigeur. Many professional service providers use compliance software, which tracks and manages regulatory changes (in the sense of implementing them into day-to-day practice). That said, technology is not a panacea and a dedicated team of in-house staff may be needed to oversee the process. Inevitably, even with cost-saving technology, regulatory compliance will require a great deal more time and expense than it has in the past. The days of the sole compliance officer or 'SIF-reporting partner' are over.

V. The Demise of Deference

The end of various professions' privileges, including their monopolies and their self-regulation, can be seen as a sign of the decline of the traditional deference once afforded to them by the rest of society. It would be foolish to believe that all members of society were once willing to accept the status and performance of solicitors, accountants and others without question. The fact that the first UK professional indemnity (PI) policies were issued in the 1920s and the volume of cases relating to claims against professionals detailed in the very first volume of Jackson and Powell, published in 1982, both demonstrate that this was not the case. Nor should we neglect the volume of negative cultural depictions of or references to lawyers, all the way back to Shakespeare.[92]

That said there is a marked difference between the long-observed willingness of clients and third parties to criticize and bring claims against, say, solicitors for their inadequate performance of professional services and the modern phenomenon of the 'social inflation' of claims. This 'social inflation' has been described by the US National Association of Insurance Commissioners (NAIC) as follows:

> Social inflation is a term that describes how insurers' claims costs are increasing above general economic inflation. This is generally thought to be due to a trend in increasing litigation costs brought by plaintiffs seeking large monetary relief for their injuries. The 'social' aspect of the term represents shifting social and cultural attitudes about who is responsible for absorbing risk (the insurer or the plaintiff). The varying demographic

[92] Who is not familiar with 'The first thing we do, let's kill all the lawyers' from Shakespeare's *Henry VI*, Part 2, Act IV, Scene 2?

> makeup of jury pools, an increasing public distrust of large corporations, and the influences of social media and legal marketing can all influence jury verdicts and awards.[93]

The factors contributing to social inflation include:

- more class actions or group litigation;
- an increase in the sums awarded by the courts to successful plaintiffs (including so-called 'nuclear verdicts');
- third-party litigation funding;
- a rise in crime (especially fraud); and
- changing social attitudes resulting in an inclination to bring climate-related and socio-political-related claims.

Although NAIC's description of social inflation is clearly US-centric (NB the reference to 'jury pools' for civil cases), the UK and other jurisdictions have also suffered from many of its factors in recent years, with the exception of so-called 'nuclear verdicts'.[94] These are jury verdicts where damages of US$10 million or more are awarded to the plaintiff(s). In its 2022 report *Nuclear Verdicts: Trends, Causes, and Solutions*, the US Chamber of Commerce Institute for Legal Reform (ILR) revealed that both the number and (median) size of such verdicts had increased over the period 2010 to 2019, the latter by 27.5%, compared to a US rate of inflation of 17.2% over the same period.[95] Half of the verdicts were in the US$10–$20 million range although there were '101 'mega' nuclear verdicts that exceeded [US]$100 million'.

Whilst nuclear verdicts are limited to the US and whilst they have not (to date) been prevalent in professional negligence cases (except for clinical negligence), they may still have a significant negative impact on the professionals involved in them. There is the possibility of satellite litigation against, say, defendant legal advisers and other litigation-support professionals. Their size may also increase the cost and reduce the availability of insurance both specifically (ie, product liability cover) and generally. They also have the potential to encourage an aggressive attitude towards litigation by claimants and their legal advisers, who may seek ever greater financial rewards at trial, rather than mediating or making reasonable settlements.[96] According to a Swiss Re institute study, this aggressive

[93] See content.naic.org/cipr-topics/social-inflation.

[94] In terms of class actions or group litigation, the so-called 'Dieselgate' litigation, Mariana Dam claim and claims by over 200 rugby union players against their professional bodies are all making their way through the English courts.

[95] See US Chamber of Commerce Institute for Legal Reform, *Nuclear Verdicts: Trends, Causes, and Solutions* (September 2022). instituteforlegalreform.com/research/nuclear-verdicts-trends-causes-and-solutions/.

[96] See also C R Cole and C Marzen 'Nuclear Verdicts, Tort Liability, and Legislative Responses' (2023) *Journal of Insurance Regulation* 35.

tendency has also been exacerbated by the participation of third-party funders in litigation.[97]

A rise in crime, especially in the form of so-called cyber-attacks, is also a growing area of concern for professionals and their insurers. In June 2023, the UK National Cyber Security Centre (NCSC) published its 'Cyber Threat Report; UK Legal Sector', in which it was noted that:

> Nearly three-quarters of the UK's top-100 law firms have been affected by cyber attacks, and for smaller firms that have little or no dedicated cyber security and IT support, the risk of incidents like ransomware attacks is on the increase.[98]

Such attacks include phishing, the compromising of email systems, ransomware and malware (ie, computer viruses) and password attacks. They may result in regulatory action and litigation by clients and third parties. Not only are law firms the targets of such attacks but their IT service providers are also vulnerable, as was seen in the recent attack on CTS, which provides conveyancing support systems to many law firms in the UK.[99] Even if there has been no cyber-crime, defective IT systems (combined with allegedly improper human conduct) may cause problems for legal professionals. Software errors in the UK Post Office's computerised accounting system, known as Horizon, led to the wrongful prosecution of over 700 sub-postmasters for fraud, theft and false accounting between 2000 and 2014. The Criminal Cases Review Commission described the affair as 'the most widespread miscarriage of justice [it] has ever seen and represents the biggest single series of wrongful convictions in British legal history'.[100] The Post Office (Horizon System) Offences Act 2024 has now quashed the convictions of sub-postmasters and others.[101]

The ramifications of the scandal continue to unfold, including – at the time of writing – 'Phases' 5 and 6 of a statutory public inquiry.[102] Ultimately, the legal advisors for both the Post Office and some of the victims may find themselves subject to regulatory and legal action.[103] The same holds true of those lawyers involved in other high-profile matters.[104] Moreover, the demise of deference is not limited

[97] www.swissre.com/institute/research/topics-and-risk-dialogues/casualty-risk/us-litigation-funding-social-inflation.html.

[98] www.ncsc.gov.uk/files/Cyber-Threat-Report_UK-Legal-Sector.pdf.

[99] See www.lawgazette.co.uk/news-focus/news-focus-cyber-attack-hits-conveyancing-firms-what-lessons-need-to-be-learned/5118101.article.

[100] See 'The CCRC and Post Office/ Horizon cases' (3 January 2024) available at ccrc.gov.uk/news/the-ccrc-and-post-office-horizon-cases/.

[101] The text of the Bill is available at bills.parliament.uk/bills/3694.

[102] The Inquiry website is available at www.postofficehorizoninquiry.org.uk/.

[103] See www.lawgazette.co.uk/news/solicitor-for-victims-says-lawyers-should-be-targeted-in-post-office-fallout/5118334.article and www.lawgazette.co.uk/commentary-and-opinion/post-office-scandal-lawyers-in-the-frame/5118335.article.

[104] Richard Moorhead will be delivering this year's Hamlyn Lectures on the theme of 'Frail Professionalism: how ethical failure is polluting justice', which will cover the Post Office scandal and other ethical lapses. See richardmoorhead.substack.com/p/hamlyn-lectures-2024.

to clients and the wider public. In a recent report 'World in motion: Why the legal profession cannot stand still', it was revealed that almost two-thirds of junior lawyers who were surveyed, stated that their firms should allow them to refuse to work on particular matters for 'ethical reasons'.[105] So, as the once-uniform ethical standards set down by the professional bodies are supplanted or by-passed by the rise of 'mega firms' and state regulators, individual professionals are choosing their own ethical standards. The potential for claims triggered by 'whistleblowers' or by disgruntled clients is self-evident, as is the appropriate response. Once again, professionals and their insurers will need to enhance staff competence, regulatory compliance and effective practice management.

VI. Observations and Concluding Remarks

One of the primary themes of this book is how law and practice should be developed by the courts, public officials (ie, ministers, legislators and civil servants) and insurers to deal with emerging risks. Insofar as the courts are concerned, their development of the law is an incremental process and there may be little change in the short term. What the courts can do is ensure that litigation is managed effectively to ensure that 'social inflation' does not lead to an imbalance between the procedural position of claimants and defendants. Moreover, any consideration of the legal rights and liabilities of professionals should be carried out with caution.[106] In particular, a move towards strict liability when AI is used by professionals must be resisted for reasons which have already been discussed. Many professional negligence claims involve pure economic loss and, as Lord Sales put it recently:

> Economic loss consequent upon breach of legal obligations arises in many different ways, and it is legitimate for the law to seek to provide a focus for liability upon those forms of injury which implicate human interests which have choate and obvious forms, particularly bodily integrity and property (a type of economic interest, but in a crystallised form recognised in a variety of positive ways by the law), limiting liability for pure economic loss (such as loss of earnings or profits) to that particularly associated with damage to those interests. Special reasons, which include reasons of the kind I have been discussing, are required to overcome this general attitude.[107]

[105] See M Fouzder 'PEP Stands for "Profit per Equity Partner" but Should Be Recast as "People, Environment and Purpose"' (16 November 2023) *Law Society Gazette*. www.lawgazette.co.uk/news/junior-lawyers-want-right-to-refuse-work-for-ethical-reasons-report/5117913.article.

[106] An example of such caution can be seen in the UK Supreme Court's decision that an AI system cannot be 'an inventor' for the purposes of granting patents. See *Thaler v Comptroller-General of Patents, Designs and Trade Marks* [2023] UKSC 49.

[107] P Sales Pure economic loss in the law of tort: the history and theory of assumption of responsibility (The Annual Tort Law Research Group Lecture, Western University, Ontario, 26 September 2022) available at www.supremecourt.uk/docs/pure-economic-loss-in-the-law-of-tort-lord-sales.pdf.

The response of public officials to these emerging risks appears to be a combination of torpor and hyper-activity. Even if one has reservations about the measures it has taken, the EU is to be commended for the alacrity with which it has sought to tackle the issue of AI liability. By contrast, the previous UK government's pronouncement on the issue (in February 2024) was:

> In the coming months, we will formally establish our activities to support regulator capabilities and coordination, including a new steering committee with government and regulator representatives to support coordination across the AI governance landscape.[108]

The new UK government's response has been little better, given that its King's Speech in July 2024 contained only the following words on the issue:

> My Government [...] will seek to establish the appropriate legislation to place requirements on those working to develop the most powerful artificial intelligence models.

Sadly, one response to the apparent increased risk of claims has been the departure of insurers and intermediaries from the PI market. In August 2019, Aon notified its UK solicitor clients that it was withdrawing from the PI market and would no longer offer cover under its Maven MGA scheme ... just a month before the September deadline for the renewal of policies.[109] In 2022, AIG withdrew from the Australian PI market.[110] Such conduct maybe understandable, given the difficulties caused by Covid 19 and the resultant economic downturn, but it is not conducive to the growth of the insurance industry.

Instead of withdrawing from markets, insurers might consider tailoring their approach to reduce their exposure to professional liability potential risks. This would include an increased use of technology, in both underwriting and claims, to identify potential risk areas (such as fraud) and reducing costs of litigation. Of course, many insurers are already following this approach, but there is scope for improvement. In addition, this tailoring process may include the development of policies which cover and distinguish between the 'product liability' and human liability elements of the use of technology, especially AI, by professionals. The wording of such cover will be dependent upon the approach to liability for AI adopted by the jurisdiction in which their policyholders operate.[111]

[108] Lord Holmes of Richmond has introduced the Artificial Intelligence (Regulation) Bill to the House of Lords. Given the UK government's stance, it is unlikely to reach the statute books. The current status and text of the Bill are available at bills.parliament.uk/bills/3519.

[109] M Cross 'Solicitors' Fury as Insurer Abruptly Quits PII Market' (22 August 2019) *Law Society Gazette*. www.lawgazette.co.uk/practice/solicitors-fury-as-insurer-abruptly-quits-pii-market/5101206.article.

[110] C Dastoor 'At Capacity: Another Major Insurer Exit Further Shrinks PI Market' (11 April 2022) *Professional Planner*. www.professionalplanner.com.au/2022/04/at-capacity-another-major-insurer-exit-further-shrinks-pi-market.

[111] There is, as one would expect, cover available to the providers of technological services such as Lloyd's longstanding Technology E&O Policy (see www.lloyds.com/news-and-insights/news/lloyds-launches-new-eo-facility-for-tech-sector) and products from Munich Re and AIG, but the market is far from fully developed.

Insurers may also have to adopt a more proactive approach towards their policyholders in terms of the maintenance of professional standards. It has been observed by many commentators that insurance provides a form of 'private' professional regulation.[112] To this end, insurers may need to increase the extent to which they engage with their policyholders, professional bodies, regulators and policy makers who establish the parameters of regulation. This may, at the very least, enable a basic level of professional conduct to be maintained within and across jurisdictions rather than an atomised approach in which multinational professional service firms set their own standards and an overly regimented approach which could result from increased state regulation.

Some commentators have also addressed the use of alternative forms of risk transfer for professionals such as mutuals and captives.[113] In so far as the UK is concerned, some readers may recall the sad history and demise of Solicitors Indemnity Fund (SIF) and conclude that a 'mutual' approach is unlikely to be adopted by UK solicitors in the immediate future. As for captives, whilst this may be a solution for multinational professional practices, it is not an option that could be chosen by, say, 'high street' firms. Similarly, some form of public-private insurance scheme (to spread the risk for insureds and insurers) seems unlikely, if only because similar proposals for pandemic risk insurance have come to naught.[114] There will be little appetite among politicians and the public for providing any public money to schemes designed to assist lawyers or accountants (among others).

If this chapter and conclusion seem conservative and cautious, it is with good reason. Thomson Reuters may well be right when they predict that 'within five years, all professionals will have a GenAI assistant, functioning as a team member' but that does not mean that *human* professional standards developed over centuries of cases law and legislation should be causally disregarded.[115] Nor should the perceived commercialisation of the professions necessitate the sacrifice of those standards. There is a place for both profit and professionalism. The decline in the influence of SROs such as the Law Society may require insures to be more proactive in ensuring professional standards but that does not mean that those standards should be diluted. Nor should those standards be raised beyond reasonable levels in the face of social inflation or political pressure. It will be the task of the professions and their insurers to ensure that the perfect does not become the enemy of the good and use a combination of traditional wisdom and emerging technology to do so.

[112] J Morgan and P Hanrahan, 'Professional Indemnity Insurance: Compensating Consumers and Regulating Professionals' (2017) 40 *UNSW Law Journal* 353.

[113] D. Smith, K Paynter and S Donley, 'Professional Indemnity Insurance' in A Tarr at al (eds) *The Global Insurance Market and Change Emerging Technologies, Risks and Legal Challenges* (Abingdon, Routledge, 2023).

[114] See G Meggitt 'Pandemics and Insurance' in T A Tarr, J Tarr, M Thompson and D Wilkinson (eds) *The Global Insurance Market and Change* (Oxford, Informa Law, 2023).

[115] Thomson Reuters 'Future of Professionals Report 2024', available at https://www.thomsonreuters.com/en/c/future-of-professionals.html.

12

Improving Insurability of Emerging Risks: The Example of Nanotechnology

CHRISTIAN ARMBRÜSTER

I. Introduction

In the following, the role of insurance for the use of nanotechnology will be shown and discussed. Thus nanotechnology serves as an example to explore the general options to enable and improve the insurability of emerging risks. While the analysis is made from a German perspective, many of the results should be valid for other legal systems as well, as the questions and legal challenges are often similar if not identical.

First of all, the analysis requires to explore the various liability risks arising from the use of nanotechnology. Once these have been analysed – based on the example of German tort law – the contractual instruments that can be used in order to improve the insurability of those risks shall be explored.

The use of nanotechnology affects various branches of liability insurance as well as other insurance lines. Moreover, it is a so-called mass risk that does not only cover specific areas. Nanotechnology is therefore particularly suitable for a study on the insurability of emerging risks. In general, the insurance of emerging risks is subject to three phases, which are a study phase, a fear phase and a maturity phase. In the case of nanotechnology, the industry is still in the study phase in which cover is granted. However, this may change quickly.

The question of the extent to which emerging risks can be covered by insurance leads to the various instruments which shape the insurability of risks. These include the definition of the insured event, time limitations, risk-related obligations, condition adjustment clauses and risk selection. They are examined in the contribution with regard to their suitability for covering emerging risks. The article then looks at the options for improving insurability in other ways, such as reinsurance, risk pooling, Alternative Risk Transfer (ART), statutory liability limits and compulsory insurance.

II. Foundations

Nanotechnology has been defined on the EU level in the Novel Food regulation (EU) 2015/2283 of 25 November 2015.[1] According to Art 3 (2) f) of this regulation

> 'engineered nanomaterial' means any intentionally produced material that has one or more dimensions of the order of 100 nm or less or that is composed of discrete functional parts, either internally or at the surface, many of which have one or more dimensions of the order of 100 nm or less, including structures, agglomerates or aggregates, which may have a size above the order of 100 nm but retain properties that are characteristic of the nanoscale. Properties that are characteristic of the nanoscale include: (i) those related to the large specific surface area of the materials considered; and/or (ii) specific physico-chemical properties that are different from those of the non-nanoform of the same material.

However, the scope of application of this definition is quite limited, and there are various differing proposals for defining nanotechnology.[2]

The risks of nanotechnology are as diverse as the areas of application of this technology.[3] Accordingly, very different branches of liability insurance are affected: It is the whole range of product liability insurance, business liability insurance, employer's liability insurance, professional liability insurance and environmental liability insurance. In addition, there are effects on insurance branches beyond the coverage of liability risks, such as health and life insurance, property insurance or business interruption insurance. This also shows that the insurance sector is affected by nanotechnology on a much broader scale compared to other emerging risks, such as biotechnology or genetic engineering. In addition, it is a mass risk that does not just cover certain areas (as is the case with, eg, asbestos or pharmaceutical risks) or a time-limited event, such as the millennium risk.

The liability risks of nanotechnology have so far been difficult to grasp. This makes the topic a controversial one not only for those who are potentially liable, but also for the insurance industry: There are no specific exclusions for these risks in the standard insurance terms and conditions. This is a consequence of the fact that in the German market the standard terms and conditions of general liability insurance generally offer so-called all-risks cover, as opposed to the concept of named perils.

This comprehensive scope of protection is related to the fact that in Germany – in contrast to the practice in the Anglo-American market – insurance practice regularly aims for long-term customer loyalty: The contract does not automatically expire at the end of the initially agreed term (so-called expiry policy) but is

[1] Consolidated version: data.europa.eu/eli/reg/2015/2283/2021-03-27.

[2] See en.wikipedia.org/wiki/Nanotechnology.

[3] For an overview, see ec.europa.eu/health/scientific_committees/opinions_layman/en/nanotechnologies/l-2/6-health-effects-nanoparticles.htm.

automatically renewed in the absence of timely cancellation (so-called renewal model). In addition, industrial insurance often is based on longer fixed terms. From the perspective of the insurer this approach offers some advantages (continuity of portfolio and premium income; reduced effort for acquisition and administration), but it also makes it more difficult to agree exclusions and, moreover, for the insurer to react quickly to a changed risk situation.

It is sometimes concluded from the fact that this is a new risk that it is a case of so-called precautionary insurance policy (in German: *Vorsorgeversicherung*). This type of insurance offers additional cover for new risks that arise due to a change in the policyholder's activities. Examples include the letting of a property previously used by the policyholder or the expansion of business operations abroad. It is doubtful whether the beginning of the use of nanotechnology in the activities covered by the insurance constitutes a new risk comparable to these cases. It can be argued that the policyholder is in principle free to use the latest technologies permitted under public law when carrying out the insured activities. The insurance does not cover the liability risk arising from the use of certain technologies, but covers more comprehensively, for example in product liability insurance, the liability risks arising from the manufacture of products. The use of nanotechnology is therefore already included in the basic cover of the liability insurance and is not only included through a precautionary insurance policy.

As mentioned above, insurance cover currently also exists for losses that can be attributed to the use of nanotechnology. However, this may change in the future. The example of terrorism risks shows how quickly an exclusion can be introduced when a risk situation has changed: Before 11 September 2001, while war risks were excluded in many classes of insurance, this was usually not the case for terrorism. Subsequently, for example, policies for aircraft were only prolonged if the policyholder accepted the exclusion of terrorism risks, so that initially only a government guarantee issued by the German federal government made it possible to continue flight operations. Similarly, the exclusion of asbestos risks, which is now a standard exclusion, was introduced when the carcinogenic effects of asbestos became known.

It is widely assumed that nanotechnology is not an evolutionary but a revolutionary development in terms of risk, which means that it is a risk whose potential damage cannot be estimated yet. At the same time, it is not a so-called phantom risk, where the cause of the damage cannot be ruled out, but it is a risk with causally verifiable consequences. This causal link is based on the fact that many artificially produced nanoparticles can be traced back to their manufacturer, unlike, for example, particles from diesel exhaust gases, which are ubiquitous in the air.

For the insurance of such risks three phases are predicted: a study phase, a fear phase and a maturity phase. We are currently still in the study phase, in which cover – as mentioned – is granted by insurers. Then comes the fear phase, in which insurers and reinsurers introduce cover restrictions. Finally, a mature phase is to be expected, in which needs-orientated insurance offers will be made at affordable premiums.

A major unknown in this forecast, apart from the actual uncertainties of liability risks, is the future activity of the legislator. For example, statutory regulation of nanotechnology could be considered in chemicals, pharmaceuticals and occupational health and safety legislation. If a specific strict liability regime were to be introduced for the risks of nanotechnology, then insurance models would be available, as they are in the area of product liability or pharmaceutical liability. In the area of traditional fault-based liability, it is more likely that standard policies with certain extensions of cover will be offered.

The question of the extent to which the liability risks of nanotechnology can be covered by insurance leads to the basic rules that apply to the insurability of risks. They will be outlined below before the consequences for nanotechnology as an emerging risk are discussed. Then the possibilities for improving insurability will be explored.

III. Some Exemplary Loss Scenarios

Nanotechnology is used in a wide variety of industries, such as pharmaceuticals, energy, IT, automotive and textiles, and the technology has considerable economic potential. The following three scenarios illustrate how consumers come into contact with nanotechnology on a daily basis, what risks are involved and what damage could potentially occur.

A. Sunscreen

Sunscreen provides protection against UV rays with the help not only of chemical products but also of mineral substances such as nano-titanium oxide or nano-zinc oxide. This makes the sunscreen appear transparent on the skin. Although no abnormalities have been observed on the market in the past, both the effects on the condition of the skin and the question of whether nanoparticles can penetrate the organism through cracks are unclear. If it can be proven that the nanoparticles have caused damage to the consumer's health, the manufacturer of the sunscreen in question will be liable under certain circumstances.

B. Laser Printers

Nanoparticles from the toners of copiers and printers can cause inflammation of the nose and cell-damaging oxidative stress due to an excess of free radicals in the body. Nanoparticles are able to overcome all the human body's protective mechanisms, and they may thus cause considerable damage to health. For example, the particles can penetrate the respiratory tract into the alveolar region (pulmonary alveoli) and thus cause an inflammatory process in the entire lung. Due to their reactive surface, nanoparticles have a toxic and carcinogenic effect.

From the manufacturer's point of view, there is a risk of liability for damage caused to the health of the user. Such damage may be particularly heavy in cases of intensive exposure, be it at work or at home. Of course, the topic of laser printers also provides an example of how difficult it can be to identify nano-specific risks. According to current sources, this is a hazard which is not decisively based on the nano-size of the particles.

C. Textiles

In the textile sector, nanomaterials are used, for example, to produce functional clothing that is water and dirt repellent, antibacterial or has UV protection. Thanks to their germicidal effect, nanoparticles prevent the development of body odours. Silver particles at nano level, for example, are used for this purpose.

In this respect, there are fears that the bacteria could become resistant to silver and thus have a negative effect on the skin flora. In any case, it should be noted that the use of nanomaterials harbours a considerable liability risk, especially in the textile industry, as textiles are mass-produced goods that are used by everyone every day.

IV. Liability

A. Overview

The main liability risk of nanoproducts lies in the area of product and environmental liability.[4] The basic problem here is the lack of knowledge about the actual effects of nanotechnology on humans and the environment. Product-related liability standards[5] must be taken into account.

In addition, production plant-related regulations such as tortious environmental liability[6] and plant-specific public protection laws[7] also play an important role.

[4] For comprehensive sources on liability in German see Armbrüster, *Nanotechnologie – Rechtliche Aspekte zur Versicherbarkeit von Produkten am Anfang neuer wissenschaftlicher Erkenntnisse*, ZVersWiss (Zeitschrift für die gesamte Versicherungswissenschaft) (2013) 102:183, 188–191.

[5] Namely Section 823 (1) of the German Civil Code (BGB), the German Product Liability Act (ProdHaftG), the German Medicinal Products Act (ArzneimittelG) and, as statutory law, the German Foodstuffs, Commodities and Animal Feed Act (LFBG) via Section 823 (2) BGB.

[6] Section 823 (1) BGB and the Environmental Protection Act (UmweltHG).

[7] Such as Section 14 BImSchG, via Section 823 (2) BGB.

The question of whether the respective liability statute provides for an exclusion of liability for such risks that are not recognisable according to the state of the art in science and technology (so-called development risks) is of particular importance.

B. Product-Related Liability Regulations

Part of the risks of nanotechnology lies in the realisation of a danger when nanoproducts are used by end users.

i. Development Risks

In principle, every manufacturer of a product – including nanoproducts – is liable for damage caused to a third party by its products in breach of duty.[8] However, such responsibility is also ruled out in the area of product liability[9] if the damage is caused by product defects that were unavoidable at the time the product is placed on the market (so-called development risks). Avoidability is measured by what is objectively not recognisable according to the state of the art in science and technology. In such a case, the manufacturer's liability fails due to the objective breach of duty of his actions, as the manufacturer is not obliged to prevent damage that cannot be recognised ex ante.

ii. Proactive Product Monitoring Obligation

Irrespective of the exemption from liability for development errors, the manufacturer has a duty to monitor the product as soon as it has been placed on the market. If he becomes aware of any damage caused by the product, the manufacturer must take all necessary and reasonable hazard prevention measures at that time. Such measures may include subsequent warnings or instructions, and in some cases even a recall of the product.[10]

The higher the danger caused by the defect, the more likely it is that such a recall obligation exists. For example, if the product poses a risk to the life and limb of its user, the manufacturer is obliged to carry out a recall and replacement campaign in order to prevent further cases of damage with potentially dangerous consequences. Particular caution is required in the field of nanotechnology, as a health hazard must also be assumed due to pending research results.

[8] Section 823 (1) BGB and Section 1 (1) ProdHaftG, with exceptions in (2) and (3).

[9] Section 1 Para 2 No 5 *ProdHaftG*.

[10] See eg, German Federal Court (*Bundesgerichtshof, BGH*), judgment of 16 December 2008 – VI ZR 170/07, *Neue Juristische Wochenschrift (NJW)* (2009) p 1080 margin no 19.

iii. State of the Art in the Industry

The state-of-the-art of production in the relevant industry at the time of placing on the market is decisive both for the assumption of a development defect and for the scope of the product monitoring obligation. In order to determine this, reference is either made to private and public law standardisations or, in the case of technical advances, even stricter standards may apply.

In the case of nanoproducts, such standardisation is sometimes lacking. In this respect, the manufacturer is all the more obliged to identify the current state of the art and to meet this standard. Manufacturers of nanoproducts shall take a particularly responsible and precautionary approach to their risk research in accordance with the Code of Conduct for Responsible Nanoscience and Nanotechnology Research proposed by the EU Commission.

iv. Distribution of the Burden of Proof

According to a general rule of German civil procedure, it is for the party asserting a claim to present all facts favourable to it. In the field of nanotechnology, this is particularly difficult, if not impossible, due to the fact that research is still not very advanced and the causal links are therefore unclear. This can be remedied by reversing the burden of proof. However, such a reversal is only justified if a defect can no longer be clearly established after the product has been placed on the market. If the injured party has to prove facts that only the product manufacturer can know, the requirements for the presentation are admittedly low; it is sufficient to show an indication from which a product defect can arise.[11]

C. Production Plant-Related Liability Regulations

Another risk connected with the use of nanotechnology lies in the realisation of a danger already at the stage of production and not just later on when the product is used. One example of this is the tortious environmental liability[12] mentioned above (see sub III A). Nevertheless, similar problems arise here – for example with regard to causation – as with product-related liability (see sub B). The fault requirement[13] – similar to the exclusion for development risks – also results in an exemption from liability, at least for any damage that was completely unforeseeable.

In any case, the injured party will have difficulty proving the relevant facts. A reversal of the burden of proof is subject to similarly strict standards as in the

[11] See eg, German Federal Court (*Bundesgerichtshof, BGH*), judgment of 8 December 1992 – VI ZR 24/92, *Neue Juristische Wochenschrift (NJW)* (1993) p 528.

[12] Section 823 (1) BGB and the UmweltHG.

[13] Section 823 para 1 BGB.

case of product-related liability; it can therefore only be considered in exceptional cases. Problems of fault, burden of proof and causality do not arise, however, if the basis of liability[14] is linked solely to the operational risk.

D. Conclusions

As far as liability for breach of contract is concerned, suppliers of goods and services have nothing to fear as long as there is no evidence that the nanotechnology used is dangerous. The situation thus differs from that in the case of a concrete suspicion of danger. In this respect, a parallel can be drawn to the case law according to which the abstract possibility of damage caused by a radiation from telecommunication masts does not constitute a defect of a nearby rental home.

It is an interesting question whether the case law on a doctor's obligation to inform patients about new (robot-supported) surgery methods that unknown risks cannot currently be ruled out can also be applied. On the one hand, it can be argued that this case law relates to a specific area in which there is a generally increased duty to provide information due to the patient's right to self-determination. In this particularly sensitive area, it may therefore also be necessary to provide information about the possible risks associated with the use of nanotechnology. On the other hand, there is a considerable difference between both situations, as the nanotechnology-related risks are still so unspecific that they are not comparable with the use of a robot in surgical interventions.

The obligations to be complied with are often based on statutory or recognised private standards and norms.[15] If these do not restrict the use of nanotechnology – unlike what is now the case, such as with regard to the use of asbestos – there is no breach of duty in this respect either. The same applies in the area of tort liability. As already explained, the manufacturer of a product is not liable for compensation if the defect could not have been recognised according to the state of the art in science and technology.[16] Liability for so-called development risks is therefore excluded.

V. Insurance Cover

A. Insurability of Risks

Whether a risk is insurable depends partly on legal requirements, but mainly on the agreement between the risk carrier and the insurer on the conditions of a transfer

[14] eg, Section 1 UmweltHG.

[15] eg the standards and norms created by the institutions DIN (*Deutsches Institut für Normung*), or ISO (International Organization for Standardization).

[16] Section 1 (2) No. 5 *ProdHG*.

of risk, and thus on the decisions of the parties involved. Accordingly, a distinction can be made between legal/regulatory, actuarial and economic requirements.[17]

i. Legal and Regulatory Criteria of Insurability

In Germany, in principle any financial, any economic interest, is legally insurable.[18] The limits to this freedom are marked by the general rules on unlawfulness and ordre public.[19] However, these statutory limits only apply to a few cases. For example, insurance against criminal fines or penalties is to be regarded as incompatible with the German ordre public; the corresponding risk is therefore not insurable.

In addition, the cover should also be compatible with regulatory objectives. This is not a restriction of insurability in the sense of a legal limitation, but rather a guideline that insurers regularly follow even beyond binding requirements. Thus, from a regulatory point of view, the insurability of entrepreneurial risk is viewed critically when an insurance cover amounts to a kind of profit guarantee through insurance cover. The risk of entrepreneurial success should not be assumed by an insurer with the consequence that the entrepreneur would be deprived of the incentive to perform.

However, this is only the legal and regulatory side of insurability. Insofar as the question of the insurability of a risk is discussed in literature, this is usually done under other, namely actuarial and economic, aspects.[20] In contrast to the legal and regulatory limits, the limits of insurability created in this way are closely related to each other.

ii. Actuarial Criteria of Insurability

The actuarial criteria for insurability are highly differentiated. These include, first and foremost, the measurability of the risk: In order to be insurable, its probability of occurrence must be known; this must not be 100 per cent – apart from life assurance, which is not in the focus here – and the distribution among the risk carriers (policyholders) must be random. In addition, the insured risks must not be too closely linked to one another; rather, the loss events should be independent of one another or at least only dependent on one another to a limited extent. The maximum loss, that is, the total loss potential of an individual insured event, must be manageable for the insurer.

[17] For comprehensive sources on insurability in German see Armbrüster, *Nanotechnologie – Rechtliche Aspekte zur Versicherbarkeit von Produkten am Anfang neuer wissenschaftlicher Erkenntnisse*, ZVersWiss (Zeitschrift für die gesamte Versicherungswissenschaft) (2013) 102:183, 192–204.

[18] See Armbrüster, *Privatversicherungsrecht*, 2nd ed (2019) margin nos 460 ff.

[19] Sections 134, 138 *BGB*.

[20] See eg, Eszler, Versicherbarkeit und ihre Grenzen (1999) p. 14 f.; Farny, in Hamburger Gesellschaft zur Förderung der Versicherungswissenschaft (ed), *Der Umgang mit den Risiken im Grenzbereich der Versicherbarkeit* (2002) p 2.

In addition, the rule of large numbers (*Gesetz der großen Zahl*) must apply to the loss. This is the case if the average loss is moderate and the loss frequency is high. That rule assists in making the future claims development more continuous and predictable. Motor vehicle accidents are one example while nuclear accidents are a counter-example.

Finally, the so-called moral hazard and negative selection must not be excessive. The term moral hazard describes the fact that the insured person behaves differently (more dangerously) due to the cover than would be the case without the cover, whether negligently or intentionally.[21] Negative selection occurs when high-risk carriers take insurance much more frequently than low-risk carriers.

iii. Economic Criteria of Insurability

In practice, certain risks are not insurable because no insurer is prepared to offer corresponding cover on the market. Such a refusal can have various motives. For example, in order to meet the actuarial requirements of a risk-adequate calculation of the premium the insurer may have come to the conclusion that it would have to accept a premium that is considered prohibitively high by the policyholders.

This is particularly the case if there is a high accumulation risk – the threat of an accumulation of losses (eg, in the event of business interruption) – or statistical uncertainties regarding the maximum loss as well as the probability that the insured event occurs so that the insurer calculates high risk surcharges. This is to be distinguished from the situation where the insured events are expected to occur but rarely. In this case, a prohibitively high premium is more likely to be due to the fact that the risk is unusual and might lead to exorbitantly high losses if it occurs, and therefore it is difficult to calculate.

It can also happen that the insurer calculates an affordable premium, but only under the condition of unacceptable coverage limits such as deductibles, maximum limits, or the like (see below sub iv for these instruments for limiting the assumed risk).

In both cases – prohibitively high premiums and unacceptable coverage limits – it is advantageous for the insurer not to enter the market with an offer of coverage. This is not only because demand will presumably be low, but also with regard to the negative impact of such an offer on the insurer's image.

Another market-related limit to insurability is the capacity of the insurance industry. This includes, in particular, the capacity of reinsurance cover available on the market, as the capacity of the primary insurer will often also depend on this. Recently, various instruments have been developed to create additional capacity by transferring risks to the capital market (Alternative Risk Transfer; see below sub D iii).

[21] See eg, Langheid, *Münchener Kommentar zum VVG*, (3rd ed, 2022), Section 19 margin no 81.

B. Conclusions Regarding the Insurability of Liability Risks from Nanotechnology

i. Legal and Regulatory Insurability

The interest in not suffering a financial loss as a result of the use of nanotechnology is legally insurable without any ado. In terms of public policy, the availability of such insurance cover is even to be considered desirable, as it facilitates the development and use of nanotechnology, which in turn is desirable from a sociopolitical point of view due to the many benefits associated with it. At the same time, nanotechnology has not yet encountered any ethical or moral reservations, as is the case with genetic engineering.

ii. Actuarial and Economic Insurability

a. Risks from Nanotechnology as Emerging Risks

In contrast, the actuarial and economic aspects of insurability are more problematic. The risks from nanotechnology are the prime example of so-called emerging risks. This term is used to describe new risks that are only just coming into focus and are not yet known in detail. These include, for example, electromagnetic fields, plasticisers, genetically modified food and functional food.

So far, there are no reliable findings on the risks of nanotechnology. Criteria for the assessment of the risks are offered in a report by the German Federal Institute for Risk Assessment.[22] In 2021 the European Food Safety Authority (EFSA) has published a revised document 'Guidance on risk assessment of nanomaterials to be applied in the food and feed chain: human and animal health'.[23] However, even these documents are only offering quite general risk assessments, so that the identification of hazard groups remains largely unspecified. This is not least due to the fact that long-term studies are still pending. In addition, it is hardly possible to draw conclusions from known risks to nanotechnology risks.

b. Conclusions for Actuarial and Economic Insurability

According to the criteria for insurability mentioned above, apart from the moral risk, which does not play a role here, insurability is problematic from an actuarial point of view. This is because it is a calculation with too many unknown factors. The insurer will normally limit the obligations it has to assume in such a way that it

[22] Bundesinstitut für Risikobewertung (ed), *Gesundheitliche Bewertung von Nanomaterialien* (health assessment of nano materials). www.bfr.bund.de/de/gesundheitliche_bewertung_von_nanomaterialien-30413.html.

[23] efsa.onlinelibrary.wiley.com/doi/full/10.2903/j.efsa.2021.6768.

can at least estimate the worst-case scenario, that is, the maximum exposure it will have to bear. This is precisely what is difficult to assess in the present situation.[24] This is not even about nanotechnology as a whole, but about specific individual areas such as certain product groups or materials.

On the other hand, it is precisely the task of the insurance industry to relieve risk carriers of uncertainties and thus enable activities and in particular innovations which may entail risks. Thus insurance offers a relevant contribution to economic growth and social welfare.

This has two implications for insurability: At the present time, as the risk potential has not been determined, from the perspective of the insurance industry there is no urgent need for action with regard to risk limitation.[25] Of course, insurers could introduce an exclusion of liability for nanotechnology risks purely as a precaution. However, this would be somewhat defensive, would not be customer-friendly and could also inhibit innovation, with negative consequences for the insurance sector as well as for society as a whole.

If specific liability risks from nanotechnology will become apparent in the future and more practical experience will be collected, a reaction from the insurance industry may be necessary in view of the actuarial requirements mentioned, which are by no means static. This explains why insurance companies, especially reinsurers, are committed to the early detection of nanotechnology risks in accordance with the principle of precaution. In this way, insurers act as 'society's early warning system'; they thus join public institutions such as the EU Commission, the German Nano-Commission set up by the Federal government in 2006, the Federal Institute for Risk Assessment based in Berlin and the Office for Technology Assessment at the German parliament (*Bundestag*). What instruments are available to the insurer to respond to an identified risk potential and how practical they are will be examined below.

C. Improving Actuarial Insurability

i. Definition of the Insured Event

a. Claims Made Principle

Traditionally, the definition of the insured event (the so-called trigger) is based on the damage, be it the causal event leading to it or the damage event itself. For the insurer, this means that it is still confronted with claims for compensation of damages that were not yet known during the contract term even after this term

[24] From the industry see eg, the statement of Sadler product liability insurance: www.products-liability-insurance.com/insuring-nanotechnology/. https://www.researchgate.net/publication/236103174_The_insurability_of_nanomaterial_production_risk.

[25] cf, also Mullins, Murphy et al, 'The Insurability of Nanomaterial Production Risk' (2013) 8 *Nature* 222–224. www.nature.com/articles/nnano.2013.53.

has ended. The situation is different if the claims made principle is agreed upon. Accordingly, the insured event occurs when a claim for damages is submitted by a third party against the policyholder for the first time during the term of the contract or within an agreed extension of the coverage period. Any such claim must be reported to the insurer in a timely manner.[26]

This definition of the insured event is used in Germany in particular in manager liability insurance (D&O insurance). However, it also occurs in certain other areas such as liability insurance for pharmaceutical risks. The predictability of the risk and thus the premium calculation is made easier for the insurer insofar as it no longer has to expect any unknown burdens after the end of the contract, subject to agreed periods of extended liability. In addition, the greater proximity between premium calculation and claims settlement makes it easier to assess risks and insurance needs.

In the area of nanotechnology, the claims made principle is considered as a suitable instrument to improve insurability.[27] In fact, the claims made principle facilitates the determination of the insured event by establishing comparatively clearly defined requirements. In addition, it makes calculation easier for the insurer, and it proves to be advantageous for the policyholder as liability for damage events occurring before the start of the insurance is also included, provided that the resulting claims are asserted against the policyholder for the first time during the term of the contract.

An important follow-up question arises as to whether the claim-making principle can be appropriately limited to the risks of nanotechnology or whether it would be consistent to generally introduce this principle for the liability risks covered by a contract. Such a broader approach would avoid delimitation difficulties. This topic cannot be delved into here.[28] However, the following should be noted: On the one hand, an undoubted advantage of the claims made principle is that it offers clearly defined temporal limits and gives the insurer short-term options for reacting to a change in the level of knowledge about the risk situation.

On the other hand, there are good reasons not to make the claims made principle the standard in liability insurance, at least beyond industrial insurance, but to limit it to some lines of insurance where there is a specific risk situation. In particular, for a policyholder who would like to have the risks arising from his actions over a certain period of time covered, significant gaps in coverage arise if the claims made principle is generally established in liability insurance policies. This does not apply if, even after the respective period of action, complete protection is

[26] For more details on the various design options in practice, see Lange, *recht und schaden (r+s)* (2006) p 177, 178.

[27] Teschabai-Oglu, *Die Versicherbarkeit von Emerging Risks in der Haftpflichtversicherung* (2012) p 220 ff, 277 f.

[28] For more information on the advantages and disadvantages of the claims principle, see in detail Schramm, *Das Anspruchserhebungsprinzip in der Haftpflichtversicherung* (2009) p 35 ff.

provided through cover based on the claims made principle. However, if an interruption occurs, for example because, due to a change in risk assessment, follow-up protection is no longer granted or is only granted under significantly less favorable conditions, the policyholder remains unprotected with regard to damages that were not claimed during the insurance period, including any grace period, and which are not yet time-barred.

If one restricts the principle of making claims to the risks of nanotechnology, this may be acceptable in view of the looming alternative of risk exclusion. However, if it is extended to other risks, this coverage limitation appears to be problematic from the perspective of the policyholder's needs. Countermeasures can be achieved through generous follow-up periods; This means that to a certain extent the design comes closer to the classic concepts.

b. Risk Exclusions

Comprehensive Exclusion

If the liability risks arising from nanotechnology prove to be very high, a comprehensive exclusion of those risks might be considered. There are examples of such a radical consequence, such as regarding the liability risk associated with the use of asbestos. Naturally, such a comprehensive exclusion only seems appropriate as a last resort in the event that the harmfulness is not already known at the time when the product is placed on the market. It could lead to the use of nanotechnology being banned in practice, as it is hardly clear why those who are potentially liable (manufacturers, etc) should have to shoulder a risk that even the insurance companies that specialise in embracing risks are not prepared to accept.

At the same time, the prognosis regarding the impending liability risks would remain with the policyholder. In addition, delimitation problems sometimes arise because there is currently no generally recognised and unambiguous definition of nanotechnology. It is difficult to linguistically distinguish nanomaterials from chemically identical but larger substances with the same name. The size difference alone cannot be decisive, especially since conventional chemistry also knows about nanoparticles. However, lawyers and especially insurance lawyers are also familiar with demarcation problems from other areas. Therefore this cannot be seen as an insurmountable obstacle to risk exclusion. A general definition could be based on the changed physical, optical and mechanical properties.

In terms of contract law, a comprehensive exclusion can be achieved in various ways: The risk of nanotechnology can be expressly named and excluded as part of an all-risks cover. Alternatively, instead of all-risks coverage, an enumerative list of the insured risks can be provided (named perils; see above sub I). For the policyholder, the second approach carries the risk that further gaps in coverage may arise. In addition, according to the understanding presented here (see above sub I), the risk of nanotechnology is included in the basic cover, as this does not differentiate according to whether nanotechnology is used.

Partial Exclusion

Instead of a comprehensive risk exclusion, it might also be considered that particularly exposed parts of the risk are excluded from insurance coverage. One example worth mentioning here is the risk of damage caused abroad. The situation with other risks is more difficult to assess. This requires more detailed knowledge of which parts of the risk should be taken into account. Further research is required on this. If a partial exclusion goes very far, for example by including all commercial liability risks, it can also have very similar disadvantages as a comprehensive exclusion. However, it is also conceivable to exclude specific types of damage (eg, certain damage to health) that have arisen through the use of nanotechnology.

The so-called testing clause should also be mentioned in this context. According to this contractual clause, in particular in the extended product liability insurance as a component of the business liability insurance, claims for property damage and financial loss caused by products are excluded if the use is not in accordance with the state of science and technology or has otherwise sufficiently been tested. By including such clauses in the insurance contract, liability insurers aim to prevent providing factual financing of the testing costs saved by the producer, and they intend to encourage the producer to carry out a careful risk analysis. However, given the uncertainties that exist regarding the risks associated with the use of nanotechnology, in this field the testing clause will currently not normally lead to a risk exclusion.

A further exclusion is to be considered with regard to so-called gradual damages (*Allmählichkeitsschäden*). This notion refers to a time-extended realisation of the damaging event through slow influences (so far in particular: the temperature, gases or humidity) with a constant intensity. Similar to environmental damage, the problem of such damage could also arise in the area of nanotechnology.

In order to avoid liability for such gradual damage over a long period of time even after the insurance contract has expired, the insurer could contractually limit its liability by excluding gradual damage caused by the use of nanotechnology.

Coverage Only Through Special Insurance

It is also possible to outsource the risk from general liability insurance by developing a special solution. The insurance industry has taken this route for certain liability risks such as recall costs, IT damage and environmental damage. This, however, does not eliminate the fundamental calculation problems. In addition, there are again difficulties in delimitation.

c. Serial Damages Clause

Series damage clauses (serial claims clauses, serial loss clauses) are an important instrument for limiting the insurer's obligation. These clauses provide that damage events from the same cause are combined into a single event and fixed at the time at which the first damage event occurred. As a typical example the serial loss clause proposed by the German General Association of Insurers for D&O policies shall be cited here:

> Irrespective of the individual periods of insurance, several claims asserted during the validity of the insurance contract by one or more claimants a) on the basis of a breach of duty committed by one or more insured persons or b) due to several breaches of duty committed by one or more insured persons, provided that these breaches of duty are attributable to the same facts and are legally, economically or temporally connected with each other, are to be considered as one insured event. This insured event shall be considered as having occurred at the time when the first liability claim was asserted irrespective of the actual time at which the individual liability claims are asserted.[29]

Calculability can be significantly improved through individual series damage clauses. This is particularly true with regard to annual limits (see sub iv c below).

An objection to the suitability of serial damage clauses for limiting nanotechnology-related risks is that this can result in far-reaching coverage restrictions for the policyholder. One could counteract this and expand insurance coverage again by requiring a close temporal connection between the damages to be summarised. However, this can in turn lead to demarcation problems. These disadvantages may suggest that it is better to use suitable sub-limits instead of a serial damage clause.

ii. Time Limits on Insurance Coverage

Insurability can also be increased by shortening the duration of the respective policy. The insurer is then in a position to react more quickly and flexibly to a change in the risk situation. In addition to a shorter fixed contract term, another legal instrument for shortening the duration of the insurer's commitment is a waiver of the contract extension, which otherwise occurs automatically if the policyholder does not terminate the contract. This would involve a paradigm shift in German insurance culture, which would also result in disadvantages for all sides, namely a loss of continuity of the insurance portfolio and higher acquisition and administration costs.

iii. Risk-Related Obligations

Risk-related obligations are rules of conduct that, if ignored, may lead to the loss or reduction of policyholders' claims against the insurer.[30] In order to formulate appropriate risk-related obligations for the liability risks related to the use of

[29] www.gdv.de (translation from German by the author).

[30] See Section 28 of the German Insurance Contract Code (Versicherungsvertragsgesetz, VVG) and the annotations to Section 28 by Armbrüster, in: Prölss/Martin, VVG, 32th ed. 2024 (in print).

nanotechnology, precise knowledge of how the risk materialises, that is, how the damage occurs, is required. It cannot be a question of outright excluding the use of nanotechnology from insurance coverage, but rather simply of imposing insurance sanctions on (particularly) dangerous types of this use.

It is possible, for example, to contractually require compliance with certain standards when using nanotechnology as part of a production process. This is also possible within the framework of a description of the insured business, which – if linked to the policyholder's behaviour – can contain so-called hidden obligations.

iv. Limitations on the Amount of Insurance Cover

The amount of insurance cover may be limited both upwards and downwards. This can be done either for the entire coverage or specifically for the liability risk associated with nanotechnology.

a. Deductible

A lower limit is the deductible (retention). In principle, this is an important instrument for shaping insurance policies. First of all, it helps reducing the insurer's administrative and compensation costs when the insured event has occurred (relief from minor damages). Another significant effect is that a policyholder who has to partially bear the damage will tend to make more intensive efforts to avoid damage.

However, this behaviour-controlling effect appears to be questionable. Unlike known risks, it is not obvious to the policyholder to what extent his behaviour is risky. As long as the risks of nanotechnology are not yet fully understood, and therefore it is difficult to argue that the users of this technology have acted negligently. In any event, it can only be a matter of strict liability. In this case, behaviour control achieved by liability is problematic. For the policyholder, it is not a matter of deciding whether to behave carefully or carelessly. Rather there is only the choice of whether to carry out the potentially dangerous activity or to refrain from doing so.

b. Maximum Sum Insured

Liability insurance is usually limited to a maximum amount. By determining the sum insured, the maximum exposure the insurer can be controlled.

c. Annual Limit; Sub-Limits

An insurer may set an annual aggregate limit for the maximum amount the policy will cover. Hence, if an insured event occurs multiple times, the insurer's liability will be limited to the policy amount. Limits of two or three times the insured sum per insured event are common. A typical example is the following model clause for general liability insurance published by the German General Association of Insurers:

> The indemnity paid by the insurer for each insured event is limited to the agreed sums insured. This shall also apply if the insurance cover extends to several persons liable to pay compensation. Unless otherwise agreed, the indemnity payments of the insurer for all insured events in an insurance year are limited to … times the agreed sums insured.[31]

A series damage clause also has an effect here: the insurer only has to settle the series damage up to the annual limit. Sub-limits can be used to further limit the insurer's obligation to provide benefits.[32]

v. *Condition Adjustment Clause*

If unexpected changes that affect the calculation basis occur during the term of the contract, the insurer has an interest in adjusting the contract. The German legislator takes this interest into account in various ways by allowing adjustment clauses with regard to the conditions of the insurance contract as well as of the premium.[33] Section 40 of the German Insurance Contract Code (VVG) expressly refers to contractual adjustment clauses which concern the premium or the extent of coverage respectively. A condition adjustment clause can also be considered in the present context.

In any case, with regard to the policyholder's trust in the agreed insurance cover it is not only the legal basis of condition adjustment clauses that appears problematic, but also their practical feasibility. As long as the risk is not specified in more detail, it is difficult to formulate in an abstract way the conditions under which the insurer should be entitled to unilaterally change the conditions in its favour.

In addition, with regard to the content of the change, there are the disadvantages that have already been mentioned: For example, an exclusion subsequently introduced based on an adjustment clause in the event that the risk manifests itself would significantly affect and devalue the insurance cover. However, an exclusion appears to be appropriate in the event that there are practically verifiable indications of a concrete potential for damage; It is then up to the policyholder to avoid liability risks.

[31] www.gdv.de (Translation from German by the author).

[32] For examples with regard to the various possibilities see Teschabai-Oglu, *Die Versicherbarkeit von Emerging Risks in der Haftpflichtversicherung* (2012) p 206 f.

[33] For details, see Entzian, *Zulässigkeit von Bedingungsanpassungsklauseln in Allgemeinen Versicherungsbedingungen*, NVersZ 1998, 65.

vi. Surcharge on the Premium

Remaining calculation uncertainties could be taken into account by increasing the premium by a safety surcharge. This can, however, only be practised to a certain extent given the impact on economic insurability.

vii. Selection when Concluding the Contract

It is also possible that the insurer, when deciding whether to conclude a contract with a particular applicant, differentiates based on how high the liability risk connected to the use of nanotechnology effectively is. If the insurer assesses this risk to be low in the specific case, it concludes the contract; otherwise it refrains from doing so.

A similar selection can also take place at the reinsurance level by offering reinsurance for some risks but not for others. Declining an insurance proposal may be economically disadvantageous for the insurer in various respects, which include loss of premium and loss of customer portfolio and possibly a negative impact on reputation as well. This is particularly true when the decision is not just about additional insurance for nanotechnology risks, but about the basic coverage (eg, product liability insurance) as a whole.

D. Improving Economic Insurability

i. Increase of the Reinsurance Cover

A primary insurer can increase insurability by passing on a higher proportion of the risk to reinsurers (reducing the gross share of the loss that it has to bear).

ii. Co-Insurance; Risk Pooling

Insurability can be increased by different insurers assuming the risk proportionately through co-insurance. A related design form is the so-called pool, which increases economic insurability by ensuring that the risk is distributed on many shoulders. This also plays a role at the reinsurance level.

In this context, state involvement can also be considered – not least in view of the socio-political importance of nanotechnology.[34] It already exists in Germany in the area of terrorism risks.[35] Here the state takes on the role of an insurer offering subordinate coverage. The insurance of nuclear risks (German Nuclear

[34] See Armbrüster, in: Kloepfer (ed.), *Katastrophenrecht: Grundlagen und Perspektiven* (2008) p. 77, 86.
[35] Managed by the public limited company *Extremus AG*, www.extremus.de.

Reactor Insurance Association, so-called *Atompool*) and the pharmaceutical pool (*Pharmapool*; see sub v for details) should also be mentioned. These risks have in common that they are difficult to calculate and that high damage may occur. The individual risks have not yet been determined when the pool is founded. Each insurer involved covers an individual risk and assigns it to the pool. In this way, every pool member engages in the cover of every risk.

iii. Creating Additional Capacity Through Alternative Risk Transfer (ART)

Additional insurance capacity can also be achieved through an alternative risk transfer (ART). This risk transfer is 'alternative' because it is aimed at risk carriers other than insurers, particularly investors in the capital market. Insurance risks are sometimes securitised in bonds (so-called risk securitisation). In current practice, this is observed particularly with regard to natural hazards such as earthquakes or storms. For this purpose, certain assessment forecasts regarding the future probability of damage can be derived from the past. However, there is a lack of such figures regarding the risks from the use of nanotechnology.

iv. Introduction of Legal Liability Limits

If the legislature introduces an upper liability limit, as is regularly the case with strict liability,[36] economic insurability can be improved by aligning the insured sum with this limit. However, given the unclear risk situation with regard to the use of nanotechnology, there is currently no reason for the legislature to take action in this direction.

v. Introduction of Compulsory Insurance

The introduction of compulsory statutory insurance actually improves economic insurability in that it forces the conclusion of a contract and thus ensures a large collective with corresponding premium income. For instance, in the area of pharmaceutical products, in response to the *Thalidomide* case, in Germany not only strict liability with high liability limits was introduced[37] and an insurance pool (*Pharmapool*) was created as a special reinsurance instrument. In addition, there is compulsory insurance for the manufacturers of pharmaceutical products.[38]

However, compulsory insurance also has serious disadvantages. In the case of a general compulsory insurance with a very different distribution of risk – which can

[36] See eg, Section 10 *ProdHaftG*.
[37] Sections 84 ff *Arzneimittelgesetz (AMG)*.
[38] Section 94 *Arzneimittelgesetz (AMG)*.

be assumed here because of the completely different areas where nanotechnology is used – there is a risk of cross-subsidisation. This is alien to private insurance law with its inherent principles of private autonomy and risk-adequate premium calculation. Accordingly, the legislator has so far only introduced compulsory insurance in those areas in which it is urgently necessary to protect third parties from the consequences of risky behaviour and in which a certain homogeneity of risk can be assumed. The outstanding example for such a situation is motor insurance, where the green card system has been introduced on a European level.[39] In this field, which concerns a mass risk, the law of large numbers also facilitates insurance.

With regard to the risks of nanotechnology, the risk situation is still far too unclear to suggest such a step to the legislator. This is all the more true because, unlike pharmaceuticals, nanotechnology is not limited to a specific area of application or industry. Last but not least, it should also be borne in mind that if a risk analysis based on the above-mentioned mathematical and economic criteria of insurability leads insurers to the conclusion that they shall not offer coverage, this might necessitate even further-reaching legislative interventions in order to ensure that there is an appropriate offer of insurance cover on the market.

These disadvantages must be taken into account if legislators are confronted with the question of whether they should introduce compulsory insurance with regard to the risks of nanotechnology. In view of the above-mentioned risk situation, there is currently no need for legislative action.

VI. Conclusions

The main liability risk of nanoproducts lies in the area of product and environmental liability. Liability for development risks regularly fails due to the manufacturer's breach of duty, but he is nevertheless obliged to closely monitor the product on the market. If a product defect can no longer be clearly identified after the product has been placed on the market, a reversal of the burden of proof in favour of the injured party appears appropriate.

As has been demonstrated liability risks from the use of nanotechnology are legally insurable. In terms of regulatory policy, their insurability is even desirable in order to make the risks manageable for market participants and thus to promote useful innovations. Nano-technology contains a so-called emerging risk, the existence and scope of which cannot yet be estimated. As a rule, this is not a so-called phantom risk; rather, the respective causer (eg, producer) will often be identifiable.

[39] See the Directive (EU) 2021/2118 of the European Parliament and of the Council of 24 November 2021 amending Directive 2009/103/EC relating to insurance against civil liability in respect of the use of motor vehicles, and the enforcement of the obligation to insure against such liability, OJ L 430, 2.12.2021, p 1.

At present, liability risks arising from nanotechnology are regularly covered by liability insurance. This is because a liability risk (eg, product liability) is insured regardless of whether it materializes precisely because of the use of a particular technology such as nanotechnology. However, in the future advances in knowledge may mean that the actuarial and economic requirements for insurability are no longer met.

Actuarial insurability can be improved by various instruments of insurance contract law. In particular, appropriate maximum insured sums and further limits as well as serial damage clauses can be considered. In contrast, risk exclusions or increased deductibles in particular appear less appropriate. The introduction of the claim-making principle is in principle a suitable instrument; However, the consequences for further liability risks must be taken into account. A shortening of the insurer's liability period would allow more flexible reactions to a changed risk situation, but would also result in disadvantages for both parties. Economic insurability can be increased in particular by pooling risks. However, the shift of risks to the capital market appears difficult when it comes to nanotechnology risks.

In contrast, legislation can improve insurability by introducing maximum liability limits or (in order to secure a sufficiently large collective) compulsory insurance. However, there is currently no reason for either of these, and the introduction of compulsory insurance would meet with considerable reservations even if the risk assessment were to change. The legislator is able to improve insurability by introducing maximum liability limits or (sub specie to ensure a sufficiently large collective) compulsory insurance. However, there is currently no reason for either. In addition, the introduction of compulsory insurance would raise considerable concerns even if risk assessments changed.

13

The Insurability of Third-Party Liability Risks Arising from the Use of Civilian Uncrewed Aircraft Systems (UAS) in the UK

GEORGE LELOUDAS

I. Introduction: A Promising New Sector

Civilian Uncrewed Aircraft Systems (UAS) (also known as drones or Remotely Piloted Aircraft Systems (RPAS)) are one of the most promising sectors in the UK. In a report that is often cited by the British government, industry and academia, PWC predicts that by 2030, the sector will 'contribute up to £45bn to the UK economy … £22bn in net cost savings may be realised, carbon emissions could be reduced by 2.4M tons [and] 650,000 jobs could be [created]'.[1]

These impressive figures explain the significant investments made by governmental, private, and academic institutions in the UAS sector. The investments are diverse, reflecting the versatile nature of UAS. For example, UAS used in infrastructure inspection brings the most economic benefits, with an estimated £2.4 billion GDP impact. UAS used in emergency response, namely hospitals, search and rescue operations, law enforcement, and son on, have the highest potential GDP impact of £14.1 billion by 2030 and enjoy the highest levels of public support.[2] One controversial yet promising area of UAS operations is last-mile delivery services, which have an estimated value of £10 billion but face significant public resistance, mainly on privacy grounds. Currently, its contribution to the UK economy is close to zero.[3] Furthermore, the crucial role UAS already play in the maritime industry, especially in the work undertaken by classification societies

[1] PWC UK, 'Skies Without Limits v2.0' (July 2022) www.pwc.co.uk/intelligent-digital/drones/skies-without-limits- 2022.pdf (PWC report).

[2] ibid.

[3] ibid.

and operators of offshore energy installations and the significant investment of the marine sector in remote inspection technologies, digitisation of operations and emission monitoring undertaken by UAS has been highlighted in a different publication.[4]

A significant portion of civilian UAS operations, especially in infrastructure inspections, emergency response and last-mile delivery, (will) take place in urban environments. To accommodate the unique characteristics of urban environments and to cope with the expected demand, innovative types of aerial vehicles are currently designed and tested, such as Vertical Take-Off & Landing (VTOL) vehicles, to supplement UAS operations; for example, the use of (uncrewed or crewed) VTOLs will enable the operation of more efficient air ambulance services, as well as the introduction of air taxis as such operations cannot be performed with UAS.

At the same time, the concept of Urban Air Mobility (UAM) has been created to address the safety challenges of operating aerial vehicles in low-level, congested urban airspaces that contain a wide range of obstacles, are near other aircraft operations and in various weather conditions.[5] UAM also addresses societal concerns about their use in urban environments, such as reducing their noise levels, making a case for environmentally sustainable operations and addressing public concerns about privacy and third-party liability.

To unlock the benefits of UAS, the UK refreshed its Airspace Modernisation Strategy in January 2023, committing, among many other things, to enabling novel aircraft operations, including UAS, to enter non-segregated airspace routinely, without the need for special permissions, as is currently required.[6] Furthermore, the refreshed strategy aims to enable the regular operations of Beyond Visual Line Of Sight (BVLOS) and autonomous UAS as they 'can facilitate more effective services to businesses and the general public, as well as to the State through medical flights, search and rescue or law enforcement'.[7] Such integration is expected to be achieved by creating a UAS Traffic Management system (UTM) and integrating it with the existing air traffic management system.[8]

In February 2024, the Law Commission of England and Wales opened a consultation on aviation autonomy to assess whether the regulatory and legal framework

[4] G Leloudas and M Chatzipanagiotis 'Use of Unmanned Aircraft Systems in a Maritime Context: Operational, Regulatory and Legal Issues' in B Soyer and A Tettenborn (eds), *Disruptive Technologies, Climate Change and Shipping* (Informa Law, 2022) (Leloudas and Chatzipanagiotis).

[5] CAA, 'CAP2272: Key Considerations for Airspace Integration within an Urban Air Mobility Landscape' (October 2021) www.caa.co.uk/our-work/publications/documents/content/cap2272/.

[6] CAA, 'CAP1711: Airspace Modernisation Strategy 2023–2040 Part 1: Strategic objectives and enablers' (January 2023) /www.caa.co.uk/our-work/publications/documents/content/cap1711/ (CAP 1711).

[7] CAA, 'What are the benefits of airspace modernisation?' www.caa.co.uk/commercial-industry/airspace/airspace-modernisation/airspace-modernisation-strategy/what-are-the-benefits-of-airspace-modernisation/#:~:text=Accommodating%20new%20types%20of%20aerial,and%20rescue%20or%20law%20enforcement.

[8] CAP 1711, n 6, p 72.

is adequate for the autonomous operation of UAS and VTOL.[9] While this Chapter is written before publication of the final report of the Commission in 2025, it aims to discuss the adequacy of the third-party liability and insurance system concerning the operation of UAS in the UK. With 900,000 UAS predicted to fly in UK airspace by 2030,[10] the third-party liability system and the insurance system that underpins it will inevitably be a part of the debate and need to be scrutinised.

Before we discuss the liability and insurance challenges of operating UAS in the UK and whether any changes to the liability and insurance system are required to facilitate their use, it is essential to review the accident rates of UAS in the UK and the regulatory system that enables their operations. This review, carried out in Part II, will inform our analysis on liability and insurance related issues.

II. UAS Accidents and Regulatory Framework

A. UAS Accidents

The official accident statistics of the Aircraft Accident Investigation Branch (AAIB) reveal some concerning trends for liability and insurance purposes. These trends will likely augment due to the increased number of UAS that will be operated in the (eventually) integrated UK airspace.

In 2022, the predominant cause of UAS accidents was the loss of control in flight (LOC-I) (53%), resulting from the UAS 'becoming unresponsive to control inputs or displaying erratic or uncommanded responses.'. The second accident cause was the failure/malfunction of the flying system (11%), and the third was the loss of communication links (8%).[11] Similarly, in 2021, the leading cause of UAS accidents was LOC-I with 34%, controlled flight into terrain (CFIT) being the second cause with 15% and system failure the third one with 12%.[12]

The first concerning trend is that UAS accidents occur due to technical failures and human errors. Technical issues, human factors, and weather conditions can cause LOC-I and CFIT accidents, indicating that product safety standards and remote pilot training must improve. This concern was also recently raised by the AAIB, which argued that the UAS industry makes 'the same mistakes that were made in the development of manned aviation a few decades ago, such as: lack of redundancy in designs; not considering all the possible failure mechanisms;

[9] Law Commission of England and Wales, 'Aviation Autonomy' (February 2024) lawcom.gov.uk/project/aviation-autonomy/ (Law Commission Consultation).

[10] PWC Report, n 1.

[11] AAIB, 'Annual Safety Review 2022' (April 2023), p 30 www.gov.uk/aaib-reports/aaib-annual-safety-review-2022 (2022 Safety Report).

[12] AAIB, 'Annual Safety Review 2021' (June 2022), p 23 www.gov.uk/aaib-reports/aaib-annual-safety-review-2022 (2021 Safety Report).

human factors not considered in design of controller; operators not expecting or training for failures'.[13]

The second concerning trend is that UAS accidents have a disproportionate share of accidents. In 2022, 18% of the accident/incident notifications received by the AAIB (138 out of 778) involved UAS, as 30% of the correspondence investigations, 21% of the safety recommendations made by the AAIB, and 7% of the safety actions undertaken by the AAIB.[14] This trend was even more dominant in 2021, with 26% of the incident/accident notifications to the AAIB involving UAS, 40% of correspondence investigations, 49% of the safety recommendations issued by the AAIB, and 13% of safety actions undertaken by the AAIB.[15] On the positive side, no fatal injuries caused by UAS have been reported. Still, a severe injury was reported in October 2015 when a child lost his eye when a recreational UA cut through it.[16]

These statistics might not be of significant concern as no fatal injuries have been reported. However, they demonstrate an apparent increase in reported incidents: 72 UAS accidents were reported between 2015 and 2020, which increased significantly to 118 in 2021 and 138 in 2022. This increase reflects the growth in the number and size of UAS operating in the UK. While it might also reflect an increased awareness of reporting UAS accidents, insurers seem to believe that the opposite is likely and the actual accident number is higher:[17]

> This data is increasing, but there are many uninsured drones, which have resulted in unreported accidents. Even where there is a mandatory obligation to report drone incidents, many are likely to be unreported. This is because they are either uninsured or the cost to replace the drone outweighs the damage it may have caused to a third party. Drone operators may lose control of a drone, which goes on to cause damage which may remain unreported where the drone and the drone operator are unable to be identified. There may also be instances where the injured property or party simply does not realise the damage sustained was caused by a drone.

UAS might not have the catastrophic potential of aircraft, yet their proximity to the ground poses significant risks of third-party damage. Focusing on their size is deceptive as the AAIB estimated that a UAS of '1.4 kg falling from 8 m could cause a fatal injury'[18] and also that a 'blunt object with a mass of 4.97 kg falling from a height of more than about 3 m could result in a fatal injury to someone wearing a hard hat'.[19] Furthermore, the ease of operating them and bringing

[13] ibid, 9.

[14] 2022 Safety Report, n 11, p 22.

[15] 2021 Safety Report, n 12, p 28.

[16] BBC, 'Toddler's eyeball sliced in half by drone propeller' (November 2015) www.bbc.co.uk/news/uk-england-hereford-worcester-34936739.

[17] M Thompson, A Tarr, J Tarr and S Ritterband, 'Unmanned Aerial Vehicles Liability and Insurance' in D Wilkinson, A Tarr, J Tarr and M Thompson (eds), *The Global Insurance Market and Change* (Abingdon, Taylor & Francis, 2023) 213, at 217 (Ritterband UAS Liability and Insurance).

[18] 2021 Safety Report, n 12, p 8.

[19] AAIB, 'AAIB Bulletin 1/2020' (January 2020) p 25 assets.publishing.service.gov.uk/media/5f69d6548fa8f507646e1ea8/AAIB_Bulletin_1-2020_Hi_Res.pdf.

them to close proximity to sensitive installations, such as nuclear plants, (air) ports, motorways and other critical infrastructures, magnifies their catastrophic potential, mainly if used by terrorists who can attempt to override geofencing restrictions and no-fly zones.

Arguably, the absence of fatal or severe personal injuries and significant property damage is to a great extent to be attributed to the current regulations governing the operation of UAS, with their insistence on keeping heavy UAS away from people and buildings, requiring a detailed safety case for close to people and buildings operations, and the reluctance of the UK Civil Aviation Authority (CAA) to permit BVLOS operations in non-segregated airspace. As such, the UAS regulations seem to manage the accident impact of UAS better than the regulations in the early stages of aviation, which developed through a long process of trials, errors and accidents.[20]

In the following two Sections, we will highlight some of the 'safety-critical' features of the current regulatory regime for UAS and address the issue of BVLOS operations, one of the main demands of the commercial UAS sector.

B. The Current Regulatory Framework of Operations

At the time of writing (spring 2024), the regulation of UAS in the UK follows, at large, EU-assimilated laws.[21] Yet, the Government is currently reviewing the inherited regulations with the aims, among other things, of simplifying their operational requirements and implementing product safety and security standards. Any amendments will be decided upon after the publication of this Chapter, so we will discuss the regulatory system as it stands at the time of writing.

To operate in the UK, a UAS needs to be classified into one of the following three categories, namely i) the Open category, ii) the Specific category, or iii) the Certified category: in which category it falls and what operational permissions are required depends on the level of risk the UAS poses to third parties.[22]

i. Open Category

Light UASs that pose less risk to third parties fall into the rules of the Open category and can be operated without authorisation from the CAA, other than

[20] G Leloudas, *Risk and Liability in Air Law* (London, Informa Law, 2009) [3.22] to [3.56] (*Leloudas Risk*).

[21] Regulation 2018/1139 on common rules in the field of civil aviation (Regulation 1139/2018), Regulation 2019/947 on the rules and procedures for the operation of unmanned aircraft (Regulation 947/2019) and Regulation 2019/945 on unmanned aircraft systems and on third-country operators of unmanned aircraft systems (Regulation 945/2019).

[22] Regulation 947/2019, n 21, art 3.

flying licences given to their remote pilots and registration of the UAS operator.[23] The overarching limitations of the Open category are that:

a. the UAS has a Maximum Take-Off Mass (MTOM) of less than 25kgs, including attached payload, such as batteries, propellers, cameras, etc;[24]
b. the UAS must be flown within 120m (400ft) of the earth's surface,[25] unless it overflies an obstacle of more than 105m, in which case it can overfly it by 15m, provided that such overfly has been requested by the user of the obstacle (for example, to perform an inspection) and the UAS is not flown more than 50m horizontally from the obstruction;[26]
c. the UAS is not carrying dangerous goods or dropping any articles;[27] and
d. the UAS is operated within the remote pilot's Visual Line of Sight (VLOS).[28]

As we explained in Chapter II.A, a 25 kg UAS can cause significant personal injuries and damages to property on the ground. One might understandably wonder whether allowing such heavy UAS to operate without prior authorisation from the CAA is advisable. The Regulation provides the following solution to this issue.

UAS of MTOM of more than 2kgs and less than 25kgs (A3 subcategory of the Open Category) are only permitted to fly *far from people*, meaning that

a. they must fly at least 150m away from residential, commercial, industrial or recreational areas (ie, areas that are densely populated or likely to be occupied by large numbers);[29] and
b. no uninvolved individuals or groups shall be present during their flight, namely people who are not participating in the UAS operation or have not received clear instructions and safety precautions on how to behave if the UAS malfunctions.[30]

In essence, the Regulation provides that heavy UAS can operate without authorisation from the CAA if they do not pose a risk to the general public by operating away from it.

[23] Depending on the weight of the UAS and its classification within the Open category, their remote pilots are required to read the user manual of the UA, get a Flyer ID or obtain an A2 Certificate of Competency. Operators of Open category UAS require registration unless the UAS has an MTOM of less than 250 g, is unable to capture personal data or is a toy (whether it can capture personal data or not) in compliance with the Toys (Safety) Regulations 2011 – Regulation 947/2019, n 21, art 14(5)(a).

[24] Regulation 947/2019, n 21, art 4(1)(b); 'MTOM' is defined in art 2(22) of Regulation 947/2019 as the maximum Uncrewed Aircraft (UA) mass, including payload and fuel, as defined by the manufacturer or the builder, at which the UA can be operated.

[25] ibid, art 4(1)(e).

[26] ibid, Point UAS.OPEN.010(3).

[27] ibid, art 4(1)(f).

[28] ibid, art 4(1)(d).

[29] ibid, Point UAS.OPEN.040(2).

[30] ibid, art 2 (18) and Point UAS.OPEN.040(1).

If an operator wants to fly the UAS closer to buildings or uninvolved people, lighter UAS must be used:

a. UAS with MTOM of more than 500 grams and less than 2 kg (A2 subcategory of the Open Category) are permitted to operate near people but not over them, meaning that they cannot overfly uninvolved individuals but can fly at a horizontal distance of at least 30 m from them (that can be reduced to 5m if the UAS is operating in the low-speed mode and certain conditions are satisfied);[31]
b. UAS with an MTOM of more than 250 grams but less than 500 grams (A1 subcategory of the Open Category) can be operated within residential, commercial, industrial, or recreational areas if the remote pilot gets the A2 Certificate of Competency (A2 CofC). Still, it cannot be intentionally operated over uninvolved individuals or assemblies of people, namely gatherings where persons cannot move away due to the density of the people present, such as people attending open-air concerts, even if it flies higher than 50m from them;[32]
c. UAS with an MTOM of less than 250 grams (the A1 subcategory of the Open Category) can be operated over uninvolved individuals (even closer than 50m) and within residential, commercial, industrial, or recreational areas. Still, UAS with an MTOM of less than 250 grams cannot be operated over assemblies of people.[33]

It is evident from the above that UAS in the Open Category are not permitted to operate close to segregations of people (assemblies) to avoid personal injuries and catastrophic events to third parties. The Regulation prioritises the safety of operations over commercial convenience and innovation in the Open category. Therefore, the Regulation further provides that UAS of the Open Category are only permitted to operate within the VLOS of the remote pilot who handles the control station.[34] The remote pilot must always retain visual access to the UA without visual enhancements, such as on-board cameras, electronic viewing equipment, binoculars, telescopes, or visual observers.[35] Furthermore, UAS in the Open category are not permitted to carry passengers or dangerous cargo, drop any articles, or operate on a BVLOS basis. Inevitably, such restrictions limit the usefulness of the Open category for novel aircraft operations:[36]

> As currently structured, the open category is of limited practical application to new forms of UAS. Most proposed uses for drones, for example, involve flying beyond the

[31] ibid, Point UAS.OPEN.030(1).
[32] ibid, Point UAS.OPEN.020(1) and art 2(3).
[33] ibid., Point UAS.OPEN.020(2).
[34] ibid., art 4(1)(d).
[35] CAA, 'CAP 722: Unmanned Aircraft System Operations in UK Airspace – Guidance' (April 2024) [2.1.1] www.caa.co.uk/our-work/publications/documents/content/cap-722/ (CAP 722).
[36] Law Commission Consultation, n 9, [3.5].

visual line of sight of the pilot (known as 'BVLOS') and would, therefore, fall within the specific or certified categories. Our other use case, VTOLs, involves carrying passengers and, therefore, would fall within the certified category.

ii. Specific Category

The Specific category is used to operate UASs outside the restrictions of the Open category. For example, it allows using a UAS with an MTOM of more than 25 kg, getting close to uninvolved individuals or buildings, or flying over assemblies of people, provided the UAS does not have a characteristic dimension of less than 3m.[37] In this case, the rule of the Certified category below applies. Also, UAS in the Specific category cannot carry passengers or dangerous goods; see the Certified category below.

For operations in the Specific category, the UAS operator must obtain an operational authorisation from the CAA, register with the CAA, and display its operator ID on the UAS.[38] To receive authorisation, the operator is required to submit an Operating Safety Case (OSC) to the CAA, which aims to evidence that the 'safety risks have been reduced to a Tolerable and As Low As Reasonably Practicable (ALARP) level'.[39] The CAA will grant the authorisation if it concludes that the mitigation measures, the competence of the personnel and the technical features of the UAS 'are adequate and sufficiently robust to keep the operation safe given the identified ground and air risks'.[40]

Most commercial UAS users require authorisation under the Specific category rules due to the restrictions in the Open category and the absence of tailor-made rules in the Certified category. This way, the CAA manages the risk of operating UAS that might pose a significant risk to third parties. It can request more restrictive measures or terminate the operation if it thinks the risk to third parties exceeds acceptable levels.

iii. Certified Category

The Certified category, which is not currently used for routine operations, is expected to become more relevant when the demand for air ambulances, air taxis, cargo-carrying UAS, and passenger-carrying VTOLs becomes more prevalent. The requirements of the Certified Category apply to UAS that i) have a characteristic dimension of at least 3 m and are designed to be operated over assemblies of people; ii) are designed for transporting people; iii) are designed for transporting dangerous goods; or iv) the CAA, following its safety assessment in the Specific

[37] Regulation 947/2019, n 21, art 5.
[38] ibid, art 14(5)(b) and art 14(8).
[39] ibid, art 5(2) and CAA, 'CAP 722A: Unmanned Aircraft System Operations in UK Airspace – Operating Safety Cases' (December 2022) p 10.
[40] Regulation 947/2019, n 21, art 12(2)(b).

category, determines that the operational risks of the UAS cannot be adequately mitigated without its certification.[41] The CAA is required to certify the design, production, and maintenance of the UAS, as well as to certify the UAS operator and impose more stringent requirements for the licensing of remote pilots.

There are no detailed rules for the Certified category yet, and the CAA requires operators to comply with the regulations applicable to manned aircraft regarding airworthiness, operations and licensing, such as the need for a type certificate and a certificate of airworthiness. The CAA expects that 'the full suite of documentation … for an equivalent manned aircraft operation' will be submitted for approval.[42] UK regulations tailored-made for UAS falling into the Certified category are expected to follow the creation of UAS-relevant Standards and Recommended Practices of the International Civil Aviation Organization (ICAO). This significant step took place in March 2024.[43]

The challenge for the future regulatory framework is to balance innovation with operational safety. While this paper does not address the future of the regulatory framework, it is essential to discuss some of the challenges concerning BVLOS operations in non-segregated airspace.

C. BVLOS Operations

The PWC study, mentioned in the Introduction, highlighted that routine BVLOS flights in non-segregated airspace are 'key to maximise growth' and the most frequent response to a 'barriers to growth' question it posed to its participants.[44] This conclusion is not surprising, as routine BVLOS operations have been the demand of commercial UAS operators in the UK for quite a while now. BVLOS operations do not require the remote pilot to maintain visual contact with the UA during flight, permitting the establishment of remote flight control centres and enabling autonomous UAS operations.

At the time of writing (spring 2024), the CAA has not authorised routine BVLOS flights in non-segregated airspace. It believes that the navigating technology is not mature enough to replicate the ability of a pilot of a manned flight to 'see and avoid' collisions.[45] BVLOS flights are only performed in segregated airspace in permanent or temporary Danger Areas (DAs) that the CAA establishes and

[41] ibid, art 6 and Regulation 945/2019, n 21, art 40 (1).

[42] CAP 722, n 35, [5.1.3].

[43] ICAO, 'ICAO Council Adopts New International Aviation Standards and Recommended Practices for Remotely Piloted Aircraft Systems' (April 2024) www.icao.int/Newsroom/Pages/ICAO-Council-adopts-new-international-aviation-Standards-and-Recommended-Practices-for-remotely-piloted-aircraft-systems.aspx.

[44] PWC report, n 1.

[45] CAA, 'Airspace Policy Concept: Airspace Requirements for the Integration of Beyond Visual Line of Sight (BVLOS) Unmanned Aircraft' (April 2023) [2.11] www.caa.co.uk/our-work/publications/documents/content/cap2533/ (CAA BVLOS integration).

the UAS uses exclusively.[46] Furthermore, for this to happen, the UAS needs to be authorised as per the Specific or Certified category rules.[47]

The CAA recently acknowledged the benefits of BVLOS operations and presented a pathway (as part of the Airspace Modernisation Strategy mentioned in the Introduction) on how BVLOS operations can be integrated into non-segregated airspace.[48] Central to their integration is developing and testing technologies (bundled together under the umbrella of Electronic Conspicuity) that will enable UAS to see and be seen by other aircraft in the same airspace and 'use the safety objectives built into the Rules of the Air'.[49] Such Detect and Avoid (DAA) technologies will combine systems installed on the UA with ground-based systems that transmit information to the remote pilot and the UAS, depending on its autonomy levels. At the time of writing (spring 2024), no DAA systems have been approved for use in the UK.

Permitting routine BVLOS operations in non-segregated airspace would require amending the UK Standardised European Rules of the Air (SERA), part of which is the 'see and avoid' rule, and the rules that the UK develops to supplement SERA, namely the Rules of the Air Regulations 2015, which are made under art 249 of the Air Navigation Order 2016,[50] as they were designed with manned aircraft in mind. With the SERA rules deriving from several ICAO Annexes,[51] their work is underway globally via ICAO to achieve a uniform amendment of the Rules of the Air, with significant developments in this context in March 2024.[52]

In principle, BVLOS operations are to be distinguished from autonomous UAS operations. While the distinction is somewhat difficult to draw, especially in light of the requirement for DAA technology to be installed on UAS, it is essential to clarify some elements of UAS autonomy.

Regulation 947/2019 defines autonomous UAS operations as 'operation[s] during which an unmanned aircraft operates without the remote pilot being able to intervene.'.[53] This definition focuses on the absence of human intervention in the operation and monitoring of the UAS. This factor seems to be the guiding principle of several aviation definitions of autonomy. For example, the Joint Authorities for Rulemaking on Unmanned Systems (JARUS) defines autonomy as a situation where 'the machine is fully responsible for function execution. The human is unable to intervene in real-time either due to practical limitations or

[46] Air Navigation Order 2016, art 239, SI 2016/765.

[47] Regulation 947/2019 (n 21) art 3.

[48] CAA BVLOS integration, n 45, [2.3].

[49] ibid.

[50] SI 2016/765 (ANO 2016).

[51] See ICAO Annex 2 (Rules of the Air) and parts of ICAO Annex 3 (Meteorology), Annex 10 (Communication Procedures), and Annex 11 (Air Traffic Services).

[52] See note 43.

[53] UK Regulation 947/2019, n 21, art 2(17).

deliberate exclusion within the operational design domain';[54] With the European Aviation Safety Agency (EASA) defining it as a situation where the 'the AI-based system performs non overridable decisions and actions'.[55]

To that effect, the CAA provided some high-level guidance on what is expected from autonomous UAS:[56]

> It will be able to follow the planned route, communicate with Aircraft Controllers and other airspace users, detect, diagnose and recover from faults and operate at least as safely as a system with continuous human involvement. In essence, an autonomous UAS will be equipped with high authority control systems that can act without input from a human.

Autonomous operations can be distinguished from BVLOS operations in that the former requires a self-contained technological ecosystem capable of responding to the challenges posed by its operational environment (including communication with ATC) without (or with limited) human interference. Levels 4 (High Automation) and 5 (Full Automation) of the CAA classification seem to fall into this concept as in both Levels, the system is responsible for the operations, monitoring and control of the UAS, with the human element playing a secondary role:[57]

	Operations	**Monitoring**	**Control/System Assurance**
Level 4 High Automation	System	System	System Humans ensure the system meets operational objectives but does not receive flight information
Level 5 Full Automation	System	System	System Humans provide high-level directives, and no human intervention is possible.

BVLOS is a broader concept that can accommodate both autonomous and non-autonomous operations, as a remote pilot operating a UAS from a remote control centre might operate the UAS in full or be able to take over functions of the UAS in flight and also communicate with the ATC. Such operations would not be considered autonomous for the Regulation as the systems are designed to support the remote pilot in Level 1, the control and monitoring of operations are shared

[54] JARUS, 'JARUS Methodology for Evaluation of Automation for UAS Operations' (April 2023) p 9 and [3.1.6] arus-rpas.org/wp-content/uploads/2023/06/jar_21_doc_JARUS_Methodology_for_Evaluation_of_Automation_for_UAS_Operations.pdf.

[55] EASA, 'Artificial Intelligence Roadmap 2.0' (May 2023) p 18 www.easa.europa.eu/en/document-library/general-publications/easa-artificial-intelligence-roadmap-20.

[56] CAP 722, n 35, [4.5.1].

[57] ibid, [4.5.4.3].

between the system and the remote pilot in Level 2, and the remote pilot can at any point intervene to manage the safety of operations in Level 3:[58]

	Operations	**Monitoring**	**Control/System Assurance**
Level 2 Partial Automation	Remote Pilot/ The system can take over particular functions	Remote Pilot / System	Remote Pilot/ System
Level 3 Supervised Automation	System	System	Humans

Yet, in Levels 1 to 3, the UAS can operate on a BVLOS basis as the remote pilot does not have the UAS within its unaided line of sight. It seems that the CAA links the two concepts in that it wants to ensure that during BVLOS operations, the system can make independent decisions to avoid collisions, set new flight paths, etc. This approach makes sense in terms of safety. It envisages emergencies where the BVLOS UA loses the connection with the remote control centre and is required to operate without the input of the remote pilot. While this might be a cautious approach to BVLOS operations, it is justified (at this stage) to protect third parties from accidents.

The classifications are not set in stone and will be adjusted according to technological developments. Yet, under any classification, it is essential to determine at which point the UAS performs the flying task to allocate responsibilities between human actors and autonomous systems. There might be situations, especially in Levels 2 and 3, where the UAS is subject to two operational regimes, depending on whether the remote pilot is in charge of its operation or the UAS operates in its capacity. This is not unlike automated cars that have issued a transition demand to the user-in-charge to take control of the driving function from the system. While operations in Levels 4 and 5 can be classified as self-flying, distinctions of responsibilities will be required in Levels 2 and 3 depending on who exercises control of the operations at any given time.

D. Concluding Thoughts on Accidents and the Regulation of Operations

The AAIB accident statistics highlight the need for more reliable technologies and better training of remote pilots. They further demonstrate that the UAS sector is still in a trial-and-error process. This process, characteristic of transport industries in general, is not as steep as aviation, which had a long history of accidents before achieving today's high safety standards.

[58] ibid.

In keeping the accident rates in control and avoiding fatal injuries and significant property damages, the current regulatory rules of operating UAS have played a crucial role. Admittedly, the rules in the Open category are rather complicated, and their proposed simplification will arguably contribute to increasing UAS appeal. At the same time, the rules of the Specific category that give discretion to the CAA in terms of authorisations have kept the risk to third parties under control while providing enough flexibility to the CAA to accommodate new applications on a case-by-case basis, provided they demonstrate a robust safety framework of operations.

The regulatory framework is not yet designed to accommodate regular BVLOS operations (with or without passengers and cargo). Such uses require significant changes to the regulatory framework and technological advances that have yet to reach maturity to reduce the risks to third parties (and passengers) to acceptable levels. When that happens (and it seems that it will not take long), flying UAS on a BVLOS basis in non-segregated airspace will inevitably lead to several current restrictions being lifted and the regulatory framework redesigned. While this Chapter does not look into the regulatory future in detail, the challenge will be to design a system that balances innovation used routinely with the safety of operations.

At the same time, such novel operations will increase the pressure on the third-party liability and insurance systems to which we now turn our attention.

III. UAS Insurance

A. Insurance Market

Like most new insurance sectors, the UAS insurance market was impeded at its beginnings by the absence of historical accident data. In many respects, these issues resemble those the aviation insurance market experienced at its birth, but the similarities end there. Multi-casualty accidents and a loose regulatory framework and enforcement characterised the beginning of aviation.[59] In contrast, the commercial UAS market, as we explained in the previous Section, is characterised by a formidable regulatory framework that has played a significant role in preventing major personal injuries and property damage from the operation of UAS. Still, UAS insurers are concerned about the underreporting of accidents (see Section II.A) and, to a lesser extent nowadays, by the limited pool of historical accident data.[60]

[59] *Leloudas Risk*, n 20, [3.22] to [3.56].

[60] They are also concerned about the low training standards of recreational (as distinguished from commercial) users of UAS.

In this context, UAS insurers were required to be innovative in collecting data about UAS and their users, including non-standard UAS operations such as swarm displays, BVLOS, etc. And creative they have been as the gradual building up of historical data was supplemented by the use of telematics and Artificial Intelligence (AI) applications with the use of sensors and LIDAR-like technologies on UAS facilitating the real-time collection of data:[61]

> Insurance underwriting models generally use historical data to predict the future risk landscape. However, drone technology is arguably moving too fast for this to be the only tool that insurance underwriters utilise. There is, however, one key characteristic of drones that will assist with underwriting drone risks in the future, which is data: Drones produce a vast amount of real-time data that can be used to analyse risks as they arise. The data that drones capture should make the task of underwriting drone insurance more accurate, and as drone technology improves and the implementation of drones expands, the data available for underwriting will also increase.

Telematics collect real-time information on the behaviour of UAS users, the reliability of their equipment, and the conditions under which UASs are operated, such as weather, location, and route conditions. Access to such information enables insurers to adjust the premium, offer rewards for safe operations, provide alternative routes for operating UAS based on the prevailing conditions and have a clear picture of the operating capabilities and deficiencies of several UASs – the use of AI in interpreting those data helped insurers to make accurate decisions in terms of ratings.

The use of telematics in the UAS insurance market was so prevalent at the beginning of the UAS insurance market that 'pay-as-you-fly' insurance policies were available to UAS operators. These policies not only offered cover based on flying hours and could have been purchased on a trip basis but also permitted insurers to give real-time instructions to remote pilots regarding routes, weather conditions, etc. The benefits of such policies were aptly described by an insurer:[62]

> It is argued that the introduction of 'pay-as-you-go' insurance assists in better promoting drone safety and ultimately will enable insurers to more accurately price drone risks using big data. This is accomplished by accessing large amounts of information and data from different sources, including weather data, building density and population density, in a way which allows insurers to assess the risk posed by a certain drone in the sky.
>
> This, it is contended, allows for an unparalleled degree of precision when assessing and pricing drone flight risks. Rather than treating all drone enterprises in the same way and providing them with an annual policy price, an exposure-based pricing approach allows for the risk of each and every flight undertaken by a drone fleet to be quantified and priced individually. The result is a more accurate correlation between risk and price.

In essence, 'pay-as-you-fly' insurance gives insurers control over the insured's behaviour, enabling them not only to provide more accurate pricing but also to

[61] Ritterband UAS Liability and Insurance, n 17, p 242.
[62] ibid, 230.

'correct' the insured's behaviour. In that respect, they can monitor and enforce compliance with the policy's 'behaviour-controlling' terms, such as warranties and conditions precedent (for which see Section III.C.f) and recommend alternative courses of action, taking, as such, the broader role of risk manager vis-à-vis the insured.

'Pay-as-you-fly' insurance is tempting for a significant part of the UAS market, especially the recreational one, where remote pilots tend to be less experienced. Yet, commercial operators of UAS are more inclined to purchase year-long policies. While data collection via telematics is still possible, it is less likely that commercial UAS operators, which usually operate under a CAA authorisation (see Section II B), will subscribe to an insurance model that gives operational control to insurers and opt for one-year policies that follow traditional methods of ratings based on the loss history of the equipment used, the operator/remote pilots and the nature of operations. In that respect, UAS insurers seem to have reached a point where they treat commercial UAS operators as a lesser risk than recreational users, similar to commercial aviation.

After several years of operation, the UAS insurance market seems to have accumulated historical data to provide insurance ratings confidently in the traditional manner. More data is becoming available through more accurate reporting of accidents and incidents to the regulators and insurers, enabling more insurers to be involved in the UAS insurance market. Some issues that affect premium rating in UAS operations are familiar to aircraft insurers, such as the risk management ones dealing with the type of UAS to be used, the geographical location of operations, the pilots' experience and qualifications, the UAS usage and the insured's loss history. Also, the distinction between ground and air risks and first- and third-party risks is also common with aircraft risks.[63] However, risks related to BVLOS operations, swarm flights and other specialist operations are unique to the UAS insurance market and also risks such as theft, flood, and other natural catastrophes, water, and transportation are more prevalent in the UAS market, considering the size of UAS, their storage places, their sensitivity to weather conditions and their potential uses in emergency situations and urban environments. At the same time, passenger and baggage liability is not yet a concern for UAS insurers, although this will change once VTOL operations are authorised.

As a result, a positive outlook has finally emerged for the UAS insurance market:[64]

> Generally … established drone insurers, such as Moonrock Drone Insurance, have now entered a period where they have much better access to historical information and new data and can more accurately identify risks and price policies fairly and transparently. For example, larger drones, such as those over 25 kg, used to require individual pricing, but many users can now be provided with an insurance policy

[63] ibid, 228.
[64] ibid, 218.

> quote online as insurers have better acquired an understanding of the risks, boundaries and parameters of drone use which can be insured. Similarly, insurers have an improved understanding of beyond visual line of sight (BVLOS) operations and its growth trajectory over the next five years. By utilising an insured's data at the end of a policy, insurers are also able to price the same insured's subsequent policy with improved accuracy.

Overall, the commercial UAS insurance market seems to flourish courtesy of a large enough pool of insureds and improved availability of accident and operational data. Its capacity to provide adequate coverage has yet to be tested (at least in the UK setting) by multi-casualty events, whether safety- or terrorism-related. The relatively easy access to UAS and their operation without many authorisations, their ability to operate in urban environments (even in breach of the Regulations), their use in swarm shows and their ability to carry significant weights of payload create a risk profile that can be attractive to terrorists for its catastrophic potential: for example, using light UASs to disseminate chemical substances over a large area of a city might not be too implausible a scenario; or targeting critical energy infrastructures, disabling the geofencing restrictions, might also not be too far off as a scenario.

Such events can test the insurance and liability systems, and we will discuss some of their implications below. But before we do so, we examine the mandatory insurance requirements for UAS operators and comment on their suitability.

B. Assimilated Regulation 785/2004

Under assimilated Regulation 785/2004 on insurance requirements for air carriers and aircraft operators (as amended), commercial UAS operators must have third-party liability insurance to cover safety and war-related risks.[65] While the Regulation also requires operators to have passenger, baggage, and cargo liability insurance, these are not relevant for UAS operators yet but will be applicable once VTOLS start carrying passengers or we have regular cargo deliveries/flights by UAS.

The assimilated |Regulation 785/2004 follows the European one, designed in 2004 with aircraft rather than UAS in mind. One issue that needs to be clarified here is that the Regulation does not determine the compensation a victim will be awarded following an accident. The relevant domestic liability laws and conventions determine that amount. It is also important to note that the Regulation does not create a right to bring a claim against an air carrier or aircraft operation with this right created by the relevant domestic liability laws and conventions.[66]

[65] Regulation 785/2004 on insurance requirements for air carriers and aircraft operators as amended by Regulation 285/2010 and further amended by Regulation (EU) 2020/1118 (Regulation 785/2004).

[66] George Leloudas, 'Montreal Convention 1999 and airline insurance: has the CJEU given insurers a cause for concern?' IISTL blog (December 2023) iistl.blog/2023/12/14/montreal-convention-1999-and-airline-insurance-has-the-cjeu-created-a-cause-of-concern-for-insurers/.

The Regulation applies, in principle, to UAS, but it has a significant exception: it does not apply to UAS of less than 20 kg exclusively used for sports or recreational purposes.[67] The exception is estimated to be so broad that most non-commercial UAS operating in the UK are not required to have insurance (see below in this Section for the implications of this exception). Still, the Regulation covers the operation of commercial UAS.

In summary, UK Regulation 785/2004 requires insurance to be purchased for every flight of a UA (whether on a VLOS, BVLOS, or autonomous basis).[68] The insurance is to be bought by the operator, defined as 'the person or entity … who has continual effective disposal of the use or operation of the aircraft'.[69] The presumption is that the registered owner is the operator unless it can prove that someone else was operating the UAS, in which case the obligation moves to the actual user.[70] This delegation would occur when the registered owner of the UAS leases it to an operator without any remote pilots or visual observers. In such instances, the insurance obligation falls on the person or entity that operates the UAS. In cases where the owner leases the UAS with the remote pilot and observers, the responsibility to insure remains with the owner. This would be the case even if the owner receives instructions from the lessee regarding the scope of the performed work.

The obligation to insure covers any UA flight 'within, into, out of, or over the territory' of the UK.[71] As such, UK Regulation 785/2004 covers domestic UAS flights, irrespective of their duration or distance flown. It also provides that aircraft operators must purchase insurance to cover their 'aviation-specific liability for passengers, baggage, cargo and third parties'.[72] With no commercial availability in terms of flying passengers and baggage yet, UAS operators must maintain third-party liability insurance. Such cover must include liability for 'death, personal injury and damage to property caused by accidents'.[73] And also war and warlike risks, such as 'acts of war, terrorism, hijacking, acts of sabotage, unlawful seizure of aircraft and civil commotion'.[74]

While we do not currently experience routine cargo operations via UAS in the UK, the requirement to purchase insurance to cover liability regarding loss, damage, destruction, or delay of cargo is controversial regarding using UAS to transport goods.[75] The Regulation requires cargo insurance of at least

[67] See Regulation 785/2004, art 2(b), which exempts model aircraft with an MTOM of less than 20 kg from its application: the CAA has interpreted the term 'model aircraft' for the purposes of the Regulation only to mean '[a]ny unmanned aircraft which is being used for sport or recreational purposes only': CAP 722, n 35, [1.3].

[68] Regulation 785/2004, n 65, art 4(2).

[69] ibid, art 3(c).

[70] ibid.

[71] ibid, art 2(1).

[72] ibid, art 4(1).

[73] ibid, recital 14.

[74] ibid, art 4(1).

[75] Leloudas and Chatzipanagiotis, n4, p 69.

22SDRs per kg,[76] reflecting the liability limits of air carriers under the Montreal Convention 1999.[77] The application of this requirement on deliveries using a UAS is questionable as the Regulation does not define the term 'cargo' with the prevailing judicial interpretation under the Montreal Convention 1999 requiring the issuance of an air waybill, which might not be the case when cargo deliveries via UA become a reality.[78]

The minimum insurance required for third-party liability reflects the UA's MTOM. Most UAs fall into the first cover category, namely 750,000 SDR per flight, as they have MTOMs of less than 500 kg.[79] Even when the weight of the payload is added, it is unlikely that their weight will exceed this threshold soon.

The Regulation requires that third-party liability cover is provided on a per-occurrence basis.[80] Yet, it permits cover against third-party war risks to be provided on an aggregate basis.[81] This exception is because the aviation insurance market cannot cover such risks on a per-accident basis following the 9/11 attacks. The practice of the airline insurance market is linked to the catastrophic potential of commercial aircraft, as witnessed by the 9/11 attacks. To avoid the recurrence of the insurance crisis that followed 9/11, third-party war risk coverage for commercial airlines is provided using several layers of excess insurance, and it is only available on an aggregate basis.

Do UAS have catastrophic potential? UASs, albeit small, can be used to carry weapons of mass destruction and other materials that have the potential to cause devastating damage, mainly if used against vulnerable targets, such as nuclear energy plants. Considering that access to UAS is considerably more straightforward than that of aircraft, it is arguable that they can cause catastrophic third-party damages against which the war risks insurance market requires protection via the aggregate limits.[82]

Overall, we believe the Regulation does not require significant amendments to accommodate the use of commercial UAS. Indeed, some adjustments are needed as there is little doubt that specific references to UAS and an amendment of the term 'flight' to accommodate rotary-wing UASs would be an improvement, as they would leave no doubt that it applies to them. When cargo and passenger flights become a reality, amendments will be required. Yet, there is no current, urgent need to overhaul it.

[76] Regulation 785/2004, n 65, art 6(2).

[77] ibid, recital (6); Convention for the Unification of Certain Rules Relating to International Carriage by Air, agreed at Montreal on 28 May 1999 (Montreal Convention 1999).

[78] G Leloudas and D B Soffin, 'Article 4 Cargo' in George Leloudas, Paul S Dempsey and L Chassot (eds), *The Montreal Convention. A Commentary* (Cheltenham, Edward Elgar Publishing, 2024) [4.46]–[4.55] (*Montreal Convention Commentary*) and G Leloudas et al, *Shawcross and Beaumont on Air Law* (Lexis Nexis, Issue 187, 2024) Vol 1, Division VII [901] (*Shawcross and Beaumont*).

[79] Regulation 785/2004, n65, Category 1 of the Table in art 7(1).

[80] ibid art 7(1).

[81] ibid.

[82] See Leloudas and Chatzipanagiotis, n4, p 70, where we examined whether continuing this practice in the case of UAS is worthwhile.

One issue requires urgent treatment, however. As we explained above, insurance is not mandatory for UAS that weigh less than 20kg and are used for recreational purposes. In contrast, insurance is compulsory for commercial users, as described herein. This is a nonsensical arrangement, considering that the impact of a UAS crash on third parties is the same irrespective of its use. One might even argue that insurance is more critical for the recreational operations of UAS as remote pilots might have less experience in operating UAS, considering that there is no minimum age for being a remote pilot of a UAS in the Open category.[83] The studies of the AAIB indicating that a 1.4 kg UAS falling from 8m height can cause fatal injuries strengthen the argument that insurance for recreational UAS users should become mandatory and not be left to the user's discretion (see Section II.A). While operations in the Open category, where most recreational UAS fall into, impose restrictions on their areas of operation and their weight, it is plausible that a recreational UAS operating in the A3 category (see Section II.B), due to a technical fault or human mistake, would crash on a moving car causing its driver to lose control and resulting in property damage and physical injuries. The remote pilot could be liable for causing such an accident. Yet, the absence of insurance would limit the recovery prospects of the car's insurers or any civil claim the injured third parties bring against the remote pilot of the UAS. Or a recreational UAS might be hijacked by a terrorist that intends to use it to cause damage to critical urban infrastructures: the absence of war risk insurance will delay the recovery of damages.

Considering the expected increase in UAS operating in UK airspace, these scenarios are not unique or implausible. While a compulsory insurance requirement might increase the cost of operating a recreational UAS, it would ensure a financial net to cover damages caused by such uses. As such, we believe that third-party insurance requirements (to include war and non-war risks) to cover all UAS need to be introduced, arguably at lower levels than the current lowest one of the Regulation, namely 750,000SDRs per flight. Such levels can be determined not only by reference to the weight of the UAS but by reference to 'the overall risk of the flight operation, and take into account the level of injury or damage an aircraft could do, the size and maximum take-off mass of the aircraft, the flight path and complexity of the operation' as the Government announced in the 'Future of Transport Regulatory Review: Future of Flight Government Response'.[84]

While the Regulation does not need urgent amendment, it is essential to reiterate that it imposes *minimum* insurance requirements on commercial UAS operators and provides for *minimum* cover terms, leaving the actual cover limits and terms to the agreement between the parties. With a burgeoning UAS insurance market, looking into current UAS insurance policies and identifying cover issues is essential.

[83] The minimum age for a UAS operator is 18 years old: ANO 2016, n50, art 265D.

[84] Department for Transport (DfT), 'Future of Transport Regulatory Review: Future of Flight – Government Response' (September 2023) p 22.

C. Insurance Policies

The UAS insurance market offers UAS cover in the UK on an annual, monthly, or 'pay-as-you-fly' basis with third-party limits of more than £ 10 million per event. Insurers can cover BVLOS operations, delivery operations, and other niche commercial activities. Furthermore, it is becoming increasingly common for UAS insurance policies to include cover for invasion of privacy and breach of the Data Protection Act.

i. The Flock Policy[85]

Flock was one of the first UAS insurers to introduce successful 'pay-as-you-fly' policies. As of late 2021, Flock moved its insurance products to commercial car fleet insurance. Still, its standard UAS policy (Flock's Fly Unlimited policy) was one of the first to provide bespoke UAS wordings and set the foundation for the buoyant UAS insurance market that we currently experience. While a bespoke policy resembled the wording of AVN1D, the standard policy for general aviation aircraft, such resemblance is expected on cognitive grounds at this early stage of the market's development. We have analysed the policy in two publications.[86] Yet a few issues of interest need to be mentioned before we move to the current wordings.

As expected, the Flock policy does not have a passenger and baggage liability section, reflecting the absence of these carriages. While the policy follows AVN1D, which does not have a cargo section, it covers damage to the UAS payload under the hull section (Section I). In general, Section I covers the loss or damage of the UAS and its payload (hull section), and Section II covers third-party liability caused by the operation of the UAS. At the same time, Section III contains the exclusions, conditions precedent, general conditions, definitions and extensions of cover. Reflecting the type of UAS operations at the time, the policy does not have a spare parts Section, which some current UAS policies offer.

Section I provides cover against the risk of physical loss or damage to the UAS and its payload whilst in flight, on the ground or in transit, up to the insured value. Two definitions of the term 'flight' are provided, one for fixed-wing and one for rotary-wing UAs; the 'rotary' wing definition, which creates a more apparent divide between 'in flight' and 'ground' risks cover, requires the UA to be switched on and the rotors to be in motion for the flight cover to apply. In contrast, the fixed-wing definition suggests that the flight cover starts when the UA is switched on, even though no power is used to move forward.

Section I also provides cover against the physical loss or damage to the UAS while it is in transit and while it is stored in an unattended vehicle (and also covers

[85] In file with the author.

[86] Leloudas and Chatzipanagiotis, n 4, pp 70–73 and G Leloudas, 'Civil Regulation of Drones in the UK' in J Hartmann, S Truxal and B Scott (eds), *Civil Regulation of Autonomous Drones in Europe* (Cheltenham, Edward Elgar Publishing, forthcoming) (Leloudas Drone Regulation UK).

damage to the unattended vehicle itself), provided the UAS is kept out of sight, and the security measures on the vehicle are in force. No such cover is provided in AVN1D to general aviation aircraft, reflecting their size and type of operations. For 'in transit' cover to be provided to the UAS, the following two conditions need to be satisfied: i) the UAS is packed and unpacked for transit by professional packers and according to the manufacturer's guidelines, and ii) all fire alarms and security measures notified to the insurer are engaged whenever the UAS is left unattended during transit.

Reflecting the increased risk of theft (compared to aircraft), the Fly Unlimited policy also provides a more elaborate but, simultaneously, more restrictive cover than AVN1D against the risk of theft of the UAS. While AVN1D does not impose any special conditions if third parties steal an aircraft, other than excluding theft by the insured or with their knowledge and consent, theft of a UAS is excluded unless i) the theft is the result of forcible entry or exit by third parties from its place of storage; ii) the security measures are in force at the time of the theft; and iii) the UAS is kept out of sight at all times. The wording is restrictive enough to exclude the clandestine theft of UAS from the operator's warehouse – a provision also standard in aircraft spare parts insurance where theft is a significant risk. It is not surprising that insurers limit coverage for theft as UAS are susceptible to it, especially during transit, because of their size.

In terms of third-party liability (Section II), the policy, in a wording copied from AVN1D, provides cover 'for all sums which the Insured shall become legally liable to pay, and shall pay, as compensatory damages (including costs awarded against the Insured) in respect of accidental bodily injury (fatal or otherwise) and accidental damage to property caused by the UAV described in the Schedule or by any object falling therefrom'. Similarly, the definition of 'bodily injury' is copied from AVN1D, covering 'bodily injury, sickness or disease including death at any time resulting therefrom'. This is a restrictive definition, as it does not cover mental injuries, the implications of which are discussed below in Section III C ii.

Similarly to AVN1D, the third-party cover is excluded when the UAS causes 'loss of or damage to any property belonging to or in the care, custody or control of the Insured'. This exclusion means that any damage to equipment used by the insured (which is not considered part of the payload) or the injury of an insured employee (e.g., the remote pilot or an observer) as a result of the UAS crash or the inadvertent drop of its payload will not be covered by this insurance. First, party insurance must be acquired to cover them. Damage to the UAS itself is covered by Section I of the policy.

As per standard aviation insurance practice (see Section II B above), an AVN52E endorsement is included, providing war risk liability cover for property damage and personal injury to third parties.[87] The cover is provided on an aggregate basis, as per airline practice, on the basis that the payload of a UAS has

[87] For a comprehensive analysis of war risk cover see Katherine Posner, Tim Marland, Philip Chrystal, *Margo on Aviation Insurance* (4th edn, Chicago, LexisNexis, 2014) Ch 19.

the potential to cause catastrophic losses. It has to be noted that the endorsement does not provide war risk cover for hull damage to the UAS and its payload, and a separate hull war cover is to be acquired. AVN52E would cover third parties for a set of risks excluded by AVN48B (the standard war risk exclusion clause in aviation policies), such as hostilities, civil war, rebellion, and so on; strikes, riots and labour disturbances; acts for political or terrorist purposes; malicious acts or acts of sabotage; confiscation, nationalisation etc. and hijacking, unlawful seizure of or wrongful exercise of control of the aircraft. For the implications of this arrangement, please refer to Section III C ii e. below.

Finally, AVN124 is included in the standard data event clause, which is also increasingly popular with airline placements. The clause essentially excludes from cover 'loss, damage, expense or liability arising out of a Data Event', which is defined as 'access to, inability to access, loss of, loss of use of, damage to, corruption of, alteration to or disclosure of Data'. For its implications, see below Section III C ii f. below.

ii. Recent Policy Wordings[88]

a. General

More recently, insurers have produced a variety of policies for commercial UAS, with some of them moving away from the standard AVN1D wording, highlighting the creation of a UAS-focused insurance market. In our analysis, we will use two UAS policies, one with wording close to the AVN1D (standard policy) and one with tailor-made wording for UAS (alternative policy).

The standard policy has four sections: Section I covers the physical loss or damage to the UAS, including its payload; Section II covers the physical loss or damage to UAS spares; Section III covers legal liability to third parties; and Section IV contains the general exclusions, conditions and endorsements. Immediately, one can see a fundamental difference with the Flock policy as it covers spare parts in Section II, reflecting the size of commercial UAS operators that keep an inventory of spare parts for their UAS fleet.

The alternative policy is divided into three sections: Section I provides the general terms and conditions, Section II provides cover for first-party property damage to the UAS and business property that belongs to the insured or for which the insured is legally responsible, and Section III provides public liability cover, which is essentially cover for damage to third-party property damage and personal injuries caused by the operation of the UAS.

b. Damage to the UAS

Section I of the standard policy covers UAS owned or used under the insured's care, custody, possession, or control and for which the insured is legally responsible.

[88] The policies that are analysed herein are in file with the author.

This wording is broad enough to cover situations where the UAS operator's fleet consists of UAS-owned or leased; it would also cover situations where a commercial party employs the services of a UAS operator and instructs the remote pilot on how to provide the required services. Section II of the alternative policy has a less detailed definition in that it covers UAS that belong to the insured or for which the insured is legally responsible. While the wording is likely to cover the same situations as the standard wording, it seems to be better addressed to operators of UAS rather than commercial parties that employ the services of UAS operators.

Section I of the standard policy provides cover against the physical loss or damage to the UAS (which is defined to include detachable and non-detachable payload) as well as theft whilst the UAS is in flight, on the ground or in transit. Yet the policy's cover is limited to photographic and video equipment carried by the UAS that are removable from it (detachable) and also photo and video equipment that the UAS carries and form an integral part of it; in essence, equipment that forms part of the hull of the UAS.

The standard policy's property cover (Section I) includes a long list of exclusions, which interest us.

The policy (as AVN1D and airline policies do) excludes 'the cost of making good wear and tear, deterioration, breakdown, defect or failure however caused in any unit of the UAS and the consequential damage to the UAS after that'. The term 'unit' is defined as '[a] part or an assembly of parts (including any subassemblies) of the UAS which has been assigned an overhaul life as a part or an assembly'. It excludes damage caused to UAS motors (units) by an internal causative factor, such as damage to the stator. Any ensuing damage caused to the UAS due to the motor failure will not be covered either; this is in dire contrast to aircraft policies, which exclude damage to engines caused by internal reasons but cover the ensuing damage to the hull.

UAS insurers also do not cover damage to a motor and any ensuing damage to the UAS caused by anything with a progressive or cumulative effect, such as dust's impact on the motor, unless the damage is attributable to a single incident. Although the standard policy does not define the term 'single incident', aviation policies define it as an incident that causes damage 'of such severity that it requires the engine Unit to be immediately withdrawn from service upon the first landing of the Aircraft to which it is attached'; a typical aviation situation, which can also apply to UAS, would be of a bird strike that requires the engine to be withdrawn upon first landing and repaired. In the case of UAS, it would require the UAS to be withdrawn from operation for repairs upon landing.

Furthermore, the standard policy contains a rather complicated exclusion of the (attempted) theft of the UAS. Complicated in that it excludes theft of the UAS by the insured or with its knowledge or consent or by third parties, unless the theft by third parties is the result of forcible entry or exit from a building, container, motor vehicle, etc., all security measures on the motor vehicle or its roof box are in force at the time of the theft, and the UAS is kept out of sight at all times. In essence, cover for theft by third parties is provided if the UAS is in a locked compartment, not visible from the outside to attract opportunist thieves, and its theft is not the result of covert action but forcible action; still, the clause does not require assault for the third party theft to be covered. Similarly, the standard policy does not cover loss or damage to the UAS in transit unless it is packed 'in accordance with manufacturer guidelines or a securely locked and padded UAS flight case'.

As expected, the standard policy does not cover consequential losses, meaning loss of use of expenses incurred due to the inability to operate the UAS (even if an insured event causes that inability). In that respect, insurers reiterate that they provide property insurance coverage (similar to aviation insurers) and are not acting as financial loss insurers. Similarly, insurers do not offer cover for repairing or replacing a scratched camera lens or mechanically deranged camera equipment unless the event that caused their damage has also damaged the UAS. In essence, insurers have carved out two popular types of damage and provide cover for them only when a major UAS incident is the cause of the equipment's damage.[89]

The alternative policy provides more comprehensive coverage than the standard policy in Section II. It provides cover against the accidental physical loss or damage of the UAS, reiterating the insurers' role as property insurers. The cover is not limited to the UA itself. It covers related accessories at a broader scale than the standard policy, as it includes, among several items, filming, scanning, mapping, infrared and x-ray equipment, including software; walkie-talkies and communications equipment; power supplies and control equipment; binoculars and photographic equipment; and laptops and tablets being used to control the insured UAS. It also covers damage to other business property that belongs to the insured or for which the insured is legally responsible, such as computers, mobile phones and PDAs, laptops and tablets not being used to control a UAS, hired-in equipment, etc. Interestingly, the policy covers the loss of money provided it takes place within the UK and is related to the insured's activities. Still, it does not cover cryptocurrencies under any circumstances or format.

In addition, the alternative policy covers the reasonable costs of restoring electronic data required to continue the insured's activities and have been lost or distorted as a direct result of property damage covered by the policy. Considering that most commercial UAS transmit data related to their operations, be they inspections or anything else, this cover is essential for most UAS operators.

In the case of a cyber attack resulting in property damage to the UAS, the alternative policy covers reasonable costs and expenses to repair or replace the affected part of any computer system if, during the period of insurance, a hacker damages, destroys or alters it. This is not a stand-alone cyber risk cover, as property damage to the UAS is required for the cyber cover to kick in. The policy widely defines a hacker as including the insured's employees. However, the hacking cover is significantly limited by the following two exclusions. The policy does not provide

[89] Same exclusion in the alternative policy.

cover for damage i) caused by viruses created by the insured, its employees, or any self-employed freelancer supervised by the insured or ii) caused by 'any virus which indiscriminately replicates itself and is automatically disseminated on a global or national scale, or to an identifiable class or sector of users', such as the WannaCry worm attack, unless the virus has been passed to the computer system of the insured by a hacker, namely someone who specifically targeted the insured's computer system and gained access to it by circumventing its electronic security systems. The term 'virus' is widely defined as malware, worms, trojans, spyware, etc. In essence, these two exclusions read together have the effect of covering damage caused by viruses that are not created by the insured's employees or subcontractors and are not self-replicating, such as certain worms, unless the self-replicating virus has been passed on to the insured's computer system by the actions of a third-party hacker that has targeted this system.

The alternative policy also provides limited consequential loss cover by covering the cost of hiring a replacement UAS to fulfil related contractual obligations of the insured affected by the UAS's damage, for example, subsequent building inspections or filming. This cover is available for six months from the date of damage or until the damaged UAS is repaired, whichever is earlier.

The property section of the alternative policy comes with a long list of exclusions, some of the important ones for our paper being the following.

The policy provides no cover while the UAS is transported as cargo unless it is packed securely in a tailor-designed protective case or is packed by professional removers. As the alternative policy does not have a cargo section, this exclusion applies to the UAS being carried as cargo by other means of transport; any damage to the UAS could still be covered under the carrier's liability policy or the UAS policy, provided the UAS has been properly packed.

Furthermore, the alternative policy does not cover damage to the UAS caused by storms or floods. At the same time, it is being stored unless the UA 'is stored in a building built of brick, stone or concrete and roofed with slate, tiles, concrete, metal, asbestos or any other non-combustible material or in a shipping container'. While the policy covers damage to a UAS in flight as a result of weather conditions, including storms or floods, the same only applies while it is in storage if it is stored in a location that is designed to protect it from such risks, and not for example under a tent, or a temporary open establishment.

Also, the alternative policy does not cover clandestine UAS thefts. Still, it will cover its theft by entering its place of storage by forcible means, or if the UAS is stored in a motor vehicle, it will cover its theft if all security measures on the motor vehicle, trailer or roof box are in force at the time of the theft; similar to the standard policy. It is a further requirement under the theft cover of the alternative policy that the insured reports the theft (as well as arson, malicious damage, riot, etc.) to the police as soon as reasonably possible and obtains a crime reference from them. As a result, 'the unexplained loss or disappearance or inventory shortage' of UAS is not covered by the policy.

It is interesting to note that, unlike commercial aircraft insurance policies, it is a condition precedent of cover under the property section for the insured to arrange for urgent repairs to be done immediately, with insurers retaining the right to inspect the damaged property but not being a prerequisite for authorising repairs. The policy also requires that backup copies of data be undertaken at least once a week and copies be kept at an alternate storage place, such as the storage place of the UAS.

c. Damage to Spare Parts

The standard policy also contains a spare parts section (Section II) replicating the structure of commercial airline policies. It provides cover for the physical loss of or damage to UAS spares, which are defined as equipment that is 'designed to be fitted to or forming part of the UAS and ancillary equipment exclusively associated with the activities covered, including the ground control station and non-detachable payload'. Like airline policies, the UAS spare section covers not only spares owned by the insured but also spares of others for which the insured is responsible whilst in its care, possession, custody or control on the ground or whilst in transit. Unlike airline policies, Section II of the standard policy does not exclude damage to spare parts of others stored by the insured for hire or reward, which leads to the argument that the policy covers the insured in its capacity as a warehouse.

In terms of the moment that a piece of equipment becomes part of the spare cover in the policy rather than the hull section, the standard policy adopts a threshold that is commonly found in airline policies, namely 'the commencement of the operations of fitting' which is defined as 'the moment the property ceases to be in contact with the ground or the trolley/stand on which it is located when the process of fitting it to the UAS is commenced'. While airline policies have several cut-off points between spares and hull cover, the one adopted by the standard policy means that the moment a spare part is lifted from the ground to be installed on the UAS, it becomes part of the standard policy's property section (Section I). So, if the equipment falls from the technician's hands upon lifting it from the ground, the damage will be covered by the property section rather than the spares section.

The spares section comes with a long list of exclusions, prominent among them being the theft one, copied from the property section of the UAS policy. Section II also excludes the 'unexplained loss or disappearance or inventory shortage of UAS spares,' which essentially avoids cover for 'inside jobs' where the insured's employees steal spares clandestinely. Not surprisingly, a condition precedent requires the insured to record its UAS spares occasionally.

d. Legal Liability Cover

In the legal liability to third parties section, the standard policy (Section III) covers all sums that the insured shall become legally liable to pay as compensatory damages for i) bodily injury and property damage to third parties; ii) unintentional invasion of privacy; and iii) noise liability, caused by an occurrence arising out of the use of the UAS.

Unlike airline policies, bodily injury is defined as '[p]hysical injury, including death resulting therefrom', but the standard policy excludes 'nervous shock or psychological injury unless accompanied by and directly caused by such physical injury to the same individual'. This definition seems to replicate the case law of the Montreal Convention 1999 on what constitutes bodily injury in the Convention, especially the case of *Eastern Airline Inc v Floyd*,[90] which does not cover stand-alone psychological injuries but only psychological injuries caused by bodily injury. Also, the term 'directly caused' is used to neutralise the effect of *Jane Doe v Etihad Airways PJSC*,[91] which held that psychological injuries accompanying (but not directly caused by the bodily injury) constitute bodily injury under the Convention.[92] While this definition will satisfy Regulation 261/2004 (if one accepts that the interpretation of *Eastern Airline Inc v Floyd* remains the prevailing one), which follows the Montreal Convention 1999, it is unlikely that it would suffice to provide acceptable cover in a domestic setting under section 76(2) to (4) of the Civil Aviation Act 1982 (for which see below Section IV.B) which enables the recovery of stand-alone psychological injuries As such, the definition of the alternative policy that covers stand-alone mental injuries (for which see below) is to be preferred.

In what is a significant extension from the Flock policy, the standard policy covers the unintentional invasion of privacy, defined as the 'unjustifiable intrusion into the personal life/lives of another without consent'. That would include any fines the insured is required to pay for '[d]ata collected from the UAS whilst in flight' and includes 'any breach of confidentiality, infringement, or violation of any right to privacy, or any statutes, laws and regulations associated with the confidentiality, access, control, and use of personally identifiable, non-public information'.

The liability section of the standard policy comes with a long list of exclusions, prominent among which are the following.

The UAS policy does not cover bodily injury or property damage sustained by any of the insured's directors, employees, or partners while acting during their employment. As a result, it will not cover the remote pilot's bodily injury. It also does not cover loss or damage to property owned, rented, leased or occupied by, or whilst in the care, custody or control of, or whilst being handled, serviced or maintained by the insured or any servant of the insured. As such, the damage to a warehouse of the insured by the UAS will not be covered by the UAS policy. It remains doubtful whether the policy will provide cover if the UAS crashes or the payload drops on the property of the contractor who has instructed the UAS

[90] (1991) 499 US 530.

[91] 870 F 3d 406 (6th Cir 2017).

[92] For a comprehensive discussion on this issue see *Montreal Convention Commentary*, n 78, Article 17.

operations, for example, the owner of a building inspected by a UAS: the answer depends on whether the said building was in the care, custody or control of the insured, that is, the UAS operator, which is unlikely for most type of UAS operations with the result being that it shall be considered third party damage.

The public liability section of the alternate policy (Section III) covers bodily injury or property damage caused by the UAS and invasion of privacy claims committed by using the UAS. As per standard practice in airline policies, bodily injury is defined broadly to include 'death, or any bodily or mental injury or disease of any person', which provides broader cover than the standard policy and would cover damages for stand-alone psychological injuries under s 76(2) to (4) of the Civil Aviation Act 1982 (for which see below Section IV.B).

The cover excludes bodily injury to any employees of the UAS operator. Also, it excludes property damage to any property belonging to the insured or being in the care, custody or control of the insured at the time of the accident. However, cover is provided for damage to employees' or visitors' vehicles or effects while on the insured premises, to premises which are not owned or rented by the insured but where the insured is temporarily carrying out its activities and to premises rented to the insured if the loss or damage is not insurable under property insurance policies and for which the insured would not be liable other than by the lease or other agreement. In that respect, any injuries of the remote pilot caused by the operation of the UAS will not be covered by the alternative policy. Still, damage to their car caused by the UAS while parked on the insured's premises will be covered, but not if the car is damaged while on the contractor's premises. Also, the alternative policy will cover damage to the contractor's premises caused by the UAS of the insured.

The public liability insurance section also covers bodily injury, property damage or invasion of privacy claims filed against any 'sub-contractor, outsourcer, employee or volunteer worker of the insured when they act on the insured's behalf in whatever capacity'. Reflecting the work undertaken by commercial UAS operators, the policy provides cover for the said risks to a contractor of the insured, provided the insured provides a service to them under contract, is liable for that claim, and, at the reasonable opinion of the insurer, the customer has not caused or contributed to the claim. For the customer to be indemnified, the policy provides that they must give control of the defence and settlement to the insurers, not to have admitted liability before notifying them, and cooperate with the insurers in managing the claim.

The policy also covers the costs of criminal proceedings, provided the breach of statute or regulation that led to the criminal action related directly to a claim under the public liability section, namely property damage, bodily injury, or invasion of privacy.

While the alternative policy does not provide cover for the cost of replacing, reinstating, rectifying, erasing, blocking or destroying any personal data (unlike the standard one), it will indemnify the insured against its liability under the Data Protection Act 1998 in connection with personal data held by it, arising as a result of its activities during the period of insurance.

e. War Risks Cover

The two policies take a different approach to the coverage of war risks. The standard policy follows the traditional airline way of excluding such risks through AVN48B. It then offers two alternative ways of covering them. The first one is the conventional way of the airline war market through the AVN52E endorsement, which covers all risks excluded by AVN48B apart from the risk of 'hostile detonation of any weapon of war employing atomic or nuclear fission and/or fusion or other like reaction or radioactive force or matter' which is uninsurable for airlines and UAS.

AVN52E would provide cover for injury or death to third parties and property damage property caused by the overtaking of the UAS by a terrorist group or a group of activists. One potential issue is whether seizing control of the aircraft by cyber means constitutes hijacking or unlawful seizure of the plane. While Article 1 of the Beijing Protocol 2010 seems to suggest so, as it provides that the unlawful seizure of an aircraft can be committed by technological means and does not require the hijacker to be on board the aircraft, its definition is not biding for insurance purposes and in addition the actual wording of the insurance clause requires that the hi-jacking is 'made by any person or persons *on board the Aircraft*'. As such, cover for the damage should be sought in other clauses of AVN52E, namely the clause covering damage caused by acts of one or more persons for political or terrorist purposes or the clause covering damage caused by malicious acts or acts of sabotage which do not require the presence of the perpetrators on board the aircraft.

Another issue concerning UAS is whether damage to third parties caused by disseminating biochemical substances carried on a UAS is covered by AVN52E. Most likely, it is covered as AVN52E only excludes (via AVN48B) damage caused by 'weapons of war employing *atomic or nuclear fission and/or fusion or other like reaction or radioactive force or matter*', which do not include instruments containing biochemical substances.

The standard policy also offers an alternative endorsement to the war risk exclusion of AVN48B by only covering the risks of 'Strikes, riots, civil commotions or labour disturbances; Any malicious act (including acts of vandalism) or act of sabotage; and Hijacking, spoofing, hacking or any other unlawful seizure or wrongful exercise of control of the UAS (including any attempt at such seizure or control) acting without the insured's consent'. This endorsement seems to cover hijackings by cyber means as it does not require the hijackers to be on board the aircraft (as AVN52E does). Yet, it does not cover damages caused by persons acting for terrorist or political purposes and also does not provide express cover for 'acts of war' and similar risks (as AVN52E does), which makes it doubtful whether this alternative cover complies with Regulation 785/2004, which requires cover against such risks (see above Section III B).

The alternative UAS policy does not have the AVN48B exclusion. Still, it provides cover in its property Section (Section II) and the general liability Section (Section III) against third-party property damage and personal injury caused by war, terrorism, hi-jacking or confiscation; those risks are defined to resemble their description under airline policies, with terrorism defined even broadly to include religious, ideological or similar purposes. It seems that those risks were chosen to comply with Regulation 785/2004, although there is no express reference to acts of sabotage, one of the risks required to be covered under the Regulation. While the terrorism risk is broadly defined to include acts of sabotage, those acts are to be committed for 'political, religious, ideological or similar purposes', which does not cover acts of sabotage committed for civilian purposes, for example, a disgruntled customer intentionally destroying the UAS. Still, it is broad enough to cover the damage caused by cyber attacks on UAS or the dissemination of biochemical substances.

f. Conditions Precedent

The standard policy contains conditions precedent to liability that are tailor-made for UAS. Also, it is interesting that UAS insurers (unlike their marine and aviation counterparts) do not contract out of the Insurance Act 2015 (IA 2015), which essentially means that coverage is suspended until any breach of the warranties included in the policy is remedied. However, insurers deal with s 11 of IA 2015 in the alternative, that is, s 11 is contracted out for some policy clauses, whereas it applies to others as follows.

For the following conditions, the standard policy contracts out of s 11 of IA2015, which means no causal link between the breach of the condition and the damage is required for insurers to exclude their liability for the claim, reflecting the seriousness of those conditions for the insurers. That applies to conditions that i) the UAS shall only be used for commercial, business and continuation of flying activities (continuation of flight referring to flying the UAS to maintain the remote pilot's ratings and for training purposes); ii) the UAS operator (which is defined to include the remote pilot) has been trained to conduct commercial and business UAS operations or has at least 10 hours of UAS flying experience; iii) the insured complies with flying restriction zones and other prohibited areas: cover will be suspended while the UAS is flying over them and the insurers will incur no liability if damage to the UAS or injuries to third parties are incurred while flying inside the prohibited zones; and iv) that the use of UAS for training purposes shall not exceed 25 hours per year of cover.

For the following conditions, s 11 of IA2015 applies, which means that insurers will only be discharged of liability if the breach of any of these conditions has caused the damage in question:

i) The insured has the relevant permissions to fly the UAS for commercial, business or continuation flight purposes; such permissions are not limited to authorisations under the Specific category, aerial work permissions, etc. The issue here is whether the absence of the permit has caused the accident in question;

ii) The UAS has not been operated for more than 500 hours per year, with the defining issue being whether the excess flying caused the accident in question;
iii) If the UAS has a 'Return to Home' function, it should be activated at all times; here, the critical consideration is whether the damage to the UAS was caused by its inability to return to its base due to the deactivation of the 'Return to Home' function;
iv) The UAS shall be airworthy at the commencement of each flight, and the insured shall maintain all log books and other records in connection with the UAS.

Finally, the standard policy contains AVN124 – the data event exclusion clause (like the Flock policy). The clause excludes cover for the financial implications of stealing data from the insured or accessing its IT network for ransom. However, it clarifies that the policy covers physical damage to the UAS, bodily injury, and property damage to third parties caused by the data breach. That would be a situation where a cybercriminal tampers with the operating system of the UAS to get access to data, leading to the crash of the UAS on property or people on the ground. As such, the policy does not cover the cost of reinstating data or hacker damage (as the alternative policy does). However, it does cover the physical damage caused to the UAS, the spares and the liability to third parties or property caused by a data event, reiterating that this is a hybrid property-liability insurance policy and not a cyber risks policy.

iii. Concluding Thoughts on Insurance

The commercial UAS insurance market is burgeoning and has moved away from its overreliance on the insurance wordings of the aviation market (airlines and general aviation) to tailor-made wordings and types of cover, such as hacker damage, invasion of privacy, etc. Combined with more accurate underwriting courtesy of new technologies, it is becoming a niche yet independent insurance sector supporting a quickly evolving industry.

Yet, it is an insurance market that has not faced any catastrophic events yet (whether safety- or terrorism-related) and underpins an industry that still operates in a strict and restrictive regulatory environment. The operational opportunities of the future, such as regular BVLOS operations in non-segregated airspace, operations in urban centres alongside VTOLs and helicopters, and an increased number of recreational UAS users, to name a few, would also bring challenges for the insurance market and are likely to trigger changes to wordings and liability limits. Furthermore, a catastrophic event might reshape the market and its wording, especially if it is terrorism-related, which tends to have a global reach in terms of insurance impact.

Overall, the UAS insurance market, predominantly with the use of new technologies, has largely avoided the trials and errors of the aviation (insurance) market. We also believe that it has successfully reached its first phase of development, with the second one following the 'opening up' of the UAS sector to routine BVLOS flights and operations in urban environments. While we await this second phase, reviewing the third-party liability framework and giving our thoughts on its adequacy is essential.

IV. Liability to Third Parties[93]

A. A Domestic Liability System

English law does not have a dedicated liability system arising from the operation of UAS. It applies the rules dealing with property damage and personal injuries caused on the ground by aircraft operation. At the same time, we have yet to see any civil cases dealing with such damage from the operation of UAS.

Rules dealing with third-party damage from the operation of aircraft are usually of domestic origin, as there is little success in ratifying international rules on third-party liability of aircraft operators. While several international legal instruments deal with such liability, the international community has not received them well. Fifty-two States have ratified the 1952 Rome Convention (RC52),[94] the 1978 Montreal Protocol (MP78), which amends the RC 52[95] has been ratified by 12 States, while the 2009 Montreal General Risks Convention (GRC),[96] which was drafted to replace the RC52 and the MP78, and the 2009 Montreal Unlawful Interference Compensation Convention (UICC),[97] that was drafted to cater for another 9/11, have not come into force yet, 15 years after their drafting.

The UK has not ratified any of these international conventions. It is part of a large group of States that are reluctant to commit to a global solution regarding the liability of aircraft operators for ground damage for two main reasons. The first one is that the RC52 and MP78 provide low liability limits. With several States, including English law, having a system of strict and unlimited liability (see below Section IV B), it was felt that the adoption of the said Conventions would undermine the protection offered to third parties, who are usually innocent bystanders and have no relation to the operation of an aircraft, unlike passengers who have consented to be carried by the aircraft operator. This argument

[93] This Section draws from a different publication of the author, namely Leloudas Drone Regulation UK, n86.

[94] The Convention on Damage Caused by Foreign Aircraft to Third Parties on the Surface, Signed at Rome, on 7 October 1952 (RC 52).

[95] Protocol to Amend the Convention on Damage Caused by Foreign Aircraft to Third Parties on The Surface, Signed at Rome on 7 October 1952, Signed at Montreal, on 23 September 1978 (MP 78).

[96] Convention on Compensation for Damage Caused by Aircraft to Third Parties, done at Montréal on 2 May 2009 (GRC).

[97] Convention on Compensation for Damage to Third Parties, Resulting from Acts of Unlawful Interference Involving Aircraft, done at Montréal on 2 May 2009 (UICC).

becomes more robust with the adoption and the wide ratification of the Montreal Convention 1999 (139 ratifications to date) governing the liability of air carriers to passengers who benefit from a strict and unlimited liability system.

The second reason is that States tend to regard the issue of third-party liability of aircraft operators as domestic, even when aircraft on international flights cause damage on the ground. They argue that the preponderance of the evidence is located within the jurisdiction, and, as such, there is little need to apply an international framework harmonising what is essentially a domestic issue. The 2009 UICC was drafted under the pressure of the catastrophic damage witnessed during 9/11. Yet, States were unwilling to ratify them once the memory of the events faded. The 2009 GRC, while providing far superior protection to victims on the ground than the RC52 and the MP78, still contains limitations of liability for personal injury and property damage claims, which are a stumbling block for several States.

States feel little urgency to ratify or update the two 2009 Montreal Conventions or create an international third-party liability regime for UAS, and it seems that any such accidents will continue to be treated as domestic incidents for the foreseeable future. When regular cross-border UAS services are established, it would be interesting to see the States' reaction, whether they will re-ignite the interest in the third-party liability conventions or continue treating third-party accidents as domestic ones. A well-publicised terrorist event involving aircraft or UAS will certainly re-ignite interest in the two 2009 Montreal Conventions. Until then, the UK third-party liability system will play a pivotal role in managing third-party liability claims arising from the operation of UAS.

B. Section 76(2)–(4) of the Civil Aviation Act 1982

In the UK, the liability for accidents resulting in death, personal injury or property damage caused by the operation of UAS is determined by the liability scheme of s 76(2)–(4) of the Civil Aviation Act 1982. This is designed to deal with the impact of aircraft accidents on people and property on the ground and was not created with UAS in mind, although they currently fall into its scope. Its endurance is explained by its simplicity. Section 76 (2) provides for a system of strict and unlimited liability when 'material loss or damage is caused to any person or property on land or water by, or by a person in, or an article, animal or person falling from, an aircraft while in flight, taking off or landing'. It is a system of strict liability, as the victim is not required to prove the negligence or intention of the owner of the UAS and is only required to prove that personal injury or property damage was caused by an object or person falling from the UA.[98] The only defence to the

[98] In that respect, the victim is not required to prove that the owner of the UAS recklessly or negligently caused the UAS to endanger persons or property on the ground as per ANO 2016, n50, art 241.

UA's owner is the victim's contributory negligence.[99] The Act makes no provision for special defences, such as acts of terrorism, hijackings or cyber interference. It creates an almost absolute liability system as it is unlikely for the victim's injury to have been caused by the victim's interference with the operation of the UAS.[100] While UAS are not carrying passengers yet, the wording would cover situations where the injury or damage is caused by the falling payload of the UA, whether it is a camera, a sensor for structural surveys, or by any propeller detaching from the body of the UA.

Furthermore, s 76(2) provides that the victim can recover for 'material loss or damage', further defined in section 105 as 'loss of life and personal injury'. The term 'personal injury' has a relatively clear understanding in that it includes psychiatric injuries and is distinguished from the term bodily injury. In the case of *Glen v Korean Airlines Co Ltd*,[101] the Court enabled, in principle, the recovery of stand-alone psychiatric damages under s 76 (2) provided the claimants satisfy the standard law test of being either primary or secondary victims with sufficient proximity and ties of love and affection with the injured.[102] As such, the standard UAS insurance policy does not cover stand-alone psychological injuries, leaving such injuries uninsured, while the alternative UAS insurance policy does (see Section III C 2 d above).

Liability under s 76(2) attaches to the registered owner of the UAS, which creates a discrepancy with the mandatory registration requirement that is imposed on the operator of the UAS, namely the entity that manages the UAS and is responsible for its maintenance, operation and ensuring that the remote pilot has the permissions to fly it (see Section II B. above). In that respect, companies that operate their own UAS would be required to register, while in the case of outsourcing the operation of UAS, the responsibility to register lies with the outsourced operator of the UAS. Currently, this legislative discrepancy does not seem to cause issues as commercial UAS are usually operated by their owners, even in cases where they are leased out. Such leases are generally arranged on a 'wet' basis, namely that the owner leases the UAS with the pilot and potential observers. As such, liability under section 76(2) falls on the operator of the UAS. Operating practices will likely change (as in the aviation industry), with owners of UASs leasing them out on a 'dry' basis, namely by providing the UA with the lessee operating the UA by using its pilots and observers. In this situation, the arrangement of s 76(2) can potentially cause unfair results as it allocates the liability risk to the owner, who does not have navigational control over the UAS.

Section 76(4) partly mitigates this issue as it makes the lessee liable in cases where the UAS has been leased out for more than 14 days without the provision of

[99] Civil Aviation Act 1982 s 76(2).

[100] One such unlikely scenario might arise if the UAS injures the person who attempts to 'jam' its operation.

[101] [2003] EWHC 643 (QB).

[102] ibid, [33] to [39]. The claimants witnessed the crash of a B747 shortly after take-off from Stansted airport and claimed stand-alone psychological injuries.

any 'pilot, commander, navigator or operative member of the crew of the aircraft'. This is a reasonable arrangement as it allocates the liability risk to the person who operates the UAS. However, this still leaves two issues unresolved. First, it does not cater for situations where the owner of the UAS provides visual observers or technical assistants, but not the remote pilot, to the lessee. Can a visual observer qualify as a navigator disrupting the allocation of liability risks to the lessee? It is likely, although by no means certain, that they might qualify as such, considering that observers advise the remote pilot about the position of the UAS and any potential collision hazards. Much will depend on whether the remote pilot retains overall responsibility for the navigation of the UAS, which seems likely to be the case. The provision of a technical assistant is unlikely to change the allocation of risk achieved as they will not, under normal circumstances, have a say over the navigation of the UAS. This also seems to be the reading of insurers; for example, in the standard UAS policy, the term 'UAS operator' excludes the 'employed observers of the insured' from its definition, focusing on the person that 'directly manipulates the flight controls of the UAS', referring to the remote pilot and 'exercises direct authority over the initiation, continuation, diversion or termination of the UAS flight', referring to the person with the navigational control of the UAS. The term operator in the Regulation is broader than the one used in the standard UAS policy as it covers the entity that manages and maintains the UAS.

The owner of the UAS remains liable for any third-party damage caused by the UAS during the first fourteen days of the dry lease. This provision seems to have been copied from the RC52, which imposes a similar requirement on aircraft owners.[103] With the mandatory registration of UAS operators, this is an unreasonable provision as it makes the owner/lessor potentially liable for a period without operational control over the UAS. The RC52 mitigates the impact of this arrangement by making the owner/lessor and the operator/lessee of an aircraft jointly and severally liable during this period, essentially enhancing the victim's protection, who has the unilateral right to bring claims against both or either of them. However, the 1982 Act does not follow the same path. Instead, it gives the owner/lessor a right of indemnity against the lessee for any third-party claims that were required to be satisfied because of the operation of a dry-leased UAS. A literal reading of s 76(3) seems to absolve the operator/lessee from direct liability for the first 14 days, giving lesser protection to victims on the ground than the RC52. Despite the wording, we believe that the reasonable interpretation of s 76(3) and (4) is that both the owner and the lessee remain potentially liable for the first 14 days of the dry lease. The owner is given the right to bring an indemnity action against the lessee in cases where they have satisfied claims arising from the operation of the UAS by the lessee.

[103] RC52, n94, art 3.

The existence of s 67(2) of the Civil Aviation Act 1982, which creates a system of strict and unlimited liability, reduces the importance of negligence as a parallel cause of action against a UAS operator. This is so as an action in negligence for surface personal injury or property damage caused by a UAS would require the claimant to prove that the operator of the UAS owed them a duty of care, that it breached that duty and that the said breach caused the injury or property damage. Negligence will likely play a more prominent role when UAS carries passengers regularly, ideally requiring the adjustment of the new domestic or international liability regime.

While the standard of care in negligence for manned aircraft pilots 'is that of a competent, prudent and qualified pilot',[104] how this would be shaped regarding remote pilots of recreational UAS is to be seen. Judging from the case law on the duty of care of pilots of manned aircraft, examples of negligent acts or omissions may include situations where the UAS is overloaded or its weight is not evenly distributed, the remote pilot does not have the necessary qualifications for BVLOS operations, drone aerobatics or other special operations, has failed to keep a proper lookout, to follow the right-of-way rules or that the UAS was not in fit-for-flying condition.[105]

C. Section 76 (1) of the Civil Aviation Act 1982

Concerning claims for common law trespass and nuisance triggered by the operation of UAS, s 76(1) of the Civil Aviation Act 1982 bars them if the following conditions are satisfied:

> No action shall lie in respect of trespass or respect of nuisance, by reason only of the flight of an aircraft over any property at a height above the ground which, having regard to wind, weather and all the circumstances of the case, is reasonable, or the ordinary incidents of such flight, so long as the provisions of any Air Navigation Order and any orders under section 62 above have been duly complied with.

The rationale behind introducing s 76 (1) was to facilitate overflights by removing 'certain activities from the realm of common law trespass or nuisance if they only resulted in disturbance or inconvenience'.[106] For this to happen, the operation of the UAS is required to comply with its statutory conditions of operation (such as the ANO 2016 or the UAS Regulations, etc.), and for the UAS to be operated at a reasonable height, what is sensible will be determined on a case-by-case basis by reference 'not only on the weather factors mentioned in the Act, but on the size, speed, and noise, of the aircraft'.[107]

[104] *Shawcross and Beaumont*, n78, Vol 1, Division VII [38].
[105] ibid, [41] to [42] and [45].
[106] ibid, Vol 1, Division V [908].
[107] ibid, [909].

Furthermore, to be barred by common law trespass or nuisance, the action must be triggered 'by reason only of the flight' or 'by the ordinary incidents of such flight'. The meaning of the former expression was examined in the case of *Lord Bernstein of Leigh v Skyviews and General Ltd.*[108] (under s 40 of the Civil Aviation Act 1949 that was similarly worded). Justice Griffiths dismissed the restrictive interpretation of the phrase, which would have equated it to a bare right of passage. Such interpretation would have the practical effect that aerial activities, such as photography, surveys, and the like, could not be undertaken while flying over someone's land without their permission. However, the aircraft was reasonably high and complied with all statutory provisions. For Justice Griffiths, such activities can be performed without triggering an action for trespass or nuisance. Yet, the phrase 'by reason only of the flight' imposes the following restrictions on them:[109]

> Although an owner can find no action in trespass or nuisance if he relies solely upon the flight of the aircraft above his property as founding his cause of action, the section will not preclude him from bringing an action if he can point to some activity carried on by or from the aircraft that can properly be considered a trespass or nuisance, or some other tort. For example, the section would not protect against the deliberate emission of vast smoke that polluted the atmosphere and seriously interfered with the plaintiff's use and enjoyment of his property; such behaviour remains an actionable nuisance.

While English courts have not issued any decisions on UAS-related actions for trespass and nuisance, it is expected that 'a single, continuous flight of a drone over a third party's land is improbable to be sufficient to amount to an actionable nuisance claim but repeated, low-level flights using recording equipment may constitute nuisance' and '[t]he landowner would need to show that the flight of the aircraft over their land has caused, by noise for example, a material interference with the ordinary use and enjoyment of that land'.[110]

D. Concluding Thoughts on Third-Party Liability

Although untested in the context of UAS, s 76(2) to (4) of the Civil Aviation Act 1982 provides a 'no-frills' third-party liability system that has served civil aviation well since its inception. The main aim of s 76(2) to (4) is not to balance the interests of aircraft operators and third parties on the ground but to provide a straightforward recovery pathway for the victims. This has been achieved by giving aircraft operators minimal defences and providing unlimited liability for

[108] [1978] QB 479, [1977] 2 All ER 902 (on the corresponding provision in s 40(1) of the Civil Aviation Act 1949).
[109] ibid, 489.
[110] Simon Phippard, 'Drones – The Legal Framework' (Lexis PSL Practice Note 2022).

operators in an era when unlimited liability was not the flavour of the month as it is today.

While the operation of this unlimited third-party liability system was not as much of a concern for aircraft operators and their insurers as the passenger liability system, as there are significantly fewer third-party accidents, the proximity of UAS to the ground and the ease of access to them are expected to involve its operation more often. Still, we believe the system (with some adjustments recommended herein) can deal with a potential influx of cases. Any possible use of UAS by terrorists to cause catastrophic damage on the ground might trigger political reactions to provide a more balanced system, maybe along the lines of the two 2009 Montreal Conventions, one of which (the UICC) was designed to deal with such events.

In contrast, s 76(1) protects aircraft operators from trespass and nuisance flights and is designed to keep a balance between third parties on the ground and aircraft operators. Again, it has worked well in that it has limited the number of claims in this context, but, similarly to s 76(2)–(4), the proximity of UAS to the ground, the ease of access to them and their (future regular) uses in urban settings will undoubtedly test the strength of this system that is predominantly designed to protect operators.

V. Conclusion

Two interesting predictions were made in the 2023 drone survey of the CAA. The first one is that the UK public expects that in the next five years, UAS will be predominantly used to facilitate the provision of public services, especially in remote areas, such as search and rescue operations (52%), medicine delivery to remote areas (51%), inspection of powerlines (49%), traffic monitoring (49%) etc. Of general uses, the UK public expects that in the next five years, UAS will be used for military purposes (46%), filming (46%), agriculture (40%), etc.[111]

The expectations of the UK public change significantly when considering using UAS in the next ten to twenty years, with commercial uses taking the lead. The UK public expects that in the next ten years, we will experience the most significant increases in UAS usage in commercial deliveries (17% increase), transport, for example, air taxis, VTOLs (14% increase), weather forecasting (14% increase) and cargo flights (14% increase). Similarly, in the next twenty years, the UK public expects cargo flights to increase by 8%, transport services by 7%, and commercial deliveries by 6%.[112]

Commenting on the results, the CAA pointedly indicated that the predicted increase of the UK public in commercial UAS use may not be driven by actual

[111] CAA, 'CAP2546: UK CAA Drone tracker survey 2023' (April 2023) p 23 www.caa.co.uk/our-work/publications/documents/content/cap2546/.

[112] ibid, 24–25.

developments but 'by what they see or read in the media rather than actual developments. This is particularly the case with drone deliveries.'.[113] At the same time, as we demonstrated in a different publication,[114] for privacy and safety reasons, the public is not yet keen on some of the predicted commercial uses, such as deliveries or air taxis.

Still, it is accurate that public services will be the main benefactors of the increased use of UAS in the short term. This development has broad and beneficial consequences for the entire UAS sector because it builds trust between the public and the new transport technologies that come together with UAS, trust that is quick to dissolve due to a significant accident that triggers critical headlines. As such, it is to be hoped that by the time the traffic management system and machine learning technologies enable the regular and safe use of BVLOS operations in integrated airspace and urban centres, the track record of the UAS operations will bring more favourable coverage to the UAS sector and will influence the UK public to accept novel UAS uses as per the current predictions.

In this context, it is essential not to underestimate the impact of a liability and insurance system, which, as aviation has taught us, can erode public trust and change public perceptions towards industry and its technologies if it does not keep up with consumer expectations and appears to be one-sided in favour of the industry.[115] While this paper has not looked into passenger accidents of UAS (and VTOLs), it is our view that, overall, the third-party liability system in the UK and the insurance products underpinning it are currently sufficient (with the adjustments proposed herein) to cater for third-party accidents and reflect current social expectations on accident recovery. At the same time, we believe the UAS sector currently operates with significant regulatory restrictions, which might be loosened to accommodate novel UAS uses. As such, we believe that introducing regular BVLOS operations in integrated airspace and urban centres and any catastrophic event involving UAS will be a better test for the adequacy of the liability and insurance system that we currently have.

[113] CAA, '2023 UK drone survey results revealed' (April 2023) www.caa.co.uk/newsroom/blogs/2023-uk-drone-survey-results-revealed/#:~:text=Some%20of%20the%20key%20findings%20of%20the%20survey%20were%3A&text=Awareness%20of%20the%20maximum%20height,and%20registration%20for%20drone%20owners.

[114] Leloudas and Chatzipanagiotis, n4, pp 82–83.

[115] *Leloudas Risk*, n20, Chapters 2 and 3.

INDEX